WILLIAM PEMBER REEVES

William Pember Reeves

NEW ZEALAND FABIAN

BY

KEITH SINCLAIR

CLARENDON PRESS · OXFORD
1965

Oxford University Press, Amen House, London E.C.4

GLASGOW NEW YORK TORONTO MELBOURNE WELLINGTON
BOMBAY CALCUTTA MADRAS KARACHI LAHORE DACCA
CAPE TOWN SALISBURY NAIROBI IBADAN ACCRA
KUALA LUMPUR HONG KONG

PRINTED IN GREAT BRITAIN BY
SPOTTISWOODE, BALLANTYNE AND CO. LTD.
LONDON AND COLCHESTER

PREFACE

THE collection of information and documentary evidence for a biography of William Pember Reeves has proved a difficult process. Some of his letters survived in various collections in New Zealand. In England, in 1955, Mrs. Amber Blanco White generously permitted me to read her father's surviving papers, which she then donated to New Zealand. They included many letters, his unfinished 'Memoirs', which were a major source for this book, and one of his clipping books. Two other clipping and commonplace books I was, by good fortune, enabled to purchase in England. In Wisconsin I discovered a series of his letters to Henry Demarest Lloyd. Mr. T. E. Y. Seddon kindly permitted me to read some of Reeves's letters to his father. Nevertheless, the total number of surviving letters is not large. Most of them relate to government business or to his public activities. His letters to his family in New Zealand, which were kept by his sister Nell, were almost certainly accidentally burned on her death and shortly before I began my search. Most of the details of his life had to be learned from newspapers, parliamentary debates and various archives.

These circumstances dictated that the first biography of Reeves should concentrate upon the public figure, especially the politician, a result which he would have desired and which is appropriate because his political work in New Zealand was the most important part of his career and, to him, the most satisfying. But this does not mean that, while the public figure lives on, in an historically-stuffed shirt, 'the man' escapes the inquiries of posterity or is ignored by his biographer, or that his emotional life is quite impenetrable, or that his inner thoughts, the 'dialogue of self with soul', are unheard.

During ten years of intermittent study of Reeves's life I have incurred numerous debts, many of them to elderly people, some of whom are now dead, who told me what they knew of him. Especially I must thank Reeves's daughters, Mrs. Amber Blanco White, of London, and Mrs. Beryl Thatcher Clarke, of Washington, D.C.; his grandson, Mr. Thomas Blanco White and, in Christchurch, his nephew, Mr. Tristram Reeves. I am grateful to the late Dr. G. H. Scholefield and to the late Mr. W. H. Montgomery, of Little River, Canterbury, for showing me letters written by Reeves. I am indebted to the trustees of the Passfield Trust for permission to read and to quote from the papers of Sidney and Beatrice Webb. I must thank the London School of Economics, the Anglo-Hellenic League, the National Bank of New Zealand Ltd and the Wisconsin State Historical Society for permission to read documents in their archives. Mr. George Macdonald of Rangiora, Canterbury, generously gave me references to many newspapers reports about the young Reeves and his father. My friends, Dr. E. H. McCormick, Mr. Maurice Duggan and Dr. R. T. Shannon read this book in manuscript or proof and proposed many improvements. Dr. McCormick first suggested that I might write Reeves's life. My wife has relived Reeves's life many times with unfailing understanding. To thank the many other people, including librarians, who assisted me would involve writing a roll. Some other debts are acknowledged in footnotes.

The Carnegie Corporation of New York assisted my research with its customary generosity. In 1954–5 I was elected to a Commonwealth Fellowship, financed by the Corporation, at the Institute of Commonwealth Studies, London. In 1955 the Corporation made me a grant to travel in the United States. Through the Carnegie Social Science Research Committee, in New Zealand, to which I am also indebted, the Corporation provided further funds for research within my own country.

KEITH SINCLAIR

University of Auckland

CONTENTS

LIST OF PLATES

ACKNOWLEDGEMENTS

I wish to thank Mr. Keith Mackenzie of 28 Ladbroke Grove, Notting Hill, London, for permission to reproduce Max Beerbohm's cartoon of Reeves. The late W. H. Montgomery gave me permission to reproduce the two other cartoons. The Alexander Turnbull Library kindly provided the photograph of the Ballance Cabinet. I found the photograph of Reeves aged about seventeen, unidentified, in an old album at Hororata, then the home of Mr. Tristram Reeves. Two people, Miss Georgie Robison and E. R. Webb, who knew Reeves when he was a few years older, confirmed my opinion that it was, indeed, Reeves without a moustache. Members of Reeves's family generously provided the other illustrations.

ABBREVIATIONS

AJHR	*Appendices to the Journals of the New Zealand House of Representatives.*
PD	*New Zealand Parliamentary Debates.*
CT	*Canterbury Times.*
LT	*Lyttelton Times.*

The following manuscript collections are also referred to in footnotes in an abbreviated form:

Alpers MSS	Papers of O. T. J. Alpers, Alexander Turnbull Library, Wellington.
Ballance MSS	Papers of John Ballance, Turnbull Library.
Grey MSS	Papers of Sir George Grey, Auckland Public Library.
Hall MSS	Papers of Sir John Hall, General Assembly Library, Wellington.
'Letters from Men of Mark'	Letters from Men of Mark in New Zealand to the Hon. W. P. Reeves, British Library of Political and Economic Science, London School of Economics.
H. D. Lloyd MSS	Papers of Henry Demarest Lloyd, Wisconsin State Historical Society Library, Madison, Wisconsin.
LSE Archives	Archives of the London School of Economics.
W.H. Montgomery MSS	Papers of W. H. Montgomery, Little River, Canterbury
Passfield MSS	Papers of Lord and Lady Passfield, British Library of Political and Economic Science.
Reeves MSS	Papers of William Pember Reeves, Turnbull Library.

Richmond-Atkinson MSS	Papers of the Richmond and Atkinson families, General Assembly Library, Wellington.
Rolleston MSS	Papers of William Rolleston, Turnbull Library.
G. H. Scholefield MSS	Papers of the late G. H. Scholefield, Wellington.
Seddon MSS	Papers of Richard John Seddon in the National Archives, Wellington or in the possession of Mr. T. E. Y. Seddon, Wellington.
Stout MSS	Papers of Sir Robert Stout, Turnbull Library.
C. O. Torlesse MSS	Canterbury Museum, Christchurch

Other manuscript sources are adequately identified in footnotes.

PROLOGUE:
A MINISTERIAL VISITATION
1857

CHRISTOPHER WILLIAM RICHMOND was paying his first visit to
Canterbury, which interested him a great deal. It was the newest
settlement, the latest to be founded on the paper model constructed by Edward Gibbon Wakefield. He was curious to see
how 'systematic colonisation', far from successful in his own
province of Taranaki, had worked out on these great plains, so
different from the rugged hills and dense bush he knew.

Ten days after landing at Lyttelton, while 'keeping house' for
his host and hostess, Mr. and Mrs. Tancred, who had gone to
church, he began a letter to his wife:

Christchurch N.Z. 25th October 1857

My dearest Emily,

Though it is probable that I shall be with you as soon as this letter
can reach you I shall nevertheless put on paper some record of my
doings here whilst the impression is fresh on my mind. Writing at the
time like sketching from nature generally seems to be more vivid, & I
find my memory is so bad that if I fail to jot down my day's works
within a week I am unable to give a consecutive account of myself....
If you will look at the map of New Zealand you will see how
curiously the oval peninsula called Banks's is stuck on to the mainland
of the Southern Island. You will also see that it is very rugged & cut
into by deep inlets of the sea not unlike in their appearance on the
map to the Norwegian Fiords. One of these deep arms of the sea, the
nearest to the main, forms the Harbour of Lyttelton called Port
Victoria, or sometimes Port Cooper. The dark hills rise steeply from
the water on every side not leaving in most places room even for a
road. But in one corner amongst these hills is stuck the Town of
Lyttelton. I say 'stuck' because it seems to have much ado to keep
itself from sliding into the waters of its Harbour. The forms of the hills
have much grandeur. In places their summits rise into craggy Tors
which recall Dartmoor. But the place is a desolate abode.... Its people
appear as disagreeable a set as I have seen in New Zealand. Fancy the
Auckland carters & Boatmen cut off & formed into a community by

themselves, privileged to levy toll on all strangers & you will understand what a nice society that of Lyttelton must be. Two or three publicans are I believe the most influential people in the place. Nobody stops there who can get out of it. Everything is dearer there than at Christchurch, although all imported goods pass of necessity through Lyttelton. Poor Hamilton the Collector of Customs condemned to reside there I pity from the bottom of my heart. He is a pleasant amicable gentlemanly man of about 32 who has not long since married a lady of a numerous house, a Miss Townsend. They have a little boy about a twelvemonth old, a neatly made delicate little fellow. Their house accommodation we should think very limited even in New Plymouth. Indeed I find Canterbury behind all the other settlements in this particular. They had not room to take me in & I could not have thought of trespassing upon them in so small a House. I put up at a Boarding House where several young men board, amongst them young Cooper brother of G. S. Cooper [a government officer in Taranaki], a Clerk in the Custom House. I was advised to avoid soiling my dignity by putting up at the Mitre—a house which it is said no gentleman likes to enter but which is nevertheless the sole Hotel. I only remained in Lyttelton two nights namely Thursday Oct 15th, & Friday—starting on Saturday morning on horseback with Hall[1] for Christchurch. My portmanteau was carried over the hill on a Pack-Horse. Carts do not use the Bridle path. Heavy goods are unladen from the ships in the Harbour into boats, which go *out* of the Harbour again round Godley Head & then over the Sumner bar at the mouth of the Heathcote & Avon into the Heathcote River, which is navigable by boats for a few miles. The head of the navigation is on the Christchurch road a short distance (two or three miles I believe) from that place....

Sat. 17 Oct.

Well I really must get over the Hill out of that dark dull Lyttelton, so Jack Hall & I will jog on; and now have reached the summit of the Bridle path. We pull up our horses & sit admiring the grand view which thence opens upon us. If you will look at your map, & put your needle into the craggy ridge which divides the deep valley of Port Victoria from the Plains you will see a little of what we saw. Before us from the foot of the hills stretched the brown Plain—a perfect level in appearance—as level as the sea itself—into the faint distance—out of which rose, sharp & distinct at their summits, though hazy purple at their bases, the snowy ranges bounding the plain with their vast sweep, terminated by the distant Kaikoras. The outer range of lower elevation, just now beautifully powdered with snow like Jeames of

<hr>

[1] Later Sir John Hall.

Buckley Square [in Thackeray's *The Yellowplush Papers*]. At the foot of the hills green corn fields & meadows showed the hand of man & further on the plain appeared dotted with Homesteads—some six miles distant lay Christchurch a little patch of scattered houses—a mere nothing in the vastness of the plain—no building of any elevation marks the Town. There is not in this Church of England settlement so much as a shingled spire. When the time comes however (if ever it does come) the Plains will afford a magnificent site for a cathedral. A great Gothic roof like Lincoln would loom like the Ark for fifty miles round. The brown of the plain melting into the purple & violet of the mountains with their 'shadowy pencilled valleys & snowy dells' makes a beautiful picture with a foreground of craggy & fantastic summits of the Port Hills, whilst to the Northwards stretches the sandy coastline, in an even curve, for miles & miles, edged with white Surf. We led our horses down & mounting at the foot of the descent were soon cantering along to the Heathcote Ferry which we crossed in a punt with 3 or 4 other mounted persons on their road to Christchurch Market. This Heathcote, understand, is a little deep narrow & (for New Zealand) sluggish stream, more like a canal (a winding one) than our rivers of Taranaki—something in the style of a Leicestershire stream, or a Norfolk one, but swifter than those. The Avon is much like it.—but clearer & swifter flowing brightly over its beds of water-cress, & dividing Christchurch Town site from corner to corner. The roads are long straight sandy. Over such a one we cantered into the Town. There is not a complete street in the place. The town site is very extensive & the houses dotted all over it. The beginnings of streets are scarcely more imposing than New Plymouth. There is not much choice in sites. The land is as flat as a pancake—treeless featureless—except the little river. You may as well build in one place as another. By the by in describing the plain I forgot to mention the patches of bush. Four or five such are visible from the summit of the bridle path drawn up like regiments on the plain. They are mostly white pine & of very limited extent. The largest at Kaiapoi (about nine miles from Christchurch) is in the hands of the natives having been reserved for them by Mr Kemp when he bought the district. We should think these patches wretched affairs at New Plymouth but here the timber alone is worth £30 or £40 per acre!!

Next morning, the weather looking threatening, Richmond sat down to describe his impressions of Christchurch. Opposite him at the same table sat his host, 'composing a Lecture on History to be delivered at the College here'. H. J. Tancred was one of the fathers of Canterbury and a prominent politician who was soon to join the Stafford ministry, in which Christopher Richmond was already the Colonial Secretary and Treasurer.

He had enjoyed himself immensely: 'With all these Canterbury gentlemen I find myself in substantial agreement on public questions, & what is of more importance in general tone of thought.... Whilst there is great liberality of feeling at Canterbury they keep fast hold of the old Formulae. In all the Houses I have yet been in they use Family Prayer.'

The 'style of living' he found quite like that in New Plymouth, more primitive than in Auckland or Wellington. Dinner parties were unknown: the settlers confined themselves to tea parties and an occasional ball. There seemed to be 'no snobbish exclusiveness at Canterbury—no such ridiculous airs as some of our half bred New Plymouth people affect to give themselves'.

Richmond had been welcomed at the Canterbury Club, by Gresson, an Irish barrister, who was Deputy Superintendent of the Province—J. E. FitzGerald, the Superintendent, being in England—and by all the local gentlemen. Many of them were Irish, and he found 'that geniality & sociability about all of them which one finds in well educated Irish people'. With C. C. Bowen, 'a clever young Rugby man, one of the editors of the *Lyttelton Times*', Richmond 'contracted an alliance'.

While he was in Christchurch there was an election for a new Superintendent. On nomination day he listened to the speeches of the two candidates, Brittan and Sefton Moorhouse.

There was not the ghost of a joke & scarcely the shadow of an idea in either speech. Both seem moderate men, holding that the Superintendents' main business is the promotion and supervision of Public Works. Both deprecate over-legislation in the Provinces. Joe Brittan is a much cleverer man than Moorhouse, who seems a softie. The show of hands was for Moorhouse—the announcement of which fact was greeted by a burst of music from a drum & two trumpets in the employ of that gentleman & by the display of several large calico flags of his colours. The whole thing very flat.

Jokes, apparently, were no better received in New Zealand politics in 1857 than they were to be thirty years or more later. A couple of days afterwards Richmond found 'Bowen in a scot because some personal epigrams upon the candidates in the Election for Superintendent & their supporters had been inserted in the *Lyttelton Times* (which Bowen edits) by his

collaborateur, Mr. Crosbie Ward. Bowen walked over at dead of
night to Lyttelton knocked up Ward & seized & destroyed the
whole of the issue of the paper which was printed ready for
publication on the morrow.' On voting day Moorhouse 'got a
great start on his adversary in one matter'—he hired the only
band in Christchurch—and won the election.

During Richmond's visit to Christchurch, W. J. W. Hamilton,
the Collector of Customs, came over from Lyttelton and on the
21st of October they rode off to visit some 'connections' of his at
Rangiora, twenty miles to the north on the Ashley river. At first
they had to take a circuitous route to avoid swamps, but soon
they were galloping over the tussock.

It is a glorious feeling of freedom one has out on these plains & nothing
to stop you for 30 or 40 miles at a stretch. Nothing indeed for a hundred
miles but the Rivers which however are formidable obstacles
enough.... Their beds are often a mile wide or more bounded by
shingly cliffs. There they range about spoiling a wide tract of country
& with their blue water threads cutting it up into little shingly islands
clothed with a scanty vegetation.

Soon they reached 'a few enclosures near one of those dark
Bush bataillons' he had seen from the summit of the Bridle Path,
where a little village was springing up. Hamilton Ward, who was
married to a second Miss Townsend, was away 'draying' wool,
but his wife was there. Richmond thought her 'a pretty little
person with the limited ideas (I should guess) of a colonial-
reared girl. She plays very fairly and has a nice voice. She may
just now be feeling that marriage is in certain respects a hard
bargain for the wife.'

With the H. Wards are living newly arrived friends who seem to be in
temporary Partnership to wit the Reeves's. W. Reeves is a stout,
healthy young fellow city bred—was in a Banking house, then tried
the Stock Exchange (where he did not succeed)—After tasting the
pleasures of London from the Opera House down to Cremorne &
Rosherville in company with friends addicted to gorgeous waistcoats
& neckties & redundant jewellery he appears to have become smitten
with the daughter of some warm city man living in good not to say
luxurious style at Clapham.... The warm city man sends his sons to
the public schools & on perchance to the university & gets the best
masters for his daughters—who put into them whatever the best

masters can put in. Altogether Reeves has not done ill for himself. His wife has the manners & appearance of a lady—plays well—very well but without much feeling—sings not very well—a plain face—dark hair & nose slightly upturned—very tall & a good figure—dresses well & has especially beautiful collars & sleeves. Mrs. Reeves so far from objecting to smoking is decidedly of opinion (all her opinions are decided) that all gentlemen should smoke. All *gentlemen* in England smoke. Edward [her brother] smoked before he married. But he never *smelt* of smoke—gentlemen never do smell of smoke but snobs do—that is the difference between gentlemen & snobs. Of course gentlemen never smoke in a sitting room—all gentlemen's houses have smoking rooms. *We* always had a smoking room at Clapham. The Reeves have a little girl & a boy born in Lyttleton just after arrival—the very heaviest little lump of lead I ever took hold of. An excellent little fellow never cries, or has anything the matter with him, & sits in his chair amusing himself for hours. NB. only seven months old! Now this is real goodness. Reeves takes kindly, & even enthusiastically, to his new work. Nothing could induce him to take to office work again. So absorbed was he in his function of Bullock driver to the plough man that he could scarcely say goodbye. These people conform readily to the public opinion of a place where no man's above his work. But enough of the Reeves's—of whom I know not why I have said so much.[1]

It was a fortunate chance that Richmond dwelt so long on his subject. Not everybody finds himself, like the infant William Pember Reeves, described by a Colonial Secretary who writes so well, who is a friend of Richard Hutton, editor of the *National Review*, and of Arthur Hugh Clough, the poet.

At thirty-six C. W. Richmond was one of the leading men in the Colony. After he was called to the Bar of the Middle Temple, indifferent health and indifferent success led him in 1853 to migrate to New Plymouth where two of his brothers had already settled. With him travelled his brother-in-law, Harry Atkinson, who became a perennial premier, and other members of their families, who formed a tribe of their own in Taranaki. Three years later Richmond was a member of E. W. Stafford's cabinet. He had the misfortune, in 1860, to be Native Minister when the Europeans and the Maoris began to fight in Taranaki

---

[1] I am much indebted to the late Dr. G. H. Scholefield for showing me this letter, most of which he later published in his edition of *The Richmond–Atkinson Papers*, Wellington, 1960.

over a discreditable purchase of Maori land by the Government. Though he had not initiated the policy that led to war, Richmond had supported it. He suffered greatly from the strain of war-time duties and from the justifiably bitter attacks on the Government by old friends. Soon, after five years of office, he retreated to the Supreme Court and to the solace of reading philosophy and poetry. His delicate constitution and sensitive nature had not been happy qualifications for a political career. 'He sometimes forgot that this world is not a system of pure mathematics', wrote a contemporary, William Gisborne:

He was a man more fitted for the study than for the rough work of political life. Earnestness pervaded ... his whole nature; and every word and act came straight from the heart. His speeches and his writings were admirable for their force of expression; he was fastidious in the choice of appropriate language; and he was a master of phrases.... In controversy Mr. Richmond was a formidable antagonist. He had great logical power, he deeply studied his subject, and, from strength of earnestness and feeling, made controversy, not a mere passage of arms, but a struggle as it were for life. At the same time, there is no doubt that this warmth of temper placed him at a disadvantage in an encounter with a cool and clever opponent.... Mr. Richmond ... though he was far from strong ... was incessantly at work. A powerful mind enshrined in a frail body, though in some respects a painful, is always an ennobling sight; the lustre which shines within and without the feeble covering shows more vividly the immortal part of man, and the possible heroism of life on earth.[1]

Many of those phrases might, equally appropriately, be used to describe William Pember Reeves. It is pleasant to imagine that something more than chance made Richmond's pen linger, that October morning in 1857; to see him as waving a wand and calling on the sturdy child to follow him to a life of law and legislation, of literature. But if this seems too fanciful, it may at least be said, though the coincidences were not surprising in such a small settlement, that Richmond's inquisitorial steps in Canterbury crossed the Reeveses' future paths at many points.

[1] *New Zealand Rulers and Statesmen*, London, 1897, pp. 92–93.

I

PARENTS AND PILGRIMS
1825–61

WILLIAM PEMBER REEVES was born a New Zealander, but (he was to observe) he 'only just managed it', narrowly escaping being born 'a native of the Parish of Stepney'. His father, William, was a Londoner, born in Clapham in 1825, the son of a civil servant who was a Receiver of Fee Farm Rents. At a private school William Reeves made friends with a boy named Coleridge J. Kennard, and later became a clerk in the private banking house of Denison, Heywood, Kennards & Co.[1] In 1848 he became a member of the Stock Exchange.[2]

The family of William Pember Reeves's mother, Ellen Pember, was altogether grander.[3] The Pembers traced their ancestry back to Robert Pember, a scholar from Hereford who was a Fellow of St. John's College, Cambridge, in the early sixteenth century. He was a tutor of Roger Ascham, the Elizabethan scholar and diplomat, whom he encouraged not only to pursue his classical studies, but to play the lute and practise archery—'an honest exercise befitting an honest and studious man'. Early in the next century, having made his fortune in London, another ancestor, Francis Pember, purchased several Herefordshire manors, including the fine property of Newport (or Neiuport) House. The family in the next generation then claimed a coat of arms—Argent: Three pheasants proper,

---

[1] On this firm, see J. Sykes, *The Amalgamation Movement in English Banking*, London, 1926, p. 31; F. G. Hilton Price, *A Handbook of London Bankers*, London, 1876, p. 76. Miss Patricia Quinn of the Bank of New South Wales, Sydney, helped me on this point.

[2] I am indebted to the Secretary of the Council of the London Stock Exchange for information on Reeves's membership.

[3] Francis Pember, *Notes on the Family of Pember of Newport House, Herefordshire*, privately printed, Shrewsbury, 1942.

PLATE I

b. W. P. Reeves's mother, Paris, c. 1854

a. W. P. Reeves's father, William Reeves

a chief Azure. Their crest: on a mount Vert, a pheasant feeding on a stalk of wheat proper.

A Pember in 1650 was High Sheriff of Herefordshire; another was a Fellow of Balliol. The church, the law, trade, the squire-archy called others to useful lives. In about 1800 St. John Pember (who had, like many of the family, 'the long Herefordshire nose'), moved to London. There his son, John Edward Ross Pember, was for many years a successful member of the Stock Exchange. He lived in a large house in substantial grounds near Clapham Park, a district then much favoured by 'warm city men'. His house doubtless did not rival Battersea Rise, the home of Henry Thornton, the banker and member of the 'Clapham Sect', which had thirty-four bedrooms upstairs; but perhaps it resembled that of another neighbour, Thackeray's Mr. Newcome—a palace 'surrounded by lawns and gardens, pineries, graperies, aviaries', a paradise 'separated from the outer world by a thick hedge of tall trees, and an ivy-covered porter's gate.... It was a serious paradise. As you entered at the gate, gravity fell on you; and decorum wrapped you in a garment of starch.'

His eldest son, Edward Henry, read law at Corpus Christi College, Oxford. He became a distinguished parliamentary lawyer and a gentleman poet who published, about the end of the century, translations of Sophocles and Aeschylus, verse plays and several volumes of verse with such titles as *The Death-Song of Thamyrus*, *The Voyage of the Phocaeans*, or *The Finding of the Pheidippides*, which reveal much learning and a faint talent. Another son, Frederick, took his degree at Christ Church, Oxford, and entered Holy Orders. George Herbert was educated at Westminster and Trinity College, Cambridge, before going on the Stock Exchange. Altogether there were nine children. Ellen, who was born in 1833, finished her education in France after private tutors had done their best. A charming drawing survives of her at that time. The slight up-turn of her nose is not disguised; her mouth petulant; her eyes dreaming; her posture dignified. She learned the piano (it is said) from Sterndale Bennett and painted careful miniatures of flowers and birds, in perfect detail and glowing colours. She, too, wrote verse. Her young lover, William Reeves, lacking this gift, sent her a few

lines from Burns, suitably revised, when he was courting her in
1851:

> Ellen, thy charms my bosom fire
> And waste my soul with care;
> But ah! how bootless to admire
> When fated to despair!

It was true, he was not altogether the most desirable match,
and had perhaps little reason to hope. But he weaned himself—
or was weaned—from the attractions of London's pleasure
gardens at Cremorne and Rosherville; gave up the fireworks and
fêtes champêtres, the grottoes and gothic ruins. He was rather
handsome, despite a prominent pointed nose. And was accepted.
In 1853 they married. Fourteen months later, in June 1854, he
was declared a defaulter on the Stock Exchange, but was
readmitted after a few days, when the Committee was informed
that he had paid all claims in full. It might be surmised (as later
events tend to confirm) that he found keeping up the with
Pembers an expensive effort which led him into unwise speculations; but whether he was rescued by his wife's or his own family
is unknown.

Two children were born at The Grove, Clapham: Annabel
Ellen in November 1854, and Coleridge Edward (who died at
three months) a year later. William was then 'attracted'—
according to one account[1]—by an advertisement of the 'New
Zealand Land Company'; more probably there was pressure
from the direction of Clapham Park. At the end of 1856 the
young couple, with their daughter and a servant, sailed for
Wellington, sad and fearful one might guess—like Ford Madox
Brown's emigrants in 'The Last of England'—yet dreaming,
too, of fortunes won and a substantial house built, with smoking
room, in the antipodes.

The *Rose of Sharon* reached its destination on 19 January 1857.
The Reeveses then took passages for Lyttelton in the small
steamer *Zingari*.[2] Not surprisingly, the first settler they met there
was W. J. W. Hamilton, the Collector of Customs. It speaks well
for both of them that he offered and Reeves accepted temporary

---

[1] Reeves MSS, small clipping book, p. 176. An article by Tom L. Mills, written in
1895 for the *Queensland Worker* and published in 1896. It is very informative about
Reeves, though possibly mistaken on this point.

[2] *N.Z. Spectator*, 21 Jan. 1857; LT. 28 Jan. 1857.

employment in the Customs House as a clerk at fifteen shillings a day. On William's birthday, the 10th of February, Ellen gave birth to another son, whom they named William Pember. At the christening, Hamilton acted as one of the sponsors.

No doubt the fact that his father and a maternal great-grandfather had long noses, or that the Pembers produced intelligent men, rightly regarded, is important. But in weighing the heritage of the child we must look at circumstances more immediate if scarcely more tangible than genetics: at family tradition. The knowledge that grandfather is rich, that uncle is famous, the doubtless later knowledge that father failed on the Stock Exchange, were to have immense influence on the formation of the child's self-regard. And at the place; for the influence of the child's environment—his social heredity—was everywhere to be apparent in his life.

Canterbury was only seven years old. Eight years before, the plains had been almost as empty of man or beast as they were bare of trees. Archaic Polynesian huntsmen, centuries before, had exterminated the giant moa, birds that grazed in herds on the tussock. Tribal feuds had reduced the Maoris to a handful. Perhaps climatic changes had hastened the decline of both. There were by 1849 no Europeans but the 'Pre-Adamites'—a few settlers on the plains, twenty French families at Akaroa, on Banks Peninsula.

It was on these plains that the Canterbury Association decided to plant a Newest England (in some ways, Olde England), a colony planted after the fashion of Greek colonies of antiquity and seventeenth-century sectarian settlements of North America. Ten or twenty years before that the very idea of Canterbury would have been unthinkable. That the ideals of John Henry Newman and Jeremy Bentham could, however tenuously, be linked; that their disciples could ever join forces, or do so for the purpose of founding a colony; would in 1833 have appeared absurdities—a year after the philosopher's death, the year when the first of the *Tracts for the Times* appeared from the future cardinal's pen, the year of the abolition of slavery. A hierarchical and utilitarian colony? Apostolic push-pin instead of Botany Bay 'two up'? Yet it had happened. Into the long silences of the plains there intruded an inspired band of Anglican Pilgrims.

The idea of Canterbury was conceived by Edward Gibbon

Wakefield, one of the most remarkable men of his day—an 'amazing genius' was the verdict of one contemporary, yet 'sulky', 'machiavellian', 'satanic'. He grew up at the fountain-heads of humanitarianism and radicalism, for his Quaker family was related to the Gurneys and Frys (Elizabeth Fry was his cousin), while his father was a friend of James Mill and Francis Place. But the idealism he imbibed always rested uneasily with his perverse, unstable character. Imprisoned in Newgate for failing to abduct his second heiress, he saw the human material that was being transported to create the Australian colonies, and thought of applying to colonization some of the ideals of the radicals and philanthropists. By planned migration, perhaps the problems of England and of her colonies could be at once solved.

Wakefield's plan of 'systematic colonization', which was in varying but moderate degrees applied in South Australia and five New Zealand settlements, envisaged the emigration of a complete 'cross section' of English society with all its strata except the lowest and criminal. In existing colonies, he believed, where land was free, the labourer became his own landlord; the people scattered thinly over the wilderness and sank into barbarism. Civilization required a concentration of population and a division of labour. By the simple mechanism of placing on land a price 'sufficient' to keep labourers labouring for a time, he argued, the class system would be maintained. The dispersal of population could be regulated by land sales, the revenues from which would bring out a steady flow of labour. A leisured squirearchy would preserve the decencies and felicities of civilized society. For the rich, colonization would become pleasurable instead of painful: capitalists would emigrate to colonies where there was more land, less competition, high interest rates and civilization.

The idea was fundamentally conservative, but most of the men who first took up Wakefield's doctrines were not. Colonial policy and founding colonies became for a time prerogatives of the radicals, utilitarians and evangelicals. Wellington, the first Wakefield settlement in New Zealand, was meant to be, the *Times* judged, a 'radical Utopia'. In the same year, 1840, Auckland was established as an evangelical capital, where humanitarian governors would solve the problem of civilizing

PLATE 2

b. William Pember Reeves and his mother

a. William Pember Reeves, c. 1904

the Maoris without exterminating them in the process. Yet why should not the High Church conservatives lend a hand?

In 1847, when Wakefield was promoting the idea of denominational settlements (the first of which was Free Church Otago in 1848), the same notion had occurred to John Robert Godley, a briefless Tory barrister and a devout young Irish squire. Godley, who had been at Christ Church in the early years of the Oxford Movement, had become a disciple of Wakefield as well as of Newman. Travel in North America had interested him in colonization; the Irish potato famine of 1846–7 had led him to see migration as the solution to the social evils of the Old World. He considered that civilization was in danger of being swept away by the rise of the ignorant masses; like Castlereagh, a generation earlier, while thinking its victory inevitable, he felt it better to retard than to encourage the dangerous principle of equality which was abroad. Perhaps, if society could not be saved at home by the emigration of excess numbers, it might at least, by the same process, be regenerated abroad. Wakefield convinced him that the Establishment could be transported. Church and state, in a colony bound by Anglican piety, would help prepare the way for 'a safe democracy'.

Inspired by Wakefield, Godley formed the Canterbury Association in 1848, under the presidency of the Archbishop of Canterbury, and with a splendid array of bishops and Tory politicians and philanthropists among its members. The plan of founding a denominational settlement based on the 'sufficient price' was soon adopted. At the end of 1849 Godley sailed for New Zealand to help prepare the way for the Canterbury Pilgrims, the vanguard of whom arrived, in the First Four Ships, in December 1850.

Though Canterbury was the best prepared, the happiest of New Zealand settlements in its early years, nevertheless its citizens soon learned the vanity of planning the future of colonies. The ideal of an exclusive community had from the first to be abandoned; there were too many Noncomformists and Catholics. Canterbury became the most Anglican Province, but the church played a relatively minor part in its leadership. There was no money for the churches that had been envisaged. The first bishop-designate, despite his coach and his silver voice, proved singularly unsuitable and departed with his flock's

cordial disrespect. Religion played no greater part than in
England in uniting the classes. One of the pioneers, C. O.
Torlesse, observed that they almost never saw a labourer at
church; churchgoers were 'mostly the upper and middle class
and women and children of the poor'. The university which had
been talked of in England had to be postponed for a generation,
though the Christ's College Grammar School was established in
1851.

There was an absence of aristocrats. Wakefield's search for a
titled leader had been unsuccessful, although the dissolute young
Lord Frederick Montagu turned up in the colony. Canterbury
did, however, have a number of younger sons and connexions of
the aristocracy. There was a similar shortage of wealthy
employers. It was curious, wrote one of the Pilgrims, Conway
Rose, that despite the high rate of interest, 'no capitalist ever
comes out to a colony'. It was, he wrote, 'with much reason
conjectured that no one with £5,000 in his pocket ever yet came
to New Zealand'.[1] Certainly such men were rare. Though a
good proportion—perhaps a quarter—of the Pilgrims were men
of comfortable means, few were rich men. Many of the leaders
were, Charles Torlesse observed, of 'reduced good Irish family'.

Far from respecting their betters, the working class soon
became 'mightily republican', as another pioneer observed on
landing in Lyttelton. Conway Rose considered that 'no man who
can think at all, is anything but an ultra radical—all for free
institutions, free trade, free church, and I never heard a solid or
serious objection raised to *universal suffrage*! For indeed you
quickly see here that one man is as good as another... .'

In a colony, as elsewhere, church and state, political
philosophy and civilization, had to wait on the table of
economics. In Canterbury, like all new settlements, the great
question was one Wakefield had not the experience to answer:
how to establish a viable economy. His writings assumed an
agricultural society, small mixed farms on English lines. But, as
Conway Rose wrote in 1852, 'Farming here is all my eye.
Labourer's wages are from 27/– to 30/– a week, your crops are by
no means good, and the price of the produce very little more

---

[1] I am indebted to the late Mr. C. R. Straubel for copies of Rose's letters. One
dated 31 May 1852, is in the Mitchell Library, Sydney. Two, dated 25 March 1852,
20 October 1853, are in the Alexander Turnbull Library, Wellington.

than in England.' The high price of £3 an acre placed on land was *not* 'sufficient': labourers almost immediately acquired a patch of land and augmented their income by market gardening and dairying. It was a truism, Torlesse wrote, 'that it won't pay a gentleman to farm'. How, then, was he to make a profitable living? And since there were no large nearby markets for perishable foodstuffs, how was the colony to earn a living; how could it pay for essential imports?

Most of the Pilgrims, landing in ignorance of local conditions, had sunk their capital in land near Christchurch. But Charles Torlesse, a nephew of Wakefield, who had been in Canterbury working as a surveyor for the Association for two years when the Pilgrims arrived, had learned from experience. Realizing the value of timber, he chose a section near the Rangiora bush. Then he leased 1,750 acres of pasturage at £14 a year, and began running stock belonging to absentee or other owners on 'thirds', a system learned from Australia, by which he received a third of the profits and increase for his labours.

The Canterbury plains seemed created for sheep. Within a few months Godley had to let in the 'shagroons', Australian stockmen, who leased pasturage and ran sheep. Wakefield had supposed that the ownership of land must be the basis of colonial life: in Canterbury it was the ownership of sheep. In less than three years, as some of the Pilgrims joined the 'shagroons', there were a hundred sheep runs; the population was scattered over a million acres. When Samuel Butler took up the Mesopotamia run in 1860, he heard a sailor maintain that the end of the world was at hand, 'the principal argument appearing to be that there was no more sheep country to be found in Canterbury'. Butler doubled his £4,000 in four years.

How could civilization be maintained in such a place? When two young gentlemen proposed to take up a sheep station in 1852, Mrs. Godley ('a lady-like icicle', Rose thought her, but a witty one) warned them that they would become 'semi-barbarous', and 'begged them to have a lay figure of a lady, carefully draped, set up in their usual sitting-room, and always to behave before it as if it were their mother'. The life of the squatter, as the sheep men were called, was for long extremely primitive. Godley found a 'shagroon', Mark Stoddard (who became one of a group of gentlemen-poets), living on his run 'in a horrible den, or cabin, into which you creep through a hole; there being neither door nor window. The floor was of liquid mud . . . .'

When Godley first thought of Canterbury, he confessed 'it pictured itself in my mind in the colours of a Utopia'. When he returned to England in December 1852, they had faded in the colonial sun. Yet much remained. The colonists soon became self-governing, as they had hoped. Land sales did not keep labourers subservient, but they yielded good revenues to pay for immigration and public works, even some churches and schools. Sheep farming, which required substantial initial capital, attracted men rich or of good credit, who grew richer or more credit-worthy. Despite the egalitarian public opinion and manners, wealth produced a local gentry, classes—and snobbery. Wool laid the foundations for a European New World civilization.[1]

How to make a living was the immediate problem confronting William Reeves in 1857. He seems to have determined to forsake the towns, but he knew nothing of farming or the merits of the various districts in Canterbury. Here his new friends, and their families, were helpful. Hamilton, Dr. Donald, the Medical Officer, and Crosbie Ward, the vivacious co-editor of the *Lyttelton Times*, had married three of the six daughters of James Townsend, who came out in one of the First Ships. Two more were married to Hamilton Ward and Charles Torlesse at Rangiora. The sixth was the wife of J. C. Boys, a friend of Torlesse, who was a settler and member of the Land Board at Kaiapoi.

---

[1] The books most helpful to me in writing this sketch of the foundation of Canterbury were: C. E. Carrington, *John Robert Godley of Canterbury*, Christchurch, 1950; J. Hight and C. R. Straubel (ed.), *A History of Canterbury*, Christchurch, 1957, Vol. 1 written by G. Jobberns, C. R. Straubel and L. C. Webb; D. N. Hawkins, *Beyond the Waimakariri*, Christchurch, 1957; J. Johnson, *The Story of Lyttelton 1849–1949*, Lyttelton, 1952; G. E. Mannering, *Eighty Years in New Zealand*, Christchurch, 1943; J. P. Morrison, *The Evolution of a City*, [Christchurch], 1948. Of early pamphlets, letters etc., the following were most useful: C. W. Adams, *A Spring in the Canterbury Settlement*, London, 1853; Lady Barker, *Station Life in New Zealand*, Christchurch, 1951; S. S. Crawford, *Sheep and Sheepmen of Canterbury, 1850–1914*, Christchurch, 1949; Charlotte Godley, *Letters from Early New Zealand*, (ed. J. R. Godley), Christchurch, 1951; S. Hodgkinson, *Emigration to New Zealand: A Description of the Province of Canterbury*, London, 1856; C. L. Innes, *Canterbury Sketches*, Christchurch, 1879; R. B. Paul, *Letters from Canterbury, New Zealand*, London, 1857; Mrs. Charles Thomson, *Twelve Years in Canterbury, New Zealand*, London, [1867].

Reeves was convinced of the attractions of that district. In June the family moved to the 'Lion', a corrugated iron hotel just opened by Captain Foster in Rangiora. Torlesse met them there. A few days later they rode round the district looking for a section. Reeves chose one near Torlesse's and Ward's, on the edge of the bush. In July he rode to Kaiapoi to see Boys about buying the land, and the family moved in with the Hamilton Wards, to 'go shares' while their own house was being built.

Reeves could hardly have met a better person to initiate him into the arts of Canterbury farming. Hamilton Ward had come out with two brothers among the Pilgrims. When his brothers were tragically drowned, Mrs. Godley took him in her care until another brother, Crosbie, arrived. She was impressed with the steadiness with which he took to the management of their farm, but soon thought him 'much too "Colonial"' for her fancy, 'much too fond, for his age (seventeen), of making a good bargain'. She wished he had learnt 'that there are things in the world to care for besides "stock" and money'. More of the Canterbury settlers did learn this than would seem at all likely; they did not all

> talk of gold and sheep
> And think of sheep and gold.

William Reeves was one of the Rangiora pioneers. There were only about six houses when he arrived; only three or four hundred acres ploughed. Torlesse's diary[1] gives a vivid impression of Reeves's first apprenticeship in New Zealand, carting firewood, fencing paddocks, searching for some wandering bullocks which Ward and he had bought. It is apparent that he was by no means penniless. His section of fifty acres cost him, at the new fixed price, £2 an acre; his house and farming implements £200 or £300 more. By the end of 1857 he was buying and selling sheep. He contributed £35 towards the cost of a direct road to Rangiora, which the settlers wanted the Provincial Government to make. It seems unlikely that he could spend the £2,000 or £3,000 necessary to purchase the goodwill of a run and a flock, but it is evident from his investments within a year or two of landing that his capital amounted to at least £1,000

[1] C. O. Torlesse MSS, Canterbury Museum, Christchurch. The information in the previous sentence is derived from a letter by W. Reeves, LT, 6 Nov. 1872.

(which we should multiply by five or more to form a comparison with the modern New Zealand pound).

From the first he entered vigorously into the public affairs of his little community. He became honorary secretary of a committee collecting funds for a church (St. John the Divine, which was built in 1860 and still stands). Soon he was in the thick of that most arcane of activities, Canterbury church politics. Torlesse hoped that his brother Henry (who was *not*, Richmond noted with amusement, married to a Miss Townsend) would be appointed as the local clergyman. When the time came to elect the church wardens, Ward, Torlesse and Reeves held a 'pre-election' meeting with their two nominees 'to settle upon our course of proceedings at the public meeting on Monday night. Conspirators met at night in the wood over a bush fire and had an interesting discussion.' At the public meeting their candidates were elected without opposition.

In May 1858 the Reeves family moved into their new house; already William was seeking opportunities bigger than were presented by a fifty-acre section, while Torlesse was on the look-out for someone to manage his run, 'Fernside', where he had just built a new house, while he visited his family in Suffolk. In August Reeves agreed to become his manager until after the shearing. The family, to which had been added another son, moved to 'Fernside', a few miles away. Their new home was made of cob (sundried bricks made of clay and straw) and wonderfully situated on a terrace on the Mairaki downs, facing towards the Ashley river a mile away.

For a few months Reeves gained a new experience of colonial life. Torlesse's diary records their routine: one day tailing lambs and draughting wethers; another washing 2,500 wethers in the Ashley; shearing; and, for recreation, hunting the innumerable wild pigs—once Torlesse put 20 pistol shots into a boar, and rode after him for an hour before killing him.

For Mrs. Reeves, 'Fernside' must have been a considerable improvement on their smaller house at Rangiora. The Bishop of Christchurch came to christen her new baby, Edmund Crosbie. Crosbie Ward and his wife and Torlesse were his godparents. The Reeveses gave a 'Bachelors' Ball' in their Rangiora house in December, and invited their guests to dinner at 'Fernside' on Christmas Day. Their life was a rural round, but they were not content. Reeves sold his Rangiora property and bought 500 ewes. He could not, however, agree with Torlesse on their future relationship at 'Fernside'. Torlesse wanted Reeves as his manager; Reeves apparently wanted a partnership. After much discussion, and a little temporary ill-feeling, Reeves left 'Fernside' in April 1859. Torlesse paid him £321 and bought his ewes for £700.

The Reeveses went to live at 'Ferry mead', the house built by James Townsend, the elderly father of so many Canterbury mothers, who had moved to Rangiora. It was a fine house, with parallel twin gables, seven rooms, totara exterior walls lined with Tasmanian timber, and with thirteen acres of grounds.[1] The little port is no longer used; a bridge has, since 1864, replaced the ferry, where traffic between Lyttelton or Sumner and Christchurch crossed the Heathcote, but the house still stands, tucked between the stream and the hills.

It was common for a new settler, whose act of migration itself indicated a certain restlessness, to 'try his hand' at various jobs. Reeves's next occupation lasted only a few months. In 1857 the Sumner Road, over the hills to Lyttelton, had been opened. It was an improvement on the Bridle path and it was briefly hoped that it would now be unnecessary to bring goods from Lyttelton into Christchurch over the Sumner bar which cost, it was said, half as much as transporting them from London to Lyttelton. But the gradients were discouragingly steep. From the crest of Evans' Pass down to Lyttelton the road was a frightful zig-zag. When the road was opened the Superintendent, J. E. Fitz-Gerald, drove a tandem over it, but his passengers had to dismount and 'let him down easy with ropes' while grooms held the horses' heads.

In June 1859 Reeves advertised in the *Lyttelton Times* that he had begun business as a carrier, with drays leaving Lyttelton and Christchurch daily. The experiment failed. In January 1860 he reduced his rates.[2] Throughout the rest of the year he was offering to sell his horses, carts, drays and harness, or to accept grain in exchange. We may presume that he was defeated by the zig-zag. The road could be used only by pedestrians and

---

[1] The name of the house was variously spelt as 'Ferry mead', 'Ferrymead' or 'Ferry Mead'. See, e.g., LT, 12 Nov. 1862, advertisement.

[2] LT, 8 June, 29 Oct. 1859 and other dates; 14 Jan., 3 March to 15 Dec. 1860.

horsemen. The transportation of goods over the bar continued until a tunnel was opened in 1863.

By 1860 Reeves had found a better prospect. He had become a partner in the *Lyttelton Times*. This bi-weekly newspaper had first been published in 1851, a month after the Pilgrims landed, under the editorship of J. E. FitzGerald. In 1856 the owner sold out to Crosbie Ward and C. C. Bowen for £5,000 (£1,500 and a mortgage). Ward, a good journalist and a witty versifier, became the editor, though Bowen occasionally wrote leaders. But relations between Ward and the more cautious, more conservative Bowen cannot have been easy, judging by the episode reported by C. W. Richmond. They were short of cash and the staff went unpaid for weeks at a time. Reeves bought out Bowen. A few years later a new partnership was formed in which Ward held 7/16, Reeves 6/16, W. J. W. Hamilton 2/16 and T. W. Maude (a friend who, like Reeves, had worked in the Customs House) 1/16 of the assets. Ward continued for a time as editor,[1] but cannot have been very active, for he was a Member of the House of Representatives and twice a cabinet minister before his death in 1867 at the age of thirty-five. Reeves was the manager. He knew nothing of newspapers, though his experience of business and farming was useful in the new apprenticeship he had to serve. He also helped with reporting and editing.

In March 1860 (C. O. Torlesse noted in his diary) Reeves revisited the Kaiapoi district to report an inquest for the *Times*. The report and the 'swingeing' leading article (which Reeves may have written too) struck a chord that would sound increasingly louder in the future of the *Times*, of Canterbury, and of three-year-old Willie Reeves.

An old man, exhausted and hungry, had begged shelter at the homestead of one of the great sheep men, G. H. Moore. Refused the customary meal and a 'shake-down', turned out in a storm, he had shot himself. His body was left where it was found for three days, and then Moore refused to permit his men to make a coffin on Sunday. The magistrate gave a verdict of suicide and condemned Moore's behaviour. The *Lyttelton Times* was

---

[1] The Lyttelton Times Co. minutes commence at a later date and shed no light on these events. Newspaper reports are contradictory: LT, 6 April 1891, 4 April 1893; *Christchurch Times*, 29 June 1935. The exact date when this partnership began is not known. 'Ward & Reeves' published the LT from 13 Feb. 1861.

indignant: 'Mr. Moore of Glenmark is the possessor of sixty thousand acres of land. In making so large a purchase it seems to have been his object, besides the growth of wool, to keep as far removed from him as possible the society and sympathies of his fellow creatures. Inside his boundary humanity has no rights: he has bought them up with the freehold at so much an acre.'[1]

[1] LT, 21 March 1860.

FRAGMENTS OF A CHILDHOOD
1861–5

WILLIAM PEMBER REEVES's earliest memory was of falling into the Heathcote River when the family lived at 'Ferry mead'. He was standing on the bank watching two sailors at work on the deck of a ketch, loaded with the odds-and-ends of coastal trade, which was mooring in the stream in front of the house. No four-year-old could resist such a sight. The bank gave way and in a moment he was splashing in a dozen feet of brownish water, running out to sea. The men heard his cries and jumped into the dinghy. As he came up a second time he felt strong hands grasp his neck and shoulders. Soon he was delivered wailing to his mother. All the rest of his life he remembered the taste of the brackish water; the pressure and noise in his ears as he went down in 'the dim grey-green swirl'; and the thump of the sailors as they tumbled into their dinghy.

He kept few memories of Lyttelton except for a little drama of royalty and the sea which might seem to contain symbols from a specifically New Zealand dream. The arrival of the mail steamer, *Storm Bird*, bringing English mail and news, had been signalled. She entered the harbour after nightfall, too late to berth at the primitive wharf, so his father went out in a boat with the Health Officer to get the news. Willie, 'an urchin of five, was allowed to crouch in the stern sheets', providing that he kept still and quiet. The boat drew up beneath the steamer's dark side, pierced by the glowing port-holes. A voice from the deck shouted, 'Death of the Prince Consort!' His father whispered that the Queen's husband was dead. It was March 1862. The *Lyttelton Times* brought out a special edition.[1]

---

[1] Reeves wrote two detailed descriptions of these two incidents and of that on board the *Parisian* which follows: 'Memoirs' and small clipping book, p. 110, clipping from *M.A.P.*, 15 July 1905, in Reeves MSS. The extra edition of the *Lyttelton Times* was published 16 March 1862. The arrival of the *Parisian* was reported LT, 19 March 1864.

Episodes from childhood remain in our minds, sometimes because of some excitement, more often for no reason that we can discern, linked by no chain of days and weeks, but by a persistent sense of joy, of mystery or loss. The adult may figure out the date, but childhood knows no chronology more precise than from breakfast to bed and the family chronicle. We must rely on our own memories and imaginations to envisage the experiences which preceded and joined these two incidents: the pleasure of learning to walk, at Rangiora and 'Fernside', where every clump of tussock was a haystack sheltering the sweet native grasses on which the sheep grazed; his first encounters with the spiny Wild Irishman and the sharp sword grass; his wonder, first watching the nippy swamp-hen, listening to the chiming bell-birds in the Rangiora bush.

In July 1862, when he was five, he was sent to board at the Lincoln Cottage Preparatory School, a 'prep' school for the Christ's College Grammar School run by the Reverend Charles Alabaster, M.A., in Cranmer Square, Christchurch, at which boys from five to ten were taught English, Latin and other subjects for £40 a year.[1] The earliest photograph of him is at about this age. He stares at us, determined, healthy, possibly a little petulant. We might guess that he was rather 'spoiled' by his mother, pensive, almost sad, who holds him near her beautiful collar.

Alabaster wrote to assure William Reeves that his son was settling down happily, and he replied:

Your letter was very welcome to Mrs. Reeves and myself. We were naturally anxious to hear how our little boy bore his first separation from home. Making every allowance for a father's feelings I think you will be pleased with the little man. He is very open and ingenuous and I shall be surprised if you do not find that he has more than average ability. Besides being very fond of play he also shows a decided fondness for his books. He has also a capital memory and when all these are combined with robust health and good spirits, I think the foundation is formed of future excellence.

I confess I have great hopes of him from his being the exact counterpart of his uncle on the mother's side who carried away prizes at all the schools he was at and afterwards took a double first at Oxford.

[1] LT, 1 June 1861; 15 Jan. 1862; 10 Jan. 1863; 21 Jan. 1865.

I dare say you will smile when you read this but you must make allowances for a father's fondness for the little man has fixed himself very firmly in my heart.

Whatever his mental qualifications may ultimately prove, be assured that my chief desire is that he may grow up a Christian and a gentleman. In this hope I trust him to you, having full faith that you will do your utmost to make him both. I need not say that I place him unreservedly in your hands and that you need fear no injudicious interference with your plans in regard to him.

Mrs. Reeves unites with me in kind regards to Mrs. Alabaster and yourself.[1]

In November Charles Torlesse, who now lived in Christchurch, where he had entered into a partnership with a new arrival from Victoria, Henry Matson, as stock and station agents, went to visit Willie Reeves and the Donald boys at school. He had more doubts than Reeves about the merits of the establishment, and wrote: 'I had an interesting talk with Mr. Alabaster whose frail body still carries on & admits of some measure of usefulness.... I have no doubt Alabaster is a good manager—but the ménage is bad & I question the propriety of bringing boys up under the rule of such a feeble shred of a man.'

Nor did Torlesse altogether accept the views of the fond father about his son. Mrs. Reeves had been seriously ill, and in December it was 'quite decided' that she should go 'Home' for first-rate medical advice, though Torlesse found her by then 'pretty well and wonderfully better than I expected....' She took her two sons to London, leaving the oldest child, Annabel, and Marion, who had been born at 'Ferry mead', with her husband and the servants. How the baby, Gertrude, who had been born in Lyttelton in 1861, was disposed of, Torlesse did not mention.

Torlesse had, at last, paid his trip to England and returned, leaving his son Arthur staying with the grandparents. By March 1863 he was beginning to worry about Arthur's return and advised his people that he would prefer his son to return with Crosbie Ward (who was in England negotiating a mail service to New Zealand) and his wife rather 'than with the Reeves boys'. When, finally, Arthur was due to sail, in the care of a friend, but on the same ship as the Wards and Mrs. Reeves, Torlesse repeated his views to his sisters: 'I trust ... you will express the earnest wish of Alicia and myself that Arthur should be kept as clear as possible of the Reeves boys.'[1]

Just what was objectionable about the Reeves boys is uncertain, but from various hints we may conjecture that they were precocious, probably high-spirited and almost certainly disobedient, not qualities generally admired in New Zealand boys then or now. One incident, at least, on board the *Parisian* in December 1863, suggests that Torlesse's fears were rooted in some understanding of the boys' behaviour. The ship was making ten knots in the South Atlantic, and had a decided list to port. As a change from learning knots and studying the rigging, or watching the milch cows, Willie was observing the entrancing process of heaving the log. He climbed on a hen-coop, the top of which was almost flush with the rails. His eyes were fixed on the minute glass, through which the sands were running, in the second mate's hands. The vessel lurched, flinging him backwards; his head was over the lee bulwarks and his hands grasped air. The mate dropped his glass and caught him by the leg just in time.

After their return from England in March 1864, Arthur and Willie both went back to Alabaster's school, now somewhat improved (Torlesse felt) by the employment of two assistants. But in the same year Torlesse died during another trip 'Home'. His son, who lived to be an admiral, was taken to England. Alabaster also died in that year and, though his wife kept the school going, Reeves took his son away. At the age of eight he was enrolled at the Christchurch High School, a 'Boys' Academy' run by the Presbyterians. His boarding school days were over, for during his absence the *Lyttelton Times* had been moved to Christchurch and was being published thrice weekly to meet the competition of the Christchurch *Press*. His home was now in Christchurch which, together with shipping and the sea, provided the principal memories he retained of childhood.

Nearly a year of his boyhood and youth was spent at sea during two return voyages to England; nine months in sailing vessels. He always recalled the sight of Tristan da Cunha in 1864, a

[1] C. O. Torlesse MSS. On the firm of Matson and Torlesse, see LT, 27 Dec. 1862 10 Jan. 1863. For Matson's arrival, see LT, 19 June 1862.

welcome and romantic 'break in the weary loneliness of months of sea and sky', he wrote when he was an old man. He remembered 'how green it looked, how small and how utterly desolate. For some reason it gave me a greater sensation of utter loneliness than any ocean island I ever saw.'

Canterbury evoked similar images. Looking back on his childhood, he was to write in 1905, 'the dominant impression remaining is that of a life amid vast empty spaces. On one side lay the ocean, on the other a bare, grassy plain, thirty miles across. Beyond the plain were high, snowy Alps, range upon range ... the plain ... was simply a sea of yellowish, wind-swept grass.'[1]

Christchurch was scarcely less empty, the slightest human imprint on a bare land. In 1869 a lady described the town: 'The inhabitants have certainly made a mistake thinking that their City ought to be a great place, they have laid it out on a large scale, and the result is that they have it far too straggling. We are in a square [at Collins Hotel] but the centre is nothing but a Common with the [Christchurch] Club and its gardens on one side, pailings and trees enclosing a large house on the other, and a church and school on the third with the hotel, while the fourth still remains unoccupied.'[2] Nearly all the houses were of wood, nearly all two-storied and gable-ended in the town. The population was only 6,400 in 1864, after fourteen years of settlement. £7,000 had been 'buried' in laying the foundations of a cathedral, but not a stone of Richmond's 'Ark' was visible above ground in 1872, as Anthony Trollope noted during his travels.[3] Nor were the cultural aspirations of the Pilgrims realized. In 1864 only 46 per cent. of the school-age children were attending school, a record no better than Auckland's, whose citizens were reputedly quite unlettered. The rate of adult literacy, 69 per cent., was lower than in Auckland. The town was very unhealthy. The site chosen illustrated Mary Kingsley's observation on Libreville: 'The English love, above all things, settling in, or as near as possible to a good reeking stinking swamp.'[4] Infant deaths were very frequent, owing to diphtheria

---

[1] Reeves MSS, small clipping book, pp. 110-11.
[2] Ellen Fox to John Phillips, 25 Sept. 1869. Letter in possession of T. A. Parker, Santa Fe University.
[3] *Australia and New Zealand*, London, 1873, ii, p. 365.
[4] Cecil Howard, *Mary Kingsley*, London, 1957, p. 84.

and other diseases, in a town where water lay for months round many houses (as W. S. Robison, a local bank manager, complained in 1870). In 1863 the main streets had not been macadamized, and six hundred school children trudged through mud in a procession to celebrate the Prince of Wales's wedding. When Willie Reeves was at school, Christchurch still fell far short of the ambitions of its founders. The main vice—Torlesse observed—was intemperance. In 1861, 52,000 gallons of spirits, 26,000 gallons of wine and 104,000 gallons of beer and cider were imported to quench the thirst of the 16,000 people in the Province—who also maintained half a dozen local breweries!

The emptiness of the village and the plains, the emptiness of human life there, had a decisive influence on a small boy. 'The earth always seemed large—one could see so far in the clear air—though the tiny settlement and its minute affairs were so small. Far across the ocean was another world, the great world of affairs, where there were nations, parliaments [New Zealand had had one since 1854], wars, big cities, and terrible crimes. The monthly mails told us of such things, and they loomed vast, vague, and fascinating.' As a result, Reeves wrote in manhood, he spent his time watching the world, so that his life was not 'narrow altogether'. 'Always a bookworm, I knew more about England, at the age of twelve, than about my own New Zealand.'[1] The immigrant pioneers were exiles. They brought up their children to feel, if not exiles too, at least a nostalgia for 'Home', an expression not perhaps concrete in its connotations, but which stood at the heart of a sense that somewhere else was better. Willie Reeves grew up, one might fairly say, to be an Englishman.

[1] Reeves MSS, loc. cit.

3

THE PROVINCIAL SCHOLAR
1866–75

IN 1866 Willie Reeves won the third prize in his class in English at the High School and the sixth in Bible knowledge. He was beaten by William Atack, who was to remain his chief rival throughout his school days. In the following year, just before his tenth birthday, he enrolled at the Christ's College Grammar School, which was the principal (almost the sole) monument to the cultural aspirations of the Pilgrims. Like the English public schools which it distantly emulated and remotely resembled, it was a rough community. Many of the eighty or so scholars were squatters' sons who had few, if any, intellectual interests. But it was possible for a boy to receive a traditional English training in Classics, with some instruction in French, mathematics and science, if he wished. A majority of the masters were graduates of Cambridge or Oxford, and some, notably Archdeacon Harris and C. C. Corfe, who taught mathematics and succeeded Harris as headmaster, were able teachers.

From the school records and from the *Lyttelton Times* it is possible to learn Reeves's place in class in every subject thrice-yearly. More interesting, however, are the examiners' reports on scholarship examinations. In 1866 the Provincial Council offered some open scholarships, including two to boys under twelve. In 1868 these were won by W. H. Atack (who was still at the High School, but in 1870 went to Christ's) and Reeves. Atack gained 213 marks out of 300 and Reeves, 163. Atack beat Reeves by 39 marks in arithmetic and 19 in Latin. The examiner, J. V. Colborne Veel (father of a future poetess) reported that Reeves's knowledge of Greek and Roman history was 'surprisingly extensive and accurate'. W. J. Habens (later Director of Education), who was the examiner in modern history, in which Reeves also beat Atack, said his grasp of the subject was 'very remarkable considering his age'.

In 1871 Reeves won another Provincial Government Scholarship for boys of his age, being beaten again by Atack and two others. In mathematics he gained only 17 marks out of 150 (having missed the algebra paper), but did well in English and Classics. In 1872 the examiners reported: 'His proficiency in history is remarkable, showing an acquaintance not only with the ordinary school books, but with the works of such authors as Prescott and Motley.'[1]

At College he was so astonishingly weak in mathematics that many people recalled the fact later in his life and after his death. 'Year after year', he related himself, he was 'left to stick on at the same wretched bit of work, making no progress whatever'. Only in his final year, under 'Old Jimmy' Corfe (a man to whom Reeves said on the occasion of his retirement: 'while masters elsewhere may teach what a gentleman should be, you showed us what a gentleman is'),[2] did he improve slightly at this subject. His other conspicuous deficiency (Atack later recalled)[3] was 'his apparently complete indifference to or ignorance of melody. Any attempt of his to whistle even an ordinary tune met with scoffing and ribaldry'. At English he did well at school, winning Mrs. Godley's prize in 1870 for an essay on 'The Anglo-Saxons'. In the following year he won the Lower VIth English prize and shared the geography prize with Atack.

In a letter to his son, possibly in 1867, William Reeves had written: 'I strongly advise you always to fix an exact minute to commence your lessons and then stick to it. It will save you a great amount of future trouble and I speak from experience.' He must have been very gratified by his eldest boy's scholastic successes. But Willie was even more impressed by his father's increasing eminence in public life. His mother was a more dominant, indeed a domineering influence, but his father was the object of his admiration, a shy, quiet and (within the family) affectionate man. Between the two there seems to have been little friction. Both parents were probably too fond, and Willie had some of the characteristics of a spoiled eldest son.

[1] *Canterbury Provincial Government Gazette*, 1867, 1868, 1871; LT, 3 Sept. 1872. I am indebted to Mr. George Macdonald of Rangiora for many newspaper references to Reeves's school and athletic career.

[2] Reeves MSS, small clipping book, p. 72, CT, 21 Feb. 1889.

[3] Christ's College *Register*, cxxxx, Aug. 1932, pp. 80-91.

The home was an infinitely greater influence on the boy than the school. He grew up among cultivated people whose talk was not entirely 'colonial', but touched as often on the arts and public affairs as on stock values (though public affairs and stock values were at times identical); in a family environment which was that of the educated English upper and middle classes, less bracing, because of remoteness, but less influenced by intellectual fashions. His father, who read widely, was especially drawn to Thackeray and Byron. He discerned the merit of Thomas Hardy, in the seventies, when he was scarcely heard of in the colony. The family read the colonial authors too, including Adam Lindsay Gordon's *Bush Ballads*. In days when people made their own entertainment, Ellen's piano also no doubt contributed much to the family pleasure. William was 'passionately fond' of music, and became president of the musical society.

They were a large family. After Annabel Ellen, Willie, and Edmund Crosbie, there came Marion, who was born at 'Ferry mead'; Gertrude, who was born at Lyttelton, and Gilbert, born at Opawa, in Christchurch. Ellen was born in 1866 and Hugh in 1869. Two other children, born in 1868 and 1872, died as babies. But eight survived. In addition there were relatives to swell the household on holidays. The Reverend Francis Pember, one of Ellen's family, had a local parish in the early seventies. Somewhat less intimate were some Reeves cousins, the family of Edmund Reeves, who lived in Christchurch.

Reeves's business interests grew steadily. The *Lyttelton Times*, of which he was probably the principal proprietor by 1867, was doing well. In 1863 it had a circulation of 1,500. Reeves estimated that the rival *Press*, which had been founded in 1861 by James Edward FitzGerald (who had brought out the first issues of the *Times*), had only 600 subscribers.[1] The *Times* was one of the leading newspapers in the country, notable in the sixties for its sympathy towards the Maoris during the racial wars in the north, and its advocacy of conciliation. Reeves himself decided on this policy, knowing that most of his readers were hostile.[2] After 1870 Reeves wrote little in its columns, though he actively directed its policy and production. He also helped to promote the Union Insurance Company and the New Zealand Shipping Company,

[1] LT, 21 March 1863.
[2] LT, 6 April 1891, obituary.

of which he was for a time chairman—resigning from the board in 1882 as a protest against the purchase of steam vessels.[1]

In the sixties Reeves was a member of the Christchurch Club, the leading gentlemen's club, which had been established by a group of squatters, and was a founder of its rival, the Canterbury Club, in 1872. He sat on the committee of the Canterbury Jockey Club, and, in about 1876, he acquired his own stud farm, 'Middlepark', and, at various times, owned some of the best known horses in the Province, including Apremont, Ravenswing and Traducer. One of his horses, Daniel O'Rorke, registered in the name of a friend, won the New Zealand Cup and the Derby.[2]

In 1864 William Reeves bought 11 acres at Opawa, on the little Heathcote river, where he built a large two-storied house, 'Risingholme', which still stands today, somewhat altered, and serves as a community centre. It was constructed of Baltic pine and roofed with Tasmanian shingles. Much of the panelling and some mantelpieces were cedar. Not quite beautiful perhaps, it was an impressive house. Its gable windows gave a superior outlook on the lowly plains. But like most of the property of most of the Colony's apparently wealthy citizens, it was not paid for. It was mortgaged to two local men for £1,400, while Joshua Strange Williams (a local lawyer who became a judge of the supreme court) held a second mortgage for £408 on behalf of his father, Joshua Williams of Lincolns Inn, the well-known 'Williams of Real Property'. On these mortgages Reeves paid 10 per cent. and $12\frac{1}{2}$ per cent. interest.[3]

The family lived in 'Risingholme' in 1865 and 1866. Reeves began to lay out the grounds, with hothouses—'graperies'—generous orchards, tennis courts and a splendid selection of trees, copper beech, alder, oak, birch, elm, lime, cedar, redwood, ash, Canadian hemlock and Australian gums, which by the eighties gave 'Risingholme' an air mellow, almost aristocratic.

In 1867, a year of falling wheat prices, when 'scab' ruined many Canterbury farmers, when the boom of the gold rushes

[1] LT, 9 May 1882.

[2] *New Zealand Stud Book*, various years; Scholefield MSS, Reeves to G. H. Schole-field, 20 Oct. 1930.

[3] The history of the 'Risingholme' property can be traced quite fully through records in the Lands and Deeds Office Christchurch. Reference 3CS/248, and deeds volumes. I am indebted to the staff for their assistance.

had died down, Reeves sold the house for £1,600 to Major
Hornbrook, a squatter who had kept the 'Mitre' hotel in
Lyttelton. The family lived for a time in Armagh Street in
Christchurch, but they still had a large house, with eight
bedrooms, a three-stalled stable, a coach-house, a servant's
room and 'a capital garden' of an acre.[1] In 1870, as the
depression grew worse, Hornbrook defaulted on the interest
payments on the mortgage and was sold up by a bank. Reeves
reacquired his property for £1,400 and immediately raised a
mortgage for £1,300. In the early seventies, during the Vogel
boom, he acquired another acre of land, and remortgaged the
property for £2,500. The gap between his mother's aspirations
and his father's money, the insecurity of indebtedness, was to
make a permanent mark on the oldest Reeves boy.

Like many of the leading men, William Reeves was attracted
to politics. He was first elected, unopposed, to the House of
Representatives in 1867, but resigned a year later, presumably
because of his financial difficulties. In 1871 he stood again,
opposing E. C. J. Stevens, another local businessman, in the
Selwyn electorate. It was a gentlemanly contest: they several
times travelled together to address the same meeting. On these
occasions Reeves's courtesy extended to giving his opponent the
headline in the *Lyttelton Times*: 'Mr. E. C. J. Stevens at Leeston'.
The main issue between them, which they politely debated, was
protective tariffs. Stevens was a free trader, but Reeves was
'not prepared ... to see the people of this young and favoured
country become hewers of wood and drawers of water for the
manufacturers of the old world'. In his demands for a tariff the
piping of colonial nationalism could be heard. Reeves won the
seat by one vote, 102 to 101.[2]

When the Treasurer in the Fox Ministry, Vogel, had proposed
in 1870 that the Colony borrow £10 million in London, to be
expended on roads, railways and immigration in a great effort
to end the prevailing depression, the *Lyttelton Times* had backed
him. In 1871 Fox appointed Reeves to the Executive Council as
Resident Minister for the South Island, with extensive control
over public works.

[1] *Press*, 10 March 1870 (an advertisement pointed out to me by Mr. Robert
Lamb).
[2] LT, 18 Jan. 1871; see also 11 Jan., 2 Feb. 1871.

Business and politics were a natural combination for a gentle-man of that time. So directly linked, indeed, were public and private advantage, that during the seventies they became scarcely distinguishable. Politics had always been about 'development'—roads and bridges—which meant that they had ultimately been concerned with land values. Land values could be increased by the expenditure of government money in a district, to the profit both of the local settlers—and voters—and land speculators. And land speculators, whether businessmen, squatters, lawyers or farmers, formed a large and probably majority group in Parliament. As Vogel's borrowing programme was implemented, a land boom set in. Astonishing profits were made overnight. Reeves joined a syndicate of capitalists who acquired a speculative holding of 20,000 acres at Lowcliffe, in the Ashburton district.[1]

Potentially Reeves's position seemed one of great power, near the heart of politics. But he did not use it. He remained a local figure, advocating, for instance, building a railway from Christchurch to Ellesmere, but doing little about it. He was extremely, indeed excessively modest. In one of his first speeches as a minister, he generously told his audience that John Hall had been offered his post first. When he spoke, at another meeting, with his friend William Montgomery, he deferred to him to an extent scarcely expected of a minister of the Crown.[2]

The experiment of a resident minister was not a success, and Reeves made little mark in politics. He was chiefly known for his Gladstonian liberalism, greatly modified by his advocacy of protective tariffs; for his criticism of the existence of the great landed estates of the runholders; and for his strong 'provincial-ism'. The ministry fell when he had held office for less than a year and he declined a portfolio in the Waterhouse ministry in 1872.[3] In 1874, in a dramatic gesture, he broke with the Vogel Government, in company with Maurice O'Rorke, who resigned from the cabinet, because they opposed the proposal to abolish the Provincial Governments. In the same year he was one of a group of politicians who met in John Sheehan's lodgings in Auckland. They aimed to help Sir George Grey in his efforts to save the

---

[1] *Press*, 4 Dec. 1890 (a correspondent).
[2] LT, 30 April 1872, 30 Dec. 1871.
[3] *Christchurch Times*, 29 June 1935, Souvenir Supplement, article by W. P. Reeves.

Provinces and to found a Liberal Party—a party 'claiming to be the defenders of the rights and liberties of the people throughout New Zealand'.[1] Reeves shared the strong provincialism, but little of the radicalism of Grey and Sheehan. He had scant sympathy for their appeals to class feeling (which fell on unready ears in the Colony, too) and soon lost faith in them. But he had helped to plant a seed that, after sixteen years, was to bear, for him, the most marvellous fruit.

Reeves was too retiring, too reserved in manner, for political success in New Zealand, and certainly too sensitive. When he was defeated in the 1875 election, William Rolleston, one of the leading Canterbury politicians (and examiner in Classics for Christ's College) wrote to Harry Atkinson, another cabinet minister of the seventies, that Reeves was 'not of a temperament to look kindly on defeat ... I am sorry for him. He is a very honestly-intentioned man, but bitter.'[2] The *Grey River Argus* judged in 1884, when Reeves was appointed to the Legislative Council: 'The truth is that he proved a failure—or at least ... was held to be so—as a Minister of the Crown; but that was more the result of nervousness than any want of ability.' R. A. Loughnan, editor of the *Lyttelton Times* 1875–89, said that Reeves had an 'austere official manner' and a 'gift of sharp speech'.[3] The first would not endear him to the voters nor the second to the small group of men who dominated politics. Moreover, his scorn of the pursuit of popularity was not an asset. He seems to have been a dignified, courteous man, too shadowy for the glaring front room of political success.

But William Reeves seemed a tremendous success to his son Willie, who later wrote that he was 'cradled in colonial politics' While a schoolboy, he conceived an ambition (one soon put aside) to enter politics. In 1872, and again in 1874, unforgettable experiences, he attended debates in the House in Wellington to hear famous leaders such as Fox and Stafford, and newer men such as Atkinson and Rolleston. William Atack remembered young Reeves's enthusiastic interest in politics:

[1] J. M. R. Young, 'The Politics of the Auckland Province 1872–76', unpub. thesis, University of Auckland, pp. 206, 281, 317.
[2] Rolleston MSS, 4 Jan. 1876, cit. J. L. Hunt, 'The Election of 1875–6', unpub. thesis, University of Auckland, p. 179.
[3] *Grey River Argus*, 23 Oct. 1884; LT, 11 Jan. 1926.

Most of the boys knew little and cared less about them, but W.P. could always tell us what was going on, and frequently rather over-awed us with his free and easy references to the Vogels, Foxes, Staffords, etc., who then bulked largely in the world of N.Z. statesmen. So thoroughly did he identify himself with the various changes of parties—mark of the budding politician—that I remember once being greatly amused by hearing him whisper in a rather anxious voice to another boy, 'I think we are safe now, don't you?' The 'we' tickled myself and other listeners not a little.

It may be inferred that Willie did not easily carry the burden of having a well-known father. Certainly he was precocious, and if not quite insufferable, at least self-satisfied to outward and deceptive appearance. At the age of eleven he made his first speech at the prize-giving at Mrs. Alabaster's 'prep' school, when he was invited to return thanks for the three cheers for the 'old boys': 'If I had been what boys ought to be, I should have shambled to my feet, blushed, looked distressed, stammered something incoherently and sat down. Being what I unfortun-ately was, I jumped up and said pretty clearly and loudly, "Boys, thank you very much for cheering us Old Boys." Then I sat down with a bump, hung my head, stared fixedly at the floor and felt hot all over.' Afterwards the 'Old Boys' discussed this 'audacious achievement': 'one said that it "was like my cheek"; another thought that it was clear that I had "the gift of the gab". I have disliked the expression ever since. Somehow I was made to feel that I had done something not quite natural and a little contemptible.'[1] Though we must remember that an old man wrote these words, they yet suggest to us, as to him, something of what his fellows thought of him.

At Christ's Reeves was called 'Quack', a nickname suggested by a slight roll in his walk, and certainly by his extremely prominent nose. According to family tradition, he hated school life outside the classroom. There is ample evidence that he was not popular. E. R. Webb, who was at school a little later, but played cricket with him and admired him, recalled that Reeves was regarded as 'snobby' and 'aristocratic'.[2] Similar views have survived in other Christchurch circles until today. Precisely why he was unpopular is matter for speculation but not merely guesswork. There was something 'different' about him, mainly

---

[1] Reeves MSS, 'Memoirs'.   [2] Interview with the present writer.

an indefinable air of superiority. In a boys' school to be merely a
little different is often enough. That he did seem 'superior' was
clearly due in part to his consciousness of the eminence of his
father; but it is not difficult to point confidently, too, at his
mother. Ellen *felt* superior; she *was* superior; and showed it.
What unfulfilled ambitions were heaped on the boy we know,
rather than guess; ambitions he was meant to achieve on a
greater stage than the Canterbury plains.

The only photograph surviving from his late teens shows a boy
sensitive, studious, but not very strong or determined. He was a
natural butt for bullies, who can make the school-days of
smaller or slighter boys a prolonged misery; he suffered, indeed,
a great deal. But he did not suffer in silence. Atack said that he
developed a gift for epigram and repartee, so that his fellows
rather dreaded his 'smartness' and he was a bold lad who would
cross words with him. Atack records some examples of his
schoolboy humour, classical puns and the like, which would not
have increased his popularity. And he was eventually pushed
into making a physical resistance which surprised the other boys.
In about 1870 he fought a 'Homeric' battle with a boy called
Frank Davie, which continued every lunch hour and after
school for a week. Atack said that it ended in a draw, and that it
was no mean feat to stand up to Davie so long. Webb believed
that Mrs. Reeves intervened to stop the fight.

Though he was studious, 'a bundle of nerves', and not very
robust, he was wiry and certainly no weakling. In 1873 he won
the two-mile walk, beating Davie and Atack. In 1867 he won the
half-mile under eleven; in 1868 the half-mile under twelve; and
in 1869 was second in a 440 yards race at the school sports.

Scholarship holders or candidates had little time for sport.
Several nights a week they attended lectures at the Canterbury
Collegiate Union (the forerunner of the University of Canterbury) in the town. The only cricket ground, Hagley Park,
though adjoining the school, was several miles from Opawa.
In the sixth form, however, Reeves began to play cricket, which
the boarders played, because he was told that he should set an
example to juniors. He 'purchased a book and tried to learn how
batsmen are made'. But his favourite exercises were riding a pony
on the sandy country between Christchurch and Pegasus Bay
and swimming—especially, he practised the 'useless and

unwholesome art' of swimming underwater, at which he had discovered he could beat everyone at school.

Richmond's healthy little 'lump of lead' was still, in 1874, moderately vigorous and agile. He made up in stamina what he lacked in brute force, but only with difficulty could he hold his own with his fellows. At school he was to some extent, though not altogether, an outsider. But perhaps he was partially reconciled to his school by the considerable success with which his days there ended.

In 1872 the University of New Zealand instituted the entrance scholarships that still continue. Atack won one of these but was disappointed to learn that he was too young to hold it and had to try again.

In 1873 Atack, Reeves and several other Christ's College boys worked hard at the syllabus for the New Zealand University scholarships; at Sophocles, Herodotus, Horace and Sallust; at Shakespeare's *King John* and Trench's history of the English language; at Creasy's *British Constitution*, Bryce's *Holy Roman Empire*, Hallam's literature of the fifteenth to the seventeenth century; at European history, 1106–1453; at German or French translation. In 1873 Cotterill and Atack of Christ's College were placed first and second in the country. Nelson College boys gained the next three places. Reeves came eighth. He was second in Latin, fourth in history, bottom in mathematics, and did not gain a university scholarship, though his school awarded him a Senior Somes Scholarship.

Atack attended the Canterbury University College for a time, but did not graduate. On Reeves's suggestion, he joined the staff of the *Lyttelton Times*, and lived to be head of the New Zealand Press Association (like William Reeves) and to write the best obituary of his old school friend and rival.

In 1874 Atack was at last out of the way and the scholarship regulations were changed so that Reeves's weakness in mathematics was no handicap. Scholarships of £20 were awarded for several groups of subjects. This time he won £40, the scholarship for Classics and that for English, French, German and history. An Otago boy won £80 for mathematics and several sciences. Several Christ's College boys won £20.[1]

---

[1] New Zealand University *Calendar*, 1872–1876; 'Minutes of the Proceedings of the University of New Zealand'; LT, 21 July, 22 July 1873; 28 July, 3 Aug. 1874.

There now followed what was undoubtedly one of the most important events in Reeves's life—perhaps, in a sense, the most important event—which is, in its most significant detail, obscure. His mother was ambitious that he should follow in the footsteps of his famous uncle Edward, who smoked. How far he was inclined to law at that time in uncertain, though as soon as he did read it he felt a positive aversion, but he certainly wanted to study at Oxford. If he had doubts, perhaps they were subdued by his mother ('a woman of strong character and great natural ability', according to a Frederick Wilding, a neighbour from 1879 onwards, 'whose chief ambition in life was the welfare and success of her children').[1] It was determined that he should 'go up' (all 13,000 miles) to Corpus Christi College to read law, a decision in keeping with his mother's instincts, her family position, her feeling that the Colony was rather a come-down; in keeping, too, with his father's eminence and his own scholarly bent.

In late 1874 he sailed for England. His adolescent 'brightness' was undimmed by the tremendous storms experienced as the ship neared Cape Horn. One night, when he came up on deck during a snow storm, he found the captain brewing a negus. He offered the young man what he called 'his humble ship's port' and he replied, 'Not at all, Captain, it's excellent. Remember, moreover, any port in a storm'. In the Gulf Stream he was leaning over the rail trying to catch gulfweed on a boat hook, when he fell over the side, but was saved by a rope fastened round his waist. His three escapes from drowning as a boy made a powerful impression on Reeves, and he wrote them down twice in later years, though it may be felt that they were too many to be very narrow. It is, however, fair to add that drowning was an ever-present danger, when to move from one town or country to another entailed a more-or-less hazardous sea voyage. Indeed, drowning was so common, especially on the dangerous bars of West Coast harbours, and in treacherous, unbridged rivers, that E. W. Stafford, the Premier, once said it should be classed as a natural death.

In England William Pember Reeves spent a winter staying with Edward Pember. He visited Paris, where he saw the

---

[1] Radio talk, 29 Nov. 1937; copy kindly supplied by Miss Cora Wilding, Kaikoura.

consequences of the 'strife of the Commune'—he saw 'the marks of the bombardment ... the print of the iron heel of the German army'—and admired the Parisians who suffered so much 'in the vain hope that by so doing they might relieve the soil of France from the invader'.[1] He spent many hours visiting art galleries, for 'in a raw, untaught way' he was 'fond of pictures'. But he did not go up to Oxford. In March 1876 he returned to New Zealand in the S.S. *Otago* from Melbourne, where he had met some of the leading politicians, including Charles Gavan Duffy, the Irish nationalist leader and writer. The young man was much impressed by his 'courtesy, culture and polish of manner'.

While he was in England he suffered a severe break-down in health which alarmed his uncle and led to his return.[2] One of his daughters believes he had 'a spot on the lung', the other that he was merely thought in danger of tuberculosis. Atack's account was that he 'became homesick, the climate frightened him', an explanation which, although inadequate, receives some support from Reeves's earliest surviving poem, written in England in November 1875, an insipid and sentimental verse called 'My Mother', which expresses his longing to see her again and concludes with her 'true eyes' saying to him:

> Go on erect my Son, nor shrink or fall,
> For, folded in my love, you pass through all.

The exact nature of Reeves's adolescent crisis is unknown. Possibly it was some sort of 'nervous break-down' not infrequently experienced by students before rather than after examinations. Although a doctor told him his lungs had been affected, afterwards he seems to have had reasonably sound lungs, while his illnesses were often nervous. His collapse led to no lasting physical incapacity, but it was followed by periodic bad headaches—reported variously as migraine or neuralgia—which, in the days before aspirin and other modern remedies, were a severe affliction. They plagued the rest of his life.

He had not retained his healthy vigour through adolescence.

[1] P.D, 1889, 65, p. 22.
[2] LT, 28 Sept. 1887.

And his first attack on the Old World, in whose terms success was to be measured both by his expatriate family and an emigrant public opinion, had been repulsed. He had, for the time being, lost heart. His schooldays had ended with a sense of failure, of frustrated ability and hopes denied. His future, his ambitions, must be sought in New Zealand.

4

APPRENTICESHIPS
1876–86

LATE in life Reeves began to write his reminiscences, which survive in a disjointed series of manuscript chapters and paragraphs. A long section describes a period in his life which would otherwise be almost a blank, when his father sent him to work on a sheep run called 'Lowcliffe' in which he had an interest. Lowcliffe was near Ashburton, some eighty miles south of Christchurch. It was hoped that there he would recover his health in the open air. For the years 1876 and 1877, biography may become autobiography:[1]

On returning to New Zealand, I was sent to vegetate on a large sheep and cattle farm. Most of it consisted of a half-drained swamp on the seaward side of a plain about 20 miles wide. The homestead, a one-storey wooden cottage of six rooms, was situated on a narrow strip of dry land between the swamp and a seafront of low cliffs overhanging a shingle beach; the beach was 90 miles long, unbroken save by rivers and lying absolutely open to the Pacific. The swamp was about two miles wide in the narrowest part, but much wider in others. Small streams or creeks ran out of it, cut their way in little gulleys through the cliffs and disappeared in the shingle of the beach. When not disturbed with draining work, their water was sweet and clear. The swamps had been covered with tall flax, toè-toè, rushes and small bushes, green and beautiful in the sunlight; but as the deep drains did their work, the peat sank, cracked and dried, the surface was systematically burnt and became stretches of black, hideous ashes and mud, poached up by the hoofs of cattle. Over this, grass seed was strewn and grass gradually appeared. In the end, rich pastures covered the surface, but in the transition time when I was there, the aspect was very depressing. Inland of the swamp, flat, tussock-covered plains sloped imperceptibly up to the great chains of the Eastern Alps. Far to the North-east one could see from the Homestead a cluster of high, blue volcanic hills, rising like an island between sea and plain.

[1] Reeves's 'Memoirs' in the Reeves MSS.

Away Southward the chains of the Southern Alps curved south-eastward in a great arc, seeming at length to be lost in the sea. Eastward, was the unbroken expanse of the Pacific. If you watched the ocean for the whole day, you might chance to see the smoke of one steamer, or the sails of a solitary ship. Always they were far out. No vessels came near the exposed beach. Five miles to the Northward, there was a much larger Homestead, with outbuildings and planta-tions of trees. Five miles to the South there was another Homestead, not very large, but still with those blessed things, trees. On our own farm, a few young plantations of eucalypts struggled against salt sea winds and the white frosts of winter, but scarcely a sapling was yet 20 feet high. Some wind or other was almost always blowing, but there was plenty of sunshine, the air was brisk and clear and the place perfectly healthy. As one lived almost in the open air, after the first month one never caught cold. There were no dangers, no diseases, no adventures, no amusements, no visitors, no real hardships—nothing particular happened. The grasses and remains of swamp vegetation might have interested an ardent botanist. I was not an ardent botanist. Speaking generally there were neither trees nor flowers. There were no wild beasts and but few birds. Our cattle were neither wild nor precisely tame. Perhaps the sheep were not the most stupid of created animals. I thought they were. It was a life of secure, unbroken monotony, the perfection of unvaried dullness.

Round the exposed little Homestead the wind, as I have said, was almost always blowing. Either it came from the North-east, steady and without rain, but chilly towards evening, or from the North-west, dry, violent, and in summer, almost hot; or from the South-west stormy, bringing deluges of cold rain and driving before it a flying confusion of scud and wild, hurrying clouds. Even now when I hear the moaning of the wind outside at night, I often seem back again on the narrow dry strip between the swamp and the sea; even now when I hear the sough of the breeze over English meadows I seem to hear the whisper of New Zealand winds over stony plains of yellow tussocks. Yet there were moments of calm and beauty in the treeless, unsheltered solitude. In the morning hours, before the wind rose, even the tussocks looked bright and one drank the fresh air like champagne. The mirage, far away over the expanse would quiver for hours. One watched trees and the Homesteads, huts and straw stacks, lifted up and trembling in air. Often the slopes at the foot of the mountain ranges were also uplifted in brown and tawny sheets shewn with astonishing clearness. In some furious storms, the rollers of the Pacific charging rank on rank like a Macedonian phalanx on the endless beach, were a fine spectacle from the cliffs. There was much more sunshine than in England and the sun was much hotter. No climate could well have been more healthy. There was not a trace of malaria in the vast half-drained swamp. During 16 months I only once caught rheumatism, and that after being wet-footed every day for 10 days in succession....

There was not much human companionship. The Manager and I of course, lived by ourselves. We had a man cook and the ploughman's wife came in every morning to tidy up the cottage. She was the only woman within five miles. In the course of a week you might exchange twenty words with her, or you might not. During the 16 months, I paid two visits to the large Homestead to the North; the smaller one to the South I saw 15 or 16 times. We were twice visited by ministers of religion. Once it was by an Anglican parson, to whom we owed allegiance, and once by a Noncomformist who passed the night in our cottage. The latter was an intelligent young man, lately come from England. Taking us from our clothing, to be barbarians in need of counsel, he began by dropping a tract or two in corners of the room and otherwise shewed a disposition to improve the occasion. After tea however, I drew him into converse about early Christian communism. Then we went on to talk about the Codex Sinaiticus and by bedtime had got as far as the Paulician heretics of Eastern Asia Minor and their alleged connection with the Albigenses of Toulouse. As I was going to bed I observed the good man stealthily resuming his tracts and slipping them into his pocket....

My rank on the station was that of a cadet. A cadet was a youth who was supposed to be learning to work a farm or station. I was there merely for my health and not anxious to learn anything in particular. Still I was called a cadet. In pastoral society, a cadet ranked very low. Still there is always a depth below a depth. I was indeed a cadet, but I was not a new-chum cadet. When in the pastoral hierarchy you came to a new-chum cadet, you came to the bed-rock. A Colonial-bred cadet might be worth his 'tucker': a new-chum cadet was, in managerial language 'simply a —— nuisance'. These derided youths were supposed to have one ambition—to learn to crack a stockwhip, and having learnt that art, to desire to practise it and nothing else. Luckily I had acquired it in boyhood and could even skin flax and twist flax 'crackers' correctly. The Manager treated me quite fairly. As I was unskilled and unfit for heavy work, he kept me employed on light jobs, such as might be done by an intelligent—or unintelligent—boy. I learnt to drive small mobs of sheep and cattle without losing them and to get them through gates. I learnt to give a very few simple orders to a sheep dog. I learnt to build a fire quickly, keep it sheltered and alight in the open air, boil water quickly and make tea. I learnt to pick up fleeces and roll them and to pare the feet of sheep suffering from foot rot. I learnt to pull sheep out of the deep peat drains, and when they were dead spread the carcases out to

dry and skin them when they were fit to be skinned. I was told that the
only approach to skill I ever displayed was in skinning sheep: the
Manager expressed the opinion that in that I was the least in-
competent cadet he had ever known. It is well to have an accomplish-
ment. I learnt to count small mobs of sheep and to judge distances so
far as to know whether sheep in the open were three-quarters of a mile
away. I was sent on long tramps through the swamps to locate sheep or
cattle and pull sheep out of the drains aforesaid. Twice a week I had
the happiness of riding for the mail; ten miles there, ten miles back,
across the tussocky plain. The mail usually consisted of three or four
newspapers and six or eight letters. I might or might not get one
letter, but I always got newspapers, and oh, the joy of those newspapers. My daily paper was a four-page affair, more than half of it
advertisements, but of the remainder one read every word. The
doctor had advised me not to work my brain more than necessary, but
to live as nearly as possible, the life of a plant. I am not sure that the
monotony I have tried to describe was really much of a rest to the
brain. In the long solitary walks and rides I thought a good deal and
I am sure it intensified my habit of brooding over subjects for hours or
even days at a time, half unconscious of surroundings. That is a very
bad habit for a politician. Our way of living was as rough as it could
be without hardship. I washed or bathed in a creek or the sea.
I brushed my hair. Every two months or so before going to town I
shaved and kept one good suit of clothes for the journey; otherwise one
wore old clothes till they began to drop off. No self-respecting English
tramp would have accepted my work-a-day suit as a gift. We lived
chiefly on roast mutton, bread and potatoes, three times a day, with
tea to drink, but always had milk and sugar, and after a time, rice or
sago puddings. It was impressed upon me that by comparison with
the fare of earlier settlers, meals like ours were almost sinful luxury....

Except when walking in the swamps, we rode everywhere. In those
days one never dreamed of walking a mile, you threw a saddle and
bridle on your horse and rode. I have often done that to get to a gate,
barely half a mile from the Homestead. We used Colonial saddles,
because with their slight approach to the Mexican shape, they were
more restful to sit in than the English. One rode of course purely by
balance. I brought out a pair of breeches and gaiters, but when they
were worn out, did not trouble to get any more. The loosest old
trousers did just as well. I have heard of men going to sleep on horseback; I only once dozed off and that out on the plain on a dark sultry
night in summer. I was awakened by riding into a wire fence. New
Zealanders who know the phenomenal slowness with which an old
station 'screw' can canter, will believe me when I say that neither the
horse nor I were hurt.

There were some amusements. Reeves practised bowling and induced the manager and some of the men to make up a cricket team to play against the Coldstream run. The manager and he practised drop-kicking to one another and played football a few times for a team forty miles away. Like all 'pastoral people', he learned to swear 'like Marlborough's men in Flanders'. He learned to swim in the dangerous surf which crashes on the beach at Lowcliffe, a great shelf of flat grey stones.

'Had I been a youth of resolution and method', he wrote, 'I should have used my spare time to master some sub-division of learning. But I was disheartened, I looked upon myself as a failure, and thought that learning would be wasted on a man who could not go to Oxford. I read every book I could lay my hands on, good, bad or indifferent.' He read a Hardy novel, Scott, Shakespeare—*King Lear* made him 'physically sick for two days'—and bound volumes of *Leisure Hour* and *Sunday at Home*, though 'after three dolorous evenings over that virtuous publication' he 'went on strike'. He lined his room with pictures cut from the *Graphic* and the *Illustrated London News*. Alma Tadema's 'An Audience at Agrippa's', which he especially admired, was given a prominent position.

Reeves got on well with the men. He felt very sympathetic towards the army of 'swaggers' who roamed the back country after the harvest—in many cases, he felt genuinely seeking work. Brooding on their lot, he began to form 'agrarian notions' such as that no one should be allowed to buy more than 1,000 acres of the public estate. In those days it was thought that a man needed 2,000 or 3,000 acres of the plains to make a decent living, and when he expressed his views to two 'Canterbury colonists', 'They rolled in their chairs, and chuckled, and laughed, and made allusions about Tiberius Gracchus.'[1]

When the day of his departure came the manager said, 'It seems to me that you are going away just when you are getting to be of some use to me.' Reeves wrote that those farewell words were the most valuable testimonial he ever received. He felt that he had, during the final months, fully earned his ten shillings a week.

So I quitted for ever the desolate beach, the half-drained swamp and the level, tussock-covered plain. Never again did I stand on the edge

[1] PD, 1893, 79, p. 530.

of the cliffs, looking eastward and thinking that there was absolutely nothing but open sea between us and South America. Somehow, as one looked eastward and southward over that sailless ocean there used to come a feeling that one was on the edge of the earth gazing out into a vast abyss where life came to an end.

Back in Christchurch, Reeves's life seemed almost as aimless as at Lowcliffe. He turned once more, or was turned, to law. At that time a lawyer did not have to study at a university but was required to spend three years as a 'barrister's pupil' before qualifying. He became the clerk of George Harper who, in partnership with his brother Leonard, practised as a barrister and solicitor. They were his father's lawyers. In September 1878 Judge Johnston examined him in 'general knowledge', as prescribed for a barrister, and passed him. In October 1880 he passed his final examinations and was admitted as a barrister and solicitor. Between those dates his studies had been, at best, half-hearted. Reading *Williams on Real Property* inspired him with a detestation of the English land system. The only law books to interest him much were Broome's *Legal Maxims*, an American work on international law, and Chief Justice Cockburn's 'charge to the jury' in the trial of the Tichborne claimant. He found greater pleasure in a book of 'leading cases done into English verse' and Darling's *Scintillae Juris*, a book of light essays. But his greatest efforts were directed elsewhere; indeed, he was to confess that he devoted 1878 chiefly to cricket, football and dancing.

At cricket his success was surprising, for he had little natural aptitude for the game, except for the advantage of a good eye and loose wrists. Atack said he was the only instance he knew from personal experience 'of a man who deliberately and of set purpose forced himself to become a first class player'. Frederick Wilding 'never knew anyone who devoted more brains and energy to cricket than Reeves'. He practised and played with great determination, and was soon a leading Canterbury bat. He had one of the highest scoring averages for the Lancaster Park Cricket Club in the mid-eighties, and represented his Province against other Provinces and visiting English and Australian teams. The standard was then much below that today; but even so, his performance was admirable. In 1882 he made 48 against Auckland, and, in 1883, 54 against Otago, facing Frank Cooke,

a celebrated bowler.[1] He was, Wilding said, 'a neat, wristy bat
with a strong defence'. His other notable characteristic was that
his nervous temperament led him, not infrequently, to run his
partner out, a failing against which he later uttered a witty
warning in some verses called 'No Judge of a Run'. His school
nickname persisted and his errors sometimes inspired loud
quacking by fellow cricketers among the spectators.

Wilding, Arthur Ollivier and Reeves used to practise at
Hagley Park a few evenings a week after office hours and
then trudge several miles to Opawa. Hearing that some
paddocks nearer home were for sale, they raised a mortgage and
founded the Lancaster Park Cricket Club, of which Reeves was
an official. He also took the lead in establishing club cricket
competition in Christchurch. There was much opposition, and
Atack was greatly impressed by a speech Reeves made on the
subject to a meeting of cricketers: it was 'the first I ever heard
him deliver in earnest, and it was rather an eye-opener to those
unaware of his latent powers.... He fairly swept the opposition
off its feet.'

Reeves played cricket on and off for sixteen years and never
lost interest in the game. He made some good friends and some of
his happiest memories were always of those days. Even in sport,
however, he aroused or stimulated antagonism, memories of
which persisted eighty years later. E. R. Webb recalled a club
game after which Reeves asked a group of players, 'Did you
chaps see the catch that put the third man out?' Asked who had
made it, he replied, 'Me.'[2] How far such recollections may be
relied on is, of course, problematical. Many of the stories still to
be heard in Christchurch about Reeves circulated among his
most bitter opponents in the nineties and have been ignored in
this book, though some of them refer, however inaccurately, to
actual incidents. Certainly they reveal what some people
thought credible, or typical, of Reeves's behaviour.

His rugby career was brief. He was good at drop-kicking, and
in 1878 played three-quarter back for Canterbury against
Otago. The Canterbury team, he wrote in his 'Memoirs', was

---

[1] See, e.g., CT, 17 Jan., 4 April 1885; LT, 19 Sept. 1887, 27 Jan., 17 Feb. 1890;
T. W. Reese, *New Zealand Cricket*, Christchurch, 1927, pp. 30, 211, 220, 227,
231.
[2] Interview with the writer.

stronger in the forwards, though their play 'often degenerated into mere shoving by tightly packed men'. The Otago team, led by James Allen, had more skilful backs. Reeves collared a Canterbury back who charged him, and 'flattered himself' that he had, for once in his life, 'saved Canterbury from defeat'. Members of his team, Wilding wrote, marvelled how he survived his plucky and successful efforts to stop the Otago forward rushes. But he was too slight for the game, and gave it up.

Throughout his adult life Reeves displayed a valetudinarian concern for his health (to which he frequently referred) which one might not expect in combination with the considerable physical courage which he several times displayed.

In May 1882 Reeves was in Timaru playing rugby with a visiting Christchurch team. On a beautiful, windless afternoon, tremendous seas suddenly began to roll up on the open road-stead, possibly caused by an earthquake at sea. Two ketches broke loose and were washed on the beach. Then a barque, *The City of Perth*, and the *Ben Venue* broke their cables. The sea was soon full of struggling seamen and broken wreckage. Lifeboats and rocket brigade failed to rescue the crews. Then (Reeves wrote in his memoirs) a district judge, C. D. R. Ward, plunged into the surf, in his frock coat and tall hat, towing a rope. Others followed his example. Reeves and another footballer succeeded in rescuing two men, despite the surf, which frequently dumped them on the bottom, and the dangerous planks and other flotsam flung at them by the waves. Then, almost exhausted, Reeves gave up, leaving the job to 'tougher men' and walked along the beach, away from the crowd, to get his breath: 'Suddenly amid the foam I saw a black struggling head. A strong young seaman came in on a wave top, got on to his feet and stood struggling with the terrible back rush, not twenty paces from me. The frothing dragging water was not much above his ankles, but he was utterly exhausted, lurched like a drunken man, and would I think have gone, had I not managed to reach him just in time.... He could not speak and merely gave gasp after gasp, the deepest I have ever heard.'

In his unpublished account, Reeves's highest praise was for Judge Ward, but Atack said that an acquaintance saw Reeves 'up to his waist in water, and spoke in very warm terms of the

pluck he and others displayed'. He never heard Reeves refer to
the incident in the many years he knew him.[1]

For a few years Reeves seemed to be wasting his time. His
earlier ambitions seemed childish dreams. But though life in a
colonial town seemed to afford no high goal, his behaviour was
yet purposeful at a level possibly below consciousness. He had
failed where the colonials most respected success, at 'Home', but
there were other fields in which they valued their own judgment
of merit. In his belated enthusiasm for sport might be sensed, not
merely a love of the game, but a determination to excel, to assert
his superiority, in a way his fellows could not fail to acknowledge.
And though he had hated school, he became a contributor to the
Christ's College *Sports Register*. He attended 'old boys'' functions,
and wrote the school song. He had certainly not surrendered;
but he had not yet found where he would fight again.

Reeves soon detested law.[2] Atack said that, as a law clerk and
lawyer, he was 'still full of unrest': 'He only appeared in one
Court case, which he won, and did a little consulting work of
which I heard very favourable opinions expressed.' His main
contribution to his profession at that time was to write up
Supreme Court cases in Christchurch for the *New Zealand Law
Reports* in the years 1883 to 1885.

Already he was being drawn to writing of various kinds, for
which he was beginning to feel a real sense of vocation. By 1880
he occasionally wrote articles and reports for his father's papers.
He also began to write political skits, often parodies, and other
light verse. One of his earliest efforts was an entry in a competition for a poem on the Melbourne Exhibition of 1880. Writing
verse, serious or satirical, was already a Canterbury tradition,
as Reeves recognized in 1883 by republishing Crosbie Ward's
anthology of 1867, *Canterbury Rhymes*. A couple of his own verses,
amusing trivia signed 'R', and Jessie Mackay's 'The Charge at
Parihaka', were included in an appendix.

In 1882 Reeves began to assist the editor, R. A. Loughnan, in
writing the political commentary in the *Lyttelton Times*. Next
year he went to Wellington to report the session of the General
Assembly as a 'Special Correspondent'. He was, at twenty-six,

[1] On the wrecks, see LT, 15 May 1882. 'Our Own Correspondent', who wrote
the reports, was possibly Reeves.
[2] LT, 9 Aug. 1887.

the youngest member of the Press Gallery, and attacked his task with an enthusiasm lacking in his legal studies, obviously enjoying sitting in 'the Chamber', a room twenty feet by fifteen where the Legislative Council used to meet, now used by the reporters.[1]

The Press Association reported the text of speeches. Reeves's task was to select the high-lights of debates and give a general impression of the political situation, liberally sprinkled with current political rumours. He did it very well, writing a breezy column or more each day, of which the following paragraph on Tom Bracken, the popular colonial bard, will serve as a specimen:

The House was pleased to indulge in no ordinary amount of laughter this afternoon. Mr. Bracken started the springs by a characteristic notice of motion. Besides gaols and gaolers the hon member for Dunedin Central has taken under his wing the oppressed native industry.... He has tried hard for flannels and other woollen manufactures; he has made Quixotic attacks ... on behalf of paper mills and the printers of telegraph forms; and today he gave notice of a last appeal for cardboard boxes, his voice being almost drowned in ironical cheers in spite of a pair of rather strong lungs.[2]

At this time Reeves, unlike his father, believed in free trade; then as thereafter, he was much impressed by 'strong lungs'.

The experience of closely watching this session was valuable to a young journalist. He gained a close acquaintance with parliamentary rules and with the politicians themselves, some of whom, of course, he already knew.

The Premier was Frederick Whitaker, a leading Auckland lawyer, businessman and land speculator; but the House was dominated by C. W. Richmond's brother-in-law, the Treasurer, Harry Atkinson, a feat not difficult, Reeves wrote later, 'where the Opposition was below mediocrity'. The Opposition was very weak and divided into factions. Grey had failed in his attempt to form a colony-wide liberal party, to oppose the dominant groups of politicians (later called 'the continuous ministry'), though he led a singularly contentious Government in 1877–9. Now he had been 'cast off' by most of his followers, who were ostensibly but quite ineffectually led by the Canterbury member,

<hr />

[1] LT, 6 Sept., 23 Aug. 1883.   [2] LT, 23 Aug. 1883.

William Montgomery. The *Lyttelton Times* supported the Opposition, but Reeves watched them 'with a feeling of despair'. He later judged the House of 1883 the weakest he ever saw, and as lacking 'every quality that a Parliament ought to have'. But, for a young man, it had its moments: some of Edward Wakefield's speeches; Grey and Dargaville attacking Atkinson, of whom Dargaville said that he called himself the Treasurer of the Colony, but that in reality he was only an accountant to the financial ring in Auckland; and Whitaker who, they said, was passing legislation to benefit the Bank of New Zealand, which he helped to direct.[1]

In 1885, upon the accidental death of the editor, John Hebden, Reeves became editor of the *Canterbury Times*, a weekly 'miscellany' established by the proprietors of the *Lyttelton Times* in 1866, which claimed the largest circulation of any weekly in the Colony. Today it seems a dull periodical, largely filled with stories and articles from other journals. It contained a ladies' page, a column of jokes, a summary of the week's news and articles on sport, agriculture, mining and literature. The political reports were often lively and provocative.

In the same year he also became a director of the Lyttelton Times Company. His salary as editor of the weekly was a handsome one for those days, £520—the editor of the *Lyttelton Times* received only £600. His fee as a director was £50, which he certainly earned, if only in worry. The Company was encountering increasing trouble, as the Colony itself entered the long depression which was to last from 1879 to 1895. In 1879 the *Press* had been reduced to a penny a copy. To meet the competition, the proprietors of the *Times*, William Reeves, W. J. W. Hamilton and T. W. Maude converted their partnership into a joint stock company with a nominal capital of £45,500. William Reeves owned 2,175 ten-pound shares. His son Will (as he had come to be called by his family and friends) acquired six, which were later increased. The *Times* was doubled in size and the Company spent £11,000 on a new building and machinery. But because advertising fell off during the depression, and because of competition with the *Press*, profits began to fall (from £8,400 in 1882 to £5,100 by 1886). The Company was heavily

---

[1] PD, 1883, 45, pp. 195, 340, 341; PD, 1890, 68, p. 520; LT, 1 Aug. 1883. For Reeves's general comments on this Parliament, see his 'Memoirs', Reeves MSS.

in debt. It had a large overdraft at the Bank of New Zealand, guaranteed by William Reeves's promissory note for £3,000, and other substantial debts. The *Press* was rumoured to be running at a consistent loss, but the battle was not going to be an easy one to win, for the *Press* was owned by a group of very wealthy men. It was clear that in Christchurch, with its population of only 40,000, four newspapers (two morning and two afternoon) and two weeklies could not all be run profitably.[1]

By 1885, through reporting political events, then helping to manage a political campaign in the newspapers, Will Reeves had become involved in politics himself. He had found a cause, to which he gave himself, in the eighties, with youthful wholeheartedness. His first cause was a railway line.

A railway to link Christchurch with Nelson and the West Coast had been suggested in 1870, foreshadowed in an Act of Parliament passed by Vogel in 1873, and in another in 1879. A Christchurch company, which soon collapsed, was formed to build it in 1880. Two years later a campaign to force the government to back the line was launched when Sir John Hall's ministry left it out of the public works estimates.

Christchurch, where the Vogel land boom had been most frantic, was one of the first towns to be hit by the depression, and it was hit the hardest. To the business community, desperate for a means of reviving prosperity, the idea of a railway to 'open up' the great districts to the north and west exerted an almost irresistible attraction—the boom of the seventies, which had enriched some and saddled others (like William Reeves) with large speculative land holdings, had been based on the construction of communications. But Governments were slow to respond. In the Oddfellows' Hall, in June 1883, the local 'Liberal' leader, William Montgomery, told his audience: 'If you want the West Coast railway—and you do ... you will have to agitate for it and enlighten public opinion, and bring the determined efforts of the people of the two Coasts to have their just rights—not by a fitful cry ... but by the strenuous and persistent cry of a people who are determined to have justice

---

[1] I am indebted to the Christchurch Press Company Limited for permission to read the minutes of the Lyttleton Times Company, which afford much information about the lives of the Reeves family.

done, and to have this money expended upon a great national work.' There was 'loud and continued applause'.[1]

William Reeves zealously supported the project. Week after week, year after year, his newspapers agitated; indeed the *Lyttelton Times* claimed that, in 1882, the campaign had been revived in its office. And, through articles and editorials, young Will Reeves did what he could to help. The *Lyttelton Times* and the *Canterbury Times* stressed the need for the line; the necessity for public agitation; and for all Canterbury Members of the House of Representatives (M.H.Rs.) to vote as a body in the House in order to get it.[2] Some politicians, like William Rolleston, were apathetic. They were denounced. Some districts, like those south of Christchurch, were indifferent too. They were appealed to by endless argument.

In mid 1884 hope presented itself in the gouty form of Sir Julius Vogel, who had supported the projected railway a decade earlier, and now returned from England to re-enter politics. He was pressed to stand for a Christchurch seat by a group that included J. T. Matson, who was running the firm, established by his father, Henry Matson, and C. O. Torlesse, of stock and station agents, wool and grain brokers and auctioneers. Matson was the most active member of a Railway League that had been formed in 1883 to organize the agitation.

To Vogel a railway was more than a great national work or a charmed electoral platform. He was interested in one himself.[3] In 1877, while he was Agent-General in London, Vogel had floated a speculative land company, the New Zealand Agricultural Company, to sell rabbit-infested land to innocent Englishmen. The names of two cabinet ministers in Grey's Government, Robert Stout and John Ballance, were on the list of provisional directors, which gave the impression that the Company had official backing. Ballance later claimed that his

---

[1] LT, 6 June 1883. On the origins of the line see, e.g., D. P. Millar, 'The General Election of 1884 in Canterbury', unpub. thesis, University of Canterbury.

[2] LT, 9 July 1884, letter; CT, 10 Aug. 1888. For the LT's arguments, see, e.g., LT, 5, 14, 23 Aug. 1882; 29 May 1883; CT, 1, 15 Aug. 1885.

[3] Apart from one or two minor references, this section is based on D. A. Hamer's unpublished thesis, 'The Law and the Prophet: A Political Biography of Sir Robert Stout (1844–1930)' (University of Auckland) and his article, 'The Agricultural Company and New Zealand Politics, 1877–1886', *Historical Studies, Australia and New Zealand*, 10, 38, May 1962.

name had been used without his knowledge,[1] but he did know-
ingly assist the Company in other ways. On learning about the
flotation, Grey forced Vogel to resign his appointment, and
Stout and Ballance to end their connexion with the Company, a
step partly responsible for their eventual resignation from his
Government, which wrecked the scaffolding he had erected for a
liberal party.

Part of the bait to induce English investors to swallow the
Agricultural Company's shares was the Waimea Plains railway,
which was to be built over the Company's land by another
private company with almost identical directors. By 1884 this
company had fallen into other hands and was threatening to
ruin the Agricultural Company by its demands for railway rates.
It is now indisputable that Vogel's main motive for returning to
New Zealand politics was to save the Agricultural Company by
arranging for the state to take over the railway, though this was,
at first, suspected by few people other than some of his friends and
Sir George Grey.

Since the fall of Grey's Government in 1879, and the dis-
integration of his following, Stout had been preaching the need
for a united, radical liberal party, but on Vogel's return in 1884
he wrote a letter, published in the *Lyttelton Times*,[2] appealing to
'liberals' to support Vogel, the apostle of big companies, and
most of the things the writer professed to oppose. The outcome
was the unholy Stout–Vogel alliance which promised to back the
Midland Railway scheme. With the support of the *Lyttelton
Times* and the 'liberals' of Canterbury, it won the 1884 election.
Stout became Premier and Vogel the Treasurer. William Reeves
was appointed to the upper house—the Legislative Council.

The new Government proceeded, against strong opposition,
to nationalize the Waimea Plains railway. It was less successful
with the Midland Railway. Since it was thought impossible for
the Government to borrow enough money to build the line as a
public work, it had to be constructed by a private company.
As an inducement, it was proposed to give the company, along
the route of the line, large areas of land which would become
valuable when it was open. In 1884 the company was to receive
land valued at half the cost of the railway. To Grey, this

---

[1] PD, 1891, 72, p.125. His name was probably added by Vogel or Stout.
[2] 10 June 1884, cit. Hamer, 'The Law and the Prophet', pp. 90–91.

amounted to giving away the rights of the future nation. He wanted the line to be built by the government. To the supporters of the scheme, including young Will Reeves, who now expressed his views in his own weekly newspaper, the *Canterbury Times*, it meant giving almost useless and valueless land to 'a great settling agency'. To him the railway company figured, as the Agricultural Company did to Stout, not as a business speculation, but as a successor to Wakefield's colonizing companies—as 'a great effort at patriotic colonisation'. The line would lead to 'closer settlement' and 'development' as it 'opened up' the land.[1]

It proved easier to plan the Christchurch, West Coast and Nelson line than to build it. The terms offered by the Government in 1884, allocating to the projected company alternate blocks of Crown land along the line, were unacceptable to the local syndicate interested in the work. Next year the Government's proposals came under heavy fire in Parliament. One opponent said that the line would not pay for the grease on the carriage wheels. J. T. Matson told Christchurch, 'There is no doubt that the City of Wellington is in flames from hatred and fear of the south. The men there are so excited that they would almost knife you over this question.'[2] The Opposition slashed the vote for the railway from £150,000 to £1,000.

It would not be easy to exaggerate how strongly the settlers felt about public works. The immediate result of this set-back was a meeting of perhaps 25,000 people, said to be the largest ever held in New Zealand, in Hagley Park, Christchurch, in September 1885. Will Reeves was inspired to write some indifferent jingles, 'The Demonstration':

> 'This Demonstration
>   Will "move e'en brutes:"
> Will rouse the nation,
>   No man disputes:
> Will be unanimous;
>   Sublime, *magnanimous*:
> Not "pusillanimous,"
>   'YOU BET YOUR BOOTS.'

----

[1] Hamer, op. cit., p. 40; CT, 25 July, 1 Aug. 1885; PD, 1887, 58, pp. 203–4, 562 ff., 581 ff.; 59, 104 ff., 563–4.
[2] LT, 7 Aug. 1885.

'So put your hats on,
    And *go and see*.'
Thus wrote John Matson,
    The bold J.T.... [1]

And some strong editorials appeared in the *Canterbury Times*.
Canterbury, one article asserted, did not care who was in the
government: 'Public opinion here cares little for parties or
Cabinets; it cares for the railway.' The Railway League, it urged,
should become a large, popular body instead of a small group of
businessmen. [2]

It is plain from occasional remarks in Will Reeves's letters,
and remarks about him, that he had entered into this campaign
with unquestioning enthusiasm. But until 1885 it is not easy to
tell which articles or editorials he wrote. From the time when he
became editor of the *Canterbury Times*, however, it is increasingly
easy to identify his writings. Its political comment became more
boldly and sharply phrased than the usual journalism of the day.
There is little doubt that he wrote the editorial just quoted, and
this passage, denouncing the selfishness of northern politicians,
who refused to spend a shilling on the Canterbury line: 'It goes
for nothing with these that this Province has been their milch
cow: that they have pocketed our land revenue ... that we have
paid for their roads, bridges and railways. Years ago, when we
were paying for the Native wars of the North, we were eloquently
assured of the reward their gratitude would some day give us.'

Whoever reads his signed writings in the eighteen-eighties can
identify, often with almost complete confidence, his anonymous
articles. With experience he became, in a very few years, an
outstanding leader writer. His phraseology, shaped sometimes
with an incisive bitterness, sometimes with a studied whimsi-
cality, became a signature. But in 1885 the tone of his prose was
more emotional and immature.

That Will was becoming attracted to politics, as well as
emotionally involved in political issues, may be guessed from the
fact that he joined the Parliamentary Debating Society, a club
which met in the Canterbury Provincial Council chambers and
followed parliamentary procedure. In 1885 Reeves was desig-

[1] G. P. Williams and W. P. Reeves, *Colonial Couplets*, Christchurch, 1889, pp. 31–33.
[2] 20 Aug., 5, 12 Sept. 1885; cf. 25 July 1885.

nated 'the Member for Coleridge' and appointed 'Attorney-General' in a 'Government' led by John Joyce, another budding politician. Reeves spoke in the Address-in-Reply and introduced a Representation Bill before resigning in July.[1] We may also guess that this interest was encouraged by his wife. In February of that year he had married Magdalene Stuart Robison, who was then nineteen.

Maud was a daughter of the manager of the local branch of the Bank of New South Wales. She was born in Mudgee, New South Wales in 1865, two years before her father was transferred to Christchurch—hopeful that 'that city would supply educational advantages to [his] growing family' quite lacking in Mudgee. Her mother was one of the talented Saunders (and Carr-Saunders) family of Surrey.

According to Miss Georgie Robison, one of Maud's younger sisters, and a bridesmaid,[2] the couple met at a 'coming-out' ball in 1883, at which we may picture Reeves's apparently confident progress from the words of a Christchurch lady who knew him a little later. He was a very good waltzer, 'but one of the rapid, inconsiderate types who rushed from one end of the room to the other, ignoring the angry glances of those he bumped against in his passage'. He courted her with a rhyming letter which informed the postman of her address in couplets. Maud was (one of the family later recalled) outside playing hopscotch when he called to propose.

Maud had a clever, handsome face; a determined face with full lips, very dark eyes and thick black hair which inspired one of his nicknames for her, 'Cetewayo', after the Zulu leader. Even a modern biographer hesitates to add that, on occasions, she called him 'monster dear'.

Her sister, Georgie, remembered Reeves as an abstracted young man, unaware of other's feelings, who used to sit in a darkened room, holding something hot against his forehead, when he had one of his headaches.

The association was as favoured by Mrs. Robison as it was frowned on by Mrs. Reeves, but the latter had met her match: Will had exchanged one dominant woman for another. On one

[1] On this club, see LT, 1, 7, 21, 28 Aug.; 4, 18 Sept., 2 Oct. 1884; 7. 14 May, 2 July, 8 Oct. 1885; 1, 8, 29 July 1886.
[2] Interview with the writer.

occasion, when Mrs. Reeves omitted to ask Mrs. Robison to a party, Maud threatened to 'turn Will against her'. Mrs. Reeves's resolution collapsed.

The young couple lived in Wilson's Road, on the border of the suburb of Sydenham, not far from 'Risingholme'. Their first child was still-born. Mrs. Robison insisted that Maud 'put her feet up for six months', and two daughters, Amber and Beryl, were successfully delivered in 1887 and 1889.

Throughout her life, Maud Reeves had many interests not fully shared by Will. For instance, she was an ardent advocate of the female suffrage, on which subject her husband in 1887 wrote some verses, 'The Ladies Triumph', prophesying its results— which included the prohibition of smoking rooms. But they shared a love of literature and politics. She became a determined intellectual. Will, though probably more intelligent, had less pretensions of that sort. In 1890, after the birth of Beryl, she enrolled at the Canterbury University College, where she was one of a brilliant set of young women, which included Edith Searle Grossmann, one of the Colony's early novelists. She passed the first section of her B.A., but abandoned formal studies when the family moved to Wellington a year later.

People measure success in dollops or teaspoonfulls, it is true, but Will Reeves might very well have thought by 1886 that he had got married; that nothing else had happened; that nothing much would; for twenty-nine is one of the measuring years in a man's life. But there was one episode that shows, gall as it was, that provincial domesticity had not swallowed the ambitious youth; that he was more than an occasionally irritating but essentially conforming young member of a remote, provincial, antipodean, middle class. In 1886 he was nominated for the Christchurch Club, the superior and more rural of the local clubs, by two leading citizens of the town—two more acceptable in Christchurch could scarcely indeed, short of royalty, have been found—but was 'black-balled' at the election. Samuel Saunders, who worked on the *Lyttelton Times*, and was an intimate enemy, later wrote that Reeves was 'pilled' because of his bitter political writings in the newspapers. Another story is that he had, while a temporary member of the club, spoken rudely to an elderly gentleman who cut the butter with his own knife before passing the dish. A further version is that he was on the premises, confidently playing billiards, on the night of the election, when a steward was obliged to inform him that he was not a member.

The third story shows Reeves being humiliated; the second demonstrates that he was not a gentleman; the first is probably near the truth. G. G. Stead, a leading conservative and one of the owners of the *Press* was 'black-balled' on the same occasion. Nevertheless, Saunders added, for good measure, that though Reeves 'had played cricket he had not assimilated the high traditions of the game'.[1]

A congeries of malicious legends, in which Reeves's weaknesses and the rebuff are magnified a thousandfold through the small, intense lens of Canterbury snobbery, has grown up round this episode, which, to local conservatives, made sense of his later radicalism. The late A. P. Harper, the mountaineer, related that, in the family law office, Reeves said: 'I'm a social out-caste. I'll make you b——s sit up!'[2] It is almost certainly apocryphal; yet it contains a psychological insight. True or false, it demonstrates what some members of Reeves's own class of people thought of him, besides explaining that any dislike became reciprocal. It reveals how high political feelings were running during the Stout–Vogel régime. And, details apart, it becomes clear that Reeves, who was very sensitive to slights, did not regard the repudiation lightly. At the same time, neither Stead nor he was snubbed because he was inconsiderable.

[1] Letters from the late Alan Mulgan to the writer, 15 Nov. 1954; 2 Sept. 1957, citing letters from Saunders. The other raconteurs shall be nameless.

[2] Interview with the author.

5

THE WORKING MAN'S FRIEND
1887

WILLIE REEVES had dreamed of political fame as he listened to
debate in the House of Representatives in 1872, but Will forgot
his boyhood ambition. It was reawakened by his interest in the
Midland Railway—which was not surprising when politics ran
on railway tracks. It was his ardent support for the Midland line
which brought him to the attention of politicians, including
Harry Atkinson,[1] who was Premier several times in the eighteen-
seventies and eighties. While journalism required him to follow
political trends and problems closely, the Midland line made
him a partisan, devoted to supporting the Stout–Vogel Government in every way he could, despite the ugly things that Grey,
J. D. Ormond and others said about the ministers and the
Agricultural Company. The railway was not, of course, the only
reason why politics became his main concern. But it was through
following those visionary tracks that he immediately entered the
life of political action. Thereafter he rapidly developed other,
more important interests. But his first political love was reluctant
to let him forget.

Despite all the efforts of the 'Times party', the construction of
the line was still unprovided for in 1887. The Christchurch
businessmen who were in 1884 empowered to build it, had
transferred their rights to an English company, the Midland
Railway Company. Parliament had approved this transfer in
1886, but the English directors were not satisfied with the new
contract. They wanted the New Zealand Government to work
the first sections of the line, when completed.[2] The Government
was negotiating through the Agent-General in London, Sir
Francis Dillon Bell, but the depression had become so bad that
the Company was demanding a very high price. The Govern-

---

[1] Reeves MSS, small clipping book, p. 101.
[2] PD, 1887, 59, pp. 104 ff., 973 ff.

ment could neither afford to build the line itself, nor to offend its Canterbury supporters by abandoning the project.

In 1884 Vogel had breezily pretended that the depression could be ignored; had proclaimed that the Colony's finances were sufficiently buoyant to satisfy the most exacting financier. But by 1887 the depression had spread from the south to the north, and covered perhaps the whole country. The Government, instead of reducing taxes as it had promised, was desperately trying to raise more money: revenues were falling with prices, while interest payments on past debt remained constant. Quite apart from a heavy burden of private debt, a population of 600,000 had incurred a public debt of some £38,000,000, on which nearly £2,000,000 was due annually in interest. Throughout the eighties (as Reeves later wrote) government finance amounted to 'little more than a series of attempts to avert deficits'.[1] Successive governments tried out a progressive land tax and a beer tax; they juggled with the property tax; borrowing was stopped by Hall and renewed by Whitaker. No one brought in an income tax—which Atkinson and Stout alike believed that the public would not accept: the former said the farmers would 'rise in rebellion' against it because of the complex book-keeping involved. In 1887, when its tariff proposals were rejected by the House for the second time, the Stout–Vogel Ministry 'went to the country'.

As the session neared its end, Will Reeves was in correspondence with the Canterbury 'Liberal' leader, William Montgomery, a man who was 'Liberal' chiefly in the sense that he had for a time supported the Grey Government; in 1892 he was to write to William Rolleston, a Canterbury leader of the 'continuous ministry', 'you are a Liberal and I am a bit of a Conservative.'[2] He was a well-to-do merchant and land-owner, a popular figure in his electorate on Banks Peninsula. In the House of Representatives, which had to put up with his ponderous speeches, he was nicknamed 'Old Mumbo'.[3] He had had close ties with William Reeves, whose extreme provincialist

[1] *The Long White Cloud*, London, 1898, p. 351.
[2] Rolleston MSS, 13 June 1892.
[3] A. M. Evans, 'A Study of Canterbury Politics in the Early 1880's', unpub. thesis, University of Canterbury, p. 86; Rolleston MSS, M. J. S. Mackenzie to Rolleston, 13 September 1895.

views he shared—indeed, in 1884 Montgomery was advocating
a revival of the provinces, even the 'separation' of Canterbury.[1]
Like William Reeves, he had become disillusioned with the Grey
Government, and had succeeded Grey as leader of the 'Liberal'
Opposition. But by 1887 he was unpopular in the *Lyttelton Times*
office. He had grown cool towards the cherished railway. Two
years before, he had broken with the Stout–Vogel Government
and voted to increase the tariff on tea, which offended Reeves,
who, like many New Zealand 'protectionists', wanted a 'free
breakfast table'—whereas some 'free traders', like members of
the Christchurch Chamber of Commerce, wanted an increased
tariff on commodities such as tea and sugar, which would tax the
poor.

On 31 May 1887, in an article undoubtedly written by Will
(it was the first sounding of his authentic note), the *Lyttelton
Times* commented on the shocking sacrifice Montgomery had
made of his reputation to his hatred of Vogel, despite his 'real
sympathy with the people in the battle of Man *versus* Money'.
The *Times* was appalled by rumours that, if Atkinson formed the
next ministry, Montgomery would join it.

Montgomery sent Will Reeves a copy of his speech on a new
Customs Duty Bill, to which he replied:[2]

                                                    Opawa
                                        Sunday 5th [June 1887]
My Dear Old Friend

I received the copy of your speech and read it carefully with much
interest. It is a good speech though not fair—from my point of view—
to the government. There are things in it difficult to answer but I
think you try to make out too harsh a case against the Ministry. If they
are to be blamed for the falling off of the revenue surely they should be
credited with any non-expenditure consequent thereupon. As for the
theoretic difference between Stout's ideal land system and Vogel's
that is an old story and doesn't, I think, matter one pin. We accepted
the coalition—and so did you—knowing this full well.

---

[1] e.g. PD, 1887, 57, p. 515.
[2] This letter and the next were lent to the author by the late Mr. W. H. Montgomery. I am indebted to Mr. W. J. Gardner of the University of Canterbury for
helping me to elucidate some of the references in these letters, and to date them.
The second was written four days after the General Assembly was prorogued.

PLATE 3

b. W. P. Reeves, c. 1887

a. W. P. Reeves, aged c. 17

I quite agree with you as to the need for retrenchment but venture to disagree as to the tactics most likely to get what we want. I am in constant communication now with men down here who know what public opinion in these parts is and they are as determined for economy as you but don't like your way. They think, and so do I, that pressure from the inside is the wisest plan; but they are not going to put the Continuous Ministry into the saddle once more. They know too well on whose backs the said saddle would be laid and who would feel the bit and spurs.

Much as I respect your heart *and head*, your long experience and shrewd judgement I think you would do better for the country as our ally than as the associate of a party comprising all the class selfishness of the Colony. Atkinson, Ormond, Readymoney Robinson, George McLean, Peacock[1] &c. &c. are queer mates for a man like Wm. Montgomery—pardon my saying so. I distrust the bulk of the present opposition utterly. To my mind Atkinson's record is far worse than Vogel's.

I write freely because we are friends and can trust each other. I am going to wade in here in a humble way—am doing so indeed. Men here mean to have retrenchment, but not Atkinson. What I fear is that retrenchment should become a catchword and a craze: the result would be a dire blow to Education. The growing hostility to the Education vote is almost alarming; I assure you honestly it is real and spreading here. I know nothing of the House, I speak only of this place. The poorer people are passing the word along against the top standards.

To sum up we mean to fight for the govt. tooth and nail, win or lose. At the same time retrenchment will be the first plank of our platform. I, so far as a humble and insignificant unit can work, mean to work for it inside our party. You will work from your different standpoint. Very keenly do I regret that we shan't be pulling together. I hope that we shall beat you (the Opposition I mean) but that when we have done so you will find us economical, just in taxation, friendly to the local industries and determined to press this Province's representatives to work together. All this is confidential but not mere words. I have been working pretty hard to find out what people think here.

Goodbye

Yours very faithfully
W. P. Reeves.

[1] Atkinson, McLean and Ormond were leaders of the 'continuous ministry'; McLean was a banker as well; Peacock a local businessman; Robinson a wealthy squatter who allegedly (and to local astonishment) paid in cash. Robinson and Peacock were proprietors of the *Press*.

Replying to this letter, Montgomery apparently annoyed Reeves by suggesting that an Atkinson ministry would support the railway project. In his next letter, it is difficult to say whether the jostling platitudes are due to hasty writing or to a natural political instinct—addressed, as they were, to Montgomery. If the emotion expressed in the letter seems excessive, it should be recalled that local feeling was quite as strong as the writer says— if less strong than his own.

Lyttelton Times Office,
Christchurch, N.Z.
Tuesday 188....[14 June 1887]

My Dear Mr. Montgomery,

Of course we shall always remain friends please Heaven, but with much of your letter I cannot agree. You say the Wellington atmosphere is calm, its newspapers and letters of correspondents to Dunedin and elsewhere tell a different tale. You may be cool and you may laugh at us for our warmth but I am truly sorry to see that you have quite lost touch of Canterbury. There is a time to be hot as well as a time to be cold. Do you know that if I could not sympathise with a brave community fighting fiercely against great odds for much less than bare justice I should not be proud—still less if they were my own people. My intelligence such as it is refuses to believe that the majority of the House would borrow money for our Railway. They would dangle the notion as a bunch of carrots before us until the ministry was out & then they would see us d——d first. As for the past we cannot cry over spilt milk. Half a loaf is ever so much better than no bread. Believe me people are roused here as they never were roused before about the line. The yell of execration that would greet your defection from the cause is a horrible thought to me. You have often said you think something of my advice—think something now sir!! throw in your lot with us before it is too late. Think of what you said in the Oddfellows Hall in May 1883[1]—that we were *never* to stay from our demand. You *know* that this is our only chance. Do not you—once our leader— now desert us. You know what I think of you how the other day I wrote an article that I knew would dismay my friends, and how I laughed at the reproof I got because I felt I had stuck by you. Don't leave me now Sir. Because you know once is for ever

Yours affectionately
W. P. Reeves.

---

[1] Presumably the speech of June 1883 quoted above, IV, pp. 52-3. The 'article' is almost certainly that of 31 May just quoted.

Two days later Reeves publicly entered politics; a month later, Montgomery retired.[1]

On 16 June an advertisement in the *Lyttelton Times* announced the formation of the Canterbury Electors' Association. The president was W. P. Reeves. Among the members of the committee were his cricketing friend, of whom he was very fond, Arthur Ollivier, a local accountant who had been at Christ's some years before Reeves, and Westby Perceval, a school-fellow who had gone to England in 1872 to 'complete' his education. There he was called to the Bar at the Middle Temple in 1878. In the eighties he was in practice in Christchurch and was on the committee of the East and West Coast and Nelson Railway League.

The policy of the Association was: 1. Substantial retrenchment. 2. Fair Taxation. 3. Encouragement to local industries (i.e. tariffs). 4. A United Canterbury.

Apparently the first meeting of the Association was held privately, for the second general meeting was announced for the next day. Although this was not immediately avowed, everyone knew that the Association supported the Stout–Vogel Government. It was equally clear that the principal architect of the Association was W. P. Reeves himself.

Two days later the Government's opponents formed the Political Reform Association. Its chairman was Peter Cunningham, one of the owners of the *Press* and President of the Chamber of Commerce. On the committee were C. C. Bowen, a leading Canterbury politician (with whom C. W. Richmond had 'contracted an alliance' in 1857), George Harper, the lawyer, and G. G. Stead, another proprietor of the *Press*. The programme of the Association was retrenchment of government expenditure, especially in education—though the national 'free' school system was to be maintained; a cessation of borrowing; and no increase in tariffs except for revenue purposes.

This was how elections had generally been organized in New Zealand, by local, *ad hoc* committees. There had been no colony-wide parties (the term 'national' would be anachronistic), though temporary controversies, such as that over the abolition

[1] LT, 5 July 1887.

of the Provinces, had occasionally created a division of opinion
throughout the country. Nor had politics been a contest between
radicals and conservatives—terms of little relevance in communities where the main political issue had been 'development',
roads and bridges. Political divisions had most commonly
arisen from competition for government expenditure on this
public work or that: a competition between, not classes, but
districts or provinces.

Politics had been managed by cliques of politicians linked by
personal bonds or by regional interest—like the large Canterbury
group that sought the Midland railway in 1884. Governments
were coalitions of cliques within an oligarchy. The shifting
alliances between these cliques, and their internal instability,
explained the endless reshuffling of personnel in the 'continuous
ministry'. Grey's unsuccessful attempt to create a Liberal Party
had merely added, to the existing congeries, further cliques
calling themselves 'Liberal', whose views were, in fact, scarcely
distinguishable from their opponents'. When Stout joined
Vogel in 1884, even that label almost disappeared from
use.[1]

The two self-appointed committees in Christchurch in 1887
certainly represented cliques, cliques associated with the two
newspaper companies—another phenomenon common when
many of the Colony's newspapers were owned or directed by
politicians. But many voters came to believe (in this case, justly)
that they stood for something more.

On June the 18th and 20th each newspaper took a first hard
look at the rival association in its editorial column. The *Press*
chided Reeves's Association for not openly avowing that it
supported the Stout–Vogel Government—and therefore a
policy of extravagance and fresh taxation. It complained that
the Electors' Association had stolen the *Press*'s cry for economy,
and scorned the suggestion that the Reform Association
supported Atkinson, who was unpopular in Canterbury. In
1884 he had lost support in Canterbury and office, after raising
rail freights on grain. The *Press* implied that he was not yet

---

[1] The general nature of politics, 1870–87, and the changes 1887–91, have been
analysed in an article by the present writer: 'The Significance of the Scarecrow
Ministry, 1887–91', in *Studies of a Small Democracy*, ed. R. M. Chapman and
K. Sinclair, Auckland, 1963.

forgiven and concluded, 'it is too soon yet for the party of economy to select a leader.'

The leading article of the *Lyttelton Times*, which bears all the marks of Will Reeves's style, boldly fastened on the Reform Association the label 'Atkinsonian Political Association': 'In and about it we see much money, some talent, and a fair amount of experience, but above all and beyond all its chief and crowning quality is its intense, impressive, and excessive respectability. Who would dare to struggle against such a weight were it not that in politics respectability, when blended with class interests and prejudices, generally manages to lose the fight.'

The article then recalled Sefton Moorhouse's claim that he had built the Lyttelton tunnel 'in the teeth of all the talent and all the respectability in Canterbury'—a reference to a struggle which (Will elsewhere remarked) was his earliest memory of politics.

At first sight (and especially to opponents of the Government) there was something distinctly odd about what followed: a catalogue of the leaders of the Reform Association demonstrating that there were nine lawyers on its committee; that its 'flower and strength' came from the Chamber of Commerce; that absentee land-owners and 'great companies' were well-represented. Coming from a paper owned by a landowner and director of several companies, in support of a group led by a lawyer and an ex-lawyer, Perceval and Will Reeves—could such stuff be regarded otherwise than as charlatanry? Yet there was something in it. A modern analysis has shown that there was an occupational and partly a class distinction between the Associations. The Reform Association was strongly backed by importers, financiers, medium and large farmers and run-holders; the Electors' Association included many manufacturers, shop-keepers, small farmers and agricultural labourers.[1] Both had their lawyers.

What gave the political conflict its sharp edge, however, was the fact that it was intertwined with a struggle between two groups of capitalists, the proprietors of the *Times* and the *Press*, which was becoming so damaging that in May 1887 the Press

---

[1] C. Whitehead, 'The 1887 Election in Canterbury', unpub. thesis, University of Canterbury, pp. 26 ff., 55, 162 ff., 181.

Company had approached the Times Company to discuss
reducing the number of newspapers. The Times Company
directors had refused, but they were becoming alarmed by
rumours that their rivals had raised £10,000 (one newspaper
said £60,000) to be spent on ruining them. At the moment the
Times was winning. Its price had just been reduced to a penny
and, as a result, its circulation had nearly doubled by October
1887, when 7,200 copies were being sold. But the proprietors of
the *Press*, 'Readymoney' Robinson, Stead, Peacock, Rhodes,
Cunningham and others were very much richer than William
Reeves and his friends. The *Geraldine Guardian* said of the former,
'All these are very wealthy men, and all of them are money-
lenders, grain-buyers, middle-men, and agents for absentees.'[1]

Will Reeves managed intellectually to subsume the Press
struggle within the political conflict. Without qualification, he
saw his paper as expressing the voice of the poor. In public
speeches delivered 'as a representative political worker', at
St. Albans, Lyttelton and Woolston, he interpreted the election
as a struggle of the people against the rich.[2]

On 5 July, in the Wesleyan School Room in St. Albans, he
addressed his first public meeting, an event which he later
described in an article on his life, seeing it as marking his turning
point from journalism to politics:

Fortunately only a few hours' notice was given me, or I should have
fidgeted into a fever. With immense care I learned my introductory
sentences by heart, and made voluminous notes. I was horribly
nervous. The little audience—it scarcely filled a big schoolroom—
seemed a portentous expanse of white faces staring at me through a
kind of haze. I began by reciting the carefully-prepared sentences.
The white faces appeared to smile good-naturedly. Then came the
pinch—I was at the end of the words I had got by rote! Could I go on?
Oh, joy! The words came faster than I wanted them. Point after point
suggested itself in proper order. I never looked at the voluminous
notes. The kindly little audience woke up and cheered the effort of the
beginner. They gave me a unanimous vote, and I went home perspir-
ing, but happier than I have ever been since after making a speech.
I made up my mind that, if I was to do anything in the way of persuading my fellow-countrymen, I had much better talk to them than write
at them. The odd thing was that this hurried conclusion was right.

[1] 23 May 1889.   [2] LT, 6, 15 July 1887.

According to the *Lyttelton Times* he spoke for over half-an-hour and 'fairly held his audience enthralled'. His main emphasis was on the need for 'party' in politics. By 'party' he meant 'the Canterbury brigade': the need for Canterbury members to stand together in defence of the Province and the Midland Railway. The Electors' Association's 'plank', a 'United Canterbury', had been invented by the *Lyttelton Times* in 1883–4 during the Midland Railway campaign. A united Canterbury bloc should be elected, Reeves urged, to fight for the line again. He was pleading for the voters to elect a solid bloc to support Stout and Vogel. But he turned away from provincialism as he explained the other proposals of his Association. They differed from their opponents, he claimed, because they did not want retrenchment to 'develop into a craze' to the ruin of numerous dismissed public servants. Above all (unlike their opponents) they did not want to cut the vote for education: 'This is the one thing that the poor should and do have the right to freely share with the rich.' Sir Robert Stout had told him that 'there could be no real economy in retrenchment on education. It would result in throwing children into the gutters, and that certainly was not economy.' Elsewhere, too, he spoke of taxing the rich landowners, and settling the poor on small farms. When he denounced 'the middleman' he was interrupted with tumultuous applause.

There was something in it; this contest was, indeed, something more than Tweedledum and Tweedledee—'Press gang' and 'Times party'. In his appeals to class feeling, however inappropriate they sounded from his lips, he expressed the beginning of a profound change in New Zealand politics.

At the end of the meeting he was rewarded with prolonged acclamation. A branch of his Association was formed. To his great pleasure, a leading politician—probably Sir Robert Stout—walked up and regarded him 'deliberately'. 'Young fellow', he said at length, slowly, 'if you have as good a stomach as you've got a head, you'll be Premier of New Zealand in a dozen years.'[1]

Will Reeves's political views were largely his father's. To his first audience he confessed that he had abandoned his youthful

[1] Reeves's account of this meeting is in the Reeves MSS, small clipping book, p. 111, *M.A.P.*, 15 July 1905 (a clipping). Because of a confusion in the text, it is not possible to identify positively the politician who spoke to him.

free trade notions, and become a convert to his father's pro-
tectionism. From him he had inherited his overpowering
provincialism—he lamented, indeed, the abolition of the
provincial governments.[1] In this respect he resembled most other
politicians and most of the settlers, who still thought of themselves as inhabiting a province (a settlement), not a country.
'Development' was conceived in provincial, or regional, terms;
was almost a synonym for 'provincialism'.

But the policy of the Electors' Association, the policies
announced in his speeches, had a further, quite different,
emphasis. 'Development' meant baking a larger cake. Graduated land taxation, though ultimately it, too, would lead to
economic growth, immediately implied redividing the existing
one. It involved an appeal not to local but to class sentiments.
In 1874, when Grey and Sheehan had uttered this call, William
Reeves had turned away. So had the voters. But by 1887, as the
depression spread and deepened, the cake had begun to shrink,
and the demand that it be cut up into more slices was
becoming insistent.

The depression was pointing to a transformation of politics,
as Reeves obscurely sensed. As the Colony's credit in London
deteriorated, as revenues fell, the extensive construction of
public works with borrowed money was becoming impossible:
the old source of political division was drying up. At the same
time, there was a growing radical movement. The desire to own
property, which had made the average settler willing to leave
politics in the hands of property-owners, was turning into
resentment against them. Unemployment and poverty were
bringing thousands of settlers to feel that something fundamental
was wrong with their society; to feel, moreover, robbed of the
fulfilment of the comfortable dream that had led them to the
antipodes.

One set of property-owners, the most conspicuous, formed a
natural scapegoat. A large proportion of the country was divided
into a few great sheep-runs: in 1883, 91 people owned 47 per
cent. of the 2·8 million acres in private hands in Canterbury.
These 'squatters', 'run-holders', 'monopolists', had earned a
large proportion of New Zealand's overseas funds, and played a
central rôle in its growth. But now they stood between the mass

[1] e.g. LT, 6 Aug. 1887 (speech). CT editorials said the same.

of settlers and the ownership of a farm. The poor could neither pay for land nor borrow the money at current interest rates; large landowners, who had bought during the Vogel boom, could not afford to sell at the prices offering in the eighties. This was a conflict intensified by the beginning of refrigerated shipping in 1882, for now there was a real possibility that capitalist small-farming would prove profitable, which it had rarely been before. The 'squatters' stood in the way of a re-organization of the Colony's resources.

All over New Zealand in the eighties associations were being formed to demand radical economic changes. There was a State Bank League; there were various Liberal Associations, survivals or reincarnations of those started by Grey; there were the Knights of Labour and the Anti-Poverty League, which promulgated the ideas of the Californian 'single-taxer', Henry George. Like John Stuart Mill, following Ricardo's theory of 'economic rent', George held that, since land values rose with the progress of the community, they represented a species of communal property, and that the 'unearned increment' in land values should be subject to special taxation. Mill wanted to tax it; George to confiscate it. This was an argument most persuasive in New Zealand, where land values had, at least before the depression, risen with 'development' paid for by public borrowing and taxation. Some groups went further than the land taxers and demanded the nationalization of the land— a policy which both Stout and Ballance, cabinet ministers again in 1887, had once advocated. The Protection League also advocated radical change. In England free trade was a radical, a liberal dogma; but in New Zealand it was, by 1887, conservative: it was calculated to bolster the position of the great landowners by providing them with cheap imports. Protection was calculated to stimulate urban industry and social change.

The depression and the rise of radicalism produced a conservative movement for the first time in the Colony, as property-owners felt challenged, and moved to defend their interests. In many parts of the country—first in Auckland, then in Christchurch—Political Reform Associations were formed to oppose the Government and to demand sweeping retrenchments in government expenditure. Their chief motive was a simple one.

Most landowners were heavily mortgaged and traders 'involved'; the 'rich' were those who had been found creditworthy by banks; in the Colony 'wealthy' usually meant 'indebted'. In their parlous state, as the depression grew ever more debilitating, middle class people felt that further taxation would ruin them. The alternative seemed to be to cut government expenditure to the bone. The Reform Associations advocated a reduction of the salaries of politicians; the cessation of borrowing; the abolition of subsidies to local bodies; the abolition of the exemption on the property tax, in order to tax cottagers; and retrenchment in the public service. Some of them wanted to reduce the education vote by 25 per cent. by such means as raising the school entry age to seven and abolishing Standards 5 and 6, the two final years of primary schooling. The Timaru and Christchurch Associations opposed further tariffs—except those on tea, sugar and tobacco: in New Zealand terminology they were 'free traders'.

These proposals were profoundly conservative, in the sense of aiming at the defence of propertied and indebted persons at the expense of the mass of the population. When Reeves spoke in terms of class warfare, he was not playing on prejudices and ignoring facts.

During the election, both Stout and Vogel favoured further taxation and tariffs. Stout wanted to avoid taxing the poor, and to maintain the education system intact 'at all hazards'.[1] So the Reform Associations hoped to defeat the Government. Their difficulty was that the policy of Atkinson, the Leader of the Opposition, was almost indistinguishable from the Government's. The *Southland Times* regarded him as 'only a milder and less unscrupulous Vogel': 'The Major [Atkinson] would lead us to perdition at a jogtrot, but Sir Julius at a hand gallop.'[2] Atkinson had once held office in a Vogel ministry. Now he frankly admitted that further taxes were needed, and favoured mild tariff protection. Consequently, much of the energies of the Reform Associations were devoted to finding a new leader, which proved a difficult task, for they were more conservative than any of the leaders of the 'continuous ministry'—now the

[1] LT, 15, 16 June 1887; *N.Z. Times*, 20 July 1887; *Otago Daily Times*, 15 June 1887.
[2] 26 July 1887.

Opposition. By July, most of the Associations supported John Bryce, a North Island politician, but in Christchurch the Reform Association continued to hesitate. It was reluctant to abandon the leading Canterbury members of the Opposition, yet could not quite accept them. Sir John Hall wanted 'unsparing' retrenchment, but leaned towards protective tariffs; Rolleston was a free trader, but believed in the radical doctrine of leasehold land tenure.

Because the Reform Associations had no one accepted leader, while their opponents were divided into Stout-Vogelites and Greyites, the political situation was as confused as ever. Indeed, it was possibly more chaotic than usual, as 'class' issues began to rival and supersede public works as the basis of political division. But the beginnings of 'class' politics could be seen clearly enough in Christchurch because there alone the Reform Association was opposed by the Canterbury Electors' Association in something approaching a conservative-radical struggle. In 1887 Will Reeves was a midwife at the birth of modern New Zealand politics.

Reeves proved a successful political organizer. He controlled, of course, the means of publicity; but he also ensured that the publicity was earned. His most satisfying effort occurred on July 18th when the Reform Association arranged for Robert Bruce, Member for Rangitikei and a leading free trader, to visit Christchurch. His sponsors issued a circular calculated—as they put it—'to appeal to the more thinking portion of the Electorate'. Reeves countered with a handbill urging supporters of the Government to 'ROLL UP' at the Tuam Street Hall to ensure that the Reform Association should not 'score a victory'. What followed is best put in Reeves's own words, which were written long afterwards, but are accurate:

'Roll-up' did it. True, the other side mustered about 800 respectable citizens who got most of the front seats and looked, I must admit it, about as decent and solid a lot as I have often seen at a rowdy meeting. But my slogan had brought together something like 1400 electors and others, a little rougher looking perhaps than the Conservatives, but reliable men who could be trusted to hold up a hand—or two hands—for the right resolution. We had, moreover a contingent of stalwart young footballers—worthy precursors of ALL BLACKS—who planted themselves in the rear part of the Hall and prepared for business.

The Hall was much overcrowded. The proceedings began with a sharp skirmish over the election of the Chairman. The enemy wanted the President of the Chamber of Commerce; we wanted the Mayor of Christchurch. They hooted the Mayor, we hooted the President. This went on for 12 or 15 minutes, then a strange thing happened. Mr. Bruce, though an excellent speaker and attractive man, had one foible, he was the most restless man I ever knew. We used to exchange bets sometimes in the New Zealand Parliament that Bruce could not keep in one place for a quarter of an hour. That is what happened that night. He suddenly stood up on the platform and to the stupefaction of his friends walked off through a side entrance. Our side laughed uproariously. Amid the general confusion a big Irishman, Mr. John Holmes, a well-known Protectionist, stepped forward. He had a voice of thunder and was able to get a hearing for 3 or 4 minutes. After reprobating the disorderly tactics of the other side he proclaimed that as they had 'so grossly mismanaged this great meeting, *we*, the people of Christchurch would now take charge!' He moved a Resolution and sat down very hoarse. I went forward to second him. I was not precisely popular with the Conservatives at that moment, and when they saw me in front of them, the tempest broke loose. Not a word could be heard. I stood looking at them for a minute. I noted how much louder, howls, booings, yells and hisses sound when they are directed at yourself than when some one else is catching it. I looked at the sea of red, angry faces, waving hands and shaken fists. Then the sea seemed to surge backwards and forwards and men from the front row began to climb on the platform. The Resolution had to be seconded and there was no time to lose. Stepping then to the front of the plat-form, I went down on my hands and knees and craned my neck over to the Reporters who were sitting in front. I bellowed in the ear of the nearest. 'Gentlemen, I second that.' It is not therefore true, as was subsequently asserted that my first attempt to address a public meeting of my fellow Colonists was totally inaudible. One man heard it.

The Resolution however, was never put. As I scrambled to my feet, we were in darkness. The enemy had turned out the lights. In the words of a veracious chronicler 'and so, in the darkened building one of the rowdiest and least creditable exhibitions ever seen in our usually well-behaved city may be said—with strict accuracy—to have terminated in disorder.'

The discomfited man who tried to chair the meeting against the will of the majority was Cunningham, leader of the Reform Association. He wrote a pained letter to the *Press*, and Reeves added insult to injury by thoroughly trouncing him in the correspondence columns.[1] The incident was reported in many newspapers, variously hailed as larrikinism or a resounding defeat for the political Opposition. It first brought Will Reeves's name to public notice outside Canterbury.

By about July Reeves had decided that he would like to stand for election to the House. In those days a potential candidate (as he plainly was) used first to be sounded out by his friends. If he showed interest, a petition was collected asking him to stand. If he accepted, his friends formed a committee to organize his campaign. Then came the day of public nomination, and finally, election day.

The invitation Reeves received to stand was amusing but scarcely flattering. Two or three 'influential local politicians' from the St. Albans electorate 'dropped in for a chat' and indicated that the sitting member, F. J. Garrick, was likely to be keenly opposed. Their spokesman said, 'People down our way are very dissatisfied with the side Mr. Garrick has taken; they're saying that they'd do anything to get him beaten. I've heard men say openly that they'd vote for a chimney-sweep to turn Mr. Garrick out. Now, Mr. Reeves, why don't *you* stand?'[2]

In late July the St. Albans branch of the Electors' Association resolved to ask Reeves to stand, and 150 signatures were immediately added to the 'requisition'. On the same day a meeting of the local Fruit Growers' Association (perhaps wanting tariff protection) also asked him to stand. Reeves was coy and would not accept unless an unusually large number of voters signed the requisition. Within a few days over 500 did so, and on 6 August he appeared on the platform as a parliamentary candidate. The *Press* summarized and commented on his speech with heavy irony: 'He would not now be seeking to enter Parliament but for the fact that a large majority of the electors of St. Albans passionately yearn to possess him as their representative. Therefore, in a truly noble self-sacrificing spirit Mr. Reeves has emerged from the seclusion of private life and is ready to satisfy this yearning.'[3]

---

[1] Reeves MSS, small clipping book, pp. 52–54; LT, 19 July 1887; Reeves MSS, 'Memoirs'.

[2] Small clipping book, p. 110.

[3] LT, 28 July, 5, 6 Aug., 24 Sept.; *Press*, 6, 9 Aug. 1887.

The electorate was distinctly promising. Though it included wealthy areas in Riccarton, Merivale and St. Albans, it mainly consisted of the working class suburbs north-west of the town, where there were many politically conscious and active people who had formed several ephemeral radical organizations in the past. When the Greyite Liberal Association of 1879 had collapsed, it had been succeeded, in 1881, by a Working Men's Political Association which advocated an income tax, graduated land tax, a state bank, the eight-hour day, tariffs, and the abolition of plural voting and of the Legislative Council. It also supported the Midland railway campaign.[1] In 1884 the sitting member, F. J. Garrick, had beaten a candidate supported by the Working Men's Association, but the victor's votes had totalled less than 400—less than the signatures on Reeves's requisition. So Reeves had every hope of beating him.

Garrick was a lawyer, whose clients included several banks and large companies. In 1884 the *Lyttelton Times* had backed him as a Stout-Vogelite. He had supported the Government and—unlike Montgomery—had voted for its tariff, but only because he regarded Atkinson as being as protectionist as Stout and Vogel. He admitted to preferring small-pox to tariff protection. During the 1887 election he expressed the most conservative views of the day, admirably fitting the upper-class stereotype that Reeves sought to fasten on his opponents. But he did not prove a colourful or impressive candidate. He did not quite know how to handle his youthful and ebullient rival, and relied on a condescending assumption that Will was acting under his father's orders. Generally both candidates avoided personal remarks, though there was a bitter undercurrent to their speeches. Garrick found the election a trial—after one of his meetings, the audience gave three cheers for Reeves.[2] Reeves, on the other hand, seemed to enjoy every minute of it.

In Christchurch as a whole, it was one of the most exciting elections for years, because of the rivalry of the two Associations. The conservatives put out an election newspaper, the *Political Reformer*, and employed paid canvassers, a practice looked down

---

[1] J. D. Salmond, *New Zealand Labour's Pioneering Days* (ed. D. Crowley), Auckland, 1950, pp. 125–7; see, also, theses by A. M. Evans and C. Whitehead (listed above), and D. P. Miller, 'The General Election of 1884 in Canterbury', p. 240 (University of Canterbury).

[2] See LT, 11 Aug., 15 Sept. 1887.

on by many politicians.[1] The Reform Association's expenses
were very heavy—£500 or more.[2] The Electors' Association
organized the suburbs and Rangiora. It requisitioned Reeves's
friend, W. B. Perceval, to stand, as well as Reeves, and several
others among its members were also candidates. The *Lyttelton
Times* pushed seven candidates, who stood for 'United Canterbury'. One of them was Vogel, but he made less impression in
Christchurch than Reeves himself. Only in Christchurch itself
did the Association fail to achieve its aim of preventing vote-
splitting. There three Government supporters stood. The
Reform Association also had its troubles. One of its most
prominent members, C. C. Bowen, a founder of the system of
compulsory primary education, resigned because it advocated
retrenchment in the Education Department.[3] Its pretence of
being a non-party organization (because it could not decide on a
leader) was a continual weakness.

The two sides discharged broadsides of doggerel. One verse
on Reeves concluded:

> In short, altho' I'm but a boy, I have a great ambition
> To become the very model of a modern politician.

Shakespeare was parodied too. Reeves was pictured as
Henry V on St. Crispian's day, leading the Electors' Association,
Protectionists and printers' devils against 'the Bruce'. Some of
the rhyming propaganda was written by Reeves himself. The
best effort, possibly his, was a long, satirical attack on 'The
Independent Member'. All his life, what Reeves most disliked in
a politician was 'sitting on a rail'. The first verse read:

> Away with your parties, their mottoes and cries,
> I scorn all political fetters and ties;
> Let others hang on to Hall, Vogel, or Stout,
> I claim the proud right to twist clean round about.
> To-day I'm a Liberal—that's if I choose—
> To-morrow my vote I am free to refuse
> To this side or that, for I'll follow no tail,
> But still 'Independent' I'll sit on a rail.[4]

---

[1] LT, 10 Sept., 28 June (W. B. Perceval letter).
[2] Rolleston MSS, P. Cunningham to Rolleston, 1 Oct. 1887.
[3] *Press*, 20 Sept.; LT, 20 June, 26 Sept. 1887; C. Whitehead thesis, *passim*.
[4] See Reeves MSS, small clipping book, for this and other election verses. Also
LT, 13 June, 29 Aug. 1887.

The campaign was not all good-humoured. Reeves's speeches, especially, aroused very great antagonism. A cartoon picturing him as Impudence was circulated; he was called 'blasé' in the *Press*;[1] in a private letter he was described as a 'stuck up little snob'. One man wrote to Sir John Hall (just after the election): 'Mr. W. P. Reeves expects to be premier in about six months time; he is a most positive young man, in fact the only thing he is not quite certain about is whether the Almighty made him or he made the Almighty....'[2] At the same time, his speeches won him a grudging respect from his opponents. He was called 'the enthralling gusher' by a correspondent in the *Press*.[3]

The *Press* was quite justified in accusing Reeves of setting class against class.[4] The tone of his speeches, almost independently of any particular words, expressed strong antagonism to squatters, banks, and Money. Apart from his advocacy of party organization—which he now believed in 'for its own sake'—and retrenchment, his speeches were aimed at the working class voter. Protective tariffs, he said, were better than cheap and sweated labour. The children of the rich were educated from the age of five to twenty-three—'If eighteen years of teaching was not too many for them, five or six years were too few for the poor.' Now it was not (as he had suggested in one letter to Montgomery) the 'poorer people', but the rich, who wanted to abolish the top classes in the primary schools. Education was essential to prepare the workers for the 'proper use' of the eight-hour day.

On the land question he was less decided. He advocated closer settlement and village settlements, while repudiating land nationalization. But as the election progressed he modified his expression of his views according to political expediency. He plainly did not want to sound too frightening to the middle class. Moreover he continued to place Canterbury before Class. Though he believed in a progressive land tax to break up the large estates, he and his friends suggested to the Government that it drop this proposal from its programme in order to unite all classes behind 'United Canterbury'.[5] What Stout thought of the suggestion is not known—but Vogel was opposed to this policy without prompting from the Electors' Association.

---

[1] LT, 24 Sept., *Press*, 9 Aug. 1887.   [2] Cited C. Whitehead, p. 64.
[3] 8 Aug. 1887.   [4] e.g. 29 Sept. 1887.
[5] LT, 6 Aug., 12 Aug., 10 Sept. 1887.

Reeves spoke with increasing fluency. He never read his speeches, which were very well-knit. He had packed, enthusiastic audiences. It became obvious that he had a gift of oratory, even some of the arts of the demagogue. In a speech at Merivale he ridiculed the Reform Association's continued pretence of being a non-party organization, and singled out a much-respected Hawkes Bay squatter, J. D. Ormond ('the one leader whom the party were not ashamed to name') for special attention. He said he could not see much difference between Ormond and Sir John Hall, except that the latter was a Canterbury man. They were both large and wealthy landowners who had 'consistently legislated for the benefit of their class'—though he did not see why they should be elected to legislate for other classes. But Ormond had opposed the Midland railway. The newspaper report continued: 'Mr. Ormond was Sir John Hall, only more so. (Laughter). He had seen the other day that a traveller had said that, if you stripped a Spaniard of every virtue, you would have a Portuguese, that a Portuguese was a Spaniard only more so; and he (Mr Reeves) would say, "Strip Sir John Hall of every redeeming feature he can have in the opinion of the people of Canterbury, and you have Mr Ormond." (Laughter and applause.)'[1]

A couple of years later Reeves gave his own account of the campaign. If he spoke on drastic retrenchment, he said, he found his audience solely interested in Catholic claims for state aid for their schools; if he spoke on protection he was asked about the 'local option without compensation' (the right of districts to vote on whether licensed hotels should be allowed); if he defended state education his audience wanted a state bank; if he opposed borrowing he was asked if his wife were a Catholic.[2] Though he did not know it, the voters were bringing up the issues of future elections.

On Nomination Day (an archaic English practice continued for the last time in New Zealand) Reeves received 'a heavy defeat'. Garrick brought a tram-load of 'voters and boys' along and, on the show of hands, he secured 120 votes to Reeves's 30.[3]

[1] LT, 10 Sept. 1887.
[2] PD, 1889, 64, 258–9.
[3] This was the last occasion when the antiquated procedure of a show of hands was adopted. In 1890 nominations were made in writing to the receiving officer, LT, 27 Nov. 1890.

But the working men turned out a week later on election day, when voting was by secret ballot. Reeves beat his opponent by 802 votes to 638. His majority came mainly from the working-class suburbs of Knightstown, Riccarton and Addington. Amidst great excitement, his committee took the horses out of the victor's carriage and dragged him a mile to the town, where he addressed the crowd in front of the *Times* office. 'Men have beaten money for once', he proclaimed. Garrick said that Reeves would not represent but misrepresent his electorate. An interjector called out, 'He's the working man's friend', and Garrick somewhat grimly observed that that remained to be seen.[1]

[1] LT, 20, 27, 28 Sept. 1887; C. Whitehead thesis.

6

MEMBER FOR ST. ALBANS
1887–9

A PHOTOGRAPH of Reeves at about the age of thirty shows a vigorous man, confident, perhaps slightly arrogant, who looks eminently capable of dealing with life. Unlike most of his photographs, it shows something of his determination. A cartoon of that time suggests rather the young-man-about-town, hands in pockets, saturnine, more markedly arrogant. Certainly not a man, to people in the crowded galleries, who looked out of place in the House of Representatives when he took his seat on 6 October 1887, nervously conscious that his 'tall silk hat' kept sliding a little to one side, relieved to observe that there was a sizeable group of new men of about his age. Among them were Joseph Ward, a thickset, swarthy, 'pleasant-looking' man from Southland, Westby Perceval and Arthur Rhodes from Canterbury, and Thomas Mackenzie, Member for Clutha. It was still sufficiently unusual for colonial-born men to sit in the House for them to be noticed and promptly labelled 'the Young New Zealand Party'.

But Reeves's eyes were mainly on the great. Sir George Grey, it was remarked, had not yet arrived, but Vogel was there, gouty and puffy, in his wheel-chair, attended by an Armed Constabulary Man. Sir Maurice O'Rorke, who was immediately elected Speaker, was there; John Ballance; and Dick Seddon— not one of the great, but certainly one of the conspicuous. Reeves had first seen him in 1882 in Hokitika. Walking past a hall, he heard a voice 'of considerable compass', and, on enquiry of a bystander, was told that it was 'Dick Seddon having it out with them'. He went in to hear, and found the speaker defending himself against the criticisms of 'certain local politicians' who, Reeves gathered, 'did not represent the higher intellect of the great heart of the people'. After listening, and observing that

immense frame and 'weather-beaten aspect', Reeves had left,
convinced that Seddon was 'worth leaving alone'.[1]

Harry Atkinson, 'a lean, wiry, tawny-coloured man', was the
main focus of attention. 'The Major' had fought in the Maori
wars and young Members used to speculate on how many chiefs
he had killed. The Opposition 'credited him with one; his
supporters hinted that it might be three.'[2] In close-quarters
fighting, whether in politics or the bush, he had proved extremely
durable. By the time the House met his victory over the Government and the rebel free traders was almost complete. Both the
enemy bands had lost their leaders: Stout and John Bryce had
been defeated in their electorates. The Government was badly
beaten. Newspaper estimates of the state of the new House gave
the Opposition up to 52 seats in a House of 95, against 30 or more
'ministerialists' and a number of 'independents'.[3] Only in
Canterbury had the Government won. All seven Christchurch
seats went to 'United Canterbury', as well as all the country
towns. Reeves had demonstrated the value of what he called
'a certain amount of machine-working' in politics.[4] But the
situation in the House was chaotic. There were Vogel and his
followers, including Reeves. Grey had 'a small tail'. Atkinson
had a quite small following—Reeves said it was the smallest of
the three 'parties'. The largest coherent grouping was the band
of militant free traders numbering about 32. It was, Reeves said,
'a new figure on the political horizon', a 'party' containing not
merely 'much of the ability, but much of the character of the
House'. Before the session they had rushed to Wellington and
tried to find a leader to replace Bryce, but had failed to find
anyone acceptable and willing. They had, in any case, little hope
of gaining power, for they were in a minority in the House: they
had been soundly beaten in the urban electorates. Moreover,
when Stout resigned, before the House met, the Governor (without asking advice) had sent for Atkinson, the Leader of the
Opposition, and invited him to form a government.[5]

His difficulties were enormous. He would not call on the free

---

[1] Reeves MSS, small clipping book, p. 184.
[2] Ibid., 'Memoirs', which describe his first day in the House.
[3] e.g. LT, 28 Sept.; Press, 27, 28 Sept. 1887.
[4] PD, 1889, 64, p. 259.
[5] See R. M. Chapman and K. Sinclair, (ed.), Studies of a Small Democracy, Auckland,
1963, pp. 117–18.

traders, who had deserted him, for support now. His old ally, Rolleston, had lost his Canterbury seat—a victim, he complained, of 'the bane of Colonial Politics—petty Localism—the Midland Railway Swindle—(that term is not too strong) and a united Canterbury'.[1] Atkinson's protectionist friend, Sir John Hall, would not join him 'for personal reasons'. He formed what the free traders called a 'scarecrow Cabinet'. It included four free traders who were prepared to swallow a tariff schedule sweetened with a portfolio, and an ex-Greyite, T. W. Hislop, as Colonial Secretary. G. F. Richardson, a 'freeholder', replaced Rolleston, a 'lease-holder', as Atkinson's Minister of Lands. No one thought it could last.

On the fourth day of the session, Reeves moved an amendment to the Premier's motion on local bills. A few days later he asked the Minister of Education, George Fisher, whether he still thought children under seven should be excluded from the schools. When Fisher replied evasively (but quoting President Garfield that education before that age was injurious) Reeves promptly moved the adjournment of the House. The motion was not seconded.

Later on that day, 14 October, Atkinson moved that the House adjourn for two weeks while the new Government prepared its business. An old friend of Reeves, on the Opposition side, 'who was a sort of guide, philosopher, and friend', came over, clapped him on the shoulder and said, 'Get up, old fellow. and pitch into the adjournment; it will give you a chance of making a beginning.'[2]

His intention, it might be guessed, was to throw the new Member back in the fray so that he would regain confidence after the earlier rebuff. And so Reeves made his maiden speech. His nervousness he confessed, and hoped Members would overlook any want of 'firmness, force, and coherence' in his remarks. He spoke for only a few minutes, describing how, during the election, the air in Canterbury 'was dark with retrenchment; the whole atmosphere was full of axes and pruning knives'; how almost none of the southern politicians supported Atkinson; how he and his friends were laughed at for saying that, if Stout and

---

[1] Rolleston to G. Fisher, 2 Oct. 1887, cit. W. R. Armstrong, 'The Politics of Development', unpub. thesis, Victoria University of Wellington, pp. 290–1.

[2] PD, 1891, 70, p. 49.

Vogel fell, Atkinson would succeed them. He likened the free traders to the young lady of Riga, and observed that the Premier was smiling.

It was fittingly modest, with a few good turns of phrase; a debating, not a prepared speech. But he was not modest himself: not many brand new Members, no matter how ardent for their cause, would have tried to move an adjournment (though it would not seem as bold then, in the absence of party organization, as it would today). It was true, however, that he was nervous. He was described as 'nervous, rapid, excitable in speech'. But he was not lacking in 'push'. A hostile description in the *Press*, though it contained elements of truth, missed this point: 'he was a profoundly nervous, blushing, and distressingly self-conscious parliamentary neophyte, who coyly disburdened himself of shrinking little sarcasms in the House, and blushed to find them heard.'[1] Though he was acutely self-conscious, his sarcasms were not shrinking. During his first year in the House his conduct was a mixture of assertiveness, tactlessness and nervousness common enough in clever young men (and he was 'as full of natural cleverness as an egg is of meat'). Above all, he showed a very powerful belief in the righteousness of his causes, even when they were railways.

In 1887 the Government had to come back to the House for approval of further legislation on the East and West Coast and Nelson Railway. The Midland Railway Company directors had refused to sign the contract approved in 1886 without a Government guarantee that the 2,300,000 acres given to them would actually be worth the estimated £1,250,000 when the line were completed. This led to further heated debates. Sir George Grey denounced giving away millions of acres, the heritage of future unborn millions, to greedy English capitalists. The action would, he believed, create thousands of paupers, and 'rack-rented tenants' on the Company's lands. To the old pro-consul, as to the young Member for St. Albans, the railway was more than twin lines of steel. Grey's mind dwelt no longer in present time, but in history, and particularly in the years of greatness ahead. He saw himself as involved in a melodramatic clash with great absentee landlords to defend the interests of a future nation. But his 'cloudy vision' seldom descended to touch the earth of

[1] 20 July 1892—referring to 1887.

everyday politics, and he had little influence. 'Every little gutter-child in Wellington', he cried, 'has a right and interest in this land': 'Why, no more monstrous thing was ever proposed to me. I think that nothing in Dante's description of Purgatory—the honourable gentleman may laugh, but I know his conscience smites him.... I say this: that nothing that Dante has conceived is more terrible than this.'[1]

Reeves twice rose to defend the line and to denounce Grey as its 'irreconcilable enemy'. George Fisher, the Minister of Education, later described him, 'with quivering frame and tremulous voice', pointing a 'rigid and scornful finger' at Grey and calling him the foe of settlement.[2] Reeves's argument was that, since the Government could not afford to build the railway, the Company must. It would open to closer settlement land at present almost worthless—what had been left by speculators who had brought up the good land under Grey's cheap land regulations of 1853, which had given north Canterbury over to 'desolation tempered by sheep'. Grey defended himself hotly. Reeves interrupted him and presently expressed his regret if he had given offence. He spoke too hastily, became confused, was laughed at, and had to make a 'personal explanation'.

Reeves later wrote that Grey's speeches at that time were 'terribly empty and insufferably tedious'—easy to deal with 'provided you remembered his ancient prestige and treated him with proper respect. The House insisted on that.' His words did not always express that respect. On another occasion when he assailed Grey, the Minister of Justice, Fergus, said the scene reminded him of the painting 'Dignity and Impudence'.[3] Nevertheless he did regard the old man, who was a legend (partly one of his own creation) in his lifetime, with admiration, if not with awe. In his 'Memoirs' he wrote as fine a description of the aged Grey as anyone has penned:

His striking talents anyone could see; his defects made him almost impossible. Yet there were moments, even as late as the earlier nineties, strange flashes that came from a mind that was not that of ordinary men. To the last he had two qualities almost to perfection.

[1] PD, 1887, 58, p. 565; cf. 203 ff.
[2] PD, 1887, 58, pp. 563, 590, 592 (Reeves); 1891, 71, p. 590 (Fisher).
[3] PD, 1888, 62, pp. 163–6.

In politics he was fearless. I never saw his physical courage tested, but old colonists who had known him as a young man in rough days told me that it was the same: he did not know what fear was. The other quality was his dignity. I have watched him daily for weeks and never saw anything get over his guard.

I used sometimes to dream of what he might do on the Day of Judgment if the Recording Angel were to sentence him to everlasting punishment. I could imagine him in that case slowly buttoning up his overcoat, deliberately adjusting a warm comforter round his throat, carefully putting on a silk hat with a broad brim. Then, taking up a walking stick, he would quit the dock without looking at the Judge or taking notice of Bar or spectators. He would quietly take the road to Avernus treading carefully, saying nothing but looking with steady gaze as though his tired brain were filled with some rather pleasant dream.

During the next session, in 1888, during the debates on Atkinson's tariff, Reeves made his first big speeches, and began to be thought of as one of the best speakers in the House. His duel with Scobie Mackenzie, the Member for Mt. Ida, which had begun in 1887, began to attract notice. Mackenzie was twelve years older than Reeves and a run-holder, but otherwise they had much in common, notably a love of literature and history and a detestation of mathematics. Mackenzie was a Scot who, as a shepherd in Australia, knew Adam Lindsay Gordon and Marcus Clarke, and himself wrote for the Melbourne *Argus* and the *Australasian*. The two men began to sit in wait during debates —each hoping the other would be led to speak first. In debate, Reeves had the better, but Mackenzie was excellent in a prepared speech.

In 1888 Mackenzie twitted Reeves for being 'the leader of a happy band of Protectionists'. Reeves happily admitted it. In his first speech on the Customs Duties Bill he praised Mackenzie and the free traders for their hopeless minority stand (even Mackenzie, the staunchest of free traders, now admitted that the country—actually the town—was 'crying out for protection'). He turned to Scobie: 'I would say, in the classic tongue so charming to the ears of the Minister of Education, *victrix causa Diis placuit, sed victa Scobaeo*. [The cause which won the day pleased the gods, but the cause which lost pleased Scobie.]'

Though there were few classical scholars left in the House, there were enough to appreciate his revision of Lucan's remark on Cato.

Much of this speech consisted of debating points scored off the free traders, but he concluded by praising Atkinson. His peroration, which was to be much quoted against him, announced dramatically that he was prepared to serve 'under King Harry'.

His next speech was thoroughly prepared. He had spent two weeks studying the tariff, and much time reading the economists, classical and modern. Most recently he had read Henry George, who, though a free trader, admitted (he said) that free trade tended to make the rich richer and the poor poorer. Reeves wanted New Zealand to develop a diversified economy, and not rely too exclusively on its agricultural and pastoral industry, lest it become, like Virginia, a place reduced to desolation, as he supposed, through relying on its 'natural industry'. He professed to believe, with Adam Smith, 'that a high standard of comfort is a much more important thing in a country than the aggregation of wealth in the hands of a few people'. He quoted Goldsmith on statesmen who survey

> The rich man's joys increase, the poor's decay,
> 'Tis yours to say how wide the limits stand
> Between a splendid and a happy land.

Reeves's choice was the one most New Zealanders have made.

Dr. Newman, one of the free traders, praised his 'charming and interesting speech': Reeves was 'certainly about the most quick-witted and keen-minded man in the House'—but hadn't he now been swallowed by the tiger himself?[1]

Reeves's praise of Atkinson led to rumours that he was intriguing for office, which Atkinson publicly denied.[2] Reeves was quite frank about his views. Atkinson was not as hard-hearted as he was painted—for instance, in announcing a fresh overseas loan of a million pounds, he explained that to stop borrowing altogether would imperil the labour market. But though the Premier's views were close to his own, Reeves would

---

[1] On these debates, see PD, 1888, 60, pp. 108-9, 121, 509-12, 538; vol. 61, pp. 409, 521 ff.

[2] PD, 1888, 61, p. 580.

not offer a 'slavish' support. Nor would he join him without the
rest of the 'Liberals'. The tariff was 'one of those great and
epoch-making measures which justify the breaking of old ties and
the dissolving, temporarily or for long, of ancient alliances'. The
Stout–Vogel alliance was not exactly ancient, but Reeves sometimes spoke as though Grey's 'Liberal Party' had existed
independently of a few Liberal Associations and Grey's rhetoric,
and had survived the seventies to enter a coalition with Vogel.

In late August Reeves went home and, on the 29th, wrote
again to William Montgomery:

Though the session still drags its slow length along like the wounded
snake I have deserted the arena. Three months and three weeks are I
think enough to give ones country and moreover I had begun to feel
the strain. Health you know has to be the first consideration with me.
I have to thank you most sincerely for your kind letters and parcels.
The papers I was always glad to get and the photographs were
delightful. The Paris ones were really fine specimens of work but I
liked the Algerian even better. Anything to give one an idea of what
the outside world really looks like always has a charm and you may
say what you like photographs are quite as useful for that as pictures.

Montgomery's son—who presently became a Member of the
House of Representatives (M.H.R.) himself—was studying art
in France.

Pray congratulate William for me on his brilliant success. There is
some one however to be still more congratulated and that is yourself.
Full well do I know that there is no earthly success you could gain
would please you half so well as his performances. Such is a father's
love which boys and young men hardly realise until in later life they
look back after they have become fathers themselves perhaps. I can
guess what it is like from the fashion in which that little morsel
[Amber] who calls me 'Dada' has wound herself round my heart
already. She is a precociously clever little monkey and I am happy to
say pretty also. I never could have endured an ugly daughter. I must
say I think that William is quite right to devote himself to art while
he can. A few months given up to it in Europe will be a possession and a
memory for the rest of his life. His return and settlement here will to a
great extent be an exile from all that he is enjoying now. Therefore he
is wise to make hay while the sun shines. When I was in England the
notion of coming back to Europe seemed easy enough, but thirteen
years have passed and I am very far off any hope of it. There are

thousands of things Europe can show and teach a young man which I would give anything in reason to have seen. Now it is getting too late. I must be judged on what I know and have seen not on what I think I could have learned if I had had the chance. I am beginning the time in life when a man succeeds or fails by justice of what he is not what he promises to be. If William uses his chances well he will thank his lucky stars many and many a time in days to come. I am glad indeed to hear improved accounts of your health and a hint that you mean to look in upon us in a few months. You wont find much change. People are beginning to talk more cheerfully though business is still deplorable. I fancy there is hope of better things.

The session has been a queer one. The Govt has been weak and despised to a degree. But the Opposition is too utterly disorganized to do anything whatever. Atkinson has been repeatedly beaten and has practically done nothing outside the Budget and the Native Bills— the latter much amended. Personally I have I think got along fairly well considering that I have *faut de mieux* had to play a somewhat more prominent part than young members usually play. We killed the New Plymouth Harbour swindle triumphantly [a government bill to rescue the New Plymouth Harbour Board, which threatened to default on its interest payments on an overseas loan]. The Council has been simply murderous and has led Stevens and Whitaker [Ministers sitting in the Legislative Council] pretty lives. On the whole I dont think much harm has been done to the Country but disorganization has meant waste of time and is destroying self respect and any feeling of trust and loyalty between members. Every man suspects his neighbour. No man knows whether his friend today will not be his enemy tomorrow. My father has been really unwell all the winter but is at last recovering. My mother and wife are in the best of health. Trusting to see you again before the year is out.

In May 1889, reporting to his constituents at a meeting in Knightstown, Reeves was able to claim that he had fulfilled his election promises. We 'disorganised our own party and deliberately gave up all thought of getting into power', he said, to support the tariff, because it was in the country's interests. But there had been no hope of power. As he admitted to his audience, his 'party' was leaderless (Vogel had now gone to England—and had led badly while he was in New Zealand[1]) and 'more or less broken up'. A Canterbury squatter, J. D. Lance, had acted as 'chairman' of the Opposition. 'We, the Opposition, were unable to get a leader. Equality soon became anarchy.'

[1] Stout MSS, Ballance to Stout, 3 Jan. 1888.

He promised that if any 'respectable Liberal' became leader, he would follow him.[1]

The disappearance of their old leaders was opening the way for new 'Liberals'. Grey could no longer be thought of as possible; Stout and Vogel and Montgomery were, at least for the time being, gone. The door was open for Ballance, for Seddon and McKenzie, and for Reeves. In 1888 he had grown considerably in political stature: in the House, as in Christchurch, he was a man to be reckoned with.

Just before the 1889 session the Opposition elected John Ballance as their leader.[2] He accepted reluctantly, and only because he could not induce Stout, the man he looked on as their rightful leader, to return to Parliament.[3] Ballance was a quiet, modest man. No one, perhaps, expected much of him. But now there was an organized parliamentary Opposition. Within its motley ranks, the makings of an effective party could be perceived. The appearance of the free trade phalanx had forced a temporary unity on the protectionists and radicals. Almost every Member who was to stand as a Liberal in the 1890 election, voted for the tariff. (The exceptions were the Maori Member, James Carroll, and the eighteen-stone Scot from Otago, John McKenzie, who were free traders, though not dogmatic ones.) Moreover the Opposition claimed that the purely protectionist (as opposed to revenue) items in the tariff had been added to Atkinson's budget by themselves, in committee.[4]

During the session of 1889 Reeves did support Ballance. There was no more talk of following King Harry. Reeves now became his persistent if respectful persecutor. His rôle, one member said, was that of the *chulos* in Spanish bullfights: 'He goes at the bull, torments and worries him with his banderillos until he is deadbeat and subdued.' The Premier was rattled by his frequent defeat in divisions, and eventually protested about Reeves's interjections. Reeves said that the Premier himself incessantly interrupted speakers and he had fancied that he enjoyed heckling—it showed Members were attending—but promised not to do it again.[5]

[1] LT, 31 May 1889.   [2] CT, 4 July 1889.
[3] D. A. Hamer, 'The Law and the Prophet', pp. 345-6.
[4] PD, 1895, 88, p. 528.   [5] PD, 1889, 65, pp. 273, 318.

Reeves was pleased to have the Premier 'box his ears'. In his reminiscences he wrote:

We usually knew what he thought of an opponent. If an attack was negligible he would read a newspaper. If he began to be roused he would pull his tawny beard and twist the end of it a little. When becoming angry he began biting one side of his moustache. During my earlier speeches he sometimes became absorbed in the newspaper. It was my ambition to make him drop it. I found there was one sure method, to make him laugh. I have seen his sides shaking behind the newspaper. He would then throw it away and look at me under his long eyebrows with a sort of amused irritation.

One day he treated me to a lecture to this effect. 'We have amongst us a young gentleman who comes here making light little speeches quite amusing. But what are they about? Nothing at all. Day after day he goes on attacking the Government, finding fault with their policy, talking about nothing in particular.'

'Do you mean about the Government' I queried.

'Of course I mean about the Government' he rapped out unguardedly.

'Then it *is* nothing in particular; that's what the country says' I replied. The laugh was against him, but he was perfectly good humoured, and meeting me in the Lobby afterwards said, 'Well, young man, you had me finely this afternoon', but added 'Why don't you try to be of some use? The country is in a mess you know.'

It was about that time that Sir George Grey spoke to me in the Lobby one day. Half closing his left eye and smiling he said slowly, almost in falsetto. 'Atkinson doesn't know what to do with you; you're too playful for him. He is like a cross old bear whose ribs are being poked with a stick through the bars of his cage.'

Grey hated Atkinson and the remark was unfair. New Zealand was, at that time, in real distress and Sir Harry had to carry the Government on his back. He had no time for light sword play with young and irresponsible members of the Opposition.

The Premier sometimes seemed to enjoy the tussles with his tormentor, and gave as much as he took. When Reeves asked the Government not to send unemployed men to work at Bealey, where the thermometer was 'perpetually below zero' in winter, Atkinson ironically called him the leader of the town party, 'the true representative of Liberalism'—'the honourable gentleman who cannot stand the temperature at 32'. The old pioneer lectured Reeves: 'It is the man who will take off his coat and turn up his sleeves and face the wilderness, and spend his life there clearing the face of the country—those are the true progressive men.'

In common with perhaps a majority of his countrymen, Atkinson thought the 'backbone of this colony is in the country'[1] (he did not ask where was its head). To praise rural virtues was a sure way of winning the majority of Members to his side, but it was not far removed from the obscurantism that was beginning to plague educated New Zealanders—that was expressed by one Member who defied the House to name one scholarship winner who had 'come to the front in business matters or anything else'.[2]

Much of the House's time in 1889 was taken up by debates on the electoral system. Atkinson first introduced a bill to set up large multi-member constituencies on the Hare plan, knowing that it would not pass, but hoping to arouse public interest. Reeves attacked this in a long, well-prepared speech, as a 'fad', a 'blind experiment—a leap in the dark ... not ... adopted in any civilised Anglo-Saxon-speaking country'. Every eccentric and faddist would gather his brother-faddists about him and they would subordinate every other issue to their fads. Parliament should be the net result of 'the threshing-out and elimination that goes on at elections'; they did not want to have every shade of opinion represented any more than a politician was expected in a speech to express all the stages of doubt he had passed through before reaching his conclusions.

Atkinson often made Reeves appear more conservative than himself. Reeves called land nationalization (which Atkinson had —Reeves alleged—once professed to believe in) a fad; and ridiculed Atkinson's proposal of 1883 for a scheme of national insurance (accident and other pensions) as a 'political nostrum', an example of quackery. The Premier replied that that was another measure which Reeves did not understand, but which they would see adopted.[3] In a phrase that oddly foreshadowed one which later made Reeves notorious, Atkinson said that the young man thought that 'if you are not a Liberal you are a pest to the community'.[4] In some ways the Premier was, indeed, the more 'liberal' of the two. For example, Reeves was so opposed to further borrowing, by 1889, that he was prepared to see public

[1] PD, 1889, 64, p. 577.   [2] PD, 1888, 60, p. 591.
[3] PD, 1889, 64, pp. 256 ff., 579; 65, p. 24.   [4] PD, 1889, 64, p. 578.

works stopped for a year or two, which would have increased unemployment. His 'party', he said, agreed.[1]

Reeves learned a great deal from Atkinson—the value of legislative 'experiment'; the value of introducing bills which would probably not pass, in order (the Premier told him) to educate public opinion. And he formed a higher opinion of Atkinson than he would admit, in debate, in 1889.

The second Representation Bill of the session led to a battle between town and country. The country members (53 in a House of 90) wanted (ignoring technical details) a 'country quota' of $33\frac{1}{3}$ per cent.—in other words, they wanted a fictitious $33\frac{1}{3}$ per cent. to be added to the rural population when seats were allocated. The Government and the townsmen agreed to stiffen the colony's backbone by only 25 per cent. Eventually 28 per cent. was agreed on after much rural stone-walling. During these debates Sir George Grey successfully moved an amendment abolishing plural voting. Property owners could enrol in each electorate where they owned enough property, but could vote only in one. Thus the constitution was made at once more and less democratic: the countrymen and the propertyless became relatively more powerful, the property owners less. These changes were to have an important influence on Reeves and his party.

Reeves was becoming not merely an entertaining but an effective speaker, who made points well and convincingly. He found that the House 'liked a good speech' and that 'it paid to take trouble and try to tell them something worth listening to'. He had 'sufficient sense' (he later wrote) to be brief and bright— and rarely spoke for more than ten or fifteen minutes. Most of the speeches were lengthy, laborious and unprepared. Like other highly-strung people, he found listening to such boring talk a quite painful trial, and he became one of the most ardent advocates for reforming standing orders so as to prevent eight-hour speeches such as he heard during the debate on the country quota. That he was 'bright' is difficult to illustrate from the printed word. As he himself once ruefully remarked to the House, all the speeches appeared in published *Parliamentary Debates* (popularly called 'Hansard' in New Zealand, as in England) in 'reporterese'—they all sounded the same in print. But perhaps

[1] PD, 1889, 65, p. 323.

it is possible to appreciate something of his wit and quickness of mind. On the spur of the moment he called one government bill 'a sort of mermaid—composed of two parts having no natural affinity, one being tacked to the other in an arbitrary and artificial manner'. Once, when Vincent Pike was raving about the fertile soil of central Otago, while advocating a railway bill, Reeves rose immediately and quoted from Pike's novel, *Wild Bill Enderby*, on the same region—'A strange wild scene. Bleak and desolate enough, God wot... .' He was capable of unusual and very appropriate flights of impromptu rhetoric. His *bête noir* was Tom Fergus, one of Atkinson's less 'liberal' ministers who had an enormous voice backed by an appropriate physique. Reeves called him 'Boanerges'—a nickname that caught on and was later transferred to Seddon. Once, in 1889, when Fergus was defending Atkinson, Reeves begged him 'in the name of the Te Kooti fiasco ... in the name of that ridiculous caravan tour through Central Otago, when the Premier was carted about like some wild beast in a cage to be shown to the people of Wakatipu,—in the name of those brass bands of Wakatipu itself ...' to be a little modest and not teach his political grandmother to suck eggs. But he had forgotten an observation in one of his favourite books, Charles J. Darling's *Scintillae Juris*, that it 'is most difficult for a wit to be aggreeable'—he is bound to offend his butts. The penalty he paid for making the House laugh was to be called 'spiteful' as well as witty and to be censured for saying 'disagreeable' things.

A circumstance that encouraged brief, 'bright' speeches was that he was listened to, was an effective guerrilla in debate, when he had little, for the moment, to say. The great issues for which he had stood in 1887—protection, the Midland line, the maintenance of the education system, moderate retrenchment— seemed won. He had not yet quite found new causes.

In July 1889 Reeves complained that his health was lately impaired by 'the oppressive and heated atmosphere' of the House. About the time Parliament was prorogued in late September, he caught typhoid, which left him quite 'done up'. But, back in Christchurch he found himself in the midst of a press battle almost as exhausting as the stone-walling over the country quota.

The Lyttelton Times Company was by now in serious difficulties. Circulation and advertising began to fall as the *Press* progressively reduced its rates. Its overdraft was nearly £3,000; several thousands were owed to a Wellington man; and Will had lent the Company £700 himself. In 1888 both companies reduced wages by 10 per cent. The compositors promptly asked permission to form a union, giving as their reason that men going to Australia (as thousands did at this time) could not get work unless they were 'Society men'. William Reeves met the leading printer and publisher, Tombs, and a representative of the Press Company, who accepted his view—not to oppose the formation of a union, but to refuse to allow their offices to be worked under union rules. A Typographical Association was formed and, in 1889, a Master Printers Association, which managed to reduce competition in printing rates. But the Times Company could not improve its position. In late 1888 William Reeves had been forced to mortgage his shares, and took over 400 then owned by his son.

The struggle between the two newspaper companies was so embittered by falling profits and widening political differences that they missed no opportunity to attack each other in their editorial columns. Early in the year William Reeves had agreed to chair a public meeting to express sympathy for Charles Parnell, who was accused of organizing the current violence in Ireland. He was unable to go, but Will spoke at the meeting. He defended Gladstone's policy of Home Rule for Ireland, which he saw as a step towards imperial federation. It won him support from Catholics at a time when their demand for state assistance for their schools, which he opposed, was giving him trouble in his electorate. But it also led to an attempt to label the *Lyttelton Times* a Roman Catholic paper—both Alfred Saunders, a local politician who had been a Greyite, and the *Press* itself, made this insinuation,[1] which gained some credence because the editor of the *Times* since 1875 ,R. A. Loughnan, was a well-known Catholic.

In mid 1889 Loughnan resigned, to edit the *Catholic Times* in Wellington. In November Will was appointed editor to replace him, which made him a lifelong enemy of Alfred Saunders, whose son, Samuel, worked for the *Times* and hoped for the position.

---

[1] Reeves MSS, small clipping book, pp. 74–5, 83.

There is no doubt, however, that William Reeves had for years been training his son for the job. At about the same time Maud became the 'lady editor'.

Will was feeling very tired. In December he showed his contempt for Protestant prejudice by speaking at a meeting addressed by John Dillon, a travelling Irish delegate advocating Home Rule, and won more Irish hearts. A Catholic paper said he made 'a really happy speech'. 'Rapturous applause, and roars of laughter, continued uninterruptedly throughout his very humorous and telling remarks.'[1] On the 19th he and his wife sailed for a holiday in Australia.

'Steamed out of Pt. Nicholson into howling nor'wester', he wrote in a scrappy journal of his trip; and, the next day: 'Heavy swell from southwest determined never again to quit N.Z. if we should be so fortunate as to get back there.'

In Sydney he noted a 'universal commonness'. But they enjoyed their stay immensely. He played cricket ('Rubbishy bowling. Made 21 in 10 minutes'). Visited vineyards. Met 'little draper Macmillan: treasurer of N.S.W.' 'Interview with Sir H. P. [Henry Parkes, the Premier] Socratic face, long white hair, ditto beard hoarse falsetto voice powerful build: tall, a strong man. Drops his h's. "Stoodious" ... Claimed friendship with Tennyson ... Has never been in N.Z. and never will.'

They then set off for the Blue Mountains, or (he wrote in an article) 'to be strictly accurate, the "Maownt'ns", for the unlovely corn-stalk twang is a thing that hits you in the face wherever you go in Sydney'.[2] In his journal, in the newspaper article and in a poem, 'An Australian Noon', he wrote many impressive words—'the loneliness, the inaccessibility, the vastness and the depth, the immensity of the expanse all these impressions hurry and jostle one another.'

In Melbourne they met more politicians before going home in mid January.

Though Reeves wrote most of the political comment in the *Lyttelton Times* and *Canterbury Times* in the late eighties, his journalism was, of course, usually anonymous. But he did

---

[1] Reeves MSS, small clipping book, pp. 92-3, 118.
[2] Ibid., pp. 85-9. The 'journal' is also in the Reeves MSS.

generally sign his verse and his more serious writings. When Freeman Kitchen founded a monthly literary magazine, *Zealandia*, in Dunedin in 1889, to encourage a national literature and provide light reading for sixpence, Reeves wrote a short story for the first number. 'A Helpless Spectator' was an attempt to disguise as fiction a polemic against the big estates. Another story, 'The Tomb in the Cliff', appeared in the *Canterbury Times* in December 1888; though it turned from Canterbury to Greece for its scenes, it was equally clumsy. He gave up the attempt to write fiction.

Early in 1889 the Lyttelton Times Company published a small book of verse, *Colonial Couplets: Being Poems in Partnership*, by George Phipps Williams and W. P. Reeves. It contained eighteen poems by Reeves and twelve by Williams, a mixture of parody, low comedy, good-natured satire and local sentiment, with a few attempts at more serious verse by Reeves. It was hailed with enthusiasm by reviewers in the newspapers as 'a miscellany of colonial experiences in fugitive rhyme', a worthy successor to *Canterbury Rhymes*. Though mainly gay, 'occasionally there is a poem brimming over with pathos, tender, touching and true; gracefulness of fancy is not wanting... .' Reviewers detected in Reeves's verse the influence of Macaulay and 'the modern school of poetry'—especially Swinburne, and Heine. The only adverse criticism, in the *Dunedin Evening Star*, was that the verses 'fail in originality'. One reviewer, who thought any fool or rogue good enough for politics, had long grieved to see Reeves 'making dismal speeches when he might be making sparkling rhymes'. The colonial bard, Tom Bracken, wrote to Reeves praising one 'charming little poem'—'Not in God's Acre'—in particular.[1] Like almost every book of New Zealand verse or fiction, *Colonial Couplets* was widely held to be a step towards a truly national literature.

What impressed the Colony most was that the poems sold. Five hundred copies were bought at a shilling each in a few weeks, and a larger second edition went almost as quickly. When a Sydney publisher said in 1891 that no book of verse had brought £5 to an Australian writer, the *Lyttelton Times* observed

---

[1] Bracken's letter (22 Feb. 1889) and reviews are in the Reeves MSS. Reviews and material about Williams are among papers in the possession of Mr. G. T. P. Williams of Rotorua, who kindly permitted me to read them.

complacently that Reeves received £15 royalties for *Colonial Couplets*.[1]

G. P. Williams was ten years older than his partner. He had had links with the Reeves family since he came to New Zealand in 1869—his brother, Joshua Strange Williams, was a judge who had held a mortgage on 'Risingholme'. He was a railway engineer, who worked for a time on the Midland railway, a sociable fellow, who was a handicapper for the Jockey Club. Though he was known familiarly as 'Strange Peter', there was no nonsense about him, as man or writer. He had been to school at Harrow and graduated from Cambridge. His views on verse may be gathered from a talk he gave to the Christchurch Savage Club, which he helped to found. He had no good to say of 'the new school of poets' with their 'erotic allusions' and obscurity. At Harrow he had to write Latin verses every day, beginning with 'nonsense verses' and progressing into sense 'by the aid of a beautiful little machine called the "Gradus ad Parnassum" or "Gradus" for short; which was simply a Latin dictionary containing every conceivable epithet which could possibly apply to every noun in the Latin language'. He concluded that it seemed to him 'that if you have been trained to write nonsense verses as a boy, it cannot be very difficult to write nonsense as a man. I know that's how I find it myself.'

His verse was manly stuff—'An Old Chum on the New Zealand Scenery', 'A New Chum's Letter Home'—inspired by a dry sense of humour and expressed in rattling rhyme and metre. The 'Old Chum' confesses that

... the terms I use are such as poets would not love to hear.
What they call a brook or brooklet, or a streamlet, or a rill,
I do only, I confess it, call a *creek*, and always will.
Then there's what we call a *gully*, which of course we take to mean
Just a small and narrow valley, in which bush is sometimes seen...
Bush, too, means the native forest; you will never, I'm afraid,
Hear a self-respecting bushman call a bush a leafy glade... .

Most of the junior partner's verses also had a local flavour. He continued to follow in the footsteps of Crosbie Ward, writing political 'squibs' and occasional verse. He agreed with Williams

[1] CT, 6 June 1889; LT, 27 Jan. 1891.

that there was no need 'to adulterate his verse with coarseness and obscenity'.[1] Besides parodies and political satire, he included verse inspired by local sentiment—'A Ball in the Old Provincial Council Chamber' and 'A Deserted School Bathing Place'—and two poems that showed his ambitions soared higher than those of Williams. 'A Dream' and 'A Sicilian Evening' were in the Victorian romantic tradition as much appreciated in the Colony as 'at Home'.

> Under the seaward-fronting castle walls
> In a green garden's ancient shade, apart
> She sat, the love whose footstep's faintest falls
>   Aye thrilled my heart.
>
> The breeze blew lightly from the western sky,
> The red-barred sky where late the sun was gold,
> And, slowly sinking on the shore to die,
>   The sea-wave rolled.
>
> Turning from these, she rose at my approach,
> And stood to meet me very calm and pale... .

Perhaps it was a dream ... but very many years later he was still 'haunted' by the vision of this dead girl. He thought, then, of her eyes as he kissed her and tried to revise his verses:

> I wake to hear the bitter wind, and know
> That round her island grave the seas are cold,
> While in a land of toil, his lamp burnt low,
>   The man sits, old.

In 1887 and 1888 it had been possible for Reeves's political opponents in Canterbury to regard his appeals to the poorer voters as demagoguism or transparent hypocrisy. A fairly large number of people must have known something of the financial position of the two papers. The spectacle of a representative of one group of capitalists (unsuccessful or indebted capitalists, indeed) setting himself up as a working-class leader against another set of capitalists was not a pretty one and it accounted

---

[1] LT leader on Tennyson, 22 Feb. 1887. This is in Reeves's small clipping book, in which many of the LT articles were written by himself. This one 'sounds like' Reeves.

for much of the very strong antagonism which young Reeves encountered. Early in 1890, however, it must have begun to dawn on his enemies in Christchurch that this view of him was too simple, but the new picture which emerged in that year and the next made him even more unpopular than before.

In April 1890 a series of articles, signed 'Pharos', appeared in the *Lyttelton Times* on the subject of socialism and communism. They were republished in the *Canterbury Times*, which also serialized a new utopian socialist novel, *Looking Backwards, 2,000–1887* by Edward Bellamy, the most widely read socialist book in the United States, Australia and New Zealand. In mid 1890 *Some Historical Articles on Communism and Socialism; their Dreams, their Experiments, their Aims, their Influence*, by 'Pharos', was published as a sixpenny booklet. 'Pharos', as became quite widely known, was Will Reeves. He explained, in a letter to J. M. Twomey, the radical Catholic editor of the *Geraldine Guardian*, the reason for anonymity:

I did not put my name to the book as my directors were rather afraid of having their editor's name openly associated with Communism and Socialism, knowing what capital the 'Press' gang would try to make of the fact. Moreover, my only object being to get people in this part of the world to study Socialism, I thought perhaps anonymity might help the book. There are many educated people who would not read anything with my name attached to it and many more who do not think a young New Zealander capable of writing about great social problems. Nevertheless several of the men up here [in Wellington] have already read 'Pharos' and speak of it in the most flattering terms. Once again I thank you for your notice [a review]. In this as in all other things you have shown yourself my good and true friend. I assure you I am not an ungrateful man. If you could send me copies of your letters on the land question I should like to have them and show them to Ballance... .[1]

'Pharos's' book, which was the first publication in New Zealand on socialism and communism, attracted a good deal of attention in the Press. The most important review was written by Sir Robert Stout for both the *Canterbury* and *Lyttelton Times* at the request of William Reeves (who informed him of the author's name).[2] It tells us as much about Stout as about 'Pharos'. He

---

[1] n.d. [c. July 1890]. In possession of Miss Kathleen Twomey, Timaru.
[2] Stout MSS, W. Reeves to Stout, 16 June 1890.

had been an advocate of extreme *laissez-faire*, but by this time his belief in individualism was weakening. He had become a supporter of trade unions and had legalized their existence by his Act of 1878. In 1889, like many others, he had learned from the Reverend Rutherford Waddell's sermons of the growth of 'sweated' labour conditions in the Dunedin clothing industry. By 1890 he had come to see the need for state intervention in economic life to protect the poor and the weak. In his review he said that the wave of individualism, which he traced from the Reformation, had begun to recede: the state would increasingly be called on to control land and capital, public health and education. But the aim, as he saw it, was ultimately to make possible a fuller life for each individual.[1]

'Pharos' was led, he explained, to write his *Historical Articles* because of the immense influence of socialist thought on legislation and the interest of 'all thinking persons' in the subject. At the same time he hoped to combat contemporary ignorance—such as the view that all socialists wished to give everyone the same income. He surveyed utopias from Plato to Edward Bellamy, communistic communities from ancient times to the experimental settlements in the United States. He discussed the ideas of Robert Owen, Lassalle, the English Fabians, the Social Democratic Federation and many other socialists or quasi-socialists. The articles revealed his very wide reading in the British, United States and German literature on the subject (he knew little of the French socialists), but they were not, in fact, merely 'historical'. No one reading them could doubt that the author was deeply involved; and his own preferences were made plain.

Reeves was mainly influenced by the views of the German 'state socialist', Lassalle, and the English Fabian Society—particularly by the *Fabian Essays in Socialism*. It seems likely that the *Fabian Essays* stimulated him to write his articles but, since they were published in England only in December 1889, it is evident that most of his reading on socialism was earlier. He had known something of socialist thought since his boyhood visit to Paris. Now the Fabians became his heroes. He sent a copy of his articles to their leader, Sidney Webb; and a few years later demonstrated his respect in a more complimentary manner.

[1] LT, 25 June 1890; CT, 3 July 1890.

There were many reasons for his attraction to the Fabians. He already shared some of their ideas; like them, for instance, he had been influenced by the views of the American Henry George. Though neither he nor they were 'single taxers', they believed in mulcting the 'unearned increment' and, ultimately, in land nationalization. But, fundamentally, given the fact that he was already moving rapidly to the left, he was attracted because, like him, they belonged to the intellectual middle class. The Webbs, G. B. Shaw, Graham Wallas and the other Fabians accepted parliamentary procedures: the ballot, not the barricade, provided the best weapon for socialists. As a parliamentarian, moreover, he was ready to follow them in seeing socialism as a process, not something to be achieved in one great stroke. Above all, they saw socialism in terms of state activity, a doctrine to which a New Zealander was peculiarly receptive, since in his colony the government had, from the first, adopted a much more active rôle (especially in 'development') than in England.

Though 'Pharos' defined socialism as the nationalization of land and capital—of the sources of production—he sees every governmental control of industry, every state enterprise competing with private capital, every state power to protect the poor, sick or aged, every interference with the rights of free enterprise, as 'a piece of socialism'. He gives a lengthy list of the state activity in New Zealand: already the state was the largest landowner, the chief rent collector, and ran the largest industry, the railways. All such activities, down to municipal lighting and roads—'All these acts are Socialistic . . . . All show that we live in an age of unconscious Socialism.' Fabians often made this identification. Like Reeves, most of them ignored Hubert Bland's impatience (in one of the *Fabian Essays*) with the notion that a hawker's licence was an example of state socialism, and his warning that 'although Socialism involves State control, State control does not imply Socialism'; that control must be exercised for the benefit of the masses.

Reeves was especially struck with the essay on 'Industry under Socialism' by Annie Besant, which developed the idea that state workshops and 'county farms' would help, through the greater efficiency of the co-operative principle, to drive private enterprise off the market. Lassalle also, he observed, had wanted the state to organize small-scale industries and farms.

Above all, 'Pharos' sought to be reassuring. Even Atkinson's scheme of national insurance and Rolleston's perpetual state leasehold were socialistic—what could be more respectable? Socialism wrapped the colonists in their infancy, an invisible shawl. He emphasized the doctrine, which had attracted him to the Fabians, that socialism could be achieved—was in fact being achieved—imperceptibly. Socialists were not generally plotters and revolutionaries, he assured his readers. In England their work was chiefly educative. The 'bombs of "social dynamite"' were penny pamphlets and Fabian tracts.

Though he appeared to accept the labour theory of value and the Marxian dogma that capitalists would decrease in numbers and leave the increasing proletariat only the bare means of subsistence, and though he acknowledged the rôle of revolution in Marxism, 'Pharos' gave an inadequate account of Marx's thought. Once production were 'concentrated in the hands of the State', he wrote, 'The State will be the People. The People will be Labour', but he ignored the Marxian dogma that the state was a class instrument which would, by definition, 'wither away' in a classless society. 'Communism' he identified with primitive (or modern and idealistic) communities withdrawn from the world, 'green isles in a deep sea of social misery'—cells, it might be, of virtuous poverty in a corrupt, capitalistic world. Marxism had not, of course, then achieved its modern pre-eminence among socialist systems, nor were Marxists the most numerous socialists, so 'Pharos's' neglect of them is not surprising.

There could be no doubt that, behind his often flippant mask, there had been forming surprising features. The Member for St. Albans, the editor of the *Lyttelton Times*, was a socialist! His father's somewhat ambiguous 'liberalism' had undoubtedly inclined him to the radical side. No doubt his observation of rural and urban working-class poverty helped to arouse a generous instinct for reform, while ambition encouraged him to follow that instinct into action. These influences, and that of his reading and thought, had led him to accept a theory which harmonized with and justified his increasing antagonism to the Canterbury traditions deriving from Wakefield and the British class structure, a repudiation evident in his speeches during the election of 1887. Consequently his new-found socialism was no

8

merely intellectual conviction. It was backed by an intense emotional drive, powered by a sense of alienation from—and rejection by—his own class, which was symbolized, to him, by 'Money' and, above all, by the 'sheep kings'.

While he was visiting Australia, one of the Amuri squatters, A. W. Rutherford, had written to the *Australasian* attacking the Sheep Department. A leading article in the *Lyttelton Times*, when he returned, denounced Rutherford—a relative of boys who had been at school with him. It was almost certainly written by Reeves. Every phrase seems his. Rutherford, it said, thought that 'no one can understand anything about the management of sheep who does not "live in the grease". Dirt, ignorance, meanness and boorishness are no doubt the qualifications he considers absolutely requisite for the proper, perfect management of a sheep property'—but nowadays, the article continued, 'men of education and refinement ... know quite as much about sheep as the coarse-mannered foul-tongued roughs who used to "live in the grease", while they represented the squattocracy of former days'.[1]

No wonder his directors preferred 'Pharos' to W.P.R.! But Reeves's conversion might not have been of any but personal and local significance, had it not occurred when it did, when many thousands of his countrymen agreed with him that society was 'a clumsy, cruel, unrighteous system', were filled with the 'divine discontent' that, 'Pharos' said, lay behind reform; and at the beginning of the greatest strikes the Colony had experienced.

[1] LT, 13 Jan. 1890.

7

INTO POWER

1890

In late February 1890 the Typographical Association pressed on
the Lyttelton Times Company a number of requests, including
one for a rise in printing rates. William Reeves told the printers
that business would not justify the increase; that the Press
Company had agreed only in the hope of ruining the Times
Company by raising costs; but he accepted their other wishes,
for a rise in jobbing rates and for a maximum of one apprentice
for every six compositors. The local printing and publishing firm
of Whitcombe and Tombs, however, flatly refused to accept the
union's conditions—to allow, in effect, their works to be run
under union rules.

This incident led to a lengthy struggle which became involved
with a complicated series of other industrial disputes throughout
the year. They were skirmishes in a class war, though one
relatively restrained, which rent New Zealand society and was a
decisive event in its development; in the life, too, of William
Pember Reeves.

In 1889 a Maritime Council, representing the seamen, wharf
labourers, and some labourers' and miners' unions, had been
formed in Dunedin. It was affiliated with the Australian
Maritime Council and led by a group of able men, including its
secretary, J. A. Millar, who was later to become a cabinet
minister. It was the most formidable labour organization yet
formed in New Zealand and it aimed at becoming a federation
of labour for the whole country. In 1890 it began to intervene in
industrial disputes in several Provinces, taking them out of the
hands of the local Trades and Labour Councils, which had been
relatively ineffectual and had acted as political rather than
industrial organizations.[1] In May 1890 it succeeded in settling a
railway strike in Petone by arranging an arbitration conference.

[1] J. D. Salmond, *New Zealand Labour's Pioneering Days*, (ed. D. Crowley), Auckland,
1950, pp. 78 ff.; 95 ff.; 127 ff.

It then took a hand in a mining dispute, threatening the owners that seamen, wharf-labourers and railway men would refuse to handle theirs goods. The employers gave in.

The Lyttelton Times Company's newspapers greeted these events with satisfaction. On the settlement of the railway dispute, the *Lyttelton Times* observed that the men beat the Railway Commissioners 'because they were able to apply the screw ... in the shape of threat of a general strike'.[1] 'Throughout the Colony labour is surging', the *Canterbury Times* proclaimed, and listed unrest among bakers, tailoresses, railwaymen, wharf labourers and wool storemen. 'The agitation is organised, and everywhere it sees clearly what it wants, and goes straight for it. The result is that capital is getting alarmed. The outspoken tone, the rigorous demands, the close, determined reasoning, all are new to the capitalist, who feels inclined to ask whether the end of the world is coming.' The voice of W. P. Reeves was evident in the tone of satisfaction and in the appeal against extremism on either side. The recent experience of the Lyttelton Times Company was evident in the complaint about over-competition and the warning to labour not to ask too much lest it 'find itself awakened by the sheer failure of the wages fund'.[2]

As tension grew, the Times Company's newspapers regaled their readers not only with 'Pharos's' articles and Bellamy's utopian socialism, but with articles on the London dock strike (the Prince of Wales's alleged words were reported: 'We are all Socialists, more or less'); profit-sharing; the need for economic 'justice'; and the May Day meetings in Paris ('Europe has felt the force of the demonstration; the spirit of understanding is moving; a new era, we may hope, is dawning').[3] These newspapers appeared optimistic that labour would win: in May 1889 the *Canterbury Times* had gone so far as to look forward to a world-wide strike which would 'be followed by a revolution of the most beneficial kind'.[4] Frightened conservatives heard the tramp of workers' boots, smelt the smoke and saw the flames of socialist revolt in the columns of the *Times*.

Reeves not only wrote about the struggle (undoubtedly many

---

[1] 26 June 1890.   [2] CT, 5 June 1890.
[3] LT, 15 Jan.; 6, 7, 14, 16 May 1890.
[4] 30 May 1889—discussing a strike in Westphalia. Cf. 16 May 1889, on Bismarck's 'state socialism'.

of these articles were his) but encouraged the unionists in other ways. In March he attended a meeting of the Miners' Amalgamated Associations in Christchurch, where, while speaking in favour of the unions, he said that 'strikes were a form of war which, though sometimes necessary, should be avoided if possible'. He looked forward to a federation of all New Zealand unions as the best preventative of 'frivolous and unreasonable strikes' yet devised.[1]

The anticipated pitched battle between employers and unionists had not occurred when Parliament assembled in June. On the 13th Reeves reported, once again, to his constituents.[2] He apologized for not doing so earlier, and explained that he had had typhoid at the end of the last session (in a speech a few months later he added that his duties as an M.H.R. taxed his limited strength). Then, in April, while playing in goal in one of the first games of Association football in Canterbury, he had been knocked out in a collision with A. P. Harper—later a well-known mountaineer—and carried 'bleeding and unconscious' to hospital.[3] His friends and supporters had pressed him to devote his energies to more serious matters, and he now promised his audience not to play football again.

Much of his talk was an attack on the weakness of the Government, which had become almost immobile. The *Canterbury Times* had summarized the 1889 session in Scobie Mackenzie's words—the House had kept the ministers in and its measures out.[4] Reeves took up this theme and said it was 'One-Man Government'; and now that man, Atkinson, was frequently too ill to attend to business. He conceded that the Premier's colleagues were not devoid of virtues: 'if they took Sir Harry Atkinson's brains, Sir Frederick Whitaker's legal knowledge, Mr Richardson's excellent digestion, Mr Fergus' unusually fine voice, Captain Russell's amiable demeanour, Mr Mitchelson's inoffensive disposition and rolled them up into one man ... and if they could furnish him with a policy, say from the Opposition side of the House... he thought they would not have a bad

[1] LT, 1 April 1890.   [2] CT, 19 June 1890.
[3] LT, 21 April 1890, Reeves describes the incident in his unpublished memoirs; Harper related it to the present writer. It was not, as is sometimes thought, the *first* game of soccer in Canterbury: some games were played in 1882. See LT, 15 May 1882 and issues earlier that year and LT, 24 March 1890.
[4] CT, 19 Sept. 1889.

specimen of their old friend, the One Man Government.' This
was one of Reeves's constant themes. The Government *had* no
policy. In *Colonial Couplets* he had published 'The Premier's
Puzzle' (to the air, 'Wanted a Governess'):

> WANTED, A POLICY. Any will do,
> Liberal, Radical, Tory true blue.
> What may we offer by way of finance?
> How shall we pipe to you, how shall we dance?
> Tell us your wishes—depression and doom
> Or, if you like it, a bit of a boom.
> Borrowing, progress, economy, rest—
> Make your choice, gentlemen, you know the best.
> One if you like not another we'll try,
> Wanted, a policy, won't you supply?
>
> WANTED, A POLICY. Wellington growls.
> Poor Taranaki, disconsolate, howls.
> Westland's placarded, 'we're starving,' of course.
> Northern petitioners bawl themselves hoarse.
> Cities the treasury seeking to rob,
> Counties demanding the usual job,
> Roads of whose uses I haven't a notion,
> Harbour-boards trying to fill up the ocean
> —These are the horse-leech's daughters who cry
> 'Wanted a policy.' I must supply.

For the rest, his speech to his constituents consisted of a list of
the eminent Canterbury families, including the Harpers, who
had 'selected' land under the Government's new regulations.
If he had his way most of these people 'would not be allowed to
purchase an acre'. And he turned to the 'labour question' and
the 'Sweating Commission' that had been investigating factory
conditions. In 1889 he had been one of those supporting its
appointment, though another Christchurch member, R. M.
Taylor, had taken the lead.[1] Now Reeves pressed for a closer
inspection of factories and supported the rise of labour organizations. Once again, he urged that a Trade and Labour Council
was 'one of the best means of preventing strikes, for it represented
large masses of men who had nothing to gain but something to
lose by any one particular body striking'.

[1] Taylor moved for its appointment; but Reeves got Fitchett to ask a question for
him in his absence.

Reeves's portrait of the 'scarecrow ministry', while a caricature, was not altogether an unfair one. Though the free-traders had tried to drop Atkinson, some of them were sore at being excluded from his government, and because he had carried his tariff with the votes of the Opposition. Consequently they gave him only grudging and unreliable support and prevented him from passing important legislation. The Con-servatives in the Legislative Council finished off many bills that did pass the lower House. But while his desire for reform was frustrated by his former colleagues, neither they nor the Opposition could command a majority and displace him.

At the beginning of the 1890 session it was discovered that the Government had found a policy but, for all effective purposes, lost its leader. A large meeting of government 'supporters' was called. Atkinson told them that if he undertook 'the active duties of his office', his doctors informed him, he was liable either to sudden death or paralysis (because of heart trouble). He offered, if caucus wished, to continue as 'nominal Premier'. Only two Members—a free trader, William Barron, and H. S. Fish, a radical who was distinctly out of his element at the caucus, though he had given Atkinson some support—refused the appeal of a man who had suffered physically and financially in the Colony's service.[1]

Throughout 1890, while Reeves teased the Government with having 'an invisible Premier',[2] its new policy failed to materialize. It had been sketched out in the report of the Sweating Commission, which had recommended reforms already advocated by some of the union organizations, including a new factory act and the appointment of Boards of conciliation and arbitration to prevent strikes.[3] Early in the session T. W. Hislop, the Minister of Education, introduced several labour bills—a Factories and Shop Hours Bill, a Truck Bill (to prevent the payment of workmen in goods, which the Midland Railway Company, for instance, was allegedly doing), and an Employers' Liability Bill. These were referred to a committee which included

[1] Reeves MSS, large clipping book, p. 93, *Otago Daily Times*, 15 Nov. 1890; p. 99. H. S. Fish speech.

[2] PD, 1890, 67, pp. 204 ff.; LT, 30 June 1890.

[3] AJHR, 1890, H-5. The Maritime Council allegedly influenced the government bills directly, following interviews with Atkinson: LT, 13 July 1890; CT, 31 July 1890.

Reeves, Perceval, H. S. Fish and Hislop, all of whom were showing a strong interest in labour legislation, or, it might be said, were bidding for the labour vote—though Reeves, at least, was not universally suspected of such opportunism: the free trader, Bruce, for example, conceded that he was, indeed, a friend of labour because he was socialistic.[1] In 1890, these bills were his chief interest. He supported them in debate; his newspaper suggested detailed amendments; he consulted with the 'parliamentary committee' of the Trades and Labour Council on the details.[2] But none of them were passed, except a Shipping and Seamen's Bill. Two were killed by the Legislative Council: the Government lost heart, and failed to push the Factory Bill through the House; a Workmen's Lien Bill was not debated at all. The industrial trouble was spreading, and the employers' antagonism to labour legislation increased with class tension. The waves of capitalist fear which had built up the Reform Associations in 1887 grew more agitated: the provision of dining rooms for employees, Wellington employers said of Hislop's Factory Bill, would 'drive capital out of the Colony'.[3]

The most interesting labour bill of 1890 was a private Strikes and Board of Conciliation Bill introduced by William Downie Stewart, a lawyer who was Member for Dunedin West. Hislop's view was that, though such a bill had been suggested to the Government, it was a matter needing study of legislation elsewhere, on which inadequate information was then available.[4] The debate made it clear that Members were, in fact, confused about the whole question. The bill provided machinery for arbitration to avert strikes, but the adoption of that machinery was permissive. Downie Stewart himself opposed the idea of compulsory arbitration, but pointed out that his bill could be made compulsory merely by changing the word 'may' to 'shall'.[5]

Much of the debate turned on this issue. Would arbitration be effective unless compulsory? Could it be enforced if it were compulsory? Grey, looking at the problem from the point of view of English liberalism, Moss, a Member who frequently spoke in terminology learned from Marx or the *Queensland Worker*, and

[1] PD, 1890, 69, p. 825.
[2] CT, 19 June 1890; LT, 22, 24, 26 July 1890; PD, 1890, 68, p. 76; 69, p. 241.
[3] LT, 5 Aug. 1890.
[4] LT, 8 Sept. 1890; PD, 1890, 68, pp. 125-6.
[5] PD, 1890, 68, pp. 118 ff.; PD, 1892, 78, p. 411.

Fish all argued that compulsory arbitration would reduce the liberties of trade unionists. Fish said that a compulsory clause would amount to an attempt to force unions into a system of arbitration, and another Member added that, if 'may' became 'shall' it would be a 'bill to suppress strikes'. It was rumoured that some sections of unionists opposed any compulsory system.[1]

Ballance agreed that if the bill were compulsory it would seem to be introduced in the interests of employers. Though he favoured optional conciliation or arbitration, he thought Downie Stewart's bill ill-considered and 'a sorry thing'.[2]

Surprisingly enough, Reeves did not speak on this bill, though he was possibly in the House and certainly in Wellington.[3] There is, however, no doubt of his views. For months the thought of arbitration had made the *Lyttelton Times* quite lyrical: 'It is the substitution of reason for force.... [It] is beautiful, being harmonious; being, in fact, the guarantee for perpetual harmony among all the orders of the State.' If the principle were applied 'every cause of friction between capital and labour would, in time, vanish.'[4] But the *Times* thought it must be compulsory to be of any use.[5] At first it was widely believed that Downie Stewart's bill would incorporate this principle; once it was found to be permissive, the *Canterbury Times* said it was not worth the waste of anyone's time. A further clue to Reeves's attitude may also be found in a remark in the same weekly, when the bill was thought to be compulsory: the editorial writer doubted whether it would pass because 'Too many members are interested in the Labour vote to allow one of their number to get so far ahead.' But the *Canterbury Times* leader writer (surely Reeves himself) hoped that one Member *would* 'get ahead': 'The man who will make arbitration compulsory in this land, will not require a statue to perpetuate his memory in a world free from industrial troubles.'[6]

In the articles in the two journals on this question there was little enough socialism; more about 'the method of pure reason', of keeping 'capital within bounds' and putting 'labour in its

---

[1] PD, 1890, 68, pp. 120 ff.; LT, 24 July 1890; CT, 17 July 1890.
[2] PD, 1890, 68, pp. 124–5; 69, pp. 394–5, 812–13.
[3] He spoke in the House on the previous and succeeding days.
[4] LT, 8 Sept. 1890; also 4 March, 11 Aug. 1890.
[5] 21 July 1890.   [6] 17 July; cf. 10 July and 24 July.

place'. It was statism rather than socialism. At the same time they published articles describing socialism and advocating unionism. It is not always possible to feel confident that Reeves wrote any particular one of these articles; but their confusion, or, rather, their bi-focalism, was also present in his thought.

The Government did not support Downie Stewart's bill. While it was held in suspense, and before it lapsed, the strikes which it was intended to prevent had begun. Whitcombe and Tombs, the Christchurch printers, had, after refusing the Typographical Association's demands about wages, apprentices and the employment of girls as compositors, sacked some binders. The typographers had struck and the Maritime Council tried to organize a complete boycott of the firm's goods. Railwaymen became involved when the Railway Commissioners refused Millar's request that they decline to handle goods for Whitcombe and Tombs. When Millar threatened a general strike, public feeling became very excited. On 9 August the *Lyttelton Times* reported, 'An impression is abroad... that a number of capitalists and friends of capitalists are anxious to "have it out" with the Unions. These gentlemen are supposed to have come to the conclusion that the sooner a battle is fought between Capital and Labour the better... .' That impression was even stronger in Australia, where some unions were very powerful and radical. In late August a seamen's and dockers' strike began there. Since both the New Zealand ship-owners and the Maritime Council were affiliated with the Australian organizations, the trouble inevitably spread. It crossed the Tasman on board Union Company ships loaded by non-union labour. The seamen and wharf labourers struck; 'special police' with white badges and batons were enrolled; there was minor rioting in Dunedin and fisticuffs in Canterbury between 'black-leg' (or 'free') and union labour.[1] For a time, when platelayers were dismissed for refusing to work the wharves, it seemed that the strike might become general, but the railwaymen did not come out.

While most of the Press, employers (who formed associations throughout the country) and farmers denounced the 'bands of conspirators' and 'self-seeking politicians and labour agitators',[2]

---

[1] J. D. Salmond, pp. 82 ff.; *Lyttelton Times* throughout August 1890.
[2] e.g. LT, 13 Sept. 1890, letter by C. Ensor, Chairman of the N.Z. Farmers' Cooperative Association.

the *Lyttelton* and *Canterbury Times*, Sir Robert Stout, Reeves and other Opposition M.H.Rs. openly sympathized with the strikers.

Reeves tried to be guarded and moderate in his public statements, to avoid inflammatory remarks, but he did denounce the Government for permitting ships to sail with untrained 'volunteer' crews, and inevitably, as what was (and is) called 'public' opinion grew hostile to the strikers, he came to be regarded by the middle classes as a possibly dangerous man.[1] Privately he thought the strike a mistake, and (mainly behind the scenes) worked as hard as anyone for a fair settlement, for which his opponents gave him little credit. The Government tried to stay neutral, but Reeves repudiated the idea that its duty was to keep law and order, while letting the two sides fight it out. In September, he and other M.H.Rs. of his mind, saw the Governor, Lord Onslow, and sought his aid. Reeves let him know that Atkinson was more inclined to mediation than his colleagues.[2] Shortly afterwards, on the motion of Perceval, the Opposition whip, the House called on the Government, as deputations of unionists had done, to mediate, but when a conference of employers and strikers was called, the former refused to attend. The Union Company demanded unconditional surrender.[3]

As in Australia, the strength of unionism proved largely illusory, while hungry unemployed were poised to jump into empty jobs. The unionists were soundly beaten. By October the strike was 'fizzling out'.[4] But embittered and now jobless men found a general election simultaneously upon them. Where boycott and strike had failed, the secret ballot might succeed.

In July, when the Knights of Labour had suggested 'concerted action' to secure the election of labour candidates, the Canterbury Trades and Labour Council had reaffirmed its previous policy not to take a direct part in politics. The *Lyttelton Times* had commended their decision: were the unionists to 'form themselves into a political association' they would 'lose ground with the moderate section of the public'.[5] After the strike, however,

---

[1] PD, 1890, 69, pp. 397 ff., 440, 798 ff.
[2] G. H. Scholefield (ed.), *The Richmond-Atkinson Papers*, Wellington, 1960, ii, p. 564.
[3] J. D. Salmond, pp. 89–90; LT, 16, 23, 29 Sept. 1890.
[4] *Evening Post*, 10 Oct. 1890.   [5] LT, 7, 9 July 1890.

though they did not form a labour party, the unionists were
determined on a more active rôle. In late August a meeting was
called at the Christchurch Trades Hall to form a political
association to organize for the election, the associations of 1887
having, as usual, folded up when they had served their purpose.
A People's (or Operatives') Political Association was established,
in succession to the earlier Working Men's Associations. One
member of its committee was Ebenezer Sandford, a compositior
employed by the Lyttelton Times Company, who had helped to
start both the Typographical Association and the Canterbury
Trades and Labour Council.[1] People's Political Associations
were also set up in the smaller towns, Ashburton, Rangiora,
Lyttelton and Kaiapoi. They were virtually the political wing
of the Trades Councils: any unionist was entitled to free membership. The 'platform' of the Christchurch Association, was
submitted to the Trades Council, amended, and then recommended to all unionists.[2] In many other towns the unionists
formed political organizations to advocate radical reforms and
to secure the election of candidates of the right colour.[3] This
widespread unionist participation in politics was unprecedented,
and made the election of 1890 very different from that of
1887.

When Reeves returned to Christchurch in late September he
found that some of his chief middle class supporters had deserted
him because of his sympathy with the strikers; but he had gained
far more. He worked in close collaboration with the People's
Political Association, and made no attempt to revive his Electors'
Association. He began his campaign, throughout October, by
speaking to groups of his supporters, a large number of whom
came to his campaign rooms in Hobb's Building to enrol on his
committee.[4] The St. Albans electorate had vanished in a
redistribution of seats in 1888, when the House was reduced
from 95 to 74 Members. He now stood for the City of Christchurch, an electorate which would return three members. When
he made his first public speech, on 1 November, he appeared on

[1] LT, 23, 25 Aug. 1890.   [2] J. D. Salmond, pp. 134–5.
[3] Ibid., pp. 127 ff.; H. Crook, 'The Significance of the 1890 Election', unpub.
thesis, University of Auckland, pp. 98 ff.
[4] LT, 30 Sept.; 3, 16, 24 Oct., 1 Nov. 1890; Press, 3 Dec. 1890.

the platform with his ally Perceval and an older man, Richard Molesworth Taylor, the Member for Sydenham, a 'frosty-bearded' Maori war veteran, who had made little impression in the House except for his drolleries. There was some doubt about whether they were conscious, but he was generally reckoned a jovial fellow. He was never one of Reeves's friends.

In Canterbury, the Opposition was quite unready for the election, which was expected in November. When the Government postponed it, the *Lyttelton Times* suspected that the ministers wanted to give discharged unionists time to leave the seaports, but later welcomed the opportunity that an extra month gave the Opposition to organize.[1]

The change in the political wind was obvious in the new slogan. Instead of standing for 'United Canterbury', Reeves and his friends presented themselves as 'United Liberals'. They urged the voters to return a solid bloc of Liberals to defend—not Canterbury's railways—but New Zealand's workers. Reeves constantly preached his gospel of party—this time, Liberal Party—unity, which now seemed, if not an imminent reality, at least more than a pious hope.

In so far as the men who called themselves 'Liberals' may be regarded as the successors of those of 1879—and the presence of Ballance and Stout among them represented an element of continuity—they were more united than ever before. But there was a real sense in which the Liberal Party of 1890 was a new phenomenon. The coalitions that formed the Grey and Stout–Vogel Governments had contained few radicals and many men for whom 'liberal' was a mere label. Most of the latter, like Montgomery, had withdrawn from politics, or, like J. D. Lance, the nominal leader of the Opposition in 1888, refused to follow Ballance. The Vogelites now opposed the Liberals, which made them a more homogeneous and radical group, especially in Canterbury, where Vogel had had most support.[2] Grey's decision not to stand in 1890 removed another source of disunity.

The Liberals had no 'national' organization; indeed there were no Liberal Associations in many electorates, and such as there were generally functioned independently of each other.

---

[1] LT, 25 Nov.; 2, 23 Dec. 1890.
[2] LT, 2 April, 23 Dec. 1890; 1 Jan. 1891.

There was no time before the election for them to co-operate in drawing up an agreed programme, as Perceval, the Opposition whip, urged.[1] Nevertheless there was an unprecedented general agreement on basic principles.

Ballance announced his views in late September in a speech which was generally accepted as laying down the policy of the Opposition.[2] It consisted of two broad parts. First there was a group of proposals to encourage closer land settlement. These included the compulsory repurchase by the state of large estates; the abolition of the property tax and its replacement by a graduated tax on the 'unearned increment'—on unimproved values; a penal tax on absentees and measures to prevent 'dummyism' (bogus applications for settlement lands by the agents of estate owners or speculators); and a ban on the further sale of Crown lands, which were to remain 'nationalized' and to be leased out. This part of the policy had been widely accepted by radicals for years—both Stout and Ballance had once gone further, and advocated land nationalization.

Secondly the Liberal programme included the introduction of some form of industrial conciliation and other 'labour' reforms, an emphasis which distinguished the Liberals of 1890 from their precursors. It derived from the policies which the Trades and Labour Councils and other groups of working men had advocated through the eighties.[3]

Ballance's proposals were listed and elaborated by other Liberals. At the same time, numerous radical Liberal and unionist groups published their own programmes, with additional or variant proposals. For example, the 'Wage-Earners' Manifesto' put out by the Wellington Trades Council and Knights of Labour, demanded an elective Legislative Council and opposed importing 'foreign labour'.[4] The programme of the Otago Workers' Political Committee was as comprehensive as that of a modern party platform, and included compulsory arbitration, the provision by the state of work for the unemployed, and several socialist proposals, such as 'State

[1] LT, 26 Sept. 1890.
[2] LT, 24 Sept. 1890; Wellington *Evening Post*, 1 Oct. 1890; *Auckland Evening Star*, 24 Sept. 1890 etc. 'Mr Ballance, of course, speaks for his party': LT, 26 Sept. 1890.
[3] J. D. Salmond, *passim*.
[4] *Evening Post*, 6 Oct. 1890.

ownership under direct ministerial control of land, railways, mines and coastal marine service'.[1]

There were, then, differences of opinion among the radicals. John McKenzie, one of the leading rural Liberals, for instance, was notoriously antagonistic to unions and had denounced them in 1890. Though he sincerely believed in closer settlement, in speaking to a rural electorate he covered with swathes of caution their plans for 'bursting up' great estates.[2] Tension between the rural and urban wings of the Liberal Party was evident from the moment it was formed. In 1890 the Party programme mainly appealed to townsmen, but while many rural workers, too, wanted farms, this conflict was minimized. Comparison of the many programmes proposed reveals widespread agreement among Liberals and other radicals on the need for the kind of land and labour reforms that Ballance proposed. He was able to write to John Joyce, a Liberal candidate in Akaroa, that the 'Basis and Platform' of the Peoples' Political Association there contained the principles 'held and advocated by the great majority of members belonging to the Liberal Party in the Colony. This platform ought to lead to the better definition of parties in the future, and prevent that confusion in Parliament, caused by personal support, which has been the principal cause of bad legislation.'[3]

The Liberals were still not sure that they had the right leader. Probably the majority preferred Stout to Ballance. Though the *Lyttelton Times* praised Ballance for his work in reorganizing the Opposition, it eulogized Stout as 'the foremost man' in the Party: his election, it said, would create 'a powerful and truly Radical party'. Ballance was not well known in the south—even the *Lyttelton Times* rarely mentioned him. Those who did know him, often thought of him as a good debater, but as lacking the popular qualities of a leader in the lobbies and in public. Reeves certainly preferred his old idol, Stout.[4] As modest as ever, Ballance again urged Stout to resume the leadership, while two thousand Dunedin voters signed a requisition asking him to

---

[1] J. D. Salmond, 'The History of the New Zealand Labour Movement', unpub. thesis, University of Otago, pp. 154–6.

[2] PD, 1890, 69, pp. 818 ff.; H. Crook, pp. 45–46.

[3] H. Crook, pp. 98–99.

[4] LT, 15 July; 4, 9 Dec. 1890; 10, 13 June 1892.

stand. He refused, while continuing to speak in public in favour of the Liberal cause.[1]

The degree of unity among the Liberals in organization, policy or leadership was not comparable with that of a party in the mid-twentieth century. They had little expectation of winning. Stout frankly thought the country not ripe for radicalism; Reeves told Stout confidentially that he thought his Party would not gain office for years—though he thought that a non-Liberal government might adopt their policy.[2] They were judging from the Party's weaknesses, underestimating the radical mood in the electorates and the extent to which the unions and other groups were acting as an unofficial party organization.

The Government was supported by no comparable organization or enthusiasm. The Reform Associations were not revived. Little was heard of the tariff question, which had united many Conservatives in 1887, though the Protection League was active on the Liberal side, while, in Otago, a 'New Zealand' Farmers' Union was formed to oppose tariffs.[3] The Conservatives still debated who should succeed Atkinson, who was too ill to offer effective leadership. He was too weak even to address his electorate, and published a long manifesto instead. He referred vaguely to conciliation, but offered nothing to rival the Liberals' programme. Indeed he abjured such a thing: 'let us have no political or financial fireworks, no great or heroic policy, no great schemes to dazzle or to lead us astray. What we want ... is a strict but not parsimonious economy, combined with cheerfulness and a firm belief in the unbounded resources of the Colony.'[4] Only the new evangelists of the left could see reasons for cheer.

Reeves was a very different candidate in 1890 from the immature young man of 1887. He still denounced 'middlemen' in his editorials. He described recent adversities as the very thing 'to unite the masses ... against the classes'.[5] But in the political

[1] D. A. Hamer, 'The Law and the Prophet', pp. 349–52.
[2] Ibid., p. 353; PD, 1890, 67, p. 569; 1894, 85, p. 134.
[3] LT, 18, 30 Oct. 1890; Reeves MSS, large clipping book, pp. 108v–109v.
[4] CT, 13 Nov., LT, 6 Nov. 1890.
[5] LT, 15 Nov., 6 Dec. 1890. The terminology and the rhetoric of these editorials are unmistakably Reeves's.

atmosphere of 1890, this sounded less radical—even Ballance in his policy speech had said the struggle was 'between the champions of the people and the champions of privilege'. Reeves's public speeches were much more conciliatory and even moderate. He was more assured. He was less on the defensive— he had less often to defend his right to speak for the working men; he was more generally accepted as a genuine radical. And he expected to win. The unions were solidly behind him. He received Catholic support both because the Catholics were generally poor, and because of his appearance at the Parnell Defence Fund and Dillon's meetings.[1] Journalists began to prophesy that, if the Liberals won, he would be in the cabinet.[2] He was recognized as the leader of the Christchurch, and perhaps, Canterbury, Liberals.[3] When the three 'United Liberals' spoke on the same platform, as they usually did, he was obviously their leader. He spoke last, and best, and received the most applause.

Their opponents were little better than negligible, for no important Conservative was willing to oppose Reeves and his supporting newspapers. J. M. Verrall, an M.H.R. who was mainly interested in a state bank, stood as an independent, but withdrew. The government candidates were not men of note, though E. W. Humphreys had been an M.H.R. in the years 1889 and 1890. He was a sheep farmer, whisky distiller and old Harrovian. J. T. Smith ran a Wesleyan book depot. He was a leading Orangeman and was supported by the best known prohibitionist in Christchurch, T. E. Taylor (whom Reeves called 'Tea' Taylor, to distinguish him from his colleague, 'Rum' Taylor). The remaining candidate, Eden George, a photographer, stood as an independent. Smith and George had the mortification of addressing meetings that concluded with a vote favouring the Liberals.[4]

Reeves and his two allies spoke at many meetings in Christ-church,[5] but they could not interview many voters, and (as in 1887) declined to follow the practice of hiring 'canvassers', which was thought degrading to the electors.[6] Generally Reeves

---

1 Reeves MSS, small clipping book, p. 121, clipping from the *Tablet*.
2 Ibid., pp. 120–1; *Catholic Times*, Nov. 1890.
3 LT, 1 Dec. 1890.   4 LT, 13, 28 Nov. 1890.
5 e.g. LT, 1, 12, 19, 27, 28, 29 Nov. 1890.
6 LT, 12 Nov. 1890 (Perceval); Reeves MSS, large clipping book, pp. 98 (T. Mackenzie) and 103–4.

spoke on the twin themes of land and labour reform, giving
rather more emphasis to the former, which had been the subject
of his main prepared speech in the 1890 session. It was, he
thought, now the most pressing issue.[1] He usually emphasized
his belief in unionism and his dislike of strikes. Most strikes
failed; not 'a single earnest and experienced Trade unionist'
believed in them, though the fear of strikes was needed to induce
employers to be just. The unions, he thought, should not be
exclusive, but should try to organize 'all the competent Labour
of the colony in their ranks', and to build up their reserve funds
as potent weapons. Above all, he looked to 'Conciliation boards
and conferences' as the solution to industrial trouble. He ignored
compulsory arbitration, which was not included in Ballance's
statement of policy, and was not an issue before the Canterbury
electors. The 'sheep kings' he denounced at length and in detail
as men who had built up their wealth not by work but by
'the unearned increment following upon the expenditure of
borrowed money'. To tax them was fair; indeed (he was prepared to flirt with the 'single taxers', though he disagreed with
Henry George) 'to put the whole burden on landed property
would be justifiable.'[2]

Though there were rowdy meetings elsewhere, in Christchurch the elections were surprisingly quiet, perhaps because
there was little doubt of the outcome.

Being fairly confident, the 'United Liberals' did what they
could to help Liberals in other electorates. They spoke in
Lyttelton, at the invitation of the local People's Political
Association, to a meeting which concluded with three cheers for
'Young New Zealand', and at Kaiapoi and Rangiora.[3] A
Wellington paper gave Reeves credit for organizing the working
men in nearly every electorate near Christchurch.[4] This was
possibly exaggerated, but he did help to arrange for suitable
candidates to stand in neighbouring electorates. When leading
Christchurch unionists, including Ebenezer Sandford, W.
Hoban, president of the railway union, F. S. Parker, President
of the Trades and Labour Council, and C. J. Rae were asked to
stand, they declined to split the Liberal vote. The United Liberals

[1] PD, 1890, 67, 204 ff.; LT, 28 Nov. 1890.
[2] LT, 1 Nov. 1890.
[3] LT, 1 Dec. 1890.
[4] N.Z. Times, 10 Jan. 1896.

helped to arrange for some of them to be nominated elsewhere. For instance, Hoban was, with their help, nominated for Kaiapoi by a joint meeting of the Rangiora Liberal Political Association (which was composed of local union representatives, the People's Political Association and the Lodge of Good Templars) and of the Kaiapoi Labour Union and People's Political Association. The list gives a good notion of the number of little organizations that helped the Liberals.[1] Parker contested another seat; Sandford and Rae did not stand.

The unionists were determined not to defeat their ends by forming a rival radical party. The Trades and Labour Council and the People's Political Association urged the voters to support the 'United Liberals'.[2] The former also urged support for Liberal or trade union candidates in other electorates. Its manifesto called on the workers to use their votes: 'Wake up, working men, to the patent fact that the so-called Government ... is a great octopus that preys on the working man. This Conservative pet arranges the taxation ... to suit the capitalist class.'[3]

In all the main towns, unionist organizations supported Liberals, or put up trade unionist candidates who agreed with the Liberals on most issues. Even the conservative Press, which usually decried talk of class, said the election was based on class warfare. The Governor, Lord Onslow, said it was 'really a fight between Capital and Labour: the strike is transferred from the financial to the political arena.' When he wrote these words to his wife, the results were uncertain, but it appeared that the Liberals had won. He would soon, it seemed, summon to his Councils 'the first avowedly Labour Government' the world had seen. It would be 'interesting to the rest of the world to see' how they would use their power, how Capital would 'have to pay for the defeat it inflicted on Labour'.[4]

The election was held on 5 December, when there was a 10 per cent. increase in the proportion of enrolled voters who voted, as there had been in 1887—an indication of the growing

[1] LT, 17 Oct., 13, 15, 20 Nov. 1890; H. Crook, pp. 101–3.
[2] LT, 26 Nov., 4, 5 Dec. 1890.
[3] Cit. J. D. Salmond, p. 135; LT, 5 Dec. 1890.
[4] G. H. Scholefield, *Notable New Zealand Statesmen*, Christchurch, [1947?], p. 171.

importance of politics to the citizenry.[1] The three 'United Liberals' won the three Christchurch seats easily:

Reeves	2,774
Perceval	2,721
Taylor	2,613
Smith	1,811
Humphreys	1,668
George	119

On 6 December there was no doubt that the Government had been defeated, but it was uncertain whether the Opposition would have an effective majority, because of the indeterminate political affiliations of some of the new Members. The *Lyttelton Times* thought the election a 'brilliant victory', and considered that 42 Opposition candidates, 26 Government, and 5 of doubtful allegiance had been returned. A modern student of the election considers that there were (excluding the Maoris) 34 Liberals, 27 Government and 9 Independents, a majority of whom favoured the Liberals.[2]

The Liberals, or 'Labour' candidates, won almost all the South Island urban and some rural seats. In the North the Government dominated the country, but the Liberals had won several urban seats. Their strength, however, was mainly in the South, where five trade unionists, the first 'Labour' Members, had been elected.[3] Ebenezer Sandford joined them after a bye-election in 1891.

Ballance told the Governor that he thought he had 36 or 37 followers out of 74, and that 5 Members were doubtful, but Atkinson questioned whether Ballance could count on more than 28. He wrote to Rolleston on 8 December saying that, though the Government was defeated, he doubted whether a strong government could be formed and was disinclined to resign until the House met in January and an attempt had been made 'to get a Government together'.[4] Impressed by the number of independent Members, he was still thinking in terms of the old shifting political alliances, oblivious to the growing spirit of party.

[1] L. Lipson, *The Politics of Equality*, Chicago, 1948, pp. 25, 172.
[2] 6, 8 Dec. 1890; H. Crook, pp. 137–8.
[3] H. Crook, pp. 119 ff.
[4] W. D. Stewart, *William Rolleston*, Christchurch, 1949, p. 177.

Though Ballance understood that Atkinson had agreed to resign if the Government was defeated in the election, to obviate the need for two sessions of Parliament (one when a new Government would be formed, the second after an adjournment while it prepared its business), 'the Major' clung to office to the last minute. Prompted by Bryce, and despite Liberal protests, he packed the Legislative Council with six extra supporters, as the Government had intended before the election.[1] That his aim was to check the radicals, as much as to reward old supporters with a life pension, could scarcely be doubted.

When Atkinson called a meeting of caucus on 21 January, twenty-four were present. He told them that he had decided to accept the speakership of the Legislative Council, so they must elect a new leader. Next day thirty-three Members were present at the Liberal caucus.[2] On the 23rd, Parliament met. On behalf of the Government one of the 'independents', Alfred Saunders, nominated Rolleston as Speaker. The Liberals made it a party issue, and the nomination was defeated by 36 to 29. Atkinson then resigned. On Tuesday, 27 January, Ballance announced his ministry.

Ballance was Premier, Colonial Treasurer and Minister for Native Affairs. Patrick Buckley, a fifty-five-year-old Irish lawyer from Wellington, was leader of the Legislative Council, Attorney General and Colonial Secretary. The Minister of Education and Justice, who was listed next, was William Pember Reeves. Richard John Seddon was Minister of Public Works, Mines and Defence; John McKenzie of Lands, Immigration and Agriculture. Joseph George Ward was a minister without portfolio. Presently he became Postmaster-General. In February Alfred Jerome Cadman, the Member for Thames, took over Ballance's Maori administration, as well as some minor offices.

In early December, Stout and Buckley had visited Ballance in Wanganui, on which occasion, it was generally thought (though he denied it) that Stout had influenced Ballance's choice of colleagues. In particular, Stout was thought responsible for the inclusion of McKenzie and the exclusion of H. S. Fish, his chief

[1] G. H. Scholefield (ed.), *Dictionary of New Zealand Biography*, Wellington, 1940, i, p. 111; G. H. Scholefield (ed.), *The Richmond-Atkinson Papers*, Wellington, 1960, ii, 565–6; Reeves MSS, large clipping book, p. 100.
[2] H. Crook, pp. 165–6.

rival as a Dunedin radical.[1] On 23 January, when the likely composition of the cabinet must have been widely known, Fish wrote a face-saving letter to Ballance saying that he did not wish to be considered,[2] but he was very disappointed. He became an hysterical critic of the Government, and of Reeves in particular. So did another radical, George Hutchison,[3] and George Fisher, who had resigned from Atkinson's ministry and now supported Ballance (though he described himself as 'a Liberal with the brake on').[4]

Caucus gave Ballance a free hand in selecting his cabinet.[5] As was customary, as far as possible he chose colleagues representing the main regions and social or other groups. The ministers held seats in Otago, Southland, the West Coast, Canterbury, Wellington, Wanganui and Thames. There were two Catholics, Buckley and Ward (while another, Perceval, became Chairman of Committees), which caused some criticism. Between them the Ministers represented a good many professions, occupations and interests. Ballance and Reeves were journalists. Reeves was included because of his debating ability, his reliability as a party man and his ability as a political organizer, but also as a representative of Labour.[6] McKenzie represented farming, Seddon mining, and Cadman timber milling, though the reason for his selection was to include an Aucklander in the government. Ward was possibly included to represent trade. He was a dapper, popular young man who had built up a very large business as a grain export merchant. His offices and warehouses at Invercargill occupied nearly an acre, while his freezing works at the Bluff were also very extensive. 'In politics' he was 'described as patriotic rather than a party man'.[7]

It was a young cabinet. Ballance, McKenzie and Buckley were just over fifty; Cadman and Seddon in the mid-forties; Reeves and Ward (and James Carroll, a half-caste Maori-European, who joined the cabinet in 1892) were thirty-four. Reeves was

---

[1] 'Letters from Men of Mark', Mark Cohen to Reeves, 30 Aug. 1900; Hamer, 'The Law and the Prophet', pp. 355–6; PD, 1893, 79, p. 107.
[2] Ballance MSS.
[3] e.g., PD, 1891, 74, pp. 985 ff.
[4] PD, 1891, 71, pp. 595–6, 601.
[5] *N.Z. Times*, 23 Jan. 1890; PD, 1891, 71, pp. 595–6.
[6] LT, 26 Jan. 1891; *N.Z. Times*, 10 Jan. 1896.
[7] Reeves MSS, small clipping book, p. 147: *The Katipo*, 24 Dec. 1892.

the only New Zealand-born minister in 1891, the third in the Colony's history.

Ballance, Seddon, Buckley and McKenzie were giants, each estimated to weigh eighteen stone or more, while the others, except Reeves, were all big men. But it did not in other senses seem a strong cabinet. Only Ballance and Buckley had previously held office; only Ballance could be thought of as a leader, and even he was more often regarded as an excellent lieutenant. Buckley had made little mark as a politician. He had had an adventurous youth. While studying at the University of Louvain he had led a band of volunteers to assist the papal forces fighting the Piedmontese, and had been wounded and taken prisoner. In Australia and then in New Zealand he had become a successful lawyer with business interests—he was secretary of the Bank of New Zealand 'Globo assets' company.[1] Seddon, McKenzie and Cadman had held seats for a decade or more, without becoming ministers.

What gave colour to the idea that a new class was in power was the education of the ministers. The country's leaders had traditionally been men educated in British secondary schools or universities. Ballance had left school at fourteen and served his apprenticeship to an ironmonger. Cadman had first worked as a carpenter, Seddon as a farm-hand and then apprentice in an iron foundry, Ward as a post office messenger and McKenzie as a farm hand. Only Reeves, of the ministers in the House, had secondary education—a qualification which was a disadvantage in the period of politics then beginning. When he returned to Invercargill to receive the congratulations of his constituents Ward said 'he was proud to belong to such a Ministry, every member of which, save one, had risen from the ranks.'[2] The 'exception' was probably Buckley, who had never sat in the House, but, perhaps not understanding this, Reeves put the newspaper report in his clipping book. Whatever Ward meant, he could be taken to refer to education. To be self-educated, to have left school at twelve, was now becoming a political asset.

Conservatives were shocked by the thought of McKenzie, a rough-spoken farmer, and Seddon, who ran a hotel, sitting in the cabinet. The Napier *Daily Telegraph* said that the Government had 'fallen into the hands of the mob', and described these

[1] PD, 1891, 70, p. 244.   [2] Reeves MSS, large clipping book, p. 130.

ministers as 'two loud-voiced, ignorant bullies ... tramping the country'. The gravest doubts of the respectable were felt about Seddon, who had been 'hitherto distinguished ... for ungovernable loquacity'. But the *Lyttelton Times* noted his 'remarkable knowledge of parliamentary procedure', his 'quickness in parliamentary tactics', his 'unflagging energy and courage in debate'.[1]

Reeves was not quite as isolated, as an educated man, as this review might so far suggest. Ballance had studied hard at evening classes at the Midland Institute and become secretary to the Birmingham Literary Society. Like Reeves, he was widely read in political and economic literature. These two were much the most radical men in the government: it was they, not their rougher colleagues, who gave intellectual substance to the idea that the 'masses', or the 'workers', were in power. But not one minister was, at that time, a 'worker'.

A frequently vituperative journalist, Joseph Evison, who, writing under the pseudonyms 'Watchman' and 'Phiz', persecuted Reeves for years, pictured him as sitting alongside the Premier 'in a white waistcoat and a smile, pinching himself to test whether it is really W.P.R. who sits there, and wondering how he got there and whether it will last'. It was true enough. All of the ministers were surprised, and so, probably, were most other people. They were an ill-assorted group. Ward and Reeves; Reeves and Seddon: little perspicacity was needed to anticipate storms. And no one could have foreseen how long they would keep power now they had it. But people did quickly appreciate that politics were changing; that Ballance was backed, as he claimed, by the nearest approximation to a united party that the General Assembly had seen.[2] In the two-storied houses, in those with servants' quarters, in the city clubs, in the high country of the 'sheep kings' and in Government House, men with money and men in debt felt cold.

[1] LT, 26 Jan. 1891 and clippings in Reeves MSS, large clipping book, pp. 42–43, 127–31.

[2] e.g. *N.Z. Times*, 23 Jan. 1891.

8

THE BATTLE JOINED
1891

In Double Harness, written by Reeves and G. P. Williams, came
out at the beginning of 1891. It was dedicated, like many
volumes of colonial verse, to the Governor—a choice of patron
Reeves would not have agreed to a year later. Though it was true,
as a journalist wrote when Reeves became a minister, that
'an honourable, unlike a poet, is a man of some importance in
his country',[1] their rhymes were welcomed by readers and
reviewers, especially those verses with a local flavour, such as
Williams's 'History of Mr. and Mrs. Miggs', some amusing
doggerel about two land selectors, and Reeves's 'The Burnt
Homestead'. Once again, most of the serious verses were written
by Reeves. Among them were an early version of one of his
better poems, 'Nox Benigna', here entitled 'Two Nights', and an
imitation Browning, 'An Old Ambassador's Pets'. Reviewers
were less certain how to respond to these. One reviewer was
coarsely humorous about young men with the '"poetic temperament"... everlastingly getting headaches, or neuralgias....'
But another liked best Reeves's 'The White Convolvulus'—
'a dainty conception, dreamily tender in its idea, and charmingly
versified',[2] a description which gives an accurate impression of
the poem. It describes many flowers—

> The rose's poetry, poppy's prose,
> The braggart peony's wrathful rows

—and personifies the convolvulus, the phantom flower:

> Cup of aërial marble made.

It is heavily loaded with highly-charged 'poetic' adjectives,
the result of his 'hardest attempt to write poetry' up to that time.[3]

---

[1] Reeves MSS, large clipping book, p. 129.   [2] Ibid., pp. 131v–133.
[3] Alpers MSS, Reeves to Alpers, 30 Dec. 1900.

A family tragedy immediately followed the triumphs with which 1891 began. When he joined the ministry, Reeves had resigned the editorship of the *Lyttelton Times*. His father, with some help, probably from Samuel Saunders, had undertaken his duties. But within two months William Reeves became seriously ill and had to undergo an operation for what was diagnosed as gallstones, but was possibly cancer. He was by now hopelessly in debt, and so was his company. The war with the Press Company still savagely continued as his rivals sought to eliminate the *Canterbury Times*, or otherwise reduce the number of competing newspapers. He made an effort to put his affairs in order. In March he sold 'Risingholme', which was advertised, to let, by his cousin Herbert Reeves.[1] Then, broken in fortune as well as health, and ostracized by many of his peers because of his political views (as Saunders related), he cheerfully said goodbye to his staff and friends.[2]

His eldest son was in Christchurch to visit the Normal School with William Montgomery and address the Educational Institute—giving the impression, according to the *Star*, that he was no longer a flippant youth, but a man of quiet dignity and good humour.[3] His constituents were to give a banquet in his honour on April the 6th. But on the 4th his father died.

The newspapers were full of rumours that Reeves would have to resign office in order to take over the *Times*,[4] but there was no such possibility. His father's estate was virtually (though not legally) bankrupt. His 2,120 £10 shares in the Times Company were valued, for probate, at ten shillings each, and they came into the hands of the mortgagee, F. J. Kimbell. A lawyer named de Malet became managing director of the Company. Reeves ceased to be a director, since he no longer held enough shares.

A cousin, Hugh Reeves, wrote to Stout that he was going 'home' to borrow £4,000, or even £8,000, from the family, so that W.P. could buy up a quarter of the shares. But it seems unlikely that Reeves knew of his plans. His cousin begged Stout to find out whether W.P. would care to have him manage the Company if his scheme succeeded. He also reported that

---

[1] *Star*, 1 April 1891 and following issues.
[2] *Christchurch Times*, 29 June 1935.
[3] 31 March, 4 April; *N.Z. Times*, 24, 30 March.
[4] *Star*, 7 April; *N.Z. Times*, 6 April.

de Malet 'avows openly that the less Reeves the better for the success of the paper'.[1]

The new directors of the Times Company had the books audited for the first time. Though it had been a limited company since 1881, William Reeves had continued to treat it as his own property. He had drawn £1,600 from the Company's account for his private purposes, apparently lending its money to his stud farm, the Middlepark Company. There were no assets in his estate from which this could be repaid and the debt had to be written off. The Company had a large overdraft, and owed £7,000 besides. It had to make a call of £1 per share.[2]

These events greatly altered Reeves's position. Previously he was generally believed to have a wealthy father—and certainly his father *spent* money; now he not only earned his living, but appeared to do so, which strengthened his political hand. He was not poorer, except in prospects. As editor he had been paid, perhaps, £600, like his predecessor. As an M.H.R. he had received £100 and £50 expenses a year. With his director's fee of £50, he thus earned some £750, not counting the expenses. Now, as a minister, he received £800 and £150 travel allowance. The Times Company re-employed him, in 1891, at £2 a week, to write a weekly leading article and to supervise the parliamentary correspondent. His mother and the younger children moved to a small house in Armagh Street after the funeral. Reeves and his family shifted to Wellington, and presently into a 'ministerial residence', a large, two-storied, wooden house in Tinakori Road. Even with a £200 house allowance that was later given to ministers, they found keeping it up very expensive. There was little money to spare.[3]

Reeves's Canterbury world had fallen: now he had nowhere to retreat from politics—as Stout sometimes withdrew to his law practice. The fact that his father died penniless, after the relentless battle with the *Press*, probably further embittered his attitude to the squatters and the Canterbury 'rich'. What wounds his father's dishonesty inflicted were mostly covered, but one remained visible all his life. All about him he saw men he knew brought to poverty or disgrace because of speculation

1 Stout MSS, 12 June 1891.
2 Lyttelton Times Co. minutes; L.T., 4 April 1893.
3 PD, 1895, 91, pp. 820, 829; 1894, 84, p. 582.

before the depression. The law firm of Leonard and George Harper, in whose office he had worked as a clerk, failed for £250,000 in 1893. It was the worst case of defalcation in the Colony's history. Leonard—who had chaired one of Will's first meetings—had for years falsified accounts sent to clients, mainly English investors, whose funds had been lost in extensive and risky land speculations. Despite the state of New Zealand business, interest had to be paid in England. George Harper and T. W. Maude, who had failed, despite suspicions, to check Leonard's dishonesty, were struck off the roll. Reeves had the unpleasant duty, as Minister of Justice, of having Leonard brought back to New Zealand for trial.

The affairs of these lawyers were inextricably involved with those of the Times Company. Maude was a director. The Harpers were its solicitors, mortgagees of some of its shares and also of the Middlepark stud—which fell into the hands of a bank, and was sold for £2,750. One of the chief unsecured creditors of the Harpers and Maude was Kimbell, now the proprietor of the Times Company. He lost £3,000.[1]

Though few people thought W. P. Reeves was personally involved in any of this—and he certainly was not—it was a notable tale of speculation and peculation that was gradually revealed. One would suppose that it aggravated one of Reeves's growing weaknesses—his touchiness. And it confirmed him in his extreme scrupulosity in financial matters, so strengthening his dislike of borrowing and gambling that financial prudence became an obsession. It was to be a major influence on his political attitudes. Statism and thrift are uneasy partners.

Parliament was in recess from the end of January until mid June to give the ministers time (in the words of a parliamentary correspondent) 'to ransack the ministerial pigeon holes, get used to the private secretaries, and learn to hear themselves addressed as ministers without blushing awkwardly—which is a great thing.'

With the civil servants Reeves immediately formed excellent relations and made life-long friends. Even his enemies admitted that he was exceedingly, almost excessively, hard-working. He was also, except in the heat of debate, very courteous. In March

[1] *N.Z. Times*, 1 April 1893; 29 May 1894; P.D., 1894, 83, pp. 192-3.

his private secretary, Frank Waldegrave, wrote to Sir John Hall: 'I get along very well indeed with Mr. W. P. Reeves. He seems to wish to work well with his officers—& he has treated me personally with a kindness and consideration which leaves nothing to be desired. He evidently intends to make a mark as a Minister and I really do not believe that he will lend himself to any of the scheming which may reasonably be expected from some of his colleagues.'[1]

The civil servants shared the apprehensions of the old oligarchy about hotel keepers entering the Executive Council.

As early as March, J. D. Ormond, one of the leading estate owners and free traders, was reporting to Hall, 'Seddon appears to rule the Cabinet and over-ride everybody.'[2] But despite Seddon's pushing ways, it was no more than appearance. Ballance proved an excellent Premier. He sometimes acted as chairman rather than commander, but when he wanted to get his own way, he got it. His conciliatory, affable manner was an essential cement for a cabinet containing several dominant personalities, men far abler than their opponents, or perhaps anyone else, believed early in 1891. Ballance's colleagues came to regard him with the highest esteem. Reeves (his 'lieutenant', he was called) felt something close to adulation for his chief, who guided and encouraged him, unsparing of his time and sympathy. 'In the various perplexities and doubts that beset a young Minister', Reeves said after his death, 'one always had a friend as well as adviser in John Ballance. If one committed a mistake he always made the least of it instead of the most; if one scored a success, he made the most of it and not the least. He was great enough to be utterly generous.'[3]

The first few months in office, following his father's death, were trying and tiring. Will replied personally to each constituent who wrote congratulations on his appointment, or hinted at needs for jobs. He met delegations. He thought up suitable serious and entertaining remarks for public functions such as opening the Wanganui Girls' College (with the women's suffrage looming it 'would be an entertaining sight to watch men educating their future mistresses').[4] Mostly he sat in his office studying the administrative details of his departments and helping to draft

[1] Hall MSS, 18 March 1891.   [2] Ibid., 24 March 1891.
[3] *Otago Daily Times*, 24 May 1893.   [4] *Wanganui Herald*, 13 Feb. 1891.

government bills for the next session. He had his first taste of the fruits of power—correspondence with Sir John Hall, for instance, over appointing a new administrator at the Cook Islands.[1] They were not all sweet. Though the Liberals had inherited a budgetary surplus from Atkinson, they had to show that their demand for retrenchment was not mere electioneering. They began by 'retrenching' staff and reorganizing some departments of the public service, changes estimated to save £100,000, and carried out at the cost of much alarm in the civil service and to the accompaniment of cries of 'corruption' and 'favouritism'.

Reeves's main interest, from the first, was in improving the lives of working men. He took up a suggestion made by Kennedy Macdonald, a Wellington Liberal businessman, for dealing with unemployment by a method already tried in the United States and France, and by the Salvation Army. It had been observed that often there was unemployment in one district while jobs were vacant elsewhere. In June, after much planning, Reeves opened a Bureau of Industries (soon called the Labour Bureau) in Wellington, with agencies in Christchurch, Dunedin and Invercargill, and two hundred sub-agencies throughout the country. Information about employment and unemployment was collected and workmen were given free railway passes to go to districts where there were vacancies. By the end of the year employment had been found for 2,000 men.[2]

The Bureau was at first managed part-time by civil servants in existing departments. It was directed by Edward Tregear, a Maori war veteran who had published a *Maori-Polynesian Comparative Dictionary*. He worked in the Department of Lands and Survey. Tregear became one of Reeves's closest associates, though they were not, judging from Tregear's later letters to Reeves, close friends. His letters are affectionate, but written from a respectful distance. Nevertheless, they had much in common and thought alike on many things. Besides being one of the best-known scholars of Polynesian language and lore in the country, Tregear was a poet and a socialist who later became president of the Social Democrat Party. Beatrice Webb, who

[1] Hall MSS, Reeves to Hall, 20, 28 April 1891.
[2] Reeves MSS, large clipping book, pp. 117v–118v; *N.Z. Times*, 6, 10 June, 6 July 1891.

met him in 1898, thought him 'a big, brawny, zealous, muddle-
headed sort of person'. He was a dreamer, about whose idealism
there was always something naïve. Like Reeves, he was not
always discreet. He once said, in public, that the declining
birth-rate was due to the fact that the toilers had decided not to
breed slaves to be ground under the iron heel of the capitalist.
Frank Waldegrave wrote to Reeves, 'I often wonder whether
he believes it all.' Something of the quality of his socialism—
though not of his best verse—may be seen in one of his political
poems:

> The stalwart troopers rode at ease,
> In scarlet, gold, and steel.
> Within the park the worker crept
> To eat his scanty meal.
> Alas! the workers' meals have paid
> For sword and horse and golden braid.
>
> The clattering troopers charge along
> The crowded city lanes.
> No medicine like steel to soothe
> The gnawing hunger pains!
> Oh! toilers for the Lords of Trade,
> These are the gods your hands have made.[1]

The strength of the Liberals lay among the voters, most of
whom continued silent until the next election, and in the House.
There they had an assured majority on most issues, despite the
presence of a few disgruntled Liberals. Grey made all the trouble
he could for Ballance. In 1892 he was 'in daily conference' with
Horton, a proprietor of the conservative Auckland newspaper,
the *New Zealand Herald*, discussing how to defeat the Premier.[2]
But his principal lieutenant, Seddon, was now in the cabinet.
Grey was a leader with scarcely a follower or a cause. Fish,
Hutchison, and Fisher formed a splinter group, the 'Bashi-
Bazouks'. Fish became especially venomous after September
1891 when Perceval, the Chairman of Committees, was
appointed Agent-General in London. Fish wanted to be

---

[1] 'Letters from Men of Mark', Waldegrave to Reeves, 9 March 18[99];
Passfield MSS, B. Webb's diary, 31 Aug. 1898. The poem is from a clipping pasted
in my copy of his *Shadows and Other Verses*, Wellington, 1919.

[2] Rolleston MSS, J. Gould to Rolleston, 16 June 1892; Hall to Rolleston, 20 Feb.
1892.

Chairman, but the Government put up Rees, another Greyite. Like Grey's, theirs was an impotent bitterness.

The Opposition was, for the first time, as plainly conservative as the Government was radical. Atkinson's elevation to the Legislative Council cleared the way for the free trade Conservatives who had fought the 1887 election. In the first session of 1891 the Opposition was led by a committee of six—Bryce, Rolleston, Russell, Scobie Mackenzie, Macarthur and Buchanan. They were all free traders and not one of them had been in Atkinson's ministry in 1887, though the gentlemanly William Russell had joined it in 1889 when Atkinson was often too ill to attend to business. For the second session of 1891, from June to September, Bryce was elected leader of the Opposition, but two months later he incurred the formal censure of the House for words used in debate, and withdrew from politics. He was succeeded by William Rolleston,[1] a kindly, well-meaning man, rather lumbering in debate. Reeves always teased him about his gloomy speeches, calling him a Cassandra, 'the most imaginative grumbler in New Zealand, and the most determined'.[2]

Though Hall repudiated the label 'conservatives' that Reeves attached to the Opposition,[3] it was accurate. Individually, some of the Opposition leaders held advanced views on particular topics: Rolleston on land tenure; Russell on labour reforms; Hall on the women's vote. But collectively they opposed most of the reforms the Liberals proposed. The forces at their command were daunting everywhere but in the House. Conservatives dominated the Legislative Council. They were backed by almost every newspaper, by the banks, by the land and stock companies, by the bigger businessmen and the estate owners. In the background, in reserve, lay the undefined vice-regal powers. For two years they frustrated the Government at almost every legislative turn.

The most bitter opposition to the Liberals in 1891 was over their land reforms. The only one to pass was that included in their land and income tax, a money bill which the Legislative Council could neither reject nor amend. It imposed a tax of a

---

[1] PD, 1891, 70, p. 48; 71, pp. 31, 51; 74, pp. 100, 384.
[2] e.g. P.D., 1893, 81, p. 495.
[3] PD, 1891, 70, p. 95.

penny in the pound on the unimproved value of land worth over
£500. In addition there was a graduated tax, beginning at an
eighth of a penny in the pound and rising to twopence, on
estates worth £5,000 or more. Absentee owners paid a further
20 per cent.

The tax was popular with small farmers, on whom the previous
property tax had fallen heavily. Six-sevenths of the landowners
escaped the new tax altogether. But Ballance did not abolish the
tax on improvements, because he could not see how to raise
enough revenue without it.[1] Small farmers with 'improvements'
worth less than £300 were exempt, however.

The graduated land tax, mild as it now seems, was, Reeves
wrote, 'greeted as a measure of revolution'.[2] It was intended to
discourage the holding of large estates, to 'burst them up', in
fact, and it reflected, however distantly, the most radical
theories of the time. As Reeves wrote, 'the doctrines of the land-
nationalisers and single-taxers were accepted to the extent of
distinguishing between real estate and personal property as
subjects for taxation.'[3]

None of the Liberal ministers were 'single taxers'. Ballance
told a deputation of 'single taxers' that he sympathized, but
could not 'go too fast' with the land tax.[4] Reeves wanted to go
much farther than Ballance: to remove the tax on improvements
and to tax large estates more heavily.[5] For the first, though not
the last time, the cabinet would not join him. But later in the year
Ballance hinted that he had not forgotten his earlier advocacy
of land nationalization, when he told an Auckland audience
that if the land tax proved the first step towards nationalization,
so much the better.[6]

Ballance and McKenzie both expressed their opinion, at this
time, that the remaining Crown lands should be kept in public
ownership and leased, not sold absolutely. This was not saying
much, for most of the good land was already held as freehold.
But they qualified even that statement by saying that among
many people 'the sentiment of freehold was deeply ingrained';

---

[1] N.Z. Times, 24 May 1893, Reeves.
[2] W. P. Reeves, State Experiments in Australia and New Zealand, London, 1902, i,
p. 260.   [3] Ibid., p. 259.
[4] PD, 1891, 71, p. 199.
[5] For Reeves's views, see PD, 1891, 73, pp. 158 ff.; N.Z. Times, 24 May 1893.
[6] PD, 1892, 76, p. 573.

10

that the public needed to be 'educated' to the value of leasehold before the Government could insist on such a policy.[1] Consequently they disappointed the thousands of land tenure reformers (and Reeves) by leaving the tenure optional in the Land Bill of 1891. It permitted land selectors the option of acquiring up to 640 acres of good land on freehold tenure by paying cash, or on deferred payment, or on a perpetual (thirty-one year) lease with a rental of 5 per cent. of the capital value. The bill passed the House but the Legislative Council turned the perpetual lease into a conditional freehold. When McKenzie visited the gallery he heard 'the largest land owner in the colony ... the manager of a Land Company ... and ... the manager of a Financial Institution in Christchurch' busily 'picking his bill to pieces'[2]. The House declined to accept the amendments; a conference with the Council disagreed; and the bill was dropped. So was a settlements bill enabling the Government to repurchase estates for subdivision and leasing to small farmers.

During the debates on the land and taxation bills, Reeves aroused very bitter enmities. Even more than McKenzie (who probably hated banks more than the estates, and used to point out that thirteen companies owned 163 sheep runs[3]) Reeves detested the great estates. He was fond of describing how far one could walk in Canterbury, or down the East Coast of the North Island, countries of the sheep and a few sheep-kings, without seeing a human being; and of listing the names of the estate owners, including the Harpers and other old friends of his family.[4] In one debate he said that a fifth of the country was held in large holdings—a bigger proportion than the aristocratic estates in France before the revolution! 'I think these estates ... are a social pest, an industrial obstacle, and a bar to progress.' Scobie Mackenzie immediately charged him with calling the great landowners themselves 'social pests'. He said that Reeves himself had been associated with 'land-grabbing' speculators who had been unsuccessful. Once he found he would not inherit their estates he became a radical. This reference to his father, two months dead, upset Reeves a great deal. He had not shared

---

[1] *N.Z. Herald*, 12 Dec. 1891, Ballance; Reeves MSS, large clipping book, p. 118v; *Te Aroha News*, 16 March 1892. Cadman agreed—*N.Z. Herald*, 4 Nov. 1893.
[2] Reeves MSS, loc. cit.   [3] Ibid.
[4] e.g. PD, 1890, 67, pp. 204 ff.

in his father's land speculations (Scobie wrongly thought there
had been a family syndicate) and replied that he had never
bought a half-acre in his life. There was a storm. The Speaker
told Mackenzie he should make allowance for Reeves's natural
feelings. But though Scobie made a qualified apology, and was
criticized for his bad taste; though Sir John Hall explained that
he had noted down Reeves's exact words at the time, and that he
had called the estates, not their owners, 'pests'; the accusation
stuck.[1] Reeves's careful repetition of the phrase, in its original
context, in a later debate, merely served to fix it in his enemies'
minds.[2] It followed him for years and did him much harm.
Though others had used the term in almost the same sense in the
past,[3] from his lips it seemed a direct challenge, the slogan of the
threat that he posed to the squatters. The Rutherfords of North
Canterbury named a horse, which won the 1898 Grand
National, 'Social Pest'.

The bills introduced by Reeves in 1891 were almost all
'labour' bills. Most of them met the same fate as the land bills,
and aroused the same, almost hysterical, alarm among the
property owners. Over these, too, he personally inspired the
greatest suspicion. The Opposition laughed at such a man being
associated with labour legislation. Fergus repeated in the House a
canard circulating in the clubs that when Reeves 'came from
Home he went about clad in gaiters like an Irish squireen'—and
at least it was true that, when he went to work at Lowcliffe for a
short time he wore gaiters on horseback.[4] But they were
frightened. Behind the slight figure of the minister, in the
imagination of Conservatives (like Buckland, Duthie or Fergus),
ranged menacing ranks of revolutionary unionists, so recently
defeated on one front, now massing on another. It was useless for
Reeves to appeal for a cordial and co-operative reception for his
bills on the ground that they were not 'party' measures, but had
been introduced, in different forms, by Atkinson's ministry.[5]
The Employers Associations hated the compulsory clauses of the

1 PD, 1891, 71, pp. 191 ff., 244 ff.; 74, p. 990; *N.Z. Times*, 24 June 1891; *Evening News* (Napier), 27 June 1891.
2 PD, 1894, 85, p. 81.
3 e.g. PD, 1878, 29, p. 64: Wason: 'a man who does not improve his land is a political and social pest.'
4 PD, 1891, 73, pp. 481 ff.
5 PD, 1891, 72, p. 596.

bills, which at best, they said, amounted to meddlesome interference; at worst to the enslavement of the people.[1] The aim of the Shop Hours Bill, which restricted the hours of female employment, was to degrade women, said Buckland, and take away their liberty.[2] And Rolleston said of the labour bills (a year after the strikes), 'I think that they presume too much upon an antagonism of employers and employed, and too little upon that mutual understanding that ought to subsist between [them].'[3] They were no happier when Reeves replied to the constant criticism that he was setting class on class by observing that the Liberals wished to abolish class altogether.[4]

The Shop Hours Bill was fought in committee until three in the morning,[5] then thrown out by the Legislative Council when it had passed the House. So was his Workmen's Lien Bill. But he managed to secure several Acts to benefit the unionists: a Truck Act, forbidding workmen to be paid in goods; an Employers Liability Act, enabling workmen injured by defective machinery, or otherwise through the employers' carelessness, to recover fair damages; and, most important, a Factories Act. The latter restricted the hours of work of females and boys to 48 hours a week, and provided for the registration and inspection of all factories. It laid down detailed requirements about sanitation, ventilation and conditions of work. The bill was mutilated by the Legislative Council, but Reeves was eager for it to pass and insisted on a conference of both Houses, where a compromise was reached. As passed, Reeves claimed it was 'the most liberal and most advanced' factory act in the Empire.[6] A further labour bill dealing with industrial conciliation and arbitration was circulated among members, Employers Associations and Trade Unions. The employers were hostile, the government busy, and the bill was left for the next session.[7]

Although some bills passed, almost all the major measures were thrown out by the Legislative Council or so amended that the Government dropped them. The Government found that it had only four or five supporters in the upper house and eighteen or more opponents. They included the six new councillors ap-

---

[1] *N.Z. Times*, 8 July 1891.
[2] PD, 1891, 72, p. 584.
[3] Ibid., pp. 582, 593.
[4] PD, 1891, 74, p. 989.
[5] PD, 1891, 72, p. 586.
[6] PD, 1891, 71, p. 152; 74, *passim*.
[7] PD, 1891, 74, p. 484; *State Experiments*, ii, p. 105; *N.Z. Times*, 12 May 1892.

pointed by Atkinson and several decrepit old men appointed in
the eighteen-sixties and seventies. The Council was, Reeves said,
'to a certain extent, representative of senility'.[1] One of the Acts
passed in 1891 was a measure, which had been introduced by
the Atkinson Government, reforming the Council by introducing
seven-year instead of life appointments. But this did nothing
to solve the deadlock between the two Houses. During the recess,
Ballance advised the Governor, the Earl of Onslow, to appoint
twelve new councillors. Six councillors had died since the
government was formed and could be replaced: the other six
would balance Atkinson's appointments.

Onslow's sympathies all lay with the Conservatives. After the
election he had written to Atkinson, regretting his defeat and
commending the luxuries that the colonists had enjoyed while
he had been premier.[2] He thought the Liberals had no right to
'swamp' the Council, and would agree to only eight appointments. Ballance's explanations that even twelve would not give
the Liberals a majority; that, at present, their bills were not even
properly discussed in the upper house, were in vain; but he
would not accept the Governor's decision. When Onslow
departed in February, he left a memorandum to his successor,
Glasgow (who did not arrive until June) urging that he adopt
the same course as himself.[3] A year after the 1890 election the
Liberals seemed not much nearer to effective power than a year
before.

[1] PD, 1892, 77, p. 284.
[2] *The Richmond-Atkinson Papers*, ed. G. H. Scholefield, Wellington, 1960, ii, p. 575.
[3] AJHR, 1892, A-7, A-9.

9

NEW ENTERPRISES
1891–2

THWARTED in Parliament, the Liberal Government decided to 'go to the people'.[1] From the end of the session in September, until the next in June 1892, the ministers addressed a series of meetings throughout the country. They began in Wellington, where there was a bye-election in which a Liberal, William McLean, was standing against Harry (later Sir Francis) Bell, the son of one of the leaders of the old oligarchy. Bell was a prominent lawyer and much more able than his opponent, an auctioneer and stock-broker. Though Bell claimed to be standing as an 'independent', the election was fought on party lines. Both sides regarded it as very important. Ballance and Reeves organized the Liberal effort, and Reeves was energetic in speaking in support of McLean.

Early in November Dr. A. K. Newman, a Wellington M.H.R., wrote to Rolleston: 'yesterday Hon. W. P. Reeves came to me & in his bitter style wanted to know if I was really backing Bell. I offered him £30 to £10 on Bell as he would not take £20 to £10. He did not like to back out so he took this.'[2] Scobie Mackenzie was equally confident that Bell would win: McLean, he said, was 'an unpopular Scotch Jew—a regular 40 per center'. After a meeting in the Wellington Opera House in December he wrote to Rolleston: 'Reeves was desperately and most unusually poor. I feel quite sure he came to the theatre nervous about the reception he would get, and Providence left no room for courage in his carcase. The big cabbage thrown at him completely knocked him out of tune.' A press report of this incident gives a different impression. When a 'full-sized cabbage' landed on the platform, it says, 'Mr. Reeves welcomed the missile [as] the

---

[1] *Otago Daily Times*, 24 May 1893; Reeves MSS, large clipping book, p. 112v, clipping 8 Jan. 1892.
[2] Rolleston MSS, 8 Nov. 1891.

first shot from the Opposition camp, and said that as usual with attacks from that quarter it fell very wide of the mark.'[1]

Reeves's meetings were as successful as ever: he drew large, generally enthusiastic audiences to hear his denunciations of the Conservatives and their allies, the Wellington 'Triple Alliance'—the *Times*, the *Post* and the *Press*. The reason for the 'hullaballoo' raised against the Liberals, he told them, was simple: 'There is a class of people in New Zealand who have persuaded themselves they have a divine right to govern ... .' He confidently awaited 'the verdict of the future' as to whether 'the mass of the people' were capable of directing their own affairs. He defended the Government against the cry of 'class legislation'—their main reform, the new taxation, did not affect the workers, who paid virtually no taxes; the Liberal labour bills had not passed. He explained the Government's demand for new Legislative Council appointments. He denied that 'capital was being driven out of the country'. He strove, in these meetings as elsewhere, to sound reassuring to the middle class: 'We have not led any crusade against private property'; the Government was not 'Socialistic from the point of view of ... Karl Marx or the author of "Looking Backwards"'. He always spoke in respectful terms of Bell, who was one of his friends.

On election day a cartoon, labelled the 'Liberal Peepshow', was circulated, showing Reeves as Tom Fool pulling two ministerial wooden puppets, Ballance and McKenzie.[2] Reeves collected his £30. The Liberals won this as they had won every bye-election, with one exception, since 1890.

Ballance and Reeves took the lead in two other important moves. The Premier decided to form an active National Liberal Federation, with branches throughout the country, as leading Liberals had long urged. Grey had made one attempt in 1879. In May 1891, Stout had formed a 'National' Liberal Association, of which he was president, in Dunedin. Now Ballance took up the work in earnest. In November 1891 a young 'labour' member, T. L. Buick, was appointed organizing secretary with a salary of £250. Ballance became president.[3]

[1] Rolleston MSS, 15 Dec. 1891; *N.Z. Times*, 4 Dec. 1891.

[2] See *N.Z. Times*, Dec. 1891–Jan. 1892 on these meetings, and Reeves MSS, large clipping book, pp. 112 ff.

[3] Hamer, thesis, p. 357; LT, 11 June 1892; Ballance MSS, Ballance to Stout, 20 Nov. 1891; W. F. Gayner to Ballance, 15 April 1892.

Reeves helped to inaugurate a branch of the Federation at Napier in January 1892, and spoke to an enthusiastic audience.[1] At the first Wellington meeting he emphasized the need for political associations to maintain their activities between elections.[2] He also addressed the new Liberal Association in Christchurch.[3] The Conservatives responded by forming a National Political Association in Canterbury, led by the wealthy squatters like John Grigg, a Rangitikei Political Association led by Macarthur and Bryce, and other organizations. They wanted 'economy and honesty of administration', 'equitable' taxes, and stood for 'Freehold tenure against the nationalisation of the land'.[4]

Reeves took the initiative in founding a Liberal newspaper in Wellington. The New Zealand Times Company was floated to purchase the local paper of that name and its weekly, the *Mail*. Reeves became managing director, with a nominal fee. Ballance, William McLean, two union presidents and several Liberal businessmen became directors. The editor was R. A. Loughnan, who had edited the *Lyttelton Times*.[5] This new task took up a great deal of Reeves's time and energy. Relations between the 'labour' men and businessmen on the board were difficult. A year later, in February 1893, Reeves wrote to Ballance:

I patched up a truce with McDonald and Jellicoe last night under which Plimmer retires from the Board at the General Meeting and is replaced by a Labour man of my nomination—other Directors to remain as before. Arthur Warburton is angry with me for not pushing matters to extremes and getting the shareholders to remove McDonald and Jellicoe by an extraordinary general meeting. He says that we cannot go on with these two men on the Board and that he will not endure them longer. However mindful of your frequently expressed injunction to me to keep the peace with them I have made this last effort though I must express my honest belief that ultimately it must come to open war. Warburton's brother—the Public Trustee—thinks so too—very strongly. I have managed, by the way,

[1] *Hawkes Bay Herald*, 30 Jan. 1892; *Evening News* (Napier), 29 Jan. 1892.
[2] *N.Z. Times*, 5 July 1892.
[3] LT, 8 June 1892.
[4] PD, 1892, 76, pp. 146 ff.; *The Mercury*, 18 Jan. 1892, in Reeves MSS, large clipping book, p. 115. Like the Reform Associations of 1887, these bodies were ancestral to the Reform Party.
[5] *N.Z. Times*, 23, 25 Feb., 26 April 1892; *Evening News* (Napier), 7 April 1893.

PLATE 4

a. W. P. Reeves and his family, *c.* 1908

b. Group portrait of the Ballance Cabinet, 1892
Back row, from left, Cadman, Carroll, McKenzie, Reeves
Front row, Seddon, Ballance, Buckley, Ward

to place some more shares so that the register is now up to 6013. It has taken us a long time to get over that 6000 hasn't it?[1]

Though he wrote little for the *New Zealand Times*, it gave Reeves a new interest at a time when his connexion with the *Lyttelton Times* was almost completely severed. In April 1892 he was given three months' notice (according to the Company minutes) as an 'economy measure'. In June, on the day Parliament met, the editor, Samuel Saunders, wrote asking him as a final service to telegraph a leader on the financial statement, as he had in 1891. He asked Reeves to send it so that it would reach Christchurch by the time the statement was presented to the House, and offered 'to regard it as sacred' and to 'sub-edit and re-write' only after that time. On 1 July, after using the article, he wrote again:

Many thanks for your admirable leader. I thought that under the circumstances (which had arisen after you wrote) it was better to omit comparisons which cd. be construed into reflections upon Sir Harry Atkinson's Administration; but I trust that I did not spoil the general sense of your article. I re-wrote the leader, as promised, and only people immediately concerned (Malet and Hull) are aware that it came from you. I hope this mild deception—which of course obtained for me considerable Kudos—will meet with your approval; it will certainly save you from any reproach.

I sincerely hope that we have not entirely lost the services of your pen; but be that as it may I hope you will do me the justice to believe that I shall always be happy to do what I can to promote your political interests.

Reeves sent the two letters to Montgomery, with these comments:

By the way talking about the Financial Statement I enclose a little note which is a sequel to the one I sent you ten days ago. It is simply what I expected viz. that those gentlemen promptly took credit for my article on the Statement. There was no need for Saunders to re-copy the article at all. It was not in my handwriting: Ballance knew I was sending it: Saunders knew that Ballance knew: I sent it under seal to Saunders not to be opened till the Statement was telegraphed to the paper.

[1] Ballance MSS. The men referred to were John Plimmer—a businessman, E. G. Jellicoe—a lawyer, and Kennedy Macdonald and Arthur Warburton—two brokers. James K. Warburton ran the Public Trust Office and drafted the 'advances to settlers' scheme.

Certainly Saunders is an astute man. You remember that the reason given for dismissing me was that Saunders was going to write the 'week' in the *Canterbury Times* now done by Loughnan. However Loughnan has now received order to go on writing the 'week' as usual.

However I am now done with the *Lyttelton Times*. My time is up today. I shall not answer Saunders letter much as I feel tempted to give him a 'stinger'.[1]

Though the new Lyttelton Times Company directors may have wanted to be rid of Reeves there were other considerations. Certainly there was need for economy: Loughnan was also dismissed in August.

During this year and the next Reeves was marginally involved in an extraordinary situation which must have few parallels in the history of journalism. A group of well-known squatters, C. G. and C. H. Tripp and J. B. Acland, presently joined by a Christchurch businessman, Sir Henry Wigram, paid the call on F. J. Kimbell's shares in the Lyttelton Times Company and then acquired them. It was evident that they would alter the *Times*'s pro-Liberal policy. Under the Company's new articles of association (drawn up after the 'call' was paid), the directors refused to consent to the transfer of shares. A long legal battle went on until the new shareholders signed an agreement not to alter the political policy of the Company's papers. Then the existing shareholders, including Reeves, agreed to register their names.[2] Thereafter he had almost no connexion with his old firm, though he wrote leading articles again for the *Times* in 1894 and 1895,[3] and owned six shares until mid 1895.

Before the session of 1892 the portfolios held by the ministers were rearranged, a change explained in a letter Reeves wrote to the Premier on 1 May:

Dear Mr. Ballance

With reference to our conversation about the proposed rearrangement of portfolios I should like to express my views to you on paper.

---

[1] W. H. Montgomery MSS.

[2] Lyttelton Times Co. minutes; interview with Mr. A. G. Henderson; *N.Z. Times*, 1 April 1893.

[3] Interview with the late Mr. G. G. S. Robison, Reeves's brother-in-law, and his private secretary in 1895.

When I consented to give up the Justice Department I did so only because it seemed to me that henceforth that Department ought when practicable to be held by a Minister having some special knowledge of Native Affairs.

I thought the arrangement by which I should take the Colonial Secretaryship in exchange was fair inasmuch as the Colonial Secretary, being leader in the Upper House, could afford to relinquish a portfolio.

As the Hon. Mr. Buckley did not see his way to do that I am now asked to give up one of my two portfolios without receiving any equivalent position of trust and importance.

While I cannot say that I at all relish this I am not prepared to decline to take a step the advantages of which to the Cabinet seem plain to me. If therefore Mr. Cadman and the other Ministers agree that it is highly desirable I should give up the Justice Department I will do so in the interest of the Government.

I am prepared to take charge of the Stamps but must respectfully decline either Charitable Aid, Customs, or the Printing Office.

If you could carry out your suggestion and appoint me Minister of Labour I think on the whole that would be a desirable thing though I am not anxious to press for it if there is any objection.

In conclusion I would like to suggest to you that if convenient I should wish to be relieved this session of as much of the work of debate as you think could be taken from me without in any way incommoding you. The Ministry is strong all round in debating power and should be stronger now that Mr. Carroll has joined. I felt the strain last session very much and rather fear the coming tax upon a health which has never been very strong. Family and private matters, of which you know something, have told on me a good deal. Moreover I have now the N.Z. *Times* to attend to. At the same time I don't wish to shirk my fair share of work or to appear lacking in personal loyalty to yourself.

Yours very truly
W. P. Reeves

P.S. I would take Marine if the Cabinet wished it but would rather not.[1]

Reeves became Minister of Labour and Commissioner of Stamp Duties as well as Minister of Education. Edward Tregear became the first Secretary of Labour.[2] Seddon took over the Marine as well as the Mines and Public Works Departments.

Reeves was not made Minister of Labour simply to save his

---

[1] Ballance MSS.   [2] *N.Z. Times*, 10, 21 May 1892.

face. The new title accurately represented the nature of his duties. Education had become a secondary concern. Though he continued to praise the education system as the country's most precious possession, and to emphasize the connexion between education and democracy, that system was no longer threatened. On the other hand, it seemed almost impossible to extend it. He several times said that he looked forward to making secondary schooling available to the poor, but his fierce insistence on non-borrowing and cautious finance prevented him from tackling the question. He was quite frank: the country could not afford it.[1] Had he tried to extend free education beyond the primary level, he would certainly have failed. Apart from McKenzie, none of the other ministers were much interested in educational reform. Reeves once wrote that Ballance's views on education were 'reactionary';[2] and certainly he was satisfied to leave it alone. His only suggestion for reform seemed to Reeves retrograde. Like Perceval, Ballance was willing to give some degree of state aid to Catholics, who refused, where possible, to send their children to state schools. Reeves thought it was 'simply a case of denominationalism against secularism', and the Premier did not press the issue.[3]

Fundamentally Reeves agreed with his colleagues that other reforms were more urgent. Consequently, though his education portfolio took up much of his time, his administration was devoted to painstaking efforts to reform the structure and improve the quality of primary teaching. He found that the national system of education which he thought desirable did not, except in a superficial sense, exist. There were thirteen systems, managed by Education Boards over which he had little influence. The inspection of schools was organized by the Boards and there was no way of ensuring anything like a uniform standard, or even of accurately comparing existing standards. Teachers were badly paid and had no uniform system of salaries. The inspectors, not the teachers, decided on the promotion of children through the standards, an influence blighting on all initiative among teachers or headmasters and encouraging a mechanical uniformity in teaching. Reeves patiently devoted himself to solving such problems. He travelled round the Maori schools,

---

[1] *Wanganui Herald*, 13 Feb. 1891; PD, 1891, 72, p. 211.
[2] *Long White Cloud*, p. 370.   [3] PD, 1891, 72, pp. 268 ff.

trying to improve the standard of English teaching. He passed, in 1891, a school committees Election Act. His work in the Education Department was hard and often unrewarding.[1] But closer to his heart were his labour bills.

The situation of the Government did not improve with the arrival of the new Governor. Glasgow took a high view of his prerogative. Appointments to the upper house were, he maintained, an 'imperial matter', vested in him as the Queen's representative. The Liberals' demand for twelve new Councillors was an 'unconstitutional interference with the liberties of the Legislative Council'. Since one Councillor had died, he agreed to raise Onslow's bid of eight to nine, but would go no higher even when another Councillor resigned and the Speaker, old Sir Harry Atkinson, died. ('The Major' left the chair, went to his room, told his friends he had 'got his marching orders' and died almost at once.)

Ballance was in a difficult position. He could bow to the Governor (and the Conservatives). He could resign. In the latter case, if no one else could form a government backed by a majority of the House, the Governor would have to accept him as premier on his own terms. Ballance wanted to take this choice, but his friends dissuaded him. Perhaps some of the ministers doubted the reliability of their followers. If a significant number of Liberals could be induced to support an alternative government, in the fashion of politicians before 1890, resignation would be a disaster. Eventually Ballance decided, and Glasgow agreed, to refer the question to the Colonial Office for decision. This submission to imperial authority was denounced by the Conservatives and by Grey.[2] But Ballance won. The Colonial Office failed to see that the appointment of twelve councillors would 'swamp' the Council, and the Secretary of State rebuked Glasgow for regarding the difference between nine and twelve appointments as justification for declining to act on the advice of ministers.[3]

Sir George Grey, who had been a governor of four colonies,

[1] See LT, 11 June 1892; *N.Z. Times*, 24 March 1891, 18 July 1892; PD, 1894, 84, pp. 602–4, for some details.

[2] PD, 1892, 77, pp. 73, 165, 248 ff.

[3] AJHR, 1892, A-7, A-9; *N.Z. Times*, 22 June, 18 Aug., 27 Sept. 1892.

hated anyone else being one and had his own notion of how to deal with such situations. He wanted the country to choose its own governor. Reeves had his last gentle brush with Grey over his Elective Governors Bill in 1892. He was extremely courteous to the old man, but feared that an elected governor would become an active politician and said he would support the proposal only if the governor's powers were clearly defined. Grey thought the goal of a governorship would stimulate the ambitions of colonial youth. Reeves believed local ambition was already strong. He conceded that there was something in what Grey said, but he felt: 'There is something higher in this argument, and that is that it [an elective governorship] should act as a stimulant to a feeling of patriotism and solidarity as New-Zealanders—that feeling which actuates men who feel that they belong to a nation, and are part of that nation.'[1]

The old governor and the young colonial minister each, in his way, believed in the desirability of 'building up a national feeling in New Zealand', but Reeves would not follow. The Bill was defeated by 28 to 27 on the second reading. Seddon voted with Grey.

The Colonial Office decision arrived in September and in October a dozen new councillors were appointed, including William Montgomery (who in July 1893 joined the Government as Minister without portfolio, an appointment generally credited to Reeves) and John Rigg, the president of the Wellington Trades and Labour Council. But the 1892 session of Parliament had just ended, so the new appointments came too late to save the Liberal bills.

Though, in 1892, the Government forced through most of its important measures, the Legislative Council was still 'murderous'. It blocked Reeves's conciliation and arbitration bill and the electoral bill, which would have introduced women's suffrage, by making amendments unacceptable to the Government. The Opposition in the lower house made very effective use of stone-walling. As Reeves said to a meeting in Christchurch:

They protracted the session to sixteen mortal weeks [nearly the longest that had occurred]; they made *Hansard* 25 per cent longer and

[1] PD, 1892, 77, pp. 190-1.

50 per cent more dismal; they nearly killed two Ministers [Ballance and McKenzie], and they prevented the discussion of a certain number of useful measures.... The seven most garrulous members of the Opposition last session spoke about 890 columns of *Hansard* between them. One gentleman spoke 88 columns ... another, 146; and one, the flower of the flock, 244 columns. Two hundred and forty-four columns of *Hansard* were equal to 52 yards 2 feet, which might not be a very great distance to run, but it was a mighty distance to talk.... There were, besides, interminable discussions in Committee, which were not reported; for instance, those over the Land Bill, which occupied days and nights... .[1]

The most important modification to the Liberals' programme in 1892 was not, however, forced on the ministers by the Opposition or the Legislative Council, but, at least in part, arose from division in their own ranks. Though Ballance and McKenzie believed in the merits of leasehold tenure, they were more convinced of the need to encourage closer settlement. They wanted to reach Goldsmith's ideal state, when 'every rood of ground maintains its man'. The ultimate, irresistible driving force behind their desire for land reform was not their intellectual adherence to the ideal of public ownership, but the intense belief, almost universal in New Zealand, that the land offered the possibility of a life virtuous, manly and independent.[2] To 'get men on the land' was a solution proffered for unemployment and urban poverty or industrial strife, which might be an alternative to Reeves's labour reforms or a measure supporting them. To get on the land was the yearning of thousands of working men. That ambition lay behind the demand for cheap money, for taxation to break up the estates, for government repurchase and subdivision of the estates. It had a political power far greater than the ideal of leasehold; one ultimately hostile to leasehold— for should not yeomen hold their land on freehold tenure? Forced to choose between close settlement and state ownership, few of the Liberals would hesitate.

McKenzie's 1892 Land Bill included a fifty-year renewable lease, but in introducing it he announced his willingness to accept a *permanent* lease, which he presently interpreted to mean

[1] LT, 15 Dec. 1892.
[2] Cf. L. J. Hume, 'Working Class Movements in Sydney and Melbourne before the Gold Rushes'. *Historical Studies*, 9, 35, Nov. 1960.

a 999-year lease without revaluations, whereby the state lost its
share in future rising land values. This 'lease-in-perpetuity' had
been pressed on him by Ballance, who was sure that the
Legislative Council would not pass a renewable lease (it had
three times amended or rejected it when the House had approved), and was not certain that it would even pass in the
House, where six or seven Liberals believed in the freehold. The
two men succeeded in inducing the cabinet and their party to
acquiesce. Reeves did so 'with a very heavy heart', being overruled, and defended the new tenure, which was in effect a
freehold in a leasehold wrapper, as well as he could: it was the
best they could get through; it was a good tenure, though not as
good as the short renewable lease in the 1891 Land Bill. But he
was not convinced that the Government did have to choose
between the leasehold and encouraging closer settlement. The
pure Liberal milk was being watered more, and more readily,
than he liked.[1]

New Zealand's first Minister of Labour (the first, it was said,
in the Empire) got a further taste of heavy political fire, which he
staunchly withstood. His Labour Bureau was denounced for
'flooding the market' with Australian immigrants. This was
untrue: the country had a small net balance of immigrants over
emigrants mainly because the 'exodus' of the late eighties had
declined suddenly. He was denounced for lowering the dignity
of the Bench by appointing three working men (including
Sandford) as J.Ps. In fact he was very fair in such appointments.
He consulted Opposition leaders like Rolleston, and accepted
some of their suggestions. He gave satisfaction to the Catholics
by appointing some Catholic J.Ps.[2]

The obstructive tactics of the Opposition forced him to drop a
Labour Department bill. The Legislative Council severely
amended a revised Factories bill and his Contractors' and
Workmen's Lien bill, which sought to make better provision for
the payment of contractors and workmen. They passed after a
conference of representatives of both Houses arranged com-
promises. He had more trouble with his Shops and Shop

[1] PD, 1892, 76, pp. 522-3, 547, 574-5; 1894, 85, pp. 63, 83-84, 95. It will be noted
that McKenzie's explanation in 1894 does not square with his introductory remarks
in 1892. On Reeves's views, see also LT, 15 Dec. 1892; *Auckland Star*, 2 May 1894.
[2] PD, 1892, 77, pp. 552-3; LT, 15 Dec. 1892; Rolleston MSS, Reeves to Rolleston,
19 Feb. 1892.

Assistants bill, a milder version of that of 1891. Reeves wanted
to close all shops on one half day a week, which caused an outcry
('a system of police inspection'). The Council hacked the bill
about so much that he did not know if it would work, but he
accepted their amendments, which gave shop assistants a weekly
half holiday while allowing the shops to remain open, and
restricted working hours of women and minors. He pledged
himself to reintroduce the bill in 1893.[1] His Industrial Conciliation and Arbitration Bill passed the House and two readings in
the Council, which sent it to a special committee. When the
Committee 'did almost nothing with it', the Council cut out
twenty-four clauses relating to the Court of Arbitration, and
refused all compromise at a conference. The Government
dropped it.[2]

This was, Reeves confessed, his 'pet measure'. There was
nothing to which he had given so much thought since 1890 as the
prevention of strikes and the protection of trade unionists. He
had studied the literature of labour problems and the legislation
of other countries, and weighed the advantages of various
methods of conciliation. His draft bill of 1890 had been endlessly
revised, in consultation with trade unionists, his colleagues, and
Edward Tregear. Tregear made many suggestions on this, as on
other labour bills, but Reeves did much of the drafting himself,
with the help of experts such as Judge Kettle.[3]

Conciliation and arbitration were being discussed in Europe
at that time. Australian unionists had several times, in the
eighteen-seventies and eighties, advocated the establishment of
conciliation boards.[4] Otago unionists had gone farther and,
before the Sweating Commission of 1889 and during the election,
argued for *compulsory* arbitration.[5] At about that time, Reeves
had come to agree with them. But compulsory arbitration had
been practised nowhere in the world (except, he said in 1893,

---

[1] PD, 1892, 77, pp. 106–7; 78, *passim*.

[2] Reeves MSS, large clipping book, p. 121; PD, 1893, 81, p. 378.

[3] Interview with Mr. G. G. M. Mitchell, who worked in the Labour Department
later, but knew Tregear and the other officials, and saw the files; also Ballance MSS,
Reeves to Ballance, 28 Feb. 1893.

[4] R. N. Ebbels, *The Australian Labour Movement 1850–1907*, Sydney, 1960, p. 96;
C. M. H. Clark, *Select Documents in Australian History 1851–1900*, Sydney 1955,
vol. ii, p. 740.

[5] J. D. Salmond, 'The History of the New Zealand Labour Movement', unpub.
thesis, Otago University, pp. 154–6; AJHR, 1890, H-5.

in the Territory of Wyoming),[1] so he could find little guidance in the experience of others. The British Acts were dead letters; the Victorian Act useless. The most successful practical measures appeared to be the voluntary boards of conciliation and arbitration in Massachusetts and the *Conseils des Prud'hommes*, which had settled thousands of trade disputes in France since 1806. Their decisions were sometimes legally binding, but they had no power over wages—and hence none over the biggest disputes.[2] Reeves had little opinion of Downie Stewart's bill of 1890. He derived one or two provisions of his bill from a New South Wales Act. Others were suggested by a draft compulsory arbitration bill submitted to a Royal Commission in New South Wales in 1890 by C. C. Kingston, himself a gentleman radical and a lawyer, who later accused Reeves of legislative plagiarism.[3] But his bill, in the end, was mainly an original product of his own mind, adapting his own and others' ideas to local circumstance.

Reeves's bill outlined a system of conciliation and arbitration much more comprehensive than any in existence.[4] District boards of conciliation, representing employers and unions, with an independent chairman, were to hear evidence on industrial disputes and make awards. Reeves believed that the majority of disputes would be settled in these boards, but if agreement proved impossible, any party to a dispute, or the conciliation board itself, could appeal to an arbitration court. The court was, in the original bill, to be presided over by a district judge or a supreme court judge, assisted by two assessors elected by the employers' associations and trades union federations. The court could, if it wished, give an award with legal force, breaches of which were punishable by heavy fines. The boards and assessors were to be elected only by unions registered under the Act (if it became law), but the Court was to have power over all other trade unions registered under the Trade Union Act. The Act would not apply to unorganized labour.

He was praised by opponents for the 'studious moderation' with which he introduced his bill; for the care he had given to its preparation. He frankly conceded that it was 'a measure ... of an

---

[1] PD, 1893, 81, p. 379.   [2] PD, 1892, 77, pp. 27 ff.

[3] *Auckland Star*, 6 March 1903; cf. *State Experiments*, ii, pp. 98–99.

[4] For Reeves's views, see PD, 1891, 71, pp. 82–83; 1892, 77, pp. 27 ff.; 78, *passim*; Reeves MSS, large clipping book, pp. 121–2.

experimental kind'. He defended the controversial compulsory element by arguing that voluntary conciliation had generally failed and that he could not see how it could work: 'All the older writers, especially in England, seem to be of opinion that arbitration and conciliation will be of no use unless ... altogether voluntary. On the other hand there is a growing feeling, especially in America, that that is not enough, and that, if you are to prevent strikes, you must arm your Court with greater power than that.' He had sought a middle course. All awards would not be binding, but the court could make them binding when it wished.

One or two Opposition members supported the Bill, notably William Russell, who was very sympathetic to labour reforms. But, one after another, Rolleston, Hall, Bruce, Duthie, and, in the Legislative Council, Downie Stewart, attacked the compulsory clauses, while upholding a purely voluntary conciliation. It should be added however, that the Bill aroused relatively little interest. Only twenty-one Members heard the beginning of Reeves's speech, and only thirty-nine the conclusion.[1] His shop hours Bill aroused far more heat. It is, moreover, uncertain what support he had in the country, among unionists. Though some backed him, there was much difference of opinion.[2]

Despite the relative calm, by the time he had finished with his favourite measure he undoubtedly felt like the 'Man with a Bill' in *In Double Harness*:

> For of objects deserving of pity,
> Meet subjects for lachrymose ditty,
>   Who wrangle or yawn
>   From noon until dawn
> In caucus, debate, or committee,
> Of all chosen victims of ill,
> All targets for spite and ill-will,
>   The sorriest sight,
>   The unluckiest wight,
> Is the member who fathers a Bill.

And, like the Bill in that 'Lay of Legislation', it was 'slain in cold blood by the Lords'.

[1] PD, 1893, 79, p. 166.
[2] See, e.g., the evidence of J. A. Millar and other unionists to the Sweating Commission, AJHR, 1890, H-5, pp. 11, 14, 15, 55.

PORTRAITS OF THE MINISTER
1892

MANY of Reeves's best speeches at this time were made in the course of his private debate with Scobie Mackenzie. Until 1890 they had been 'real cronies', who were sometimes seen walking along Lambton Quay arm-in-arm, at a time when that custom was dying out.[1] But now a marked bitterness had turned friendly rivalry into an 'oratorical vendetta', perhaps since Scobie's unfortunate reference to William Reeves in June 1891. Nevertheless, whoever spoke second usually began with friendly praise of the other's speech.

Both men had sharp, inquisitive faces. Neither had an impressive or resonant voice. Reeves's voice was English, Scobie's Scottish. Reeves's voice was generally low, Scobie's more studied and oratorical, though both were sometimes 'jerky' in delivery. Reeves's speech was rapid—rapid, on one occasion, 'beyond the experience of the sharpest note-takers'.[2] He was called 'fidgety'. His enemy, 'Phiz', said he popped about 'like a parched pea on a hot pan'. But what his speeches lacked in quality of sound or delivery, they more than gained from the intense force of personality. He could draw his audience to him, dominate it and carry it off.

Scobie was noted for his ability to invite an interjection and then flatten his critic with a prepared rejoinder; in general for prepared speeches. Reeves was brilliant at the unprepared reply when, 'swollen with thought', he let his words run on, though it was on such occasions that he ran the risk of saying more than he ought. Then he expended 'a fearful amount of nervous energy',

---

[1] *Evening Post*, 24 May 1932, 'Memories of W. P. Reeves' by F. W. W. The reporter may possibly have confused Scobie with Thomas Mackenzie, who was a friend of Reeves. Once, when Reeves and he were swimming in Wellington harbour, they rescued the occupants of a swamped dinghy ('Memoirs').

[2] *N.Z. Times*, 15 July 1893. Reeves's clipping books contain many descriptions of his (and Scobie's) speeches.

and people guessed that he 'suffered for it afterwards'. 'He slashes without mercy and with very little prudential calculation, so that he is a dangerous foe, and at least an equally dangerous friend', a parliamentary reporter wrote. 'He is sensitive, excitable and irritable, with a constitution unfit to sustain the wear and tear of such a mind. But his excitability adds to the effect and power of his best speeches, and evidently supplies him for the time being with great resource of imagination and happy facility of expression.'

Beneath the sword-play of personality and word, between fairly matched antagonists, lay the deeper drama of squatter fighting hard, though in retreat, against the landless poor.

By 1892 Reeves had provided Mackenzie with a good number of targets: his cry that he would serve 'under King Harry'; his 'social pests'; the Governor's speeches, written by Reeves yearly while he was a minister, in which he 'sought to combine discretion with optimism', to 'unite the style of a diplomatic despatch with the spirit of an auctioneer's advertisement'.[1] But Reeves delivered many a riposte that stayed in the minds of his audience. Once, when his right to speak on farming was questioned, Reeves offered to bet that he could skin a sheep faster than Scobie. (He had skinned them daily at Lowcliffe during an epidemic of footrot.[2])

One of Reeves's most successful onslaughts on Mackenzie was made during the debate on the Financial Statement on 21 July 1892. His critics said Scobie was never in the House unless he could shine; but when he spoke, everyone wanted to hear him. On this occasion a reporter wrote:

When the word 'Scobie' is wafted round the galleries there is a rush to get within view of the sport. Mount Ida [Mackenzie] is armed with a neat sheaf of papers, blue, white, and grey, pinned together in one corner.... It is the Mount Ida arsenal, which remains in custody of his left, while he keeps up the war on the enemy with his right.... Every now and then he transfers the arsenal to the other hand, and then his left devotes attention to the enemy.

Like most political speeches, the printed version of his speech offers little that is memorable. A denunciation of the Liberals'

---

[1] Reeves MSS, 'Memoirs'.
[2] Interview with the late W. H. Montgomery.

pretence of retrenchment: 'as fast as public servants in a high position were removed in a striking and dramatic fashion ... all the nooks and crannies of the public service were quietly filled up with the followers and hangers-on of the Government.' A detailed survey of finances, with much hansarding of ministers. A denunciation of a letter by Seddon about a bridge: 'a meditated act of unblushing public corruption'. When ordered by the Speaker to withdraw, Scobie enquired innocently how it was possible to impeach a minister for corruption if the word was unparliamentary. His speech moved from quiet detail, to emphatic denunciation, to 'sarcastic banter', to his peroration on 'Liberalism without liberty'. Reeves was not spared. Scobie began by saying that he had waited for three days in the hope of following him, and later remarked the irony that the Minister of Labour was 'probably the only man in the House who never did a day's labour in his life' except that he 'laboured as hard as any man could to set the labourers of the colony against the employers'. During the strike, not 'one solitary unpopular truth did the Minister of Labour ever utter', but encouraged the strikers until the strike had spent itself, when 'the honourable gentleman, true to the instincts of a pallid nature, retired frightened from the storm he had himself aroused.' Then, Scobie alleged, Reeves urged the strikers to make peace. When he concluded, some of the Liberals joined in the congratulations.

Reeves was up immediately:

It is said of the British army that its course through the deserts of Egypt could be traced by the empty soda-water and brandy bottles it left in its track. Just so the honourable gentleman's track could be traced through the pages of *Hansard* by the epithets he has used.... Everything is 'cadging', 'unblushing', 'vicious' ... except where it represents 'corruption', 'ignorance', 'fustian' and 'sycophancy'.

He slyly represented his opponent as a comic character, and related how Scobie had demonstrated to an audience at Kaitangata the fearful consequences of travelling in a train fired with West Coast coal. On seeing Scobie's blackened hands, Reeves alleged, a miner observed that 'if he only blacked his face ... he'd be the best Christy minstrel in New Zealand.' Scobie was, Reeves said, 'the corner man of debate. He is the

Ethiopian humourist, the sable songster, and the African delineater of the Tory troupe. So perfect is his art that when he is speaking we have but to shut our eyes and we see a vision of exaggerated shirt-collars, striped unmentionables, and burnt cork. We feel that the honourable gentleman ought to begin with the banjo and conclude with a clog-dance.'

While Reeves 'revelled in the idea' the House 'became very lively' and the Liberals shouted with delight. Rolleston he pictured as the serious and ponderous 'Mister Johnson', while Scobie was the capering 'Bones, Sambo, or Charlie', who unsuccessfully tried to explain things to him. But Scobie quite misunderstood his rôle; took comedy, or at best melodrama, for tragedy. Having 'studied the tremendous language of Sheridan when he denounced the oppression of India, the brilliant periods of Burke when he lamented the French revolution.... He comes here with all this oratory jingling in his head, and in tremendous tones and ornate language he tells us about the dismissal of some subordinate servant in some subordinate department ....'

Few were spared. James Allen was 'a paragon of certainty, cocksureness and positiveness'. In Rolleston's speeches, 'Lamentation, thunder and sabbatarianism seemed to be the flavouring tone.' He out-hansarded Scobie by quoting one of his rival's earlier speeches, which he had now contradicted, and then identifying the speaker. He reviewed the finances and answered criticisms. When supper time came he evidently wished to continue, and both sides of the House willingly agreed. He concluded a speech lasting an hour and forty minutes with a long examination of the rôle of the state. Neither he nor his colleagues were communists, as they were labelled. But socialism was another matter. He did not expect that the theories of Marx, Lassalle or Bellamy would ever be 'exactly realised'. But he was sure that 'Humanity does not favour individualism.' As the world grew 'in civilisation and in education' he believed that the functions of the state would grow. He ridiculed the claim that the rural settlers did not want government interference. The recent resolutions of an Agricultural Conference, he showed, were a long list of requests for state aid. And it was natural enough—a settler in the bush needed the help of the community to survive. 'I believe in the State because the State is now the people, and the people the State, and because the people are orderly and well educated.'

He preferred, he confessed, a benevolent despotism to an uneducated democracy, but he expressed his faith in his country-men. And concluded by remarking that at least Scobie, unlike some of his colleagues, but like the Roman of old, did not 'despair of the Republic'.

Members rushed to shake his hands. One reporter thought such satire and impassioned eloquence combined had seldom been heard in the House. He had held the floor and the galleries completely. Even Fish admitted that Reeves had had the better of Mackenzie. He was less bitter, more eloquent, more telling. Nothing in Scobie's speech had the depth of Reeves's perora-tion.[1]

Though he was enjoying his new position, in some photo-graphs taken about this time Reeves looks peaky and slightly peevish. Many reporters tried to describe his appearance and personality. Though 'dark', he was also 'pale' or 'sallow', and was said to have 'a firm mouth and dreamy eyes'. He was called 'caustic', 'tart', 'cynical', or 'sneering'. He had, it was thought, a tendency to 'superciliousness and intellectual hauteur'; 'a bilious disposition' or 'a bilio-nervous temperament'. Such unfriendly descriptions, even when substantially discounted, give some notion of the impression he made on some people. One journalist came near the mark in suggesting that Reeves probably ate too quickly, thinking of other things, and suffered from dyspepsia.[2] He was a man completely absorbed in his work, in his thoughts, who was often quite abstracted in manner, and oblivious of his company—or their feelings. His sister-in-law, Miss Georgie A. Robison, relates that, asked at table if he wanted bread or the like, he would accept but not eat it until they 'woke him up'. Once he served himself soup first and started drinking it without serving the family.

Partly, at least, for the same reason, he was not self-conscious about his appearance. His 'incorrigible neglect of dress', he conceded in his 'Memoirs', got him 'into some awkward little plights'. Late in 1891, for instance, 'a tall, grave, kindly-looking

---

[1] PD, 1892, 76, p. 13 ff.; Reeves MSS, small clipping book, pp. 122–3; *N.Z. Times*, 22 July 1892.
[2] *Hawkes Bay Herald*, 30 Jan. 1892.

English tourist of aristocratic bearing' met him coming out of the parliamentary library and enquired whether he could see Parliament House. Reeves showed him round and the gentleman produced a sixpence. Reeves nearly took it, to hang on his watch-chain, but a Messenger drew near and he fled. The tourist was the Earl of Meath, founder of Empire day, who learned who his guide had been and called next day. In his *Memories of the Nineteenth Century*, many years later, he recalled the Reeveses' kindness.

It was asperity, not kindliness, which most often impressed his associates in 1892. He did not strive to please. He suffered fools badly. Few New Zealanders have more fully embodied the New Zealand ideal of the all-rounder, but he lacked what is commonly supposed its product—an easy, genial personality. 'Phiz' wrote in the Christchurch *Press*:

> Of his genuine cleverness, his capacity for hard and sustained intellectual toil no one can have the slightest doubt. In all that regards education he is head and shoulders above his fellow Ministers. He has the brain to conceive, the energy and knowledge necessary to carry out difficult affairs, and he has some pluck. But he has not tact, and he does not inspire affection or even personal enthusiasm.... It may be that the knowledge of this fact has ... made him bitter.[1]

Like most of the press comment on Reeves, this is hostile—published, indeed, in the newspaper of the Canterbury gentry. It expresses a dislike largely inspired by the feeling that Reeves was a renegade, which sometimes appeared in another form—prophecies that he would mellow and become a conservative. But it remains true that such a view of Reeves was widespread, too generally believed, perhaps, to be quite misguided. There was, however, more to be said. Reeves's hot, hasty words were news. The Press often ignored evidence of generosity, tact, or a conciliatory manner. It was Reeves, in 1892, who successfully moved that the vote of censure on Bryce should be expunged from the journals of the House. Again, when Fergus apparently called Seddon a liar and Seddon threatened violence if he repeated his words outside the House, it was Reeves who stepped in and soothed them down.[2]

[1] 20 July 1892.
[2] PD, 1892, 76, p. 507; *N.Z. Times*, 10 Sept. 1892.

In the *New Zealand Graphic* in 1892[1] there appeared a
sympathetic portrait of Reeves written by 'Birdseye' (Mrs.
Bullock of Wanganui), which stressed his 'indomitable will, a
possession not often found in a frame so frail-looking', his
'buoyancy of temperament'. Among friends he was gay, witty—
'the most amusing and agreeable of companions'. It described
Maud, too, 'a pretty, girlish figure industriously employed in
needlework'—sitting in the Peeresses' Gallery: 'Mrs. W. P.
Reeves is a living protest against the gratuitous masculine
assumption that a liking for politics must of necessity have a
deteriorating effect upon woman. She is young and pretty, with
slightly reserved yet engaging manners.... She is fond of society,
and is possessed of the graces and accomplishments necessary
to adorn it.'

Though devoted to her husband and two daughters, she yet
felt 'a strong inclination towards political studies', and had
'from early girlhood been an enthusiastic advocate of female
suffrage'. Maud was, indeed, as unusual a cabinet minister's
wife as he was a minister. At twenty-seven, she was becoming a
formidable young woman whose tactful ease of manner often
smoothed her husband's relations with his colleagues and society
in general.

Though 'indomitable will' was too high-pitched, Reeves was
beginning to show one quality in which he surpassed his
colleagues—one which, looking at the ministers, an observer
would have been unlikely to discern. He was extremely determined to pass his bills in the shape he desired; extremely
unwilling to compromise beyond a certain point. He would
accept half a loaf one session; but he would demand the other
half the next. Unquestionably he felt a stronger desire to pass his
reforms than to hold power. He believed completely in their
cause: 'to do what we believe to be best for the advancement
and raising-up of the poorer and less fortunate of our fellow-
men'. The insults the Liberals received were nothing, he
consoled himself, in comparison with the sufferings of past
reformers. And saying these words, he turned to his Factory Act,
which had rescued women and children from foul air and filthy
surroundings: 'Think of the overwork, the life of degradation,
and the increasing wretchedness and misery from which that

[1] 27 Aug.

Act has rescued whole generations of workers to come. Surely that is consolation enough. If, as I think, we cannot enjoy popularity, or rank, or wealth, at any rate we can feel that we are doing good to our fellow-men.'[1]

Many of his opponents admitted that he was sincere. But to prefer principles to power is, in a politician, often a step to keeping the first and losing the second: he may gain more respect than votes. Reeves did not, in fact, pay the same attention to the politician's arts as some of his colleagues. Criticism, plain hostility, were mounting. He did little to assuage them, and was less equipped than his colleagues to stand the strain. He was, indeed, for a politician, extraordinarily thin-skinned. As Atack put it:

For a man who had been accustomed to use the rapier on his opponents ... the new Minister was surprisingly sensitive.... He was prone to take all hostile comment as a purely personal matter. In his first year or two I frequently used to receive a message asking me to see him. Going up to the Government Buildings expecting to receive a piece of news for circulation, I would find him with a newspaper cutting in front of him, containing some comment he disliked, and not always on himself, but merely directed at the Government generally. Sometimes he would ask me to publish a denial for him through the Press Association of which I was then Manager. Sometimes he was fuming to the extent of threatening a libel action. Never that I can remember were any of the attacks libellous which he, as a barrister, ought to have known. I had some trouble, occasionally, in persuading him to ignore them, pointing out that to start a libel action was just what his opponents would love to see him do. He did not actually go to that length, and by and by simmered down, but he never really got used to criticism.[2]

A misunderstanding in October 1892 shows that Reeves could be punctilious to a point near absurdity. Glasgow was going north to New Plymouth (by train) and then to Auckland (by boat). Ballance told him that Reeves was ready to accompany him as 'minister in attendance'. Glasgow thought it a pity to inflict this duty on Reeves 'so soon after the exhausting work of the session', and since Ballance agreed that it was unnecessary, the Governor asked him not to trouble Reeves. But the Executive

---

[1] PD, 1892, 78, pp. 185–6.
[2] *Christ's College Register*, cxxxx, Aug. 1932.

Council decided that a minister ought to go, and Glasgow then wrote to Ballance requesting Reeves's company. Reeves misunderstood what had occurred, and wrote to Ballance:

The very courteous letter written to you by His Excellency this morning has left me in a difficulty. Under any ordinary circumstances I should have had the greatest possible pleasure in complying without a moment's delay with His Excellency's request for my attendance. After what has passed however let me with the most absolute respect say this.— If I were on Monday to present myself as minister in waiting it would be with the uncomfortable impression that I was an official whose presence had not been originally desired but had been requested after certain representations had been made. I should feel this somewhat acutely and am convinced that if the position were explained to His Excellency he would with his customary kindness excuse me.[1]

Glasgow soothed him with an urbane note to Ballance explaining that it was not that he had not *wanted* Reeves, but that he had not wanted to *bother* him; that Reeves was 'therefore "the official whose presence was originally desired"'. Reeves went, and made his first speech in Auckland.

Some of the elements in Reeves's reputation and character were illustrated in another episode, which became widely known. At the beginning of 1893 two of his acquaintances offered to put him up for the Wellington Club. One was L. O. H. Tripp, a Cambridge graduate and barrister-at-law of the Inner Temple, who had been at Christ's with him for a time. Tripp was one of the family of squatters who had bought the *Lyttelton Times*. The other was Jim (later Sir James) Coates, of the National Bank. Reeves flatly refused, until they virtually promised him that he would not, once again, be black-balled. They 'canvassed a few votes'. It was reported that the respected old political leader, Sir Francis Dillon Bell (father of Reeves's friend Harry) had let it be known that he would resign if Reeves were not elected.[2] The extent of the feeling, both of Reeves's enemies and of his gentlemen friends, is shown by a letter that William Russell wrote to W. B. Edwards, a lawyer whose appointment as a judge, by the Atkinson ministry in 1890, had been successfully contested

---

[1] Ballance MSS, 14 Oct. 1892.
[2] Interviews with Mr. L. O. H. Tripp and Mr. G. G. S. Robison; letter from Secretary, Wellington Club, 19 Feb. 1954.

in the Privy Council by the Liberals—Atkinson having made one judge too many.

I must say that you should feel intense and righteous indignation at the treatment you have received from the Ballance Government is only natural and that you should desire to give effect to that indignation at every opportunity is equally so and that every Member of a Club has an absolute right to vote against the introduction of any man for whom he has a personal dislike is unquestionable, the more intimate friends of a blackballed candidate will of course be much annoyed but to a large proportion of the members the subject is usually a matter of indifference.

In your own case—I cannot think that Reeves has been antagonistic to you personally, on such occasions as I have spoken to him about your Claims I certainly have formed that impression, but loyalty to his colleagues would prevent his allowing his own opinion to appear at variance with their united action.

I have argued in favour of Reeves election to the Club but I have been completely misunderstood by anybody who fancies I dispute the right of every person to act precisely as he deems proper in the matter, nor would my esteem be in any degree affected by his action.—

Individually I have a far higher opinion of Reeves than you say is entertained by some, he does hold very advanced theories, but I believe he is quite sincere in his convictions, unfortunately for himself he argues in their favour in an intolerant tone and in the excitement of Debate uses words and phrases he may well regret when he gets calm again; I fear his theories have been intensified by some social rebuffs he has experienced and I have felt sorry for him the gift of personal popularity is for the few only.

At the Bar opposing Counsel I understand are pretty 'rough' on one another when they consider it in the interest of their clients, yet at Bar mess good fellowship prevails. The same may be said of the Politician, and at Bellamys both sides of the 'House' chat over the dinner table in the happiest of moods and difference of opinion proves no obstacle to friendliness. Clubs in this Colony are non-political, *but* membership tends to make men less rabidly radical and personal intercourse among its members rubs down many asperities. I incline to the opinion that Reeves election to the Club would be beneficial rather than the reverse to your interests; that it could directly or indirectly be construed as a sign of approbation of the treatment you have received could not possibly be the case.[1]

[1] Russell MSS, 23 Feb. 1893. This letter was kindly given to me by Mr. W. J. Gardner.

Reeves was elected, a process in some ways nearly as painful as being black-balled. G. P. Williams, who wrote a column in the Christchurch *Press* under the pseudonym 'The Bohemian', pictured him in a swallow-tail coat telling 'funny little stories' about his colleagues, including Dick Seddon—'my colleague don't cher know, good fellah but awful raw...not at all a gentleman'. A couple of years later he followed this up with a description of his poetical collaborator as 'your dine-at-the-Club, like-m'-wine-dry type of socialist'.[1]

Reeves could not evade the contradictions in his nature and his rôle. He *did* like belonging to the club; he came to love it, and many years later said that he was never happier in New Zealand than when he stayed there. If not, as George Fisher thought, 'a Tory by instinct and tradition',[2] he certainly was a *gentleman* on both counts. It was significant, though it was natural, that his friends should include a banker, lawyers, club-men, rather than trade unionists. He was, as Russell wrote, 'by instinct exclusive'; but he was also, as Russell added, 'by reading and emotion a genuine Socialist'.[3] It was not altogether unfair to call him, as the crude Fergus did, 'the minister of Lab-ah'.[4]

[1] Reeves MSS, small clipping book, p. 126; *Press*, 21 Feb. 1895.
[2] PD, 1893, 79, p. 84.
[3] Russell MSS, Russell to Horner, 27 Nov. 1894. Reference provided by Mr. Gardner.
[4] Reeves MSS, large clipping book, p. 8.

11

THE CAPTAIN CALLED AWAY
1893

IN 1893 Ballance's Liberal Party was nearly torn apart during a series of internal struggles which did as much damage to Reeves's programme of reforms as the Legislative Council had managed to do. They began in September 1892 with the first round of a long contest between Seddon and Reeves himself. Reeves took a body-blow which appeared for a time to have hurt only his self-esteem but which proved, in the end, to have weakened him and upset his political balance. Few of the fascinated and expert spectators, however, could have doubted what the outcome would be.

During the second session of 1891 Ballance had been at times ill. Next year he grew worse until, early in September, when he had a bad breakdown, the other ministers felt obliged to choose one of their own number to act as leader of the House during his absence. Officially Seddon was elected unanimously, but it was reported in the lobbies and in the Press that there had been 'a considerable difference of opinion on the subject' and keen rivalry between Reeves and Seddon. It was, one newspaper added, commonly assumed that the 'acting premier' held the right of succession[1]—not that that title had been conferred on Seddon by cabinet.

---

[1] *New Zealand Herald*, 7 and 8 Sept. 1892, cited R. T. Shannon, 'The Liberal Succession Crisis in New Zealand, 1893', *Historical Studies*, 8, 30, May 1958, pp. 186, 189.

When I began work on the life of Reeves, two of the questions that most interested me were the 'succession crisis' and Reeves's reasons for going to England. Dr. Shannon, who was then studying the Liberal Government, has since published articles on these very questions. We were of material help to each other. I am indebted to him for newspaper references I had missed, and, to some extent, influenced by his general interpretations, while he made use of the Reeves MSS which I arranged to be brought to New Zealand. It is a useful illustration of the merits of historical research that, while working independently, we arrived at identical conclusions on (what had long seemed a mystery) the nature of the 'succession crisis'.

Reeves had been named ahead of Seddon in the cabinet in 1891; he certainly could not easily accept the precedence of his rough (but not unionist) colleague. Whether Ballance took sides is unknown, but he very soon regretted that Seddon had secured a position from which he might succeed him, and quite possibly he opposed Seddon's elevation from the start. (As early as January 1891 some disaffected Liberals had talked of replacing Ballance with Seddon.[1]) Two weeks later Ballance was back on the front bench, but he collapsed again late in September, leaving Seddon in charge.

There is no doubt that Reeves was very put out—'disturbed', a newspaper said, 'by the weight of the shadow of his greater colleague ... greater in the art of saying pleasant nothings, and preferred before him in the Cabinet'; Alfred Saunders said that he was 'sulking and pouting'.[2] In part, Reeves felt he had a better claim to act as Ballance's lieutenant. But, more strongly, he was determined not to allow Seddon to become premier. By November, and probably earlier, it was known that Ballance had cancer. Even in September his death must have seemed a possibility. There is no shred of evidence that Reeves had any expectation of becoming premier himself, though the ambition must naturally have occurred to him, as it did to others: in January 1892 a hostile newspaper had forecast that he would be premier in a very few years, and then (the highest goal of colonial politics) agent-general in London.[3] The person Reeves wanted to succeed Ballance was Stout, the man Ballance looked to himself. In September 1891 Ballance, McKenzie and Reeves wanted Stout to stand for a vacant seat in Christchurch[4] (which Sandford won). He refused, but the association of those first four names was to prove significant. In 1892, with customary modesty, Ballance told the House that if Stout re-entered politics he 'would be gladly given any position he desired to have'.[5] In opposing Seddon, then, Reeves was fighting not only for himself, but for

---

[1] Shannon, article cited, pp. 195–6.

[2] Reeves MSS, clipping 20 Dec. 1892, small clipping book, p. 101; Saunders to Kate Sheppard, 30 Sept. 1892, cited Patricia Grimshaw, 'The Women's Suffrage Movement in New Zealand', (unpub. thesis, University of Auckland), p. 148.

[3] *Hawkes Bay Herald*, 30 Jan.; for a similar forecast see Reeves MSS, loc. cit.

[4] Stout MSS, Stout to Ballance, telegram 19 Sept. 1891.

[5] PD, 1892, 76, p. 466.

his old hero, Stout; for his whole conception, moreover, of a Liberal Party led by theorists.

In November, referring to Ballance's fatal illness, one of the Conservatives, Dr. Newman, wrote to Rolleston:

I hear Seddon and Reeves have effected a reconciliation—without the aid of his Bill—& are jointly to guide the Labor Party. Seddon I know will not be shunted from the lead.... He has set his heart upon being Sir Richard Seddon K.C.M.G. My opinion is that he will struggle with all his dogged strong will to stay there. You see the *Cabinet* would have to invite Stout—& Seddon I believe would fight hard against it. Ever since he took office he has played for the Leadership.... Why then should he turn round & ask Stout?[1]

It may be inferred that Seddon's lack of sympathy for one of Reeves's bills—probably the arbitration bill—was a further cause of conflict.

The 'reconciliation' did not convince many politicians. In March 1893 Fish told Scobie Mackenzie, as he related to Rolleston, 'that Seddon and Reeves are at daggers drawn—held together solely by the bonds of the sordid'.[2] In the terminology of Scobie, who fought all governments and joined none, 'the sordid' meant office.

For a few months after the session, while ministers were busy in their departments, and addressing meetings to explain their policy, there was an uneasy quiet. But Ballance knew now that death might be near. In February he arranged to meet Stout. He told him that he would probably have to resign and asked his friend to stand for Parliament.[3] Stout apparently agreed. By April Ballance was much worse and had to have an operation. He anxiously asked for Stout and reminded him of his promise. On 27 April, after a second operation, while Stout, Seddon, Buckley, McKenzie, Cadman and Reeves were with him, he died. There followed the most extraordinary cabinet crisis in New Zealand's history.

On Ballance's death—but, indeed, for some months earlier—Seddon saw before him almost the greatest prize he could conceive of. He was aggressive, grasping—of course he would

---

[1] Rolleston MSS, 2 Nov.
[2] Ibid., 31 March 1893.
[3] *Evening Post*, 11 Aug. 1894, cit. Shannon, pp. 184–5.

get it. But how? The answer now seems simple—simply hold
what he already held. But his acting leadership was quite
precarious, and even to him, to keep it must have seemed
difficult and daring. Premiers had been men of education, wealth
or profession. No one like Seddon, who in manner (but not
ability) was a rough fellow off the diggings, had ever been
premier. To the gentlemen who had hitherto ruled the Colony,
it was almost unthinkable; yet not quite; they knew 'his dogged
strong will'.

Not only did some of Seddon's colleagues oppose him, but so
did Stout—a traditional leader, an ex-premier, the leading
Liberal of the past decade. Yet Seddon had a high card to play.
He appealed, by telegraph, to Sir George Grey, an older Liberal
leader, a greater leader still, saying that he had no idea what the
Governor's or his colleagues' wishes might be, but that he would
hesitate to accept the premiership, if it were offered.

On 1 May the Governor sent for Seddon and asked him to
consult his colleagues and notify him who could form an
administration. Seddon telegraphed Grey again, this time
asking pretty plainly for his blessing as well as advice. Seddon
had been elected as a Greyite; had followed Grey almost to the
last ditch. Like Grey, he had not been pleased with Ballance's
election as leader in 1889. But the last ditch had lain in front
of Ballance's cabinet, and he had yielded before it was reached.

Grey hated Stout and Ballance. Of course he wired back urging
Seddon not to 'shrink', adding shrewd advice—'two are
enough to start—if there is any difficulty others will soon join
you', and suggesting that, if necessary, Seddon could ask the
Governor for a dissolution and seek the approval of the people.[1]
So armed, Seddon went to meet the rest of the cabinet.

The exact number of ministers on each side is uncertain.
Seddon's published version of this telegram reads 'five are
enough'. Reeves later wrote, and McKenzie said, that they
supported Stout,[2] which leaves Cadman, Carroll, Buckley and
Ward supporting Seddon. But the copy of the telegram kept by

---

[1] Shannon, pp. 186–7. The telegrams are in the Grey MSS, but evidently some
are missing, presumably including one in which Seddon told Grey how many
supporters he had.

[2] For McKenzie's views, see PD, 1896, 92, p. 50; for Reeves's see his memo on
Seddon cited below.

Grey among his papers plainly reads 'two are enough to start'.[1]
In retrospect it appears improbable that a gentleman-politician
like Buckley, who had served in Stout's ministry and was—like
him—a lawyer, would have favoured Seddon. Ward, moreover,
was a close friend and protégé of McKenzie. Either at this time,
or a few months later, Stout wrote to McKenzie suggesting that,
if Ward cared to support him, he could succeed to the premiership when he retired in a year or two. Ward claimed to have
spurned the offer,[2] but he may have been tempted. If these two,
as well as Reeves and McKenzie, inclined to Stout, then only
Cadman and Carroll at first favoured Seddon. A significant
piece of evidence suggesting this line-up presently appeared.

It seems likely that Seddon had only two reliable supporters
when the crisis began, four (and two strong opponents) when it
ended. But 'two' or 'five' is immaterial. Though Seddon was
stronger than either in the House, Reeves and McKenzie led the
two greatest blocs of voters, the unionists and the small farmers.
Reeves was next to Seddon in cabinet—had chaired it, in his
absence, shortly before.[3] Together, McKenzie and Reeves were
enough to constitute a great obstacle before Seddon, and a
powerful support for Stout. Moreover, Seddon was in the
embarrassing position (which even he felt) of having to press his
own case. But Stout had an almost insuperable handicap. He
could not become premier immediately because he was not a
Member of the House. There was a safe Liberal seat vacant, but
the election was a month away.

The cabinet met in an atmosphere of great emotion, for
Ballance was loved, not only by some of his colleagues, but by
thousands of voters. There was a 'great struggle'. What arguments Seddon used are uncertain. Probably he referred to Grey's
support. According to Stout he 'threatened and cajoled'. It
seems that he threatened to ask for a dissolution. One minister
told Stout that he threatened to form a new cabinet of his
supporters rather than surrender, but this he denied.[4] After a
time, almost (but not quite) incredibly, Seddon came out (in

---

[1] Shannon, p. 187, n. 38.
[2] PD, 1896, 92, pp. 31, 50.
[3] *N.Z. Times*, 19 April 1893.
[4] Grey MSS, Seddon to Grey, 29 Nov. 1893; also Grey to Seddon, 1 May 1893;
Stout MSS, Stout to Seddon (draft letter), 12 Aug. 1894; Shannon, pp. 190, 195.

Stout's words) 'crying like a child and asking me to consent'.[1]
On Seddon's invitation, Stout entered the cabinet room and
joined in the discussion. An almost inescapable compromise was
reached and summarized in a cabinet minute which was (a year
later) published:

1st May, 1893.

We to hold office until the party meet—two days before the meeting
of Parliament. The party then to decide who is to be leader. We to
loyally support whatever that decision is. Sir R. Stout to stand for
Inangahua. All portfolios as at present.

Ward, Treasurer.[2]

The portfolios were, in fact, rearranged. Ward had become
Treasurer, the most important post after the premiership, though
his name was listed after Reeves's and McKenzie's.

According to Stout, Seddon promised to resign two days
before the new session, and after the Inangahua election, and
allow caucus to choose a leader.[3] But this Seddon denied; and it
is not what he told the Press. After forming his Government, he
announced that he was carrying on the administration until
Parliament met, when the party would be asked 'to determine
as to whether the present arrangement shall further continue'.[4]
The conduct of the other ministers, when that occasion arrived,
was strongly to suggest that Stout's interpretation of the agreement was correct.

On 6 May Colonel Trimble, a retired politician, wrote to
Rolleston that Seddon was to be Premier until Parliament met:
'I believe him, or try to believe him, for bold Dick may refuse to
part with his duties just then. Think of the degradation of
having Seddon presiding over our "best and noblest".'[5]
The Honourable Richard Oliver, a Councillor and ex-
minister, was even franker in a letter to Hall, in which he
deplored the death of Ballance, who, in his view, had at least
some dignity and fairness. Better him, he wrote, than 'an
ignorant rude clown endowed only with natural astuteness &

[1] Stout MSS, Stout to Seddon, 12 Aug. 1894—a draft letter cit. D. A. Hamer,
'The Law and the Prophet', p. 363.
[2] N.Z. Times, 16 Aug. 1894.
[3] Stout MSS, loc. cit.
[4] Shannon, p. 188; cf. Grey MSS, Seddon to Grey, 1 May 1893.
[5] Rolleston MSS.

a diarrhoea of words frequently used without a particle of truth'.[1]

If one ignores some metaphorical confusion, his was a common view, but it was not that of common voters; nor was it the only view that a conservative could take. 'Seddon's instincts', Sir John Hall wrote, 'are by no means socialistic.... Ballance was infinitely more dangerous.'[2]

It was widely assumed that Stout would, once elected, become Premier. The *New Zealand Herald* judged that 'Grit and bluster may gain for a man a certain position in public life, but when pitted against culture and trained ability, the result is a foregone conclusion',[3] a view which seems naïve only in the light of after-knowledge. On 17 May Seddon indirectly revealed, in a speech in Napier, how much intention he did have of parting with his duties:

Without taking any credit from Mr. Ballance his lamented chief, he might say that the Ballance Government was in no sense a one man Government. On the contrary, every member of this Government knew his work and fearlessly did his duty. The position was that of a ship; when the

CAPTAIN WAS CALLED AWAY

the first mate took his place. He (Mr. Seddon) was recognized as the first mate of the ship in this case, and when their lamented captain was removed by death he had been called upon to take his position *until the colony should declare that somebody else should fill it; until then he hoped and intended to remain the Premier of New Zealand.* (Loud and continued applause.)

It was 'the most enthusiastic meeting ever held in Napier'.[4]

Seddon's suggestion that 'the colony' (not caucus) would have the final say did not go unremarked. Reeves put the speech in his clipping book. Rolleston wrote to Hall, 'Seddon's speech at Napier out Seddon's Seddon for audacity & mendacity.'[5]

The Press observed that Seddon was growing impatient at the prolonged obsequies for Ballance—which were being conducted chiefly by Reeves. In Dunedin the latter delivered a long and moving speech which was widely quoted.[6] McKenzie was less

---

[1] Hall MSS, 16 May 1893.   [2] Ibid., Hall to Russell, 19 Dec. 1893.
[3] 2 May 1893, cit. Shannon, p. 189.
[4] *Evening News* (Napier), 18 May 1893 (my italics).
[5] Hall MSS, 28 May 1893.   [6] *Otago Daily Times*, 24 May 1893.

expansive on this theme.[1] It was also noticeable that Reeves did not mention Seddon, while McKenzie did so quite cursorily. On the other hand, they did not explain the cabinet agreement, which would have made Seddon's position more difficult.

On 19 June, in a pre-session speech in Christchurch, Reeves again ignored Seddon, praised Ballance, his party and Stout, whose recent election for Inangahua he saw as due to 'the recognition of the fact that he was a man to be trusted at the present juncture'.[2] By this time, however, Reeves and McKenzie knew that Seddon was not going to fulfil the letter, nor even the spirit, of the cabinet agreement, and that they would have to 'give way'.

Apparently many Liberals ignored a summons to a caucus to be held two days before Parliament met on 22 June. As a result, the caucus which was supposed to decide on the leadership did not meet until five days after the session commenced. And Seddon did not resign. Thus he met his party, not as a candidate for the leadership, but as the Premier in office, and in the parliamentary firing-line.[3]

Forty Liberals attended the meeting, but astonishingly, not one other minister came except Carroll. Only Cadman, who was resigning over a libel case, explained his absence.[4] Perhaps these were Seddon's original 'two'. Some of the ministers were said to be 'disgusted'. They stayed away because they knew that Seddon was not going to allow any election for the premiership.[5] Stout refused to attend because he 'understood his name was to be mentioned', but he encountered Seddon on his way to the meeting. Seddon told him plainly that he intended to ask the party to approve his continuing as leader.[6]

Seddon took the chair and explained the Government's position, which he compared with that of a ship's crew who had lost their captain and placed themselves under the first officer while awaiting the decision of the directors. In his metaphor, thus varied, the 'directors' had become the members of the

---

[1] *The Globe*, 27 May 1893.
[2] LT, 20 June 1893.
[3] Shannon, p. 191; *N.Z. Herald*, 17 Aug. 1894.
[4] *N.Z. Times*, 28 June 1893. His resignation was accepted after the caucus.
[5] *Evening Post*, 11, 16 Aug. 1894; Stout to McKenzie, 15 Aug. 1894, cit. Shannon, p. 196.
[6] *Evening Post*, 16 Aug. 1894; Stout MSS, Stout to Seddon (draft), 12 Aug. 1894.

party, not the public, but he gave them little scope for choice. He explained that he was the spokesman of the absent ministers and gave the impression (according to one Member there) that they supported him. He did not explain the cabinet agreement, though he mentioned that Stout had been suggested as their leader. He then, at great length, expounded the Government's policy, *his* policy, and pleaded his case to continue as Premier. Only one man, Eugene O'Conor (who was called 'the Buller Lion') urged Stout's claims. No motion was put, no vote taken, but it was 'tacitly understood' that Seddon should continue in office. After the caucus Seddon offered Stout a place in his government. Stout publicly stated that 'under no circumstances' would he join the present ministry.

It is obvious that the majority of the party thought, as one said, that Seddon had 'won his spurs' and deserved a chance to prove himself in the elections later in the year.[1] But why had Reeves and McKenzie given up their resistance?

Many years later Reeves set down the case for Seddon and the case against. The former, he then thought, was much stronger:

It may be put thus; though he seized the Premiership, he only did what nineteen men out of twenty would have done in the case. When Mr. Ballance fell ill he was asked to take charge of Government business in the House. When he dubbed himself Acting Premier everyone laughed but no one objected. When Ballance died, the Governor—Lord Glasgow—sent for Seddon and asked him to form a Ministry, the minority, John McKenzie and myself, had to give way.

We had to give way for two reasons. If we had made it impossible for Mr. Seddon to form a Government, Sir Robert Stout would not have been sent for. Lord Glasgow would have sent for the Conservative Leader, Mr. Rolleston. This gentleman would have formed a Ministry, obtained a dissolution from a friendly governor and gone to the Country. The Liberal Party out of office and divided into two sections would have had to fight at a great disadvantage. The second reason was that the policy of the Government, held back by the Upper House, was in the air. To McKenzie the Land portion of this policy was his very life; to me, the Labour Laws ... seemed everything on earth. The rank and file of the Party accepted Seddon almost without objection.[2]

[1] On the caucus, see *Evening Post*, 27 June; *N.Z. Times*, 28 June, 29 June 1893; PD, 1893, 81, p. 322.
[2] Reeves MSS.

The first point is conjectural, but it is true that Glasgow's
sympathies with the Conservatives were as strong as Onslow's.
He could be expected to help them if he could. And there was the
other possibility, that Seddon would form a cabinet of his
supporters and 'go to the country'. Whether the Liberals were
in office or opposition, the prospect of an election following a
party feud was scarcely cheering to Reeves and McKenzie.

Reeves's last point was very weighty. There was strong support
for Seddon in the Party. As Reeves conceded even in 1893,
Seddon had fought for the Liberals, in Parliament, during years
of adversity, while Stout was a private citizen. It was by no
means certain that the caucus would choose Stout. One of the
Labour Members, Earnshaw, publicly supported Seddon,
though later he became a follower of Stout.

Probably the decisive factor was McKenzie's and Reeves's
desire to pass their bills. Seddon wanted power; they wanted
reforms. A bargain was clearly possible and, between the death
of Ballance and the June caucus, it was struck. Reeves wrote to
an American friend in 1899 that, when Seddon became Premier,
he agreed not to 'interfere' in any way with his labour administration.[1] McKenzie, too, was not, it seems, to be 'interfered
with in his own Departments'.[2] A consequence of this situation
was the spectacle, over the coming two years, while collective
cabinet responsibility was in practice abrogated, of Reeves being
left to push labour bills without help from his colleagues.

Stout naturally felt that Reeves and McKenzie, as well as
Seddon, had let him down,[3] but there was little he could do.
He had incurred much criticism for letting people know
privately that Ballance wanted him to be premier. Rolleston
thought this was 'an indecent thing', and told him so.[4] Oliver
wrote to Hall: 'How poor a figure Stout cuts in these late
events! Where is now the boasted democratic principle? Put
aside for the moment apparently in favour of another policy—
the devolution of government of the people by bequest.'[5]

[1] H. D. Lloyd MSS, Wisconsin State Historical Library, 2 Dec. 1899.
[2] 'Letters from Men of Mark', F. Waldegrave to Reeves, 6 Dec. 1902.
[3] e.g. PD, 1896, 92, p. 50.
[4] Hall MSS, Rolleston to Hall, 15 May 1893; Rolleston MSS, Stout to Rolleston,
12 May 1893.
[5] Hall MSS, 16 May 1893.

Stout had been scrupulous, however, not to mention publicly Ballance's wishes. They were, indeed, relevant to the issue only in the sense that, if known, they might have influenced some Liberals' views. For the time being Stout was helpless. He could only watch and wait.

The coronation of King Dick, by his own hands, marked a stage in its way as decisive as the 1890 election in New Zealand political history. In 1890 radicals came to power; in 1893, someone who seemed very like the average voter. This was a change as significant for the radicals as for the conservative gentry. The majority of New Zealand voters, though radical, were not very radical. In this respect Seddon was typical. He had some radical views and prejudices, but he was not intellectually committed to any reforming programme. For all his association with Vogel and company promotion, Stout was, in opinion, to the left of the new Premier. In summarizing the case against Seddon, Reeves emphasized the effect of his leadership on the party:

The case against him may be stated thus; it may be said that by seizing the Premiership in 1893 he kept out Sir Robert Stout, a man in many ways better suited for the position than himself. Stout could have prevented the mischievous split between the prohibitionist Liberals and the rest of the party. One of the results of this split was to divide and weaken the more progressive section of the Liberals of which I was at the time spokesman. Mr. Seddon had to lean on the more Conservative Section of the party with the result that the Party became much less progressive. It is complained that Seddon vulgarized the Party and that by rampant platform speeches and foolish self-advertising pronouncements he made New Zealand Liberalism a laughing stock in England and elsewhere. Furthermore it is said that by vanity, suspiciousness and jealousy he antagonised most of the able men in his Party and especially the younger and more ambitious men. He took weak men into his Ministry, and whereas in 1891 he entered a strong Government, he died leaving a very weak one. It is said that by a fondness for small dodges and petty jobs he irritated numbers of right-thinking people and gained for his Party and himself a reputation for corruption which neither he nor the Party really deserved. Finally, by neglecting Labour in the last years of his life, he helped to bring on the division between Liberalism and Labour in New Zealand, the results of which have been, in the opinion of Liberals, something like disastrous.

What Reeves did not write was the case against Stout. He was the leader of the High-Minded—not a Christian but a 'free-thinker' like Ballance and (though he kept off the topic) Reeves. He was a public moralizer. At that time his integrity was questioned by few besides Grey, and it was easier to think that his hostility was senile than that Stout confused private with public business.[1] Now it seems that, though Seddon was some-times transparently untruthful, his moral inferiority to Stout is debatable. Certainly, in retrospect, Stout seems quite as unscrupulous a politician as his rival. Whether he was likely to carry more radical measures than Seddon is also questionable. Though he was more 'progressive' in opinion, and though it is true that he would have derived his support from the left wing of the Party, his previous record as Premier reveals little per-sistence in radical courses. It is difficult not to conclude that much of the opposition to Seddon derived from the feeling that Stout was a gentleman and he was not.

[1] D. A. Hamer, *Historical Studies*, 10, 38, May 1962.

12

RIDING THE WHIRLWIND
1893

SEDDON announced that the new Government would carry on with Ballance's policy. The Liberals had borrowed no money and he saw no need to borrow. Their land policies would be more fully implemented. He supported arbitration, a question on which he wished to be 'well and clearly understood': the 'time had come' when it should be compulsory. The notoriously rough-and-tumble politician began his career as Premier by assuring a sceptical House that his fighting days were over. He would leave fighting to his lieutenants: 'It is now my duty to direct and to guide.'[1] Stout soon made him prove his ability to lead, and made him fight too, by raising the most contentious issue in the country.

The prohibition movement had been rapidly growing in importance since the late eighties, led by the New Zealand Alliance and the Women's Christian Temperance Union. The consumption of alcohol was steadily declining, and New Zealanders now drank less than the British,[2] but zeal collects its own statistics. Prohibition had become the most fervent religious and moral movement the country had (or has) seen. New Zealand was flooded with prohibition tracts, temperance reciters and prayer-books; awash with 'dry' novels and drier verse. The prohibitionists pressed on Reeves that 'scientific temperance' should be taught in the schools. The Colony, in their eyes, was a battlefield, not of Capital and Labour, but of God (helped by bands sporting the blue ribbon) and the Devil (leading ranks of brewers and drunken wife-beaters).

When Reeves gave his pre-sessional speech in his electorate, for the first time in his experience, his meeting ended in a narrow victory over disorder. Christchurch was the chief centre of

---

[1] *Evening News*, Napier, 18 May 1893; PD, 1893, 79, p. 53.
[2] W. P. Reeves, *Long White Cloud*, 1899 ed., p. 363; LT, 20 May 189

prohititionist agitation, and its leaders, T. E. ('Tea') Taylor, a radical Liberal, and the Reverend Leonard Isitt lived there. At the conclusion of his speech, Taylor climbed on the platform and challenged Reeves's views on the liquor question. Reeves replied that his hands were tied by a pledge to the electors in 1890 not to support alterations in the liquor licensing laws during the forthcoming Parliament. Isitt's brother, the Reverend F. W. Isitt, added to the disturbance. Reeves begged the audience not to vote for an amendment moved by Taylor and Isitt to the vote of confidence, and thus give him a slap in the face for keeping his pledge. He made it plain that (like Seddon) he favoured moderate temperance reform, not prohibition. In the end he received his vote of thanks and cheers.[1]

It is clear that licensing reform was soon going to become a major problem for the Government. It is equally certain that it would have been easily evaded until the election, but for the succession crisis and Stout. He chose to give it a priority which no one else could have done.

Stout had long believed in temperance. Suddenly, without warning even during his recent election campaign, he assumed the rôle of parliamentary leader of the prohibitionists. He had not pressed the reform of liquor licensing when he was Premier,[2] and it seems fair to agree with Seddon that he took up the issue in order to embarrass (or wreck) the Government. Shortly after the session began he introduced a licensing bill giving the prohibitionists almost all they wanted. Already licensing committees elected by rate-payers had power to issue licences to sell liquor, and withdraw them without compensation. The prohibitionists wanted the 'direct veto'—power for a majority in any licensing district to close all licensed premises without compensation. Stout's Direct Veto Bill was read only once. In August he tried again with a licensing bill which, while more moderate, still permitted a simple majority to abolish liquor sales in a district.

For a moment he succeeded in disorganizing the Government. Seddon announced that, as an individual, he would vote for the bill. If it passed its second reading, the Government would take up the question and bring in a bill of its own. Because of his public 'pledge', Reeves explained, he was obliged to vote against 'his

[1] LT, 20 June 1893.   [2] D. A. Hamer, 'The Law and the Prophet', p. 390.

chief'. If the House decided that legislation was necessary, however, he would allow himself to be overruled, and would try to secure reasonable reforms.[1] Whereas Seddon treated the issue from a tactical viewpoint, Reeves condemned prohibition strongly, while conceding that he risked defeat in his electorate for doing so. He denounced Stout's 'revolutionary' views and demanded moderate reform.

Licensing reform had not been on the Government's programme, but a Government bill was hurriedly drawn up and substituted for Stout's. Thus Seddon out-manoeuvred Stout, but he was scarcely justified in claiming that the Government was leading and not led.[2] The new bill enabled a bare majority of voters in a district to close only a quarter of the hotels; a three-fifths majority was needed for total prohibition. Unless a majority of enrolled voters voted, a poll was not effective. No compensation was paid to the owners of hotels closed down. The bill passed, but Seddon had a struggle with some of the left-wing prohibitionists, including the 'labour members' Pinkerton and Earnshaw, who voted against the Government.

The 'liquor question' gave Reeves endless trouble in other ways. Followers of the Salvation Army were causing disturbances when, for instance, they wrote 'This is the road to hell' on the pavement outside a pub and were pelted with stones by sturdy drinkers. Several 'Sallies' were gaoled by magistrates, one (at Milton) for playing a cornet in the street without a permit. Reeves introduced a bill to revise local bye-laws and prevent such magisterial zeal, but the Legislative Council threw it out. Privately he would have been happy to consign all 'Salvationists' and Bands of Hope to the lock-up.[3]

One part of Ballance's policy was introduced despite his lieutenants. The prohibitionists had been demanding the female franchise, convinced—as were their opponents—that New Zealand women were dry at heart. Others believed that they would vote conservative.[4] Tens of thousands of women wanted the vote for its own sake and for equality's and signed the biggest petitions in New Zealand history up to that time.[5]

---

[1] PD, 1893, 80, pp. 388 ff.   [2] PD, 1893, 81, pp. 168 ff.
[3] Ibid., *passim;* 82, pp. 1003 ff.   [4] *N.Z. Times,* 9 June 1892.
[5] Patricia Grimshaw, 'The Women's Suffrage Movement in New Zealand', unpub. thesis, University of Auckland, p. 176.

The ministers were opposed to the enfranchisement of the women, partly because of fear about the way they would vote, but were unhappy at the prospect of sounding less democratic than Sir John Hall or Stout. Seddon pronounced himself in favour of votes for married women. Reeves, even in 1890, had confessed that he was a 'half-loaf man'. He believed in the principle, but thought it should be extended cautiously. He was willing to begin by enfranchising women (like Maud!) who had matriculated. [1] Maud was an active feminist, who had collected many signatures for the petitions. Any doubt about her influence on Will may be dispelled by an ominous note she wrote to Hall, the parliamentary leader of the feminists, and a leading member of the Opposition, in 1893:

> We are going to have our franchise after all. Isn't it glorious? Could you prick a card for me & send it up? My husband is to be relied on. I have seen to that.

A few days later she followed this up with a letter:

> I must congratulate you on the success of your amendment on Tuesday night. I had hardly expected so large a majority. I regard it as an honour to the cause that men like Mr. Fish oppose it. As far as I am concerned they may make women out to be as inferior as they like as long as we get our vote. I liked your speech very much. Privately I think that our Queen might have done more than she has for the rest of her sex. As far as women not wanting the franchise goes, I can only say that most of the women I come in contact with are intensely anxious for it & others only require to know that it is possible for them to get it to be quite as anxious in their turn. On the whole it is very cheering & I can only thank you, as a woman, for the part you have played on our behalf. [2]

The Government covertly opposed the women's vote. [3] Reeves made an embarrassed speech favouring it: 'The time has come when women will have the vote, and I hope they will make good use of it. I believe myself that in a little time they will make good

---

[1] PD, 1890, 68, pp. 392 ff.

[2] Hall MSS. The note is not dated and the second is dated 'Wednesday'. The dates added to these letters in another hand are wrong. The letter appears to have been written on 9 Aug. 1893 (referring to the Committee of 8 Aug.) and the note possibly on 1 Aug. 1893. 'Pricking a card' may mean marking a list of Members voting in a division on the women's vote.

[3] Grimshaw, pp. 137, 183 ff.

use of it.'[1] Seddon let the measure pass in the House, hoping (and trying to ensure) that the Legislative Council would do its usual work, but it passed by two votes, to the ministers' evident chagrin.[2]

The rest of the Electoral Bill was a government measure. It completed the democratic franchise by preventing property owners from registering in several electorates and then choosing in which one to vote. This was an important reform in marginal seats. In 1890 Ballance won his seat by only twenty votes, and allegedly only because some conservatives went to vote for Atkinson in Egmont.[3]

Seddon defeated Stout in the tactical skirmishing of the 1893 session, but Stout held the initiative long enough to unsettle a government already weakened by the succession crisis and in which the conflicting views of the ministers were no longer reconciled or harmonized by Ballance's conciliatory leadership. Liquor and the ladies took up a great part of the session. Nevertheless, the Government's reforming drive was by no means halted. There were no radical reforms comparable with those of 1891 or 1892, but a large number of measures were passed.

Reeves got through an Act codifying the whole criminal law, a revised version of a measure that had been thrown out almost every session for years. A new Customs Act was passed, and two banking acts, one to protect bank notes and one to enable the Bank of New Zealand, which was sliding to disaster, to raise extra capital. An Act to separate the Maoris from their lands more rapidly, in the interests of European settlement, went through. Seddon assured the House that 'no sufficient attempts [had] been made, to give the Natives an opportunity of disposing of their lands ... .'[4]

Reeves at last had his way over the land tax. The tax on improvements was abolished, and the graduated tax on estates stiffened to make up for the revenue lost. Scobie pictured him in cabinet, pleading with his colleagues not to 'legislate in favour of the social pest'. Reeves unguardedly remarked that Scobie's taunts might 'help to stiffen the graduated tax a bit', and in a public speech he allegedly referred to 'giving another turn to the

---

[1] PD, 1893, 80, p. 546.
[2] R. M. Burdon, *King Dick*, Christchurch etc., 1955, p. 113.
[3] PD, 1892, 76, p. 571.   [4] PD, 1893, 81, p. 518.

graduation screw'.[1] In their letters and speeches, many estate owners expressed what was becoming an unqualified hatred of him.

Only one of Reeves's own assortment of labour bills became law in 1893, a Workmen's Wages Act, providing for weekly payments. His bill to amend the law of conspiracy, which rested on an English Act of 1825 and virtually prevented 'combinations' of workmen, was lost. Though most of the unions now publicly supported compulsory arbitration, the Legislative Council again deleted pages of the bill, and it was dropped again. Old Christopher Richmond, now a judge, who was watching the progress of 'the Reeves baby' with interest and of 'Social Democracy' with distaste, wrote in a letter: 'Willie Reeves probably never read Hood's story ... of the wether conciliated by the butcher who tugged him tail foremost to the slaughterhouse. "There (says the butcher) I've conciliated him." '[2]

Over his Shop and Shop Assistants Bill, Reeves had a tremendous struggle. He was learning the immense difficulty of legislating on social questions, for this was not merely a matter of work hours. The reform of shop hours, long demanded by the Early Closing Association, affected the shopping customs of the entire populace. Modern New Zealanders could scarcely imagine the hostility that Reeves's proposals aroused. In 1892 he had given shop assistants a half holiday, but had been forced to drop the compulsory closing of the shops for a half day (as well as Sunday). Some shopkeepers in Auckland were giving one or two of their staff a half holiday each week-day, and running their shops with a short staff. Now Reeves returned to the fray with a bill closing most shops on Saturday afternoon, unless the local authorities chose some other afternoon. Even some Liberals, like the editor of the *Auckland Star*, T. W. Leys, deprecated his persistence in meddling with legislation already passed.[3] His critics were hysterically angry. Fish prophesied that the gaols would have to be enlarged to accommodate recalcitrant shopkeepers.[4] Fish, Duthie, Buckland and others fought the bill in

---

[1] PD, 1893, 79, pp. 530, 575–6; 80, pp. 209–10.
[2] G. H. Scholefield (ed.), *The Richmond-Atkinson Papers*, Wellington, 1960, ii, p. 591. On his arbitration bill of 1893, see PD, 1893, 81, pp. 364 ff.; 82, pp. 961 ff.
[3] *Auckland Star*, 27 May 1893.
[4] PD, 1893, 82, pp. 568 ff.

committee from 7.30 one evening until nearly 9 a.m.—an occasion which Tregear always remembered as one 'like the struggles of the Titans ... when W.P.R. rode the whirlwind'.[1] Duthie stone-walled for two hours to get fruiterers' shops excluded. When Reeves managed to get a word in, at 8 a.m., he explained that he had come to the committee intending to move the exclusion of fruiterers and fishmongers. Seddon and Ward went home, but McKenzie and Cadman stayed with Reeves.[2] Then the Legislative Council threw out the bill. It was causing immense trouble for the Government, particularly because so many small shopkeepers were Liberals.

In *The Long White Cloud*, Reeves blamed licensing reform for blocking radical measures in 1893.[3] But that was not the whole truth. The other ministers did not regard his labour bills as having first priority, which they gave to land and taxation reforms. His bills were pushed into the background. Partly this was a result of the succession crisis. Reeves's relations with Seddon continued very strained, even in the House. For instance, Reeves voted for Stout's bill to set up an Institute of Journalists, against Seddon and McKenzie (and, next year, against Cadman and Ward as well).[4] Sometimes there was open friction. In a discussion of a railways bill, Reeves discomfited Seddon with his interpretation of a legal point. The Premier asserted that Reeves was not speaking as a lawyer—'as a lawyer he would know better'. Shortly afterwards, when McKenzie advocated 'a good big bonfire on the tennis-court' to burn May's treatise on parliamentary procedure, so that they could run Parliament on common-sense lines, Reeves was at odds with Seddon and McKenzie.[5] He found their disrespectful attitudes to legal—or other—niceties very trying.

But there was something much deeper than personal relations. New Zealand had a rural economy. Its towns were small—the largest, Auckland, had only 50,000 inhabitants. The unionists were a minority. Even Reeves did not imagine that the Liberals were a labour party—'we claim to be', he said, 'a national party.' But Seddon saw the unionists as having a much smaller

[1] 'Letters from Men of Mark', Tregear to Reeves, 23 Jan. 1905, 25 Nov. 1897.
[2] PD, 1893, 82, pp. 64 ff., 568 ff.; 1894, 83, p. 126.   [3] p. 364.
[4] PD, 1893, 80, pp. 578–9; 1894, 83, pp. 445–6.
[5] Ibid., 82, 414, 428, 434–5, 657–68.

13

rôle than Reeves supposed in the Liberal scheme. He agreed with majority opinion. In a sense, he had less sympathy for the unionists and the unemployed, more for the small farmers, small townsmen, shopkeepers, clerks—the great majority, and not, in those days, notably washed. But in another sense his sympathies, less impeded by intellect or by theory, were broader. In his Napier speech in May he made a remark about the unemployed that, in its intimacy, its impact, Reeves—who had never lived with the poor—could not have matched: 'Unhappily, many of those present knew quite well when out of work they got credit from the storekeeper for the week; in the second week the storekeeper was cool towards them; in the third week he had not got the goods they wanted; in the fourth week the wife was sent to buy them; in the fifth week the children were sent, and finally they were near starvation.'

It would be a mistake, then, not to see Seddon's 'big heart' beneath the politician's genial, yet hard, exterior. His sympathies were much more malleable according to expediency than Reeves's, but they were abiding. Still, the fact remained that neither the man nor the politician shared Reeves's preoccupation with unionism. He would not take the risk of offending middle class and rural voters by giving prominence to Reeves's bills. Moreover he took the first opportunity of reassuring those voters that he was 'not a socialist'. In June 1893 he was welcomed in Auckland by Ballance's Liberal Association, which advocated policies very radical and bordering on socialist, including the 'Land tax pure and simple'. Seddon bluntly said that its programme was 'a very nice little pill', but not one he could swallow, and that it would alienate all the country districts. To the delight of the conservative Press, he announced that the Government's policy 'ought to be one of moderation'. He lectured the Association on its duties, which did not include the Government's job of leading.[1]

On one occasion in 1893 Reeves spoke as though he stood with his back to the wall, facing the new Liberal spirit of moderation. In the debate on his shop hours bill, he said he had been told that some Liberals were growing 'luke-warm' towards his bill. He did not believe it, but if it were so, he knew that people 'outside'

1 See R. T. Shannon, 'The Fall of Reeves', *Studies of a Small Democracy*, ed. R. M. Chapman and K. Sinclair, Auckland, 1963, pp. 128–9.

were very warm indeed. Governments (and he pointed to the Opposition) had often underestimated the strength of public opinion before elections. He declared that he would never cease to introduce such bills while his party supported him. If his party ceased to do so, he would try to form another; if he failed he would fight alone.[1] He would not have made that speech in Ballance's day.

The political landscape was changing very rapidly. New features were thrusting up. Prohibition threatened to dwarf labour reform. And an issue, which was to dominate both, was becoming an insistent problem. It was the oldest stuff of colonial politics, taking a new form.

As in all colonies, there had been in New Zealand a perennial demand from farmers for cheap credit. Credit was dear in a remote colony in any case, and since English bankers regarded land and fixed property generally as the most risky security for loans, farmers paid more than anyone else. During the eighties, while bank interest rates rose as high as 10 per cent., while old mortgages kept land prices high and many men wanted small farms, the demand for cheap credit was institutionalized in a State Bank League, led by Reeves's old friend, J. M. Twomey.[2] Though he might have regarded the idea of a state bank as a step towards socialism, Reeves in fact regarded it as a fad: it would involve government borrowing and risky lending— another example of his financial caution moderating his radicalism. But Seddon once flirted with the idea, and McKenzie hated bankers with a small farmer's hatred. In 1890, at a meeting of a New Zealand Farmers' Union (established in Otago in 1889), the latter advocated allowing the Life Insurance Office to lend more money to farmers.[3]

In 1893, during the Australian banking crisis, with banks closing their doors, with the Bank of New Zealand and the Colonial Bank (the only 'New Zealand' banks) in trouble, with the minimum bank lending rate at 7 per cent., there was an increasing need for cheaper credit: the shaken or shaky banks

---

[1] PD, 1893, 82, p. 580.

[2] LT, 11 Aug. 1884; J. M. Twomey's clipping book, in possession of Mr. E. M. Twomey, Wellington.

[3] Reeves MSS, large clipping book, undated clipping pp. 108v–109v. Internal evidence shows the date was 1890.

were unlikely to come to the farmers' aid. The farmers do not seem to have been importunate—certainly their representatives in Parliament said little. But they spoke to a more receptive audience. In 1891 Reeves had told a parliamentary questioner that the Government would look into the problem of state loans to farmers. In 1893, however, to the same question, Ward's response was much less conventionally evasive.[1] Ballance was dead; an election approached.

In 1893 McKenzie had his greatest success, when the Government bought the Cheviot estate in Canterbury after the owners refused to accept its official valuation for tax purposes. Reeves and the radicals wanted to keep it as Crown land and lease it to small farmers. The majority of the House wanted to sub-divide and sell it. McKenzie and Seddon were content to compromise. A third was sold and two-thirds leased.[2] Within a year nine hundred people were living where there had been perhaps forty.

Cheviot, too, pointed with dramatic emphasis towards the election. State loans to farmers, government repurchase of estates (already permitted, when owners agreed, under the 1892 repurchase Act and the Land and Income Tax Act) offered a basis for a powerful rural programme. But they necessarily involved state borrowing—overseas borrowing for 'development', the old core of politics, in a new guise; they involved dropping the Liberal programme of a complete cessation of borrowing. Reeves was its only defender left in the cabinet, and he did not have a chance.

In his opening election address in Feilding on 13 October Seddon produced two bombs. One of them eventually blew up in his face, the other in Reeves's. First of all, he felt it necessary to deny the spreading rumours about Ballance's views on his successor. He said it was untrue that Ballance had wanted 'another'—it was clearly understood that he, Seddon, should 'take the lead'. And, he added, in a pathetic attempt to mislead and convince, 'Mr. Ballance gave him certain papers previous to his undergoing the operation.' Of course Ballance had given his deputy 'papers'—but not, as his listeners might reasonably have been expected to infer, letters approving of his succession. The conservative Press ridiculed Seddon's claim, which simply

---

[1] PD, 1891, 72, p. 617; 1893, 79, pp. 472–3; 80, pp. 102, 114.
[2] LT, 31 Oct. 1893, Reeves speech.

spread the story further. Stout still kept silent, though he publicly warned the Liberals against being used 'for the purpose of aiding the personal ambitions of any one man', and announced that he would accept the premiership if offered it.[1] Possibly it was at this time and not in May that Stout tried to induce Ward to desert Seddon for him. Not until a year later did Seddon learn that his rash assertion had led Mrs. Ballance to write to Stout confirming what her husband's wishes had been. Then, after another brush with Seddon, Stout published her statement.[2] The most that could be thought of in Seddon's favour was that, though plenty of Liberals knew of Ballance's wishes, he probably had not told Seddon. He was so generous with praise that it is just possible that Seddon supposed he had his blessing.

Seddon's second weapon was more effective. He urged that the Government should be able to lend money at low interest to lessees. On 1 November, while boasting that the Government had not borrowed, McKenzie took up the same theme. Next day Seddon promised to arrange for money to be borrowed in England, on the security of New Zealand lands, and lent at 5 per cent. The Government would simply act as agent and take a commission. Then the Government leaked the news that in Ballance's papers was found just such a scheme. A Mortgage Office in London, not the Government, would raise the money. Ward, too, played the new note, again stressing that the Government would not be borrowing: it would merely guarantee repayment. And the denunciations of the conservative Press spread the glad tidings among the farmers.[3] That Reeves found all this distasteful, if not abominable, is obvious. He seems not to have mentioned the new plan—which had little appeal in his electorate. And when Seddon spoke in Lyttelton in November, with Reeves on the platform, he ignored it too.[4] It was the first big break with the Ballance programme.

In his draft 'Memoirs' Reeves wrote his own recollections of the 1893 election. He described how he went down to Christchurch, 'full of hopes and dreams', his head full of 'Land

[1] *N.Z. Times*, 1 Aug., 14 Oct., 18, 25 Nov.; *Evening Post*, 18, 19 Oct.; *N.Z. Herald*, 19, 20 Oct. 1893.
[2] *Evening Post*, 11, 13, 16 Aug. 1894; *N.Z. Herald*. 17 Aug. 1894; *N.Z. Times*, 6, 13, 16 Aug. 1894.
[3] *N.Z. Herald*, 14 Oct.; 1, 2, 3, 6, 8, 27 Nov. 1893.
[4] LT, 21 Nov. 1893.

Questions', arbitration, and of the Government's achievements, Cheviot and factory inspection. As in 1887, he learned that the electors were thinking of other things. His supporters explained that everything would turn on his answer to several questions:

1. Would I or would I not vote for shutting up all public houses at once without compensation by what was called a Bare Majority—i.e. by a single vote?
2. Would I or would I not vote for giving grants to the Roman Catholic Church schools?
3. Would I express sympathy with a popular preacher of—goodness knows what—who was then enthralling large audiences in an edifice known as the Temple of Truth?

   (This gentleman was just then the subject of a lively correspondence in the public Press. There was, I am afraid, some story about an attractive lady disciple of unquestioning faith and statuesque proportions.)
4. Would I consider the case of a doctor who had been sent to gaol for professional misconduct and, having served his sentence, wanted to resume practice? He had sympathisers and they had votes.

I set to work. I refused to vote for the Bare Majority. I refused to vote for grants to Catholic schools. I sent a guarded communication to the friends of the persecuted Apostle in the Temple of Truth. They were asking that he should be given the right to solemnise marriages. I told them that I was gratified to know that he was giving attention to that question. I told the erring doctor that I could only promise to look into his case but hinted that as a matter of personal feeling I rather sympathised with a man who wanted to earn his living. After that I turned my attention to the platform and at meeting after meeting talked to the people about the policy. At first they were reluctant to listen. But after a while they did listen.

Because of the unknown quality of the women's votes, the Government regarded the election with some apprehension. Everywhere the 'wowsers' were at work, trying to turn the Liberal Party into an instrument for Sir Robert Stout. Reeves's position in his electorate was weaker because he now lived in Wellington, and had lost the *Lyttelton Times*, his main political weapon, and the powerful support of his father. His mother and sisters were so conservative that they would not let him stay with them when he was campaigning.[1] The new editor of the *Times*,

---

[1] Information from Mrs. Beryl Clarke.

Samuel Saunders, was the son of Alfred Saunders, one of the leading prohibitionists. On the other hand, the fact that Reeves was a minister strengthened his hand. And he discovered in the family an ally of previously unsuspected strength.

The Electoral Bill was signed by the Governor on 19 September. The day before T. E. Taylor wrote to Stout that Mrs. W. P. Reeves was in Christchurch calling on the electors 'evidently to feel their pulse on behalf of her husband. The ladies are thus early in the field.' A few days later he added that she was still 'moving around quietly'. Various rumours, such as that Stout would not stand for Christchurch because he would not oppose Reeves, were circulating—'all claiming to have originated with that lady—for whom I have the greatest respect'.[1] On 11 October, in the Temperance Hall, the Women's Section of the Canterbury Liberal Association held a large meeting, one of the first political meetings of enfranchised women in the country—and perhaps in the world, for only in Wyoming did women have the vote earlier. Mrs. Reeves had founded the Women's Section of the party, and she chaired the meeting. Next day the members were going about inducing the women of Christchurch to register as electors.[2]

Mrs. Reeves was becoming as good a politician as her husband. But it was plain that he had lost the control over Christchurch politics that he had twice exercised. Ballance's National Liberal Association had not worked as an instrument to enforce an agreed party policy in all electorates. In April 1893 Ballance had written that it had almost no funds and would be of little use in the election. He was too ill, he confessed, to 'galvanise' it into action.[3] On his death Seddon rebuked the Auckland Liberals for their presumption. Then the Stout–Seddon battle and liquor reform had split the Party from top to bottom. Several Liberal Associations and their allies, the Knights of Labour, had 'come out' for prohibition. In Christchurch the Association broke in half.

At the annual meeting in June one 'plank' in the Christchurch Liberal Association's platform, which gave all adults a vote on

1 Stout MSS, 18, 21 Sept. 1893.

2 *Press*, 12, 13 Oct.; LT, 12 Oct. 1893.

3 Ballance MSS, Ballance to Sievwright, 15 April 1893, (reference kindly supplied by Dr. R. T. Shannon).

licensing, was amended to include the possible abolition of public houses. A special meeting was then called and, according to T. E. Taylor, 'bogus' tickets were issued, while some members received their ballots too late to vote. The amendment was repealed by twenty votes. This 'disgraceful burlesque' led the prohibitionists, foiled in the existing Association, to found a Progressive Liberal Association, led by the ex-president of the parent body. Taylor asked Stout to stand for Christchurch, because Reeves could 'be regarded as the champion of the conservative interests as far as the liquor interests are concerned—he has departed from Liberal principles.'[1] By 'liberal principles' Taylor meant the right of a majority (or even of a minority, in a small poll) to deny the minority (or even majority) the right to drink alcohol. Fortunately for Reeves, Stout decided to stand for Wellington, where he lived.

Both Liberal groups called combined meetings with Labour and other radical organizations. Both nominated candidates for Parliament. In the ballot of the Liberal Association, Reeves came first, but he was followed by W. W. Collins, a 'free thought' lecturer and prohibitionist, with Sandford third. The Progressive Liberals nominated three candidates of their own.[2] The (original) Liberal Association had dropped old R. M. Taylor, a sitting member, possibly because he was too strongly opposed to prohibition—and thought to be too fond of liquor.[3] The Conservatives also put up three candidates, including Reeves's journalistic persecutor, J. S. Evison ('Phiz'). R. M. Taylor and W. Hoban, a Catholic left wing Liberal, another of Reeves's old allies, stood as independents. Eleven candidates, eight of them 'Liberals', whether Catholic, prohibition or government, were standing for two seats. To add to the confusion, the Catholic bishop asked all Catholics to vote for the three candidates who supported the demand for state aid for Catholic schools—Hoban and two of the Conservatives, George and Evison. The last, though he once edited the *Catholic Times*, also wrote rationalist pamphlets under the pseudonym 'Ivo'.[4]

Reeves had to walk with extraordinary caution. He had no

[1] LT, Sept.–Oct. 1893; Stout MSS, Taylor to Stout, 18, 20 Sept. 1893.
[2] LT, 20, 21 Sept., 3 Nov. 1893; PD, 1893, 82, pp. 465–6.
[3] Reeves hints this, PD, 1894, 83, p. 125.
[4] LT, 6, 23, 25, 27 Nov. 1893.

hope of winning the extreme prohibitionists, who called him the 'Brewers' Candidate',[1] but he had to woo the 'temperance' voters by stressing the great advance made in licensing reform by the Government, solicit the Catholic vote, court the unionists, defy the Conservatives. He worked hard, and successfully. Hall wrote to Rolleston, of Reeves, 'He is a prince at election time—more's the pity....'[2] He abandoned Taylor and ignored Collins, the third Liberal Association candidate. Sandford and he acquired their own committee, and rooms, and spoke together at meetings.[3]

At his first meeting, before three thousand people, Reeves showed that he had not lost his platform arts, and in circumstances trying beyond the ordinary. Reeves liked to sip something during long speeches, and, as a concession to prohibitionists, he took care that that something was gin: 'gin and water have an innocent look.' This seems to have been the occasion that he later described when his supporters thought a bottle of gin contained water and filled his tumbler with it. Before he spoke, Reeves swallowed half of it.

It was my first experience of raw gin and I thought I had swallowed blue fire. The alcohol and the shock made my head whirl round and my eyes grow slightly dim. For a minute or two I thought I was drunk. I gazed hopelessly at the audience while the Chairman droned on. The front benches were all packed with relentless prohibitionists led by my bete noir Mr. 'T.E.A.' Taylor; they had also swarmed on to the platform, collaring the seats and leaving my leading supporters to stand up against the walls. Looking round I could see no prospect of mercy anywhere. As an old journalist I instinctively thought of next day's newspapers. I could see black head lines in big caps. WHAT SEDDONISM IS BRINGING US TO! SCANDALOUS INCIDENT IN CHRISTCHURCH! MINISTER OF EDUCATION DRUNK ON A PLATFORM!!! I stood up and fancy that I swayed a very little. With a great effort I stepped forward and delivered the first sentences. They came out all right, but sounded in my ears as though someone else was speaking. Fortunately the effort and the heat of the night threw me into a perspiration and in five or six minutes my head was clear.

[1] *Press*, 4 Sept. 1893.
[2] Rolleston MSS., 19 Nov. 1893.
[3] e.g. LT, 14 Nov. 1893.

He soon won the laughter that cheers the orator near the beginning of a speech by remarking that he was surprised to see such a large audience 'when he reflected that so many of his constituents were themselves candidates'. But the meeting was 'rowdy and unfriendly'. The Reverend F. W. Isitt and other prohibitionists created an uproar. There were so many interruptions that Reeves was momentarily rattled. A voice called out 'Keep your rag in!' According to the *Press*, he 'floundered and plunged, stuttered and spluttered'—a state produced, no doubt, more by gin than Prohibition. In the end he 'got into his stride and held his own'. The meeting ended triumphantly with a vote of thanks passed by a majority of seven or eight to one.[1]

On election day Reeves rode a charger from booth to booth. He topped the poll, and his friends drew him in a cab to the *Lyttelton Times* Office, as of old, where he spoke from a window and dodged a few rotten eggs.[2] But the prohibition candidate, Smith, beat Collins, and Collins beat Sandford. Reeves received 5,431 votes, Smith 4,577, Collins 3,873, the three Conservatives, including Evison, less than 2,000 each. It was a personal victory. He was helped perhaps (it could not be proven) by the ladies, who voted in large numbers.[3] But the rise of prohibition spelled the end of his 'party' of 1887 and 1890.

The election was a victory for Seddon. The Conservatives were massacred. In Waihemo John McKenzie beat Scobie, whose parting words here may be his remark to Rolleston, when he rejected everyone's advice not to fight the great John: 'I lack the moral courage to a be coward.'[4] Only three Opposition members (all in Otago) were elected in the South Island. Even Rolleston, their leader, lost his seat. (Glasgow wrote to him: 'I am *very sorry*. I don't think I should say any more.')[5]

It was not, outside Christchurch, a victory for Reeves (and the ghost of Ballance). The Liberals increased their share of the votes from 54 per cent. to 57 per cent.; they doubled their rural seats; but in Wellington, Bell this time beat McLean, and in

---

[1] Reeves wrote two accounts of this incident, in his 'Memoirs' and in a journal (entry 25 Oct. 1904). See also LT, 31 Oct., 1 Nov., 3 Nov.; *Press*, 31 Oct. 1893.

[2] LT, 29 Nov. 1893.

[3] LT, 10 Feb. 1894; *Press*, 29 Nov. 1893; P. Grimshaw, Appendix and pp. 215 ff.

[4] Rolleston MSS, 11 Sept. 1893.

[5] Ibid., 29 Nov. 1893.

Auckland, the largest town, where the Liberal Association was very radical and strongly supported Reeves's bills,[1] the Liberals were battered by the Conservatives who were organized in a National Association, one member of which was their future leader, William Massey.[2] In 1890 the town had elected three Liberals: now it elected Grey—an independent—and two Conservatives.

The *Lyttelton Times* estimated that the Conservative Opposition now numbered only about fifteen. The Liberals, wet or dry, numbered fifty-one or two, depending on how many (Grey, Green, Earnshaw, Stout?) were called 'independents'.[3] But almost all the left wing Liberals, other than Reeves, were prohibitionists. The Ballance Liberal Party was no more. The supporters of the Government were mainly rural members.[4] It was true, as Reeves wrote, that Seddon had to rely on the more conservative section of the party. But who was Reeves to turn to? He had lost much of his trade union support to Stout. He now had only the Seddon Government and the parliamentary Liberal Party. Yet, on the other hand, the election had triumphantly vindicated the Liberal policy—and Reeves's policy—against the Governor, the Legislative Council, and the conservative Opposition. Carefully read, the election results spelled Reeves's future.

His mood may be judged from a letter he wrote in mid November to Sir John Hall, who had retired from politics after the dissolution: 'The hurly-burly will be over in a fortnight thank goodness. My friends seem to think I will head the poll but I don't feel at all exultant. The fact is I want a holiday rather badly and feel as though I didn't care what happened so long as the fighting were honourably over and one could go to sleep.'[5]

[1] *N.Z. Herald*, 6 June, 26 Oct. 1893.   [2] Ibid., 17 Nov. 1893.
[3] LT, 29, 30 Nov. 1893.
[4] See R. T. Shannon, 'The Fall of Reeves', *Studies of a Small Democracy*.
[5] Hall MSS, 14 Nov. 1893.

13

VICTORY

1894

In 1894, especially from Reeves's point of view, there was an extraordinary change in the tone of the House of Representatives. Most of his old enemies were gone. Only a demoralized handful of Conservatives remained. William Russell had to confess in June that they were unable to form any recognizable organization, though he began to act as Leader of the Opposition during the session.[1]

Russell had in the past, as chairman of the Labour Bills Committee, been very helpful to Reeves. Now he conceded that Reeves's bills had been placed before the country and that 'this House was elected by an overwhelming majority' to pass them. It was a happy day for Reeves and the Liberals when the Opposition leader could describe his duty as to be 'among the less enthusiastic supporters of the Government'.[2]

The prohibitionists virtually formed a third party, which put up a stronger resistance to the Government than the Conservatives; at times, indeed, Stout seemed effectively the leader of the Opposition. It was not, however, a conservative opposition. Almost all of the left wing Liberals, with the conspicuous exception of Reeves himself; almost all the trade union members; followed Stout. They opposed Seddon at every opportunity. They openly resented his 'coup d'état'. But they supported Reeves's bills in principle. So, though he was in a difficult situation, with Russell and the prohibitionists on his side his bills were safe.

There was no prospect now of Seddon losing his premiership. When Stout challenged a government appointment at the beginning of the session, to Stout's discomfiture Seddon made it a question of want of confidence. The Government won by

---

[1] PD, 1894, 83, p. 164.
[2] Ibid., p. 38.

forty-eight votes to nineteen. Most of the prohibitionists voted with the Government, but it would have won without them.[1] The 'extreme left wing of the party', as Seddon called the prohibitionists, pestered him continually. He complained about their 'mutiny', and eventually refused the whip to G. J. Smith, from Christchurch, after he voted against the Government sixty times in three months.[2]

One other obstruction the Government now effectively reduced. Reeves had for years protested against the prolixity of speeches. Now he carried a motion to reform the standing orders of the House by limiting the length of speeches and the number of speeches by any one Member in Committee.[3] It was, henceforth, much more difficult to 'stone-wall'.

Reeves's relations with Seddon outwardly improved. He was pushed towards the Premier by the prohibitionists. Moreover, he was too strong a party man to relish exhibitions of cabinet discord. He regarded loyalty as a major political virtue, and believed Seddon felt the same: 'My chief may have his faults ... but it was never said of him that he ever turned upon a man who had stood shoulder to shoulder with him.' And he loyally supported Seddon, despite these (no doubt galling) concessions that he had faults. If ministers, he said, 'are loyal to their chief.... They wash their dirty linen behind the scenes.' There was plenty of it, but Reeves was very discreet.[4]

His honest endeavour to stick by his party was shown in his attitude to Ward's Government Advances to Settlers Bill, which the Government had to fight to pass. Stout hated the thought of New Zealand 'taking a stimulant'[5]—in this case in the form of credit. Some of the prohibitionists and Conservatives fought long hours in Committee. After obvious hesitation, and several revisions of the Bill, which apparently resulted from differences of opinion in cabinet, Reeves supported it strongly. It was difficult to reconcile with his boast, early in the session, that the Government had not borrowed in three-and-a-half years; with his assertion that the Government would be liberal and gradual in reform, conservative in finance.[6] However, some features of the

---

[1] PD, 1894, 83, p. 84.   [2] PD, 1894, 86, pp. 303–6.
[3] PD, 1894, 83, pp. 482 ff.; N.Z. Times, 16 July 1894.
[4] PD, 1894, 84, p. 468; 86, p. 1,110.   [5] PD, 1894, 85, p. 705.
[6] PD, 1894, 83, p. 47; cf. 84, p. 467 ff.

new policy appealed to him. He agreed with McKenzie that small settlers could not succeed without capital;[1] he was as keen as McKenzie that they should get it. He was attracted to the idea, as he wrote in the 'Governor's Speech', of the state sharing in the work of colonization, helping private enterprise to secure English capital, which the state alone had the security to borrow cheaply. Finally, he saw the 'cow cockies' as poor men oppressed by the money lender.

In the financial debate, he spoke in reply to George Hutchison, a lawyer who had defeated Bryce in the 1887 election, in whom he found an opponent almost as worthy as Scobie. 'Phiz' said 'Reeves is nettles, Hutchison scorpions.' Hutchison lamented the lack of 'purity of government'—a cry which was to follow the administration to its fall—'The New Democracy expects its public men to be men of probity and honour—men who dare not, will not, lie.' Then, turning from Seddon to Reeves, he suggested that if the future historian ever took pains 'to inquire how it was that the first Minister of Labour was a gentleman who previously had no sympathy whatever with the labourers', he would find it difficult to answer. He conceded that Reeves had written a pamphlet on socialism: 'Honourable members may remember the title that the honourable member took as the compiler of these philosophies. It was "Pharos", and I need not recall that Pharos [the Alexandrian lighthouse] was one of the seven wonders of the world.' He made sport of Reeves's condescension in taking the great philosophers in hand. Plato, he went on, had gone; Socrates had passed away; Herbert Spencer had ceased to write; and Reeves was not looking very well.

Reeves had been lying in wait for Hutchison, as he used to wait for Scobie. He managed nothing to top his opponent's joke, but he hit him a few times (not 'one drop of human blood' was in his speech—a description true enough of Hutchison and his oratory alike). Then he concentrated on answering the charge that the Government's policy was nothing but borrowing. He distinguished between previous borrowing, when the Colony had to pay interest and principal from taxation, and the present scheme, in which the principal and interest were paid by the borrowers, while the principal was secured by mortgages. He

[1] PD, 1894, 85, p. 97.

pictured the 'eternal burden of interest' 'weighing down our toilers'. It was not one of his best speeches; but it was the best he could do.[1]

The Government tried to raise an old-fashioned loan as well. This time they failed, and Reeves helped to bury, at least for the time being, his first great political cause.

The Midland Railway Company had run into difficulties from the start. In 1892 its problems had kept Seddon and Reeves very busy. It wanted a new contract whereby it abandoned the rest of its land grant, in exchange for which the Colony was to guarantee its profits. The Government in 1893 offered to permit it to issue debentures in exchange for its land. This was refused, and now the Government was asked for £600,000 instead of the land. Very reluctantly, rather than allow construction to cease, the Government sought authority to raise the money in London. This was too much for the House to swallow and, despite Seddon's and Reeves's pleas, the Bill was defeated by six votes. A year later, when work on the line had virtually ceased, the Government took over the Company's operations for breach of contract. Only eighty-seven miles of Canterbury's iron vision had materialized. The line was not completed until Reeves was an old man; the Nelson section is not laid yet.[2]

Reeves's nightmares in 1894 and 1895 must have been about bankers, interest rates, balance sheets and illiquid assets, subjects to which, despite his profound prejudices, he had not hitherto devoted much attention. As the depression hung over the country, year after year, even the wealthiest individuals sank into debt. Probably the majority of the great leasehold runs had fallen into the hands of mortgage companies and banks.[3] Then, as prices for produce, and therefore for land, remained low, the finance companies themselves began to suffer in their turn. Through the eighties the 'local' banks, the Colonial and the New Zealand, were obviously struggling to keep afloat. In 1893 the Bank of New Zealand secured authority to seek further capital, but could not raise it. Then its subsidiary, the Loan and

[1] PD, 1894, 84, pp. 460 ff.
[2] *Nelson Evening Mail*, 6 Feb. 1893; *N.Z. Official Year Book*, 1895; AJHR, 1893, D-6, D-6A, I-6C; PD, 1894, 86, pp. 808 ff., 1122.
[3] LT, 7 July, 1887.

Mercantile Agency Company, went into liquidation and its directors into an English court. In the same year almost all of the banks in Australia closed their doors, temporarily (for reconstruction) or for ever. There was a panic 'run' on the Auckland Savings Bank.[1]

The shakiness of the banks and the extreme nervousness of depositors created a tense situation, for the collapse of one bank could easily lead, as in Australia, to runs on all the others; a situation on which the Bank of New Zealand capitalized, when no other source of strength remained. The Bank brought an expert out from England to discuss its situation with its local officers. When Parliament met on 22 June, the Government had no idea of the crisis that was being prepared.[2] A week later, John Murray, the General Manager, informed the Government that the Bank would have to close its doors next day, unless the state came to its rescue. Seddon acted with immense energy. On the same day the Government rushed through all its readings in both Houses and a Committee of the Legislative Council, and presented for the Governor's signature, a bill giving a government guarantee to an issue of £2,000,000 of preference shares.

There is little doubt that the Liberals acted rightly, for the failure of the largest bank would have had incalculable consequences. There is no doubt that they were 'taken for a ride'. Murray held a pistol to their head. As a conservative Wellington member said in the debate, the Government intervened to support a private trading company of whose affairs it knew nothing that Murray did not choose to tell. And it soon appeared that he had told very little. What was known, however, was enough to cause grave anxiety. The principal, though not the sole difficulty of the bank was that it had invested a large part of its funds in increasingly dangerous and often speculative property transactions. The long depression had obliged it (like the Colonial Bank) to 'write up' the value of its assets while property values fell. Like the Colonial Bank, it had been paying dividends out of capital. In 1888 it had 'written off' much of its capital and transferred its mass of unsaleable properties (it was

---

[1] For a fuller account of the banking crisis, see Sinclair and Mandle, *Open Account*, ch. VII.

[2] Glasgow to Ripon, 10 July 1894, confidential despatch, National Archives, G26/4; PD, 1894, 83, p. 492, (Duthie).

now the largest landowner in the country) to the New Zealand
Estates Company. These properties were valued at quite un-
realistic levels, and the bank continued to pay unjustified
dividends. The Opposition expressed dismay at accepting the
bank's estates as part of the security, and Ward confessed that he
would have preferred to see the Assets Company quite separated
from the bank. The Government had, he said, looked into
the security offered 'with not the most pleasant feelings'; 'I
express my individual opinion that... the security is adequate
enough.'[1]

Though Seddon thought criticism of the Estates Company was
'unpatriotic',[2] the Government was nervous at the prospect of
its reputation, and the credit of the Colony, being tied to the
heavy burden, remaining from old land speculations, which was
pulling down so many institutions. When Murray's letter arrived,
Reeves was in the midst of the second readings of his labour bills.
Though he later defended the Government's action, he remained
aloof during the debates on the banking bills, even, on one
occasion, failing to vote and returning to the House immediately
after the division.[3] Within a few months, his distaste and
suspicion matured to antagonism, not towards what the
Government had to do, but who was doing it; for Ward's
involvement with the bankers was too close for his actions to
escape close scrutiny. He was, in fact, in no position to resist the
most outrageous proposals of the bankers, while, as Treasurer,
he was in a perfect position to make arrangements to their
advantage—or his own.

The rumour was spreading that Ward was in financial
difficulties. He and the Ward Farmers' Association, which he
virtually owned, had developed an extensive business in frozen
meat, grain and other exports, and engaged in some highly
speculative and increasingly unsuccessful enterprises which the
Colonial Bank had financed. In 1893 a Wellington newspaper
asked whether his Farmers' Association was running the bank,
or the reverse.[4] He replied to this, and similar criticism in 1894,
by boasting that he earned one of the largest incomes in the

[1] PD, 1894, 83, pp. 162–3, 173, 496–7.
[2] Ibid,. p. 490.
[3] Ibid., p. 517. For his defence of the Government, see vol. 84, p. 468.
[4] N.Z. Times, 30 Aug. 1893, citing the Evening Press, 26 Aug.

country, being one of seventy-five people who paid tax on incomes over £3,000, and that his Association owed no one a penny.[1]

The rumours, at least, were known to Reeves. How much more he knew or suspected is uncertain. In fact, Ward was on the verge of bankruptcy and the bank of liquidation. It had recklessly advanced almost any credit he wanted, until, in 1894, his debts to the bank totalled at least £50,000, and perhaps nearly twice as much—so confused were his affairs that it is difficult to be sure. Both his Association and the Colonial Bank falsified accounts to keep the facts from the public. The former, for instance, inflated its assets by including worthless cheques signed by Ward, and a draft on fictitious oats, which the bank accepted. Both companies continued to pay dividends.[2]

The government guarantee of the Bank of New Zealand suggested a solution of Ward's troubles and his bank's. In September 1894, after months of uneasy whispering, the Honourable George McLean, the chairman of the Colonial Bank and a Legislative Councillor, who had held office in Vogel and Atkinson ministries, proposed to the Government an amalgamation of the Colonial Bank and the Bank of New Zealand, for which parliamentary approval was necessary. On 12 September Ward wrote to Seddon about his general worries in connexion with the Bank of New Zealand's Estates Company, which was making it impossible for that bank to recover. The solution to this problem, he suggested, was to separate these two concerns, and to amalgamate the Colonial Bank with the New Zealand, thus enlarging the latter's business. Although both banks were to clear 'all bad or doubtful debts', the proposals he outlined also included the following condition: 'Each proprietory to be held responsible for and

---

[1] *N.Z. Times*, 30 Aug. 1893; also 21 Jan. 1895; PD, 1894, 85, p. 6.

[2] See, e.g., the *Press*, 29 Jan. 1897. There is an immense amount of published information on the banking crisis and Ward's affairs. A clipping book in the possession of the late W. H. Montgomery of Little River was especially valuable. In addition there are the reports of the liquidators of the Colonial Bank and the Ward Farmers' Association, the judgments of Mr. Justice Williams on Ward and the Association, and the parliamentary enquiries of 1897–8. The famous anonymous 'Black' pamphlet, *Unauthorized Biography of Sir Joseph Ward, Premier of New Zealand*, Auckland 1910, and V. M. Braund, 'A Romance of Trade and Politics', Wellington, 1905 (cyclostyled), are substantially accurate and mainly based on newspaper reports.

to provide for any losses made on any accounts now held by either.'[1]

What Ward was proposing was the amalgamation of a practically worthless concern with one now state-guaranteed. What he hoped is equally obvious. He had recently tried unsuccessfully to induce the Bank of New South Wales to take his accounts:[2] now he hoped that his debts would be taken over by the Bank of New Zealand. If he could rescue the Colonial Bank he could reasonably hope that its directors would protect his interests while the amalgamation was in progress.

Immediately there were rumours of dissension between Ward and Seddon, which Ward denied.[3] In fact, the real trouble, once again, was between Seddon and Reeves. Ward hoped to save himself; Seddon the Government's power; Reeves its reputation. On 20 September Reeves and Montgomery wrote a joint memorandum to Seddon:

Since the last discussion in Cabinet on the suggested amalgamation of the Colonial Bank and the Bank of N.Z. we have very carefully considered the position.

The issue involved in the suggested scheme seems to us sufficiently grave to affect the reputation and standing of the Cabinet. A successful amalgamation upon sound lines is probably desirable, but we are distinctly of opinion that the settlement of the scheme should by no means be left to the two Banks concerned. It must be virtually controlled by the Government.

Disliking as we do the proposal that the future of that very doubtful concern the N.Z. Estates Co should be laid directly on the Cabinet, certain as we are that the discredit of any future failure there will be laid to the charge of Ministers, and will be constantly contrasted with any success that may attach to the management of the Amalgamated Bank as separated from the Estates Co;—we are still prepared to assent to the amalgamation under certain conditions.

These are first, that any bill shall leave it to the option of the Government to sanction amalgamation, only in the event of the arrangements therefor being found satisfactory.

Second that before any further step is taken in the matter of the

---

[1] This letter, and that following, by Reeves and Montgomery, are in the late W. H. Montgomery's papers. Ward's was published AJHR, 1896, I–6, pp. 296–297.

[2] K. Sinclair and W. F. Mandle, *Open Account*, pp. 126–7.

[3] *N.Z. Times*, 24, 25 Sept. 1894; PD, 1894, 86, p. 241.

Bank of N.Z., a trustworthy President and Auditor be appointed to
that Bank. By 'trustworthy' we do not of course mean merely
commonly honest, but men in whose skill, and judgement, and
independence, full confidence can be placed.

Third it is a sine qua non that a Government Valuator or valuators
shall independently scrutinise and assess the accounts and assets of
each Bank, and of the N.Z. Estates Co.; and shall be generally
satisfied with the proposals of the Directors as to these.

Fourth we think it right that we should know who these valuators
shall be before we accept any responsibility for any Govt. action in
the matter.

We are quite aware that to address this letter to you is to take a
somewhat unusual course, which can only lead to one result in the
event of our requests being thought unreasonable, or such as cannot
be acceded to: but we are compelled to think that the position with
which the Government is face to face is one so unusual and of such
importance that we can see no other course to adopt than that we
have indicated.

Reeves and Montgomery probably had it in their power, by
resigning over such a grave issue, to wreck the Government,
particularly because they were supported by Stout (who
introduced a Guaranteed Banks Amalgamation Prohibition
Bill) and the prohibitionists, as well as the Conservatives. What
occurred in the cabinet is unknown, but the result was that Ward
regretfully informed the House that though amalgamation would
have been desirable under proper safeguards, the Government
could not accept the banks' proposals.[1] Nevertheless, he was
not beaten yet. When the Government rescued the Bank of New
Zealand, it gained the right to appoint the president and auditor.
Reeves and Montgomery at first got their way over this point, and
the Government tried to induce Reeves's friend, a banker of
high repute, James Coates of the National Bank, to run the
Bank of New Zealand. When he refused, however, Ward
succeeded in securing the appointment of William Watson, Chief
Inspector of the Colonial Bank, one of the men who had him in
their power, as head of the Bank of New Zealand. When challenged, he assured the House that the appointment was no job.[2]
The preposterous volunteer laureate of the Liberal parliament-

---

[1] PD, 1894, 86, pp. 241–2, 449.
[2] PD, 1896, 92, p. 22.

arians, 'He Hem' Smith, might almost have read Ward's
thoughts (but did not):

> With a state bank at our command,
> What cannot we achieve?[1]

Cabinet disputes occurred at a political level below public
consciousness: they were known only in rumours which, like
dreams, indicated some unidentified disturbance. In 1894 there
were frequent hints in the Press that Reeves wanted to go to
London as Agent-General to succeed Westby Perceval, whose
three-year term was up. In February the *New Zealand Graphic*
published a series of cartoons on this theme, showing him, for
instance, dreaming of a knighthood. Eventually he felt obliged
to deny the rumours—not, however, very positively: 'I have
never expressed a desire or hinted to my colleagues that I wanted
that position, although I do not think it would be a disgrace
either to the country or to me if I took the position.' Attentive
listeners at a meeting in Auckland in May might have pricked
up their ears at another remark by Reeves when, describing
himself as 'a Fabian socialist', he added: 'He was not to be
hounded down, or to be hurried off the stage of public life
because he advocated these opinions.'[2] But, outwardly, the main
influence of the banking crisis was that it interrupted and, like
the succession crisis and the liquor issue in 1893, for a time
threatened to delay the Liberal progress. This time, however,
Reeves was not denied. He had his old bills ready, and a few new
ones, including a masters and apprentices bill, an immigration
bill, and a workmen's wages bill. These three bills had to be
dropped for the time being, but six of his labour measures,
including an amended Factory Bill, Industrial Conciliation and
Arbitration, a Shipping and Seamen's Bill and his Shops Bill
were passed. 1894 saw the most important set of new laws
passed by a New Zealand Parliament up to that time.

Reeves was a little too jubilant at 'the very novel reception'
his labour bills received in the House, but even the *Evening Post*
thought he had every reason for pride, after fighting consistently
and courageously for several sessions and meeting defeat with

1 PD, 1894, 84, pp. 292–3.
2 PD, 1894, 86, p. 1114; *Auckland Star*, 2 May 1894.

'unwearied persistence'.[1] It gave him immense encouragement to think that his Shops Bill now seemed in some respects to be behind rather than ahead of public opinion—Stout and his cohort wanted a compulsory Saturday half-holiday, whereas Reeves left the closing day to be decided in each locality.[2] As a result, he was, throughout the 1894 session, markedly more conciliatory, cautious in speech, courteous and generous to his opponents. The new temper of the House—and his own—did not, however, mean that his measures were unopposed.

One of the new measures, which had not been debated during the election, led to almost unanimous indignation in the newspapers. On his own initiative, Reeves had an Undesirable Immigrants Bill drafted privately (the government draftsmen being too busy to touch it). Its aims were several. First of all he wanted virtually to prohibit Asian immigration, as the radicals were demanding, in the interests of racial purity and the trade unionists' standard of living. He also intended to protect the unionists by hindering the immigration of 'paupers', especially from Australia, who were arriving in such numbers (he felt) as to frustrate his efforts to 'raise the condition of our people'. No one who did not possess £20 was to be allowed into the country. Finally the bill excluded the immigration of cripples and people with certain diseases. The public protest was mainly aimed at the last two sections. Even Seddon, though he publicly defended the restriction of Asian immigration, thought that the bill had 'one or two undesirable clauses': he, himself, he confessed, could not have landed in New Zealand if he had had to possess £20![3] The ridicule of such clauses embraced Reeves himself and the newspapers began to call him Undesirable Bill Reeves. The Bill was read once and dropped without debate, though it had been extensively debated in the Press, if mainly from one side.

Once again he met his greatest difficulties in the House with the Shops and Shop Assistants Bill. He was kept up until two in the morning in committee, where the prohibitionists managed to pass an amendment closing hotels at the same time as shops, so

[1] 29 June 1894; see Reeves's remarks, PD, 1894, 83, pp. 124 ff.
[2] PD, 1894, 83, p. 124.
[3] On this Bill, see PD, 1894, 83, pp. 91-2, 121, 155-6; 86, pp. 80, 611-12; 1895, 89, pp. 345 ff.; *N.Z. Mail*, 1 March 1895; *N.Z. Times*, 10 Jan. 1895.

that shop assistants could not enjoy an alcoholic half-holiday. The casting vote of the Chairman of Committees, A. R. Guinness, an ex-Greyite Liberal who had been appointed by Seddon, was given against Reeves. When this amendment was later thrown out by the House, by a majority of 34 to 30, Guinness attacked Reeves in terms which were to gain wide currency. He warned the Government that Reeves, 'by his radical and hasty legislation in the interests of what he called the cause of labour, was doing what would ultimately ruin the Liberal party: that was to say, he was legislating in a direction that was unfair, and would have a most detrimental effect upon the liberty of the subject'. Even more ominously, in committee, Ward, Cadman and McKenzie all voted against Reeves on detailed amendments—giving, for instance, a lunch hour to shop assistants.[1] The other leaders of his own party were beginning to find Reeves's reforms indigestible.

Reeves claimed that his Shipping and Seamen's Act was an improvement on legislation in the United Kingdom or anywhere in the Empire. It cut down penalties for breaches of discipline, improved sanitary provisions, and laid down the proportion of skilled seamen necessary in ships at sea.[2] His Factory Act, which in some details resembled the British Act and legislation in the United States, he claimed to be, in certain respects, in advance of that in any other country.[3] No child under fourteen could be employed in a factory, nor under fifteen unless he passed an education test. A forty-eight hour week was the maximum for women and children. They could work overtime only on a limited number of occasions and with the approval of a factory inspector.

The Industrial Conciliation and Arbitration Act is the measure with which Reeves has rightly been associated ever since. He was, William Russell said, 'saturated' in it. Whenever the subject arose he found it difficult to restrain his enthusiasm for expounding its origins, methods and aims, for it was central to his conception of the art and philosophy of politics. Its origins have

---

[1] PD, 1894, 84, pp. 611–12; 85, pp. 232 ff., pp. 387 ff.; 86, pp. 318–30; *Journals of the House of Representatives*, 1894, p. 196.

[2] PD, 1894, 85, p. 231.

[3] Speech to the 'Eighty Club', *Reform and Experiment in New Zealand*, (pamphlet), London, 1896.

been briefly glanced at. Its aims were two. First of all it was an
Act 'to facilitate the settlement of industrial disputes'; secondly,
as its title indicated, it was intended 'to encourage the formation
of industrial unions and associations'. To prevent strikes and
encourage unionism might seem, at first glance, oddly assorted
objectives, but they arose from his experience of life as well as
ideas, and were linked in a single vision. He wished to benefit
employees both immediately and prospectively.

He began from the assumption that there was 'a natural
warfare between classes', but was convinced, in the light of 1890,
that labour was too weak to wage it. Consequently, it was
essential both to strengthen labour, and save it from itself, by
limiting the likelihood of strikes. Yet he saw that, though in the
colonies unions generally lost, their interests were nevertheless
advanced by striking and the threat of striking, and he denied
that 'the strike is the suicide of labour'. In 1891, he added to this
remark: 'But I say a strike is industrial war, and like all other
war it is a thing to be avoided as far as possible. I am not a
peace-at-any-price man, but I am a peace-at-*almost*-any-price
man when it becomes a question of an industrial war.'[1]
Thus he did not attempt to abolish absolutely the right to strike.
The Act merely made strikes illegal while a dispute was under
consideration by a Board or the Court. Reeves seems, to judge
from his correspondence in 1901–5, to have supposed that it went
farther and prevented a registered union from striking, but this
may indicate a change in his opinions, not his opinion in 1894.[2]
In any case the term 'compulsory arbitration', he later explained,
was only a nickname.[3] Arbitration could be compulsory only
after conciliation failed, when any party could have a dispute
referred to the Court. Because of their reluctance to accept
arbitration it was employers who first felt this compulsion.

Reeves saw that his measure could be regarded as being as
much in the interests of employers, since industrial harmony and
a generally high standard of living were to their advantage, as of
employees. He professed to be puzzled that it was almost
universally denounced by businessmen, but proud that it had

---

[1] PD, 1891, 71, p. 82.
[2] See below, pp. 306–7.
[3] Reeves MSS, typescript lecture, 'Compulsory Arbitration', written while
Lloyd George was in power.

originated with 'labour'.[1] Once he presented it to the public as 'designed to fairly hold the scales between employer and employed'. Fundamentally, however, he was careless of the interests of employers. He thought that, in the short term, they could well look after themselves, while, in the long run, he hoped they would disappear from the earth.

In his basic intellectual conviction Reeves was a socialist—not a theorist, but a practical politician who believed in ultimate socialism. In his speeches he surrounded his profession of faith with sincere defining qualifications, which did make his doctrine sound as nearly innocuous as possible. He proffered socialism embedded in honeyed phrase. The aim of his arbitration Act, he said, was '*a kindly solution* of the natural warfare between classes'.[2] But he did believe in the reality of class warfare and that its final solution was socialist. In discussing unemployment in 1894, he said that all they could do was palliate the evil: 'I believe that so long as the world sticks to the present method of exchange, and so long as the world is ruled by what is called the capitalist system, so long shall we see these extraordinary industrial crises and panics.'[3]

This thought was constantly in his mind in the eighteen-nineties. In 1894, attacking a private bill to introduce an elective executive, he said that, in 'Anglo-Saxon' countries, 'you will always have a party of resistance and a party of progress, —as long as you have the capitalistic system.'[4] And, in talking of the trade depression and the bank crisis, he said to an Auckland audience in the same year that thinking people were asking whether 'civilisation and the State' could not 'restrain the commercial anarchy that led to these frightful disasters'. Because he thought that the State could and should, he told the meeting, he was called a socialist. There were, he assured them, good and bad socialists: 'For his part he claimed to be a Fabian socialist.'[5]

The decisive influence on Reeves's views had been reading the *Fabian Essays in Socialism*, when they first appeared. He had also

---

[1] *Auckland Star*, 2 May 1894; cf. PD, 1894, 83, pp. 128 ff.; Reeves MSS, large clipping book, p. 121.

[2] PD, 1893, 79, p. 171.   [3] PD, 1894, 83, p. 47.

[4] PD, 1894, 85, p. 136. W. K. Hancock later applied the same terms to Australian political parties in *Australia* (1930).

[5] *Auckland Evening Star*, 2 May 1894.

been influenced by the arguments of writers, such as Henry George,[1] who had inspired the English Fabians, but he was not, he readily conceded, an original thinker. He continued, in 1894 as in 1890, like the leading English Fabians, to regard every state regulation of the individual, from the registration of his birth to that of his death, as steps towards socialism. It is an adequate shorthand symbol to label him a Fabian.

Socialism appeared to him a consequence, in fact a necessary corollary, of democracy. In the past, he said in 1892, the colony 'had been governed by the middle classes, on the sufferance of the democracy'. 'He believed that government by the democracy—direct government, as we must have it, would mean a very large extension of the functions of the State ... in that sense, and that sense alone, he was socialistic.'[2] He sometimes took 'that sense' a long way. In 1895 he observed: 'Our policy has for its object the increase, enlargement, and multiplication of the functions of the State.'[3] But though he sometimes sounded as though he believed in state activity for its own sake, he was perfectly clear about the ultimate objective. The 'collective power of the community' would be used to defend the weak:

If they were going to raise the masses of the people, and to raise the scale of civilisation, it was to the collective power of the community, the State, that they would have to look. Co-operation, organisation, unionism—call it what they would, it was not a question of getting a shilling more in wages, or regulating the number of apprentices or the hours of labour—these things were only the means to an end, and that end was to raise the masses of the community and to improve their condition.[4]

The duty of the state was to promote a moral society—as Frederic Harrison, another thinker who influenced the Fabians, had written. Reeves agreed with Dr. Johnson's observation: 'Where a great proportion of the people (said he) are suffered to languish in helpless misery, the country must be ill policed and wretchedly governed: a decent provision for the poor is the true test of civilization. —Gentlemen of education, he observed, were pretty much the same in all countries; the condi-

---

[1] On George's influence, see E. R. Pease, *The History of the Fabian Society*, London, 1916, *passim*.

[2] Reeves MSS, large clipping book, p. 121v, speech in Auckland in late 1892.

[3] PD, 1895, 87, p. 48.   [4] Reeves MSS, loc. cit.

tion of the lowest orders, the poor especially, was the true mark of national discrimination.'[1]

In an article in the *Independent Review* in 1903, Reeves put his aim, the aim of his party, in a question: 'Is it possible to have a civilisation which is no mere lacquer on the surface of society? Can a community be civilised throughout, and trained to consist of educated, vigorous men and women; efficient workers, yet not lacking in the essentials of refinement?'[2]

The question embraced those asked by most socialists in modern times. He would have been astonished to know that some Marxists were later to detect Fascist tendencies in his thought, and particularly in his Industrial Conciliation and Arbitration Act.[3] It is possible to support such a view, because he did sometimes verbally identify the state with society or the nation in a way later characteristic of Fascists; but he did not believe that his legislation would or could produce a permanent reconciliation of class interests; his bills he regarded as temporary palliatives. His identification of state control with socialism was a natural (and very general) error at that time, despite Bismarck's or Louis Napoleon's example and Hubert Bland's warning. To regard him as a proto-Fascist is anachronistic thinking which makes sense only to some dogmatic Marxists. Reeves was a socialist who saw no alternative to accepting the wages system for the time being, and trying to get as much as possible from capitalism for the worker. That endeavour, through progressive state encroachment on employers' powers, he thought would ultimately lead to socialism. That endeavour, which he called the state's civilizing mission, we now label 'the Welfare State'. Whether it will, in fact, lead to socialism, or to a 'capitalism' indistinguishable from 'socialism', remains to be seen.

In his 'Memoirs', Reeves wrote of his political rôle:

I was not an original thinker and never flattered myself that I was, even when a young man. It is true, that like all men who have the

---

[1] J. Boswell, *Life of Johnson*, (Oxford Standard Authors), p. 446.
[2] Dec. 1903.
[3] In two pamphlets, W. Rosenberg, *Compulsory Arbitration: Barrier to Progress?*, Modern Books, Wellington, 1952, (a very confused argument), p. 29 and *passim*; W. T. G. Airey, *New Zealand Foreign Policy, Related to New Zealand Social Development and Current World Trends*, New Zealand Student Labour Federation Occasional Paper No. 2, July 1954.

habit of brooding intensely over certain matters for hours at a stretch, I sometimes hit upon notions which seemed to be fresh. But experience has taught me that there has been nothing fresh in them except in the minor way of supplying links for piecing together other men's ideas and fitting them for use. That was my business between 1890 and 1896. There were plenty of ideas about. Labour questions were in full discussion in England, America, Germany and Australia. The air was thick with schemes and suggestions; there were even suggestions in New Zealand. What one had to do was to form a view as to what was wanted and desirable in New Zealand. Then one looked round to see whether there were any schemes or suggestions that would be useful. From these you selected what seemed likely to be of service, taking one, rejecting many. What you took you pieced together, modified and endeavoured to improve upon. The result was something added to a bill, sometimes one clause, sometimes several. The work was interesting but extremely laborious. The amount of adapting, revising, adding and taking away was very great; over and over again one changed one's mind.

But it must not be inferred that he was a mere eclectic legislator. His political philosophy permeated his legislation. When speaking, with Reeves, to the distinguished Eighty Club in London some years later, the Fabian leader, Sidney Webb, asked why it was that, though not premier, Reeves 'occupied so commanding a position' in New Zealand politics; and answered that it was because he did his own thinking. Reeves's measures, he said, 'all hung together'; they were not 'merely isolated experiments, devised to meet particular emergencies', but 'parts of a definite, systematic, far-reaching policy of social re-organization'; they had 'the inspiration, the breath of life, which comes from real, intellectual conviction'.[1]

It was true, though only a few New Zealand politicians like Stout, Ballance and Atkinson had read widely enough in political theory to appreciate it. His defence of the compulsory education system, his advocacy of protective tariffs, his labour legislation, were all parts of his ideal of the state as midwife to a civilized community. His enthusiasm for leasehold land tenure arose from his desire for state ownership of the means of production. His desire to benefit the poor, together with his dislike of capitalists, led him to advocate breaking up the great estates. The 'land monopoly was the parent of the unemployed and the

[1] 'Eighty Club', *Reform and Experiment in New Zealand*.

swagger system';[1] subdivided, the estates would provide land for
the unemployed and other would-be farmers. But this involved
him in what proved one of the contradictions of the Liberal
policy of 1890. Closer settlement, which fitted in with the growth
of dairying following the invention of refrigerated shipping,
meant creating a 'yeomanry', a capitalist class, which soon
proved, as opponents of the Liberals had foreseen, antagonistic
to Crown leasehold tenure.

To subdivide the great estates was a policy leading to economic
development, which was also partly an aim he had in mind when
he advocated protective tariffs, but it was not an objective in the
forefront of his labour policies. In this respect his views were
typical of New Zealand radicalism then, and during the next
intense depression of the early nineteen-thirties. André Siegfried,
who later knew Reeves and visited New Zealand, remarked:
'The conception of the country as a cake, which it is to one's
interest to divide among as few mouths as possible, seems to be
almost universal in the Colony.'[2] Siegfried was thinking of the
falling birthrate and the antagonism to immigration (which
Reeves shared). He might have said that Reeves's (and the
radicals') aim was to divide the cake evenly among as *many*
mouths as possible. Reeves generally thought of redividing the
existing cake instead of baking a larger one. And beyond that,
he distrusted large industries, and did not mind if the economic
development of the country were retarded by his legislation, as
long as the workers' conditions improved. He frankly preferred
to see the country inhabited by a million people, 'happy,
prosperous and satisfied', than twice as many living in 'dreary
poverty', if that were the price to be paid for industries.[3] He did
not, perhaps, ask how far the general standard of living *could*
improve without as much attention being paid to economic
growth as to welfare. Siegfried condemned this dog-in-the-
manger attitude. The Government, he wrote, 'should realize
that a young country which, in spite of its youth, is already
trying to preserve itself rather than to expand, is by that act
condemning itself'. It is impossible to ignore this criticism.
Sir George Grey dreamed of creating a great country; Reeves

[1] PD, 1894, 86, p. 623.
[2] *Democracy in New Zealand*, trans. E. V. Burns, London, 1914, p. 267.
[3] Ibid, p. 108; PD, 1894, 86, p. 1113.

of a happy one. Describing New Zealand to the Eighty Club, he said that 'though it is not a great nation, it has in it the element of a stable and comfortable civilised nation'. There was, indeed, something *domestic* in his picture of the future New Zealand utopia.

In this perceptible contraction of the radical vision, he was typical of his radical compatriots. But the diminution was not in the degree of radicalism. His views were far to the left of anyone who had ever held cabinet rank in New Zealand, and probably to the left even of any prominent member of the Labour Government which came to power in 1935, or of anyone since. Largely as a result of his drive, New Zealand legislation no longer followed that in Great Britain, but led. Asquith, introducing Reeves to the Eighty Club, said he had carried a series of measures of social and industrial reform to which, in an equal period of time, he believed it would be impossible to find a parallel. He had helped to make his country 'a laboratory in which political and social experiments are every day being made for the information and instruction of the older countries of the world'.

Reeves's part in that transformation exceeded that of any other individual. Seddon, in particular, had contributed little to designing the legislative programme (though a major part in the tactics that got it through); in particular, he had had nothing to do with the arbitration bill. With all the caution owed to the idea that important events usually have important causes, deep-rooted in human society, it may be said that it is improbable that compulsory arbitration would have been introduced but for Reeves's personal effort. There was wide support for a voluntary system; little demand at first for compulsion, but strong opposition from employers. It would have been easy to give in, as McKenzie and Ballance did over the perpetual lease with periodic revaluations. Reeves's Act influenced later arbitration legislation in New South Wales and Western Australia as well as the first Australian Commonwealth Act, besides leading to much thought and debate in Great Britain.

Isaiah Berlin has written: 'The notion of greatness, unlike that of goodness or wickedness or talent or beauty, is not a mere characteristic of individuals as more or less private personalities, but is, as we ordinarily use it, directly connected with social effectiveness, the capacity on the part of individuals to alter things radically on a large scale.'[1]

It is an idea which is relevant to a consideration of Reeves's political importance. Though in a small country and among a small population, he did 'alter things radically on a large scale'. It is largely owing to his efforts that at an early stage industrialization and urbanization were regulated by the community so that it never had to experience their worst horrors. The structure of industry and industrial relations in New Zealand have ever since 1894 developed within the framework provided by his Arbitration Act. Even some of his less important legislation had far-reaching social consequences. His Shop Act of 1894 eventually led to one of the salient features—to visitors, an astonishing feature—of New Zealand life: the inert week-end, with scarcely a shop to be found open from Saturday noon until Monday.

[1] *Historical Inevitability*, London, 1954, p. 6 n

14

ON THE DEFENSIVE
1895

EARLY in 1894 Maud Reeves left the two girls with her parents in Christchurch and went, with Mrs. Ballance, on a trip 'Home'. The family vacated the 'ministerial' house in which they lived in Molesworth Street, Wellington, as they had previously left that in the Tinakori Road, because it was too large and expensive to maintain. The Seddons presently moved in.[1]

While his wife was away (and he enjoyed the political triumphs of that year) Reeves lived happily in the Wellington Club. One of the favourite family stories about his absent-mindedness dates from this time. One morning he left the Club, dreaming, he alleged, of compulsory arbitration, carrying an umbrella, and dressed in a tall silk hat and a dressing gown instead of an over-coat. When his messenger gasped at him 'in dismay' Reeves (so he later recalled) said to him hastily, 'White, how late you are! I thought you were never coming! Here, take this dressing gown down to the tailor's and tell him to put a new girdle on it.' White was later heard to observe, 'It's lucky 'e can't take 'is 'ead off at night: 'e'd leave it be'ind 'im every blessed morning.'

At the end of November, he went over to Australia to meet his wife on her return from England. He spent a month visiting various 'village settlement' projects, and was particularly impressed with the attempt of the Kingston–Cockburn Government in South Australia to plant 'a body of the unemployed' in 'co-operatives' in the wilderness on the Murray River. He thought this the 'most interesting social experiment the world has seen for some time', and a promising cure for unemployment.[2] He met Kingston, with whom he had much in common,

---

[1] See *N.Z. Times*, 23 Feb. 1892, 21 Jan. 1895; PD, 1894, 83, pp. 436, 547; 84, p. 582. On Mrs. Reeves's trip, see *N.Z. Times*, 7 April 1894.

[2] *N.Z. Times*, 22 Nov.; 31 Dec. 1894; 4 Jan. 1895. Throughout Dec. this newspaper quoted comment on Reeves from the Australian Press. See also *State Experiments*, i, pp. 305 ff.

and became ebullient from the constant, though not always favourable, attention he received in the Press. While being interviewed in the Grosvenor Hotel, Sydney, by J. Tighe Ryan, the local correspondent of the *Westminster Gazette*, he committed another of his famous indiscretions. Ryan wrote an article that was reprinted and quoted by the New Zealand newspapers. He said that he 'had met scores of irresponsible politicians who talked Socialism', but that the 'opinions of a politician out of office have generally but little relation to his policy when in power'. He had 'despaired of meeting in the flesh an out-and-out Socialist as a Crown Minister. This is what Mr. Reeves professes to be, and this is what he is.' Ryan reminded him of his 'History of Socialism and Communism': 'I suggested that he had perhaps modified his views before taking office, and remarked that the articles on "Wealth and Want" which brought forth the Labour Party were written by Sir Samuel Griffith [the ex-premier and then chief justice of Queensland], who was afterward the most determined opponent of that party. But he [Reeves] replied: "I took office to carry out my ideas."'

Ryan asked about some of the New Zealand reforms, and Reeves told him that 'all the world over the female franchise will have a Radical and Socialistic effect': he had himself defeated two clergymen in the last election, which showed women did not vote for 'the clerical party': 'The domestic servant, the needlewoman, and the factory hand have to work as hard as and harder than men, and they get less pay for their work.... They have, therefore, less reason to be satisfied with the world as it is.... They will try to change it.'

Ryan quoted an Australian politician who said of Reeves that a cabinet minister 'who talks about factory hands, servant girls and washerwomen as if they were human ... would be amusing if he were not so terribly serious'. His article concluded that Reeves seemed to believe that 'all the dreams of a Socialist' would be realized in New Zealand.[1]

Reeves had often described himself and been described as a socialist before, but this interview, telegraphed from abroad, caused a minor sensation in New Zealand where already a storm was brewing for his return. For three months he was

---

[1] *N.Z. Mail*, 1 March 1895.

subjected to a full-scale onslaught, with no insults barred, in the Press. The attack concentrated on his 'socialist' interview, his undesirable immigrants Bill, which he had, for the first time, publicly defended in talking to Ryan, and his shops Act. The latter had worked reasonably well in most places, where Wednesday or Thursday had been chosen for the half holiday, but in four towns that chose Saturday, and especially in Auckland, there was continual agitation and unrest. The trouble, which Reeves had foreseen in 1894, arose in part from badly-drafted amendments, relating to exemptions, made to the Act by the Legislative Council. Some exempted shops, hairdressers' and greengrocers', increased their trade while rival shops were closed by selling 'sidelines' (tobacco and groceries respectively). But all sorts of other difficulties had arisen. Some shopkeepers defied the law and were prosecuted. There were disputes about the penalties imposed by the Act. A magistrate ruled that shopkeepers' wives were not shop assistants. Thus there was great dissatisfaction in a section of the community that included many Liberal voters.[1] The socialist message from across the Tasman sounded to them, as to the Conservatives, like a challenge.

In late January 1895 Reeves spoke to a meeting in Wellington. He said that New Zealand was politically a generation ahead of Australia, where the Labour parties were only beginning the work that the New Zealand Liberals had accomplished. Australians hearing him had thought he was describing a utopia, not a sister colony. When he was last in Australia, five years before, New Zealand visitors had had to sing very small; but now they could boast of the best labour code in the world. The Government hoped that in the next few years as many new labour laws would be passed. He hoped that a Saturday half holiday would eventually become universal; he meant to persevere with his Undesirable Immigrants Bill, despite 'the howls of execration', until he had converted the public; he also listed Masters and Apprentices, Servants Registry, Eight Hours and Labour Department Bills as coming up in the next session.[2]

It was a great shock to Reeves, though he later made light of

---

[1] PD, 1895, 91, pp. 441 ff., *Auckland Star*, 6, 11, 14 Feb., 5 March 1895; *N.Z. Herald*, 25, 26 Jan.; 6, 11 Feb. 1895.

[2] *N.Z. Herald* and *N.Z. Times*, 26 Jan. 1895.

the criticism by calling it 'not unfriendly' advice, that this speech led T. W. Leys, perhaps the most influential Liberal editor in the country, to turn on him. Leys's newspaper, the *Auckland Star*, came out 'strongly objecting' to bringing down 'a sheaf of Labour bills', and 'legislating ahead of public requirements'. It suggested that New Zealand should first try the Acts already passed, and especially denounced the immigration bill as 'a scandal to any Liberal Government'.[1] That this opinion was held by even more august Liberals became plain a few days later. A deputation of Reeves's strongest supporters, the Wellington Trades and Labour Council, of which John Rigg, a Legislative Councillor, was President, met Seddon and pressed for further labour legislation. He told them that they must not ask for too much or 'there might be a reaction detrimental to the interests of the men themselves.' 'New Zealand was more of an agricultural than a manufacturing colony.... The Government could not, he said, be expected to legislate only for one class; it had the colony to look to.'[2]

Once again Reeves put the best gloss he could on unwelcome words. He explained to a Christchurch meeting that, though the statement 'had not been pleasant reading to him, or to anyone who had the labour cause at heart', Seddon had not suggested that labour reforms should cease, but that they should not come too fast—an unexceptionable sentiment. On this occasion, at a meeting in the Theatre Royal in Christchurch, he again adumbrated his measures for the forthcoming session, though he thought it would be mainly 'a tariff session'. The only significant addition to his programme was a call for old age pensions, which the local Progressive (prohibitionist) Liberal Association wanted, but which had not previously had ministerial backing. He took the opportunity of replying to T. W. Leys and Seddon:

If the wish of the Liberal party is to pause now and wait for years before going on further with labour legislation, then, if I know that, I will give up the position of Minister of Labour and see what I can do to hasten the work on as a private member. I have been the staunchest of party men since I first took office in politics ... but I will not consent to hold office merely for the sake of doing so, merely to

[1] 28 Jan. 1895.
[2] *N.Z. Herald* and LT, 9 Feb. 1895.

remain an inactive observer of the working of existing laws, to rest and be thankful when so much remains to be done ... I will not stay in office and stand still.

Once again the prohibitionists tried, in alliance with other 'malcontent Liberals' and Conservatives, to disrupt his meeting, but he received a resounding vote of confidence from his constituents.[1]

Reeves's uncompromising statement again made him the centre of editorial attention. Even the *Lyttelton Times*, in a sympathetic editorial article, conceded that his arbitration and conspiracy Acts, though 'invaluable pieces of legislation', might 'be called theoretical and in advance of actual requirements'.[2] The *Herald* revealed that, for some time, members of cabinet had been tired of Reeves's 'persistent endeavours to pass more and more labour and Socialist measures'.[3] The *Auckland Star* fired a damaging salvo. If it were true that there was a serious difference between Reeves and Seddon, it would 'be so much the worse for Mr. Reeves'. The editor said Reeves was 'a source of weakness' to the ministry, while Seddon was 'its backbone and chief source of strength'. He condemned Reeves's 'craze for theoretical and experimental legislation', while praising his more valuable measures. 'Mr. Reeves has a fatal facility for making enemies and creating a feeling of distrust'—especially, through his use of the word 'socialism'—among employers. His ill-advised utterances and ill-digested bills had damaged the ministry and been even more injurious to the workers and to industrial progress.

Leys repeated the old criticism that Reeves had 'been too prone at times to give unqualified heed and ready assent to the extreme demands of irresponsible and selfish agitators'. (Reeves was, quite erroneously, thought to have introduced his immigrants' bill at the instigation of the unions.) Leys added that the 1894 Factories Act had increased the legal working hours of women and children without Reeves being aware of it. This seemed evidence supporting the accusation that Reeves's bills were carelessly drafted—a criticism difficult to test: so many amendments were made to these bills in committee and in the Legislative Council that it is hard to say how far Reeves can be

---

[1] LT, *N.Z. Herald* and *N.Z. Times*, 12 Feb. 1895. On the old age pensions proposal, see LT, 1 March 1895.

[2] 12 Feb. 1895.   [3] 13, 22 Feb. 1895.

held responsible for their details. Leys thought Reeves must adopt a slower pace, for too many restrictions on industry might prevent economic expansion.[1]

The reiterated support of the Wellington unionists[2] cannot have been much consolation. Reeves was being hit with every weapon that editors could lay their hands on. He was denounced for appointing his young brother-in-law, G. G. S. Robison, a new graduate of Canterbury University College, as his private secretary.[3] The Department of Labour published a monthly journal that sold for twopence. The conservative National Association in Auckland noticed that it included some articles describing a socialist colony in Peru which allegedly had unorthodox marriage laws. A member of that Association, William Massey (whom Reeves quite underestimated, and thought merely 'a decent country member; what we called "a roads and bridges" man'), took this up in the House in 1894 and obliged Reeves, who was extremely puritanical in his views on sexual morality, to defend himself by showing that, as 'Pharos', he had described the Oneida 'complex marriages' as 'revolting'. Now the *New Zealand Herald* took up the cry and insinuated that he believed in 'free love', a libel repeated in its correspondence column.[4]

In March, accompanied by his wife, her cousin, Miss 'Edie' Carr-Saunders, and John Rigg, Reeves travelled to Taranaki on an important mission, to visit the Maori 'prophet', Te Whiti. Since his imprisonment in 1881 for passive resistance to the survey of confiscated land, he had resisted all official attempts at conciliation and maintained 'passive opposition' to the government. On the 23rd, Reeves visited him at Parihaka. He was greeted by a Maori brass band and entered the settlement to the strains of 'Sherman's March Through Georgia'. According to a family tradition, he was shocked to find some of the male members of the welcoming party wearing V-necked sweaters as trousers—a detail which, if it met the notice of the reporters, they did not think fit to print. Te Whiti's speech of welcome was

---

[1] 20 Feb. 1895. The 1894 Act permitted slightly more overtime, but whether intentionally or whether Reeves knew this is uncertain.

[2] *N.Z. Times*, 15 Feb. 1895.

[3] Ibid., 9 Jan. 1895.

[4] PD, 1894, 83, pp. 461 ff., *N.Z. Herald*, 28 Jan., 13 Feb. (letter from a draper), 22 May 1895.

interpreted by the local Press as evidence of his intention to
abandon his isolation. Reeves was praised for his part in bringing
Te Whiti 'under the Queen's mana'.[1]

Two days later he won less favourable headlines when he
addressed a meeting in New Plymouth. He took the opportunity
once again of carefully defining his brand of socialism—he was
'one of those Socialists who believed that the functions of the
State should be extended as much as possible'. Towards the end
of the meeting a local wag lowered from the 'flies' a placard,
'THE ONLY TRUE AND ORIGINAL SOCIAL PEST'.
Reeves was at that moment talking of the drink traffic and—his
wits either failing him or being carefully adjusted to local humour
—he quipped that liquor was, indeed, the only social pest, which
was thought a capital reply.[2]

By this speech Reeves exposed himself on two sides. He was
immediately abused as a confessed socialist, and sneered at for
his careful qualifications, which were interpreted as a retraction
of his alleged claim in Sydney that he was a 'straight-out'
socialist.[3] This latter view was expressed in some verses by the
local Member, 'He Hem' Smith, which were actually quoted
in the House a few months later by Thomas Mackenzie:

> Who to Melbourne gay did go?
>   Rambling R——s the Ranter, O!
> Who burned with Socialistic glow?
>   Rambling R——s the Ranter, O!
> Who, started forty overproof,
>   Came back, reduced, with stealthy hoof,
>   And tapered down to shun reproof?
>   Rambling R——s the Ranter, O....

The rest of the verse—and the remaining six about 'Wriggling
R——s' and 'Wrecker R——s' repeated the common sneers
that he 'learned in luxury's lap to grow'; that he voted each
squatter 'a social pest'; and they sank to coarseness and
absurdity.[4]

His tour through the small towns had happier moments. He
was, as usual, pestered for a bridge. He was presented with

[1] Reeves MSS, medium clipping book, pp. 1–8.
[2] Ibid., pp. 4, 4v. For his speech, see *N.Z. Herald*, 25 March 1895.
[3] *Evening Post*, 27 March 1895.
[4] Reeves MSS, loc. cit., p. 5v.

carefully hand-written addresses by groups of Liberals, working men and Knights of Labour. They are evidently sincere and quite moving in their gratitude for his efforts to make 'the path of life easier for the majority' and for his 'interest' in the working classes—'recognizing as we do that labor is the source of all wealth'.[1]

He assured the Stratford settlers that Seddon was always courteous and considerate, but added that the other ministers had minds of their own. The local *Egmont Settler* found Reeves, in his turn, 'courteous and considerate'—not at all the 'dangerous enemy of the state' that he was painted by some newspapers.[2]

During the session of 1895, Reeves was a reduced figure, while Ward had swelled, at least in the eyes of the public, to almost Seddonian dimensions. Shortly after the session opened in June, Ward returned from a triumphant visit to Great Britain and the U.S.A. In London he had raised a large loan for advances to settlers at the unprecedentedly low rate of 3 per cent. The *Australasian Insurance and Banking Record* saw nothing remarkable in this, for the money market was 'extraordinarily easy', and accused him of issuing misleading figures about New Zealand revenues,[3] but the low rate demonstrated that the Colony's credit was improving. Ward was given a splendid reception, with addresses of congratulation, bunting, the Police Force, Garrison and Jupp's bands, and a procession of brakes, thirty or forty carriages and a dozen 'expresses containing women and children'. Memorial trees were planted and he was banqueted in grand style. Everyone quoted the Governor of the Bank of England's praise of Ward's financial acumen, a testimonial of which he was, indeed, in much need.

Reeves joined in the mutual back-slapping, and the crowd cheered at Seddon's mention of his name, which, the Premier said, 'made his heart warm.... In all great reforms those who persevered and insisted on those reforms were very unpopular....' When Reeves spoke towards the end of the banquet, he received 'a great ovation'. Perhaps he recalled a quip he had made a year before, that he 'looked upon political banquets as funereal functions consisting of equal parts of sham pleasure and

[1] Reeves MSS, pp. 1 v, 6.
[2] Ibid., p. 2; *N.Z. Herald*, 30 March 1895.   [3] 19 July 1895.

champagne'.[1] But he contented himself by referring to the occasion (for which Sir Walter Buller was chairman of the reception committee) as 'the Buller gorge'.

Ward was walking along the edge of a financial and political abyss, and dragging the Government after him. Instead of letting the Agent-General, now Sir Westby Perceval, raise the new loan, he had, almost without warning, decided to go to London himself. Seddon apparently heard of his plan only at the last moment, and the other ministers learned it from the newspapers.[2] Business and political circles buzzed with rumours that his chief intention was to raise money for another of his own businesses, an investment company that was meant to rescue him from bankruptcy. Ward later retaliated on Stout, one of his chief tormentors, by claiming that, when he was about to sail, Sir Robert Stout and Walter Guthrie (one of Stout's business associates) had asked him to push in London the shares of a company in which they were interested, in return for a directorship.[3]

The Government was soon in the thick of further banking trouble. John Murray had quite misled the ministers about the extent of the Bank of New Zealand's difficulties—though it would be difficult, Reeves wrote, to prove 'conscious deceit'.[4] Murray was brought back temporarily from Coolgardie, where he had fled. After hurried consultation he retreated even further to, it was believed, Mashonaland. A Select Committee of both Houses, which included four ministers (Seddon, McKenzie, Montgomery and Ward), Stout and George McLean, the Chairman of the Colonial Bank, recommended further state aid. The Government provided another £500,000; a further half million pounds was raised by a call on the shareholders; and £900,000 of the bank's capital was wiped off its books.

The new Act was not merely one to strengthen the Bank of New Zealand but also to rescue the Colonial Bank, whose directors, foiled in 1894, still pressed for amalgamation. The Act enabled the Bank of New Zealand to purchase other (un-

[1] *N.Z. Times*, 11 July 1895; PD, 1894, 85, p. 118.
[2] R. T. Shannon, 'The Fall of Reeves', *Studies of a Small Democracy*, ed. R. M. Chapman and K. Sinclair, p. 141. I had read this article in MSS before writing the present chapter, and am indebted to Dr. Shannon for several newspaper references I had missed and for the stimulus of his ideas on this topic.
[3] PD, 1896, 92, p. 31.
[4] H. D. Lloyd MSS, Reeves to Lloyd, 20 Sept. 1900.

specified) banking business. Everyone knew that the Colonial Bank was meant, and there soon followed a bill to provide for the sale of its business to the Bank of New Zealand. This time Ward kept silent and left the fighting to Seddon. Meanwhile, still denying that Watson (who was a shareholder in the Colonial Bank) had been made President of the Bank of New Zealand in order to facilitate amalgamation, he helped to arrange for the General Manager of the Colonial, Henry Mackenzie, to take the same position in the New Zealand.[1] The terms of agreement immediately aroused the strongest suspicion. The Colonial Bank accounts were divided into three lists. The 'A' list was to be taken over unconditionally by the Bank of New Zealand, but it was to take over the 'B' and 'C' lists on the condition that the Colonial Bank reimbursed it for any losses incurred in adjusting or realizing on the accounts included. Some members of the House became most persistent in enquiring whether these accounts had been certified as good by the auditor, as required by the new Bank of New Zealand Act. Seddon parried their enquiries very successfully.[2] What was suspected was, a couple of years later, discovered to be true. The 'C' list, of £98,000, included Ward's debts, which the Colonial Bank had 'reduced' by accepting his worthless promissory note for £55,000.[3] Obviously he still hoped that his account would secretly be taken over by the now sound Bank of New Zealand.

It is unlikely that Reeves knew for certain about Ward's account in October, when the sale of the Colonial Bank was effected, but he naturally knew why George Hutchison and others were so curious about the 'B' and 'C' lists. Once again he was very unhappy, but he defended Ward against Hutchison's 'sandpapered sarcasm' (Hutchison compared Ward with a notorious criminal). 'Do not', Reeves said, 'serve your country, because if you do your character will be attacked, your reputation will be traduced, you will be accused of fraud, of telling lies, and you will be compared with the vilest felons and criminals.'[4] It was scarcely possible to exaggerate how intolerably personal the level of parliamentary and Press discussion then was:

---

[1] See PD, 1895, 89, 90 and 91, *passim;* AJHR, 1895, B.27 and B.27A.
[2] e.g. PD, 1895, 91, pp. 580–3
[3] W. H. Montgomery MSS, clipping book, judgment of Mr. Justice Williams.
[4] PD, 1895, 88, pp. 25–29.

Seddon's and Reeves's wives and Seddon's daughters were dragged into political argument.[1] Reeves deeply sympathized with his colleagues in this respect, for he suffered so much himself, but he added to the ill-feeling. Bell described his speech replying to Hutchison as 'personal, malicious, vindictive vituperation'.[2]

Though he defended Ward, he was increasingly suspicious of him, and regarded the whole business with growing distaste. Some of his feelings he relieved by writing one of his best political verses, which he circulated confidentially. He never published it.

Bonnie McLean

> To the lords of the Council 'twas Geordie who spoke:
> 'Ye maun pass ma wee bul or the Bonks will be broke;
> Vote Absorption the day: 'twill be a' richt as rain;
> An' ye'll chuck up your bonnets for Geordie McLean.'
>
> 'Wad ye hae Jock McKenzie and Seddon ride forth?
> They hae freends in Dunedin and votes in the North;
> If ye shatter the Bonks then will thoosands complain,
> An' ye'll wush ye had lustened to Geordie McLean.'
>
> 'Wi' new Liberal notions ma manly breast heaves.
> Ere I face liquidation I'll chum up wi' Reeves;
> An' the Mariteem Cooncil wi' cheerful acclaim
> Will hurrah for Jock Millar *and* Geordie McLean.'
>
> 'Amang African negroes Jock Murray's awa'
> —May his body mak' broth some for blackamoor's maw.
> Soon the Bonk'll pay fine: we'll be a' free from pain;
> An' they'll pit up a statue to Geordie McLean.'
>
> 'So finish your speeches and tear up your notes,
> An' burn your amendments and gie me your votes;
> Pit it through—the bit bul—wi' a sma' guarantee;
> Ye may leave a' the rest to Wull Watson an' me.'
>
> 'Stop the thief,' Shrimmy shrieked and Republican Rigg,
> And Macgregor divorceful, and Reynolds the big;
> But Charles Bowen, douce man, just said: 'Heed not the cranks,
> Let's be rid, once for all, of McLean and his Banks.'

[1] PD, 1895, 91, pp. 204-5.   [2] Ibid., 88, p. 30.

The Councillors heard and made little ado;
They swallowed the clauses; they put the bill through;
And the country was saved;—and oh! never again
Will yours truly pull chestnuts for Geordie McLean.[1]

Much of the session was taken up with banking legislation and the new, more highly protective, tariff. But Reeves managed to get through eight bills. Though five were labour measures, only two were new, the Wages Attachment Act and Servants Registry Offices Act, minor measures in comparison with those of 1894. There were also amending Acts dealing with arbitration, shop hours and shipping. Even so, he was certainly in a hurry and might well have taken more notice of Seddon's attitude, expressed in its plainest form in a remark addressed to Ward in cabinet a few years later, which Waldegrave reported to Reeves: 'You are too young Ward. You want to give everything at once. You should always keep something up your sleeve for next year. Keep the b——s on a string & then they'll keep you in office.' [2] Seddon's view that too much labour legislation at a time would prove indigestible was certainly true of the House, if not of the country.

Though, in writing the Governor's speech, Reeves was able to say that the depression was—almost unbelievably after so many years—passing away, as prices began to rise, one of his main worries was still the unemployed. An influx of workmen from Australia, where conditions were worse, aggravated the problem. Both Seddon and Reeves, on several occasions, felt obliged to speak plainly to deputations demanding work, and expecting it, as the latter said, 'at their back doors'. The two ministers were bluntly explicit that the Government had never promised to make work or to find work for all. Seddon requested the Australian governments to warn men not to go to New Zealand.[3] Nevertheless, though the Labour Department was initially meant merely to advise the unemployed on where vacancies existed, its function grew. The Government's aim was to move urban unemployed into the country. They were engaged on 'co-

[1] Reeves MSS, small clipping book, p. 22. 'Shrimmy' was S. E. Shrimski. He, John Macgregor and W. H. Reynolds were members of the Legislative Council.

[2] 'Letters from Men of Mark', 16 Oct. 1901.

[3] Reeves MSS, medium clipping book, pp. 6v, 8, 8v, 10; PD, 1893, 79, pp. 75, 92; 1894, 86, p. 623; *Press*, 19 Oct. 1893.

operative works' in rural areas, and by 1894 the state was
subsidizing some of these jobs.[1]

Reeves's main hope lay in closer land settlement based on
'village settlements' of the sort he saw in Australia, in which
he unsuccessfully tried to interest Seddon. Reeves already had a
small pet project of this sort. In 1892 he had bought 800 acres for
a 'state farm', an idea derived directly from Annie Besant's
essay in the *Fabian Essays*. He did not expect any immediate
results in the way of socialism superseding capitalism through the
superior efficacy of co-operative effort, but adapted the theory
to the practical problem of 'getting men on the land'. On the
Levin state farm the workers were engaged chiefly in bush
clearing. They were paid five to seven shillings a day on contract
and were permitted to sell the timber they cut. They paid no rent
for their cottages.[2] The project was small, unimportant, and as
far from the socialist ideal as the French workshops of 1848, but
Seddon did not like it and McKenzie detested it.[3] Reeves, on the
other hand, hoped to start several more, for which he had
Crown land set aside.

The Asiatic and Other Immigration Restriction Bill of 1895
was partly directed to the same end, of reducing the number of
unemployed, besides seeking to protect the New Zealand workers
from the competition of 'cheap' labour: 'Chinese competition
is not fair competition', Reeves said. But his motive was not
purely economic. In preaching to the Anti-Chinese League, and
in speaking to the House, he expressed in its most vehement form
an Anglo-Saxon racialist fervour. His vision of New Zealand's
future was of an exclusive and healthy people—and the term
'healthy' included the idea of 'racially pure'. Chinese civilization 'was no civilisation in the European sense of the word, it was
arrested development'. He conceded that the Chinese were
industrious, but in a civilized country people should be capable
of something beyond 'the dull round of toil'. He hoped they were
not 'to have a race of labourers in the country whose sole
qualification was that they were strong and industrious and

---

[1] PD, 1895, 87, p. 47.

[2] LT, 15 Dec. 1892; PD, 1894, 86, p. 613; *N.Z. Times*, 20 Feb., 12 April 1893,
27 Jan. 1894. In later years they paid from 1s. to 3s. a week rental for cottages.
Auckland Star, 17 May 1899.

[3] 'Letters from Men of Mark', Tregear to Reeves, 27 Nov. 1896, 8 Dec. 1896,
17 Jan. 1897, 31 Aug. 1900.

cheap. Only that day he had read of an incident in South Africa, where a baboon had been trained to work at a railway station, and it worked very well.' He pictured Chinese 'quarters' in New Zealand as dens of vice and stench. All Chinese, he seemed to think, took opium and played fantan.[1]

This was a time when the Australian and New Zealand Europeans were becoming conscious and frightened of 'the Yellow Peril'. Reeves entered so emotionally into denouncing the Asians that his sincerity was questioned. The *Press* suggested that his enthusiasm was an attempt to regain his 'waning popularity',[2] but it was not artificial. All his life he felt a powerful prejudice against Asians which would seem a sign of personal psychological instability were it not then so widely shared by British people, and indeed a 'respectable' opinion.

In the debate on his immigration bill Reeves received a severe beating, for there were men there like Willis, Ballance's successor in Wanganui, with 'a kindly word for some Chinamen'. George Hutchison asked, 'Is it worthy of our boasted civilisation that it cannot improve or ameliorate the lives of these persons?'[3] The fact that there were only 4,000 Chinese in the country, and that their number was decreasing, made Reeves's alarm appear absurd to calmer and more balanced observers.

The clauses of the bill restricting European immigration were also roughly handled. They gave great offence to many British immigrants, which Reeves exacerbated by complaining, 'It has seemed to be the maxim for generations in England that anything is good enough for the colonies, and the rubbish of the Old World is constantly being shot into this corner of the earth... .' The House ignored his pleading that, by one of the unquestioned 'laws of nature', criminal, pauper, and imbecile immigrants would breed their kinds.

The immigration bill of 1895 was a version of the Undesirable Immigrants Bill. Although it had been modified in the hope of securing public support, it met a very mixed reception. After a heated debate it was committed by a narrow majority on 22 August. Later the Government was defeated over an amendment in Committee and an attempt to recommit the bill failed.

[1] PD, 1895, 89, pp. 345 ff.; *N.Z. Times*, 5 Aug. 1895.
[2] 25 April 1895; see also LT and the *Star* (Christchurch) of that date.
[3] PD, 1895, 89, pp. 366, 375.

When a deputation, led by Stout, urged Seddon to insist on passing it, he said that, though he approved, it was too far ahead of public opinion, and that the Government risked defeat over it.[1] Reeves introduced another bill which merely restricted Chinese immigration, but this was killed in the Legislative Council after passing in the House.[2]

If Reeves had any doubts about the way the political wind was blowing, they were finally removed on 23 August, when he introduced two relatively minor labour bills. A bill to prevent the attachment of workmen's wages for debt was fiercely opposed in committee, and passed only with great difficulty. The attack on the bill was joined by three Liberal members from rural and country town constituencies, Willis, Meredith and McLachlan.[3] Reeves was evidently put out, and immediately afterwards made a most injudicious speech introducing his Public Tenders, Contracts and Works Bill, which regulated working hours and wages of employees working for the Government and local bodies. He began by saying that no doubt 'the usual tirade' would be raised against it, and the House would be told it was 'brought in from the lowest and most discreditable motives'. His tone, at once contemptuous and self-pitying, led Stout to suggest that the minister was inviting opposition, and certainly the bill aroused unexpected heat. The rural local bodies disliked it, and the Liberal country members denounced it on their behalf. Willis said he was 'getting sick and tired of so much labour legislation', and especially with Reeves' 'continual tinkering'. The House was unmoved by Reeves's reply that all legislation was 'a continual tinkering with the great social questions'.

The speech of Robert Thompson, the Member for Marsden, brought out the essential respect in which Reeves's public image was changing. In 1891 he was seen by Liberals as leading the fight of the poor with the rich. Now he was seen as leading the urban unions against small capitalists, shopkeepers and, more particularly, against small farmers. Thompson felt that when 'the small struggling settler' wanted to augment his income by securing minor contracts from local bodies, he would find that

[1] *N.Z. Times*, 24 Oct. 1895.
[2] PD, 1895, 91, pp. 608, 716–17, 772, 816.
[3] Ibid., 89, pp. 379–80.

they had been placed, by this legislation, under the 'iron heel of some union that is probably located a hundred miles away'. This hit Reeves very hard. He warmly denied the suggestion that there was, in New Zealand, a division between the trade unionists and the small farmers. There was scarcely a union member who was not related to small settlers. He pointed out that the second to largest union, the New Zealand Workers, was mainly of rural labourers: 'I say it is to the country Liberals I look always for reasonable support of labour legislation. And, Sir, I have never failed to get that support. I have addressed meeting after meeting ... in the country districts, and I have never failed to meet with the kindest and most courteous consideration in explaining my labour legislation; and ... to receive expressions of thanks and confidence from the country settlers.'

He was attacked by allies, such as W. H. Montgomery, the son of his old friend, and completely abandoned by his colleagues. In the end he had to accept an adjournment of the debate in order to avoid outright defeat.[1] The *New Zealand Herald*, in an article headed 'Revolt of Ministerialists', quoted a Liberal member who declared that 'any more Bills of this sort would create a rebellion in the camp and cause a split in the party', and called on Reeves to make good his 'threat' of resigning his office and going into opposition.[2]

It was the same with his amended shops bill, which passed after a long struggle in committee.[3] The prohibitionist radicals and rural Liberals gave him as much trouble as Scobie and the squatters had. The House was evidently tiring of his perfectionism: though revision of the Shops Act was essential, it could not be overlooked that this was the fifth consecutive session in which Reeves had brought up a shops bill. His Eight Hours, Masters and Apprentices and Fair Tender Bills were silently dropped.

Reeves was by now almost completely isolated in an exposed and beleaguered position. Nothing made that plainer than his action in voting against the other ministers on a private bill to revise McKenzie's lease-in-perpetuity by adding a periodical revaluation of lands. McKenzie implicitly rebuked him by announcing, 'I must define myself as a member of the class of Liberals who wish to carry out something practical, and

[1] PD, 1895, 89, pp. 381–409.   [2] 26 Aug. 1895.
[3] PD, 1895, 91, pp. 441 ff., 900.

something which the people of this colony are prepared to accept'.[1] Reeves also again voted with Stout and his band for the Institute of Journalists' Bill, which Seddon and McKenzie opposed as likely to restrict entry to the profession.[2] In a speech on temperance, too, he seemed to be moving towards Stout's camp.[3] But, more frequently, he was attacked by Stout and deserted by his colleagues. He showed his feelings by too personal replies, for which the Speaker once rebuked him,[4] to the endless spiteful attacks on himself. Though he could still be judicious, and cool on occasion,[5] he was losing his sensitivity to the mood of the House. But that was merely a reflection of the rapidly changing mood of the country. The depression was passing. The trade union influence on the Liberal Party was declining. Loans to settlers, co-operative dairy companies, the rapid sub-division of a large part of the North Island into small dairy farms, were changing the nature of New Zealand society. Urban radicalism was fading almost as fast as the squatter-dominated conservatism it had defeated. Reeves's position in the party had become precarious, not merely because of his disputes with Seddon, but because, while he was a radical general without troops, the party as a whole no longer faced a formidable conservative Opposition. He was at the mercy of his Liberal rivals and their cohorts.

The question arises whether his bills were, in fact, introduced ahead of public opinion. It is true that they were not adequately supported, but this was because of the growing hostility towards any new measures introduced by him, as well as of unfamiliarity with their principles. It seems a fair inference, from the fact that some of his measures were accepted in the next few years, that he was advancing only a little way ahead of public demand. By his actions, in failing to pass bills, he helped to make opinion.

The diminished rôle of the Minister of Labour left more room for the Minister of Education, who was very much more popular. George Hutchison said Reeves was probably a 'heaven-born' Minister of Education, and his administration of this Department, in which there had scarcely been a hitch, was frequently praised in the Press. Even so, when he introduced three education

---

[1] PD, 1895, 88, pp. 201, 271.   [2] Ibid., 87, pp. 359, 363, 373.
[3] Ibid., 88, pp. 356–60.   [4] Ibid., 91, p. 332.
[5] e.g. Ibid., pp. 755 ff.

bills in 1895, he was accused of intending one of them to provide a job for a friend.

His Technical Education Act had been drafted long before, but some of the Education Boards had protested when he circulated it. Now, when an Education Conference urged him to pass it, he expressed pleasure that 'public opinion had now overtaken the Bill'.[1] It set up technical schools providing classes outside ordinary school hours. Reeves had kept in close touch with the Educational Institutes, and now he met the teachers' wishes by incorporating their institutes and setting up a teachers' appeal board. His third Act set up Industrial Schools for neglected children and delinquents.

Many of the reforms he desired were out of his reach. Not 2 per cent. of primary school children went on to secondary schools. He wanted to improve this situation. In 1895 he circulated a bill to provide for a certain number of free scholars in endowed secondary schools, but it was dropped,[2] like old age pensions, for Seddon to pick up years later. He failed, too, to secure central control of inspectors, who were directed by the Education Boards, or a uniform teachers' salary. His achievements were important but unspectacular. He reorganized Maori schools, and regarded the increase of 10 per cent. in the attendance of Maori school children, in 1894 to 1895, as a 'ray of hope' for their race.[3] His Act of 1894, making school attendance compulsory, also led to a large improvement in the attendance of European children. When he became Minister, he found that school children were supposed to read over 130 textbooks, a list he reduced to 50 by putting pressure on the Boards.[4] He revised the system of government payments to schools, which was based on attendance. While the country was still depressed, larger aims were pipe-dreams. He continued to think that the administration of education must be 'conservative' and, for instance, told a deputation led by Stout that there was no prospect of the state finding money for a university in Wellington.[5]

One educational measure in which he took keen interest (he

[1] N.Z. Times, 10 Aug. 1895.
[2] PD, 1894, 85, p. 371; H. Roth, George Hogben, New Zealand, 1952, p. 111.
[3] Long White Cloud, p. 58; PD, 1895, 89, p. 337.
[4] LT, 11 June 1892; Reeves MSS, medium clipping book, p. 13v.
[5] Reeves MSS, medium clipping book, p. 14v.

16

had worked on it since 1891) was the publication of a national *School Reader*. The English readers in use sometimes contained quite fatuous statements about the Colony. With the help of his departmental officers, he gave a great deal of thought to this project. Passages from Tasman's journal, contemporary accounts of episodes such as Hone Heke's rebellion and the gold rushes, verses by New Zealand writers, were collected and in 1895 10,000 copies of the *Reader* were published, excellently printed and bound, to be sold cheaply to school committees. Reeves read the proofs himself. He hoped the book would 'tend to make our children more patriotic and foster love and pride for their country'.[1]

Reeves, who was very widely—indeed almost comprehensively—read in published New Zealand literature and history, probably selected most of the passages in the *Reader* himself. He also continued to write when he could find time. In his verse written while he was a Minister may be found some of the first evidence of an evolving national consciousness. In 1893 he wrote his national (and Liberal) anthem, 'New Zealand', which contained some lines which help to explain why it never became very popular:

> Though least they and latest their nation,
> Yet this they have won without sword,
> That Woman with Man shall have station,
> And Labour be lord.

'The Passing of the Forest', which was for long his best known poem (indeed, in New Zealand, it was second in public esteem only to Thomas Bracken's mawkish 'Not Understood'), was written in 1894 or 1895. Several of his other popular poems, including the 'Egmont' sonnet, 'In Pember Bay' and 'Hokianga' (which he wrote while visiting northern schools), were written in 1894.[2] These poems, published generally in newspapers, received favourable notices. One reviewer thought 'The Toe Toe in Church' 'an exquisite little poem' worthy to

[1] PD, 1891, 72, p. 213; AJHR, 1896, E-1; E-10; Reeves MSS, medium clipping book, p. 13v.

[2] A copy of 'In Pember Bay', inserted in the Alexander Turnbull Library copy of *In Double Harness*, is dated 'February, 1894'. 'The Passing of the Forest' and 'The Rivers of Damascus' appeared in *Tom Bracken's Annual*, 1896.

rank with Shelley's 'Ode to a Skylark'[1]—though Thomas
Mackenzie told the House that Reeves was worse than Nero,
writing odes to *toetoe* grass in a temple while the unemployed
were starving.[2] This sort of thing, which was not necessarily
ill-humoured, and which he might almost have said himself,
hurt Reeves absurdly. He referred to it very many years later in
a letter, wondering whether 'a public man' were 'rash to let his
name be linked with verse in a country where provincial taste
and middle-class feeling' were so strong.[3]

[1] Reeves MSS, small clipping book, p. 40. For another longer review see *Otago
Witness*, 2 May 1895.
[2] PD, 1894, 84, p. 477.
[3] Reeves to Miss G. Colborne Veel, Alexander Turnbull Library, 25 April
[probably 1925].

15

RETREAT
1895–6

ON 31 July, when Reeves referred to the next election, he obviously had no definite intention of leaving politics,[1] but his ordeal over the next few days, as his labour bills were assaulted by Liberals, must undoubtedly have helped him to change his mind. That he had done so by the end of the session was made at least symbolically clear by an odd little incident on 1 November, when Seddon moved the adjournment of the House. As though thumbing his nose at the Premier, Reeves voted against the other ministers.[2] His valedictory address had (necessarily) already been delivered before the public knew he was leaving, when a branch of the New Zealand Workers' Union was formed in Wellington in October. He told the meeting that the work of unionists was only half done, and that they must not 'imagine that their cause had been won because they had carried one or two general elections'. 'There was never a time', he said, 'when there was more necessity for them to be awake and watching their interests in Parliament and in the country.' If they relaxed, 'they would not win any victories in the next two or three years, such as they had won in years past'. Above all, 'the gospel of labour must be preached in the country districts as strongly and as perseveringly as it was preached in the towns. A majority of the members of Parliament were elected by the country districts ... .'[3]

In January, Seddon had reappointed Perceval as Agent-General for a year. During November it was widely believed that Reeves was to succeed him, while rumour also made Ward a candidate. By December it was known that Reeves was to go, though he was not appointed until 6 January. Once again he was the centre of a paper storm of epithets. Although it was

[1] PD, 1895, 88, p. 358. [2] Ibid., 91, pp. 972–3.
[3] *N.Z. Times*, 8 Oct. 1895.

understandable that his colleagues wished to be rid of him, the *New Zealand Herald* sneered at his alleged desire for 'entry into courtly and aristocratic circles' and to assume 'the most splendid position in the gift of Ministers'. Having concluded, the *Herald* thought, that socialism could not be established in New Zealand, 'he retreats from the field of effort to the gay and splendid office of Agent-General, with £1,500 a year and the rank of an ambassador at the Court of St. James.' The *Herald* trusted that Seddon had talked to him severely about expressing his socialist views: 'What would be said on the Stock Exchange if the Agent-General of New Zealand became a public advocate of free-love?' Even the *Lyttelton Times* was critical;[1] few editors thought Reeves at all a suitable representative of his country 'at Home'.

While the Press was denouncing him, but his new appointment was still merely rumoured, Reeves provided his enemies with fresh ammunition by acquiring, jointly with a brother-in-law, a small sheep run of 5,000 acres at Awakino. It was Maori leasehold land, with the periodical revaluations of which he approved, but (it was said) with a right of purchase. Naturally he was called 'a political hypocrite and charlatan', though the *Evening Post* (for once) defended him. It said his purchase was made through thrift and hinted of private circumstances, known to the writer, which justified the purchase.[2] It may be that Reeves joined in this venture to help his relative, or perhaps, like many New Zealanders going abroad, he wanted to keep 'a stake in the country', but it was politically the least judicious step he could have taken. (When, a couple of years later, John McKenzie acquired a large estate for his sons, the sincerity of the Liberals' radicalism became even more in doubt.[3])

For Reeves, once again, almost everything pointed towards London. In colonial estimation, the agent-generalship was a post fit for ex-premiers and at least equal to the premiership in prestige, so his appointment was not a plain mark of failure. As a public servant, he was effectively silenced while, as a staunch

[1] *Auckland Star*, 3 Jan.; LT, 5 Nov.; *N.Z. Times*, 29 Nov.; *N.Z. Herald*, 14, 23 Nov., 21, 28 Dec. 1895, 11 Jan. 1896.

[2] *Evening Post*, 3 Dec.; *N.Z. Herald*, 10, 18 Dec. 1895.

[3] LT, 10 June 1898; 'Letters from Men of Mark', M. Cohen to Reeves, 29 Jan. 1897.

Liberal, he was at the same time suitably rewarded, both to
Seddon's satisfaction. As we have seen, and as he later wrote, his
position in politics had 'become intolerable'.[1] A note of self-pity
was creeping into his speeches: it was to sound increasingly
louder, in years to come, when he spoke of his political career.

His discouragement is understandable enough in political
terms, but it must be added that his political isolation was largely
a consequence of his social isolation. Among the pioneering
immigrants there had been only a minority of well-educated
men, but they had dominated politics and exerted a pervasive
influence in society. At least some of them, like William Russell,
understood Reeves, if they did not agree with him. Now they had
lost their power, a process Reeves had helped, and were, indeed,
a dying generation. Democracy proved, at first, less sympathetic
to intellectuals than oligarchy for, with the spread of primary
schooling, while ignorance was becoming less common,
philistinism was growing more assertive. The uneducated had
respected learning and the arts more than the barely schooled.
Neither the tiny universities nor any other institutions had
established positions where independent opinion might be defended. Most men of intellectual interests, like Edward Tregear,
acquired government jobs which restricted their freedom of
speech but protected them from the denunciations of conformity,
which exercised an effective tyranny over opinion.

The educated minority of immigrants was being succeeded
by an even smaller number of people at all interested in ideas or
the arts, and few of them had any sympathy for radical reforms.
In 1903 Reeves was to write to one of them, O. T. J. Alpers, in
whom he discovered an unexpected sympathy, on reading
Irvine and Alpers' *Progress of New Zealand in the Century*. 'I have
always thought (till I saw your book) that you merely looked at
our work from the individualist and irreconcilable standpoint',
Reeves said, and added, 'one of the great wants of the colonial
democracy is criticism from educated yet sympathetic men. It is
a bad thing altogether, an unmitigated evil, that social and other
influences should have ranged the educated class in a hostile
body on the side of sheer obscurantism.'[2] The educated minority
was unfriendly and provincial. 'Public opinion', as expressed in

[1] Reeves MSS, Reeves to Charles Wilson, 9 April 1919.
[2] Alpers MSS, 11 Jan. 1903.

the Press and in Parliament, revealed an intolerable pettiness, generally unable to credit any motive that might not be understandable in a semi-literate Taranaki land agent pursuing a commission, or an Auckland draper's wife angling for an invitation to Government House.

Any New Zealand intellectual suffered from loneliness as an occupational disease, but an educated middle class socialist was doubly isolated from his countrymen. Although he was respectable himself, Reeves ignored Disraeli's observation that it never paid to affront respectability. In New Zealand, as in England, what Reeves had proclaimed in 1887, that respectability was usually beaten in politics,[1] was simply untrue.

On the other side of his social contacts, Reeves's relations with 'working men' were not personally close. Though he continually corresponded with and talked with their leaders, many unionists were suspicious of him. Tom L. Mills, a correspondent of the Brisbane *Worker*, wrote, late in 1895, that the workers said, 'For our sakes he put away his pride, yet who can ever think of him as other than "a cut above us!"', though he confessed that, by calling Reeves 'W.P.', they betrayed a lurking affection for their champion, and some pride. Mills called him 'a recluse'.[2]

Reeves was often criticized for being aloof in his manner towards the public (except at election time). An incident that was remembered against him in the Labour Department for many years was that after Mrs. W. White, the wife of one of his chief Christchurch supporters, called on him in his office, though he had greeted her warmly enough, he asked his staff why they 'let that horrible woman in'.[3] Seddon would not have made that mistake, though he was no more sincere in welcoming such visitors than other politicians and businessmen. Even Reeves's jokes were not of a kind popular with his audiences. In his 'Memoirs' he recollected one unfortunate incident:

I was foolish enough once, when in the Government, to make a joke to a deputation of country settlers. I happened to be in an out-of-the-way district where there was a large bridge. The people there had got it into their heads that the piles of the bridge were rotting. They wanted a Commission to examine them and fresh piles put up. A Government Engineer had warned me that the whole thing was

---

[1] See above, p. 67.   [2] *The Worker*, 11 Jan. 1896.
[3] Interview with Mr. J. W. Collins of Wellington.

nonsense, saying that he thought they only wanted some money
spent on the place. I therefore treated the matter rather light-
heartedly and proposed that they should give the piles a chance.
'Gentlemen, I suggest that instead of being examined by experts, the
bridge should be "tried by its piers"'. The joke fell dismally flat, and
the local member complained of my manner to Mr. Seddon.

Once when the *New Zealand Herald* denounced the ministers
as uncultured, he retaliated by pointing out in this very editorial
a plural verb attached to a single noun, and said (to his Auckland
audience) that the local school inspector, W. H. Airey, would
fail a sixth form boy for such an error.[1] He won a laugh but it
was not a joke well-chosen for his audience.

Most of Reeves's difficulties found at once expression and
symbol in his relations with Seddon who, as early as 1894, was
being called 'the King', 'King Richard', and 'King Dick'.
Seddon and Reeves each possessed qualities the other lacked,
while failing to appreciate the other at his worth. The former had
mastered the arts of exercising and keeping power; he stepped,
indeed, from the pages of the *History of England* by Macaulay,
who had described Wharton in these words:

As a canvasser he was irresistible. He never forgot a face that he had
once seen. Nay, in the towns in which he wished to establish an interest,
he remembered, not only the voters, but their families. His opponents
were confounded by the strength of his memory and the affability of
his deportment, and owned that it was impossible to contend against
a great man who called the shoemaker by his Christian name, who
was sure that the butcher's daughter must be growing a fine girl, and
who was anxious to know whether the blacksmith's youngest boy was
breeched.

Nothing could more clearly underline the differences between
Reeves and Seddon than a letter Seddon wrote from Kumara
in 1883 to Montgomery, who was then the Liberal leader.
Discussing the chances of a parliamentary candidate, Seddon
suggested:

Enjoin upon him the necessity of a house to house canvass, nothing
goes down so well with the sturdy tillers of the soil as a personal chat—
an oration from a veritable Demosthenes would only bring the
interjection My word he talks like a book—whilst ten minutes talk on

[1] He repeated this remark in the House: PD, 1894, 84, p. 473.

Irrigation and a little judicious flattery as to breed of stock crops etc. and to wind up with the cost of carrying grain as compared with that of Timber and Minerals etc. on our railways with a promise to have a searching enquiry made into the same, would fetch the vote. Tell Richardson [the candidate] not to be too heavy on [his opponent] Sir John Hall but to praise him if anything. . . .

Seddon concluded, 'I am well and full of fight and though in an obscure corner am not asleep.'[1] He was never, politically speaking, asleep.

In public more 'democratic', in private Seddon was more cynical about politics than Reeves. As we have seen, Reeves was much more concerned with reform than power. It was to be some time before he realized that Seddon was not averse to reform once he found that leading had become easy. But it was true that Seddon was primarily a politician. In his 'Memoirs' Reeves was to write that Seddon gave himself untiringly, day and night, to politics:

Though I knew him well I never saw him amuse himself or take up a book that was not a blue book. Once, only once, a brother member told me that he had seen Seddon reading a book which had nothing to do with politics but that he only read it for a short time. I have often been alone with him when we were not doing business and when we might have talked on any subject. I cannot recall that he spoke of anything except politics and politicians. A man who is capable of working at politics or talking about them for sixteen hours out of the twenty four and who does not want to do anything else has advantages over competitors. Moreover, he was not a mere talker or worker at details. My conviction is that when he was not talking about politics he was thinking about them. His next quality was his striking skill in understanding and handling third-rate men, sympathetically or otherwise. As most men are third-rate this is an important quality in a leader. He grudged no time or pains over dealing with such men. In the third place he devoted systematically a large share of his restless energies to cultivating popularity. He did not neglect politicians but he attended specially to that large element in a population which neither knows nor cares about the details of politics. He pursued popularity and won it and having won it never lost it.

Reeves never managed to establish a tolerable relationship with Seddon. Though he appreciated some of his 'chief's'

[1] W. H. Montgomery MSS, 12 March 1883.

qualities, to a person as formal as Reeves, Seddon's familiarity
and occasional vulgarity were distasteful. His bullying manner
and his evasive bluster were more than Reeves could stand.
A year after Reeves left, his friend and ex-secretary, Frank
Waldegrave, wrote reminding him of the atmosphere in 'the
antechambers of the Great one'—'Telephones going, Private
Secretaries running hither & thither, messengers flying for
their lives, a few Heads of Depts. & others all with an air of
business, outside all the dead-beats in the country waiting for
billets, & over all the dreadful bell of the King himself which now
& anon gave forth its furious sound'.[1] Reeves must have
shuddered at the thought.

There is no doubt that dislike of Seddon weighed heavily in
Reeves's decision to accept the agent-generalship. To this point
Tregear and other friends often returned in writing to him in
London. Tregear, too, 'had resented the needless rudeness &
crude roughness with which both Seddon & McKenzie treated
everyone; rudeness that often annoyed you exceedingly and
made official positions almost unbearable'. While Reeves stood
near Seddon, Tregear wrote to him, 'every prickle and roughness
became abhorrent to you by the continual and irritating intercourse.' But though Tregear knew that Seddon regarded him as
Reeves's man, and though he had no illusions about the Premier
('Think what he was—the rude forcible politician, with
"flashy" ideas, mainly in the direction that men & women were
pawns on a chess-board, to be pushed here & there just to make
the game for RJS.'), he nevertheless reminded Reeves that
'little things that jar the fastidious mind only endear him to the
crowd.'[2]

Yet it would be a mistake to exaggerate the personal aspects of
Reeves's differences with Seddon. Beneath there lay fundamental
disputes about the nature of politics and the nature and aims of
their party. The two men might still, today, be thought the
pre-eminent New Zealand examples of the reformer and the
politician.

John McKenzie was, to the end, a friend, though not always a
political ally. But there was one other colleague with whom
Reeves's relations were cold: he was not taken in by Ward's jaunty

[1] 'Letters from Men of Mark', 3 July 1897.
[2] Ibid., 17 Jan., 15 Sept. 1897; 18 July 1906.

charm—an immunity connected with one other aspect of politics that lay behind Reeves's departure. It can be perceived only in faint, almost conjectural, outline. It is the thread of business enterprise, of profit, often twisting into dishonesty, that runs through nineteenth-century New Zealand politics.

By December, but probably months before, Seddon learned that Ward's debts were included in the suspicious 'C' list of the Colonial Bank's accounts that the Bank of New Zealand was conditionally to take over. On 30 December he wrote to ask the advice of the Otago 'Liberal' banker, W. J. M. Larnach, who was a shareholder of the Colonial Bank. Larnach described to him his anxiety for the Government and their party. Were it not for this, he assured Seddon, 'not even £2,000 p.a. would tempt me to do the work that may have to be done.' He advised Seddon that the Bank of New Zealand must take over Ward's account and his promissory note, to get them out of the hands of the liquidators of the Colonial Bank and the court. If not the liquidators would call on the Bank of New Zealand 'to *liquidate* and *realise*—the immediate result being "the fat in the fire" and the reputation of everybody connected with the party blasted and soiled for all time.... *The Treasurer must remain Treasurer* if possible....'[1] Seddon scarcely needed the advice; indeed, his conduct during the 1895 session strongly suggests that he was shielding Ward.

But Ward's plans came apart. The Colonial Bank directors were horrified when they learned the true extent of his assets; the Bank of New Zealand refused to continue his accounts. Ward went bankrupt. Mr. Justice Williams observed that the conduct of the Ward Farmers' Association should be investigated and that 'those who were responsible for its management should no longer be permitted to roam at large through the business world.'[2]

About this time Seddon lost most of his cabinet; only McKenzie and he remained of its original leaders.

Reeves resigned in January 1896; Ward in June. Old Montgomery resigned in November 1895, and Buckley in

---

[1] A transcript of this letter, and of another dated 13 Dec. 1896 from Larnach to Seddon were kindly provided by a New Zealand historian who must remain anonymous.
[2] W. H. Montgomery clipping book.

December, when he was appointed a judge of the Supreme Court. All of these men had been closely associated with the banking legislation, whether as supporters or critics. It is difficult not to believe that their resignations were connected with it too, though Buckley's appointment may have been consolation for missing the agent generalship, and it must be added, too, that W. H. Montgomery (who was a very old man when interviewed by the writer) did not recall hearing that his father resigned because of the bank proceedings. His father, however, was reported in 1896 to be 'disgusted' with the Seddon Government.[1]

How much Reeves knew of the 'C' list and of Seddon's and Ward's motives may never be known. But he remained for many years hostile to Ward (as he did not to Seddon). Indeed his suspicion of Ward, the idea that he was untrustworthy and positively dangerous in financial matters, was to become 'a sort of mild obsession', as W. H. Atack observed. When Atack, an old acquaintance rather than a close friend, met him in Christchurch a few days before his departure, he 'expressed his fears of Ward's financial policy'; ten years later, when Atack met him in London, 'his theme was still the same.'[2] At the end of 1899 McKenzie insisted on bringing Ward back into the ministry, even threatening to resign to get his way. Seddon sent Ward off to England with McKenzie (who was going for medical treatment) to get him out of the way during the election. Reeves's friend Waldegrave then wrote to him, 'It will not be very pleasant for you to have to endure J.G.W. in London after all that has passed.'[3] Only such broad but inconclusive hints point towards what, in the opinion of his present biographer, may have been the decisive circumstance leading to Reeves's retreat.

There was one quite different pressure impelling him towards London. Though he confessed to Rolleston that 'the London post' had attractions, not least the prospect it held out that he could continue his 'work' (his writing and study), 'with comparatively little interruption',[4] the fact remained that he went reluctantly. His recollections of England were unhappy. He decidedly did not want access to aristocratic or royal circles.

[1] Hall MSS, A. Saunders to Hall, 21 Sept. 1896.
[2] *Christ's College Register*, cxxxx, Aug. 1932, pp. 80–91.
[3] 'Letters from Men of Mark', 9 March 1899.
[4] Rolleston MSS, 6 Jan. 1896.

He did not want to go; and going, he announced that he would
certainly return.[1] Despite the battering he had received, the
question may still be thought unanswered, why did he go to
London? Part of the answer has been seen in the fact that the
agent-generalship had such prestige as not merely to save faces
but to seem the crown of colonial success. The rest of the answer
is provided by his daughters, Amber and Beryl (now Mrs.
Blanco White and Mrs. Eric Thatcher Clarke). Their mother
had enjoyed immensely her visit to England in 1894. She had
had considerable social success, and wished to return. At the
same time she was very worried about Will's health, and the
strain he felt in politics. She was convinced that he could not
stand it much longer. She arranged an interview with John
McKenzie, Mrs. Clarke relates, and asked him to see that
the agent-generalship was offered to her husband. She told
McKenzie to ignore Will's views—she would see that he took it.
McKenzie admired Maud, who was about to give birth to her
third child—later he said she was 'the pluckiest little woman in
New Zealand'. And she had her way.

Maud stayed behind with the girls and their new son, who was
named Fabian. John McKenzie was his godfather. Early in
January Reeves sailed alone, in the *Wakatipu*, for Australia.
Seddon, Tregear and a few officials and friends saw him off.
In Australia the Labour Parties, like the New Zealand Liberals
and unionists, presented him with complimentary addresses and
a public dinner was given in his honour. But despite his optimistic
words, a reporter thought he looked 'atrabilious and despondent.
He has nothing sanguine about him, He looks as if he thought
very badly of human nature in general, and as if the majority of
his fellow-creatures were "undesirable immigrants".'[2] With
gleeful malice the *Herald*, in Auckland, republished this
description, a parting shot at New Zealand's rejected son, the
first great European New Zealander.

Nothing speaks more clearly of Reeves's own thoughts and
feelings than a poem he wrote as soon as he reached England.
He went to stay with his uncle, Edward Pember, at Boldre, in
the Isle of Wight. There, though he found 'tranquillity', a

[1] 'Letters from Men of Mark', Mark Cohen to Reeves, n.d. [Jan. 1896].
[2] *N.Z. Herald*, 18 Jan. 1896.

'scholar blest' and 'not with the world at odds', yet (as during
his visit in 1874—but in how different circumstances!) memory
at once turned to 'fortunate isles', to shores 'beyond the wave'.
On this occasion, however, illness could scarcely take him back;
there remained the life of exile.

AT VICAR'S HILL[1]

March, 1896.

A sky of rest is here, a realm of ease,
A land of gently spreading swell and vale,
Moist, grassy, sloping; thickly studded trees
Bathed in a placid sunlight mild and pale
Gleaming from skies of pearl; and matching these
A lightly dwelling haze on down and dale,
—A quiet, misty coast of green and gray
Where bird-notes deepen silence all the day.

. . . .

Thin vapour veils the sky, soft, low in air,
As though to bid the restless soul not soar
But turn to earth and dwell contented there.
No vault of height majestic, arching o'er,
Is this caressing heaven, but tender, fair,
Brooding on wings above the still, green shore.
And all the kindly land and cool, gray sky
Breathe one wide-whispered word—tranquillity.

What though fond memory wings rapid flight
To loftier coasts amid a wider deep,
Fortunate isles of clearest golden light,
Where peaks far seen o'er ancient forests keep
Ward from on high, and alpine crests are white!
Yet may this silken, dreamful sky of sleep,
This friendly, restful scene console, nor cease
To smile and soothe with sweet-remembered peace.

How pleasantly, to stir the day's repose,
The old port by the river murmurs still.
How temptingly yon half-seen topmast shows,
Swaying where tidal waters shrink and fill.
How wistfully the eye led seaward goes
To where, far past the clock-tower on the hill,
The island heights the touch of magic have,
The spell of shores that rise beyond the wave.

1 Reeves MSS. The poem appears in *The Passing of the Forest*, London, 1925.

Here from the leafy brow with genial looks,
Through firs and limes and cedars of renown,
And quaint exotics filling garden nooks,
A house in creepers cloaked is gazing down,
A house of flowers, good talk and many books,
Peace of the country, lightness of the town,
Roof not too vast to bid a welcome warm,
Too old for comfort or too new for charm.

Under his trees let us their master seek,
Advocate, poet, student, gardener,
Lover of rhymes and music, birds and Greek.
With eye unwearied and attentive ear
For Nature, he yet hears the city speak.
Not with the world at odds, yet can prefer
His verses and his garden; scholar blest
For whom this corner of the earth smiles best.

THE AGENT-GENERAL
London, 1896–9

In later life Reeves used wryly to recall his reception in England in March 1896. He left the *Ormuz* at Naples and travelled overland with the mails, catching a cold besides enduring a rough passage from Dieppe to Newhaven. As the ship neared England he paced the deck, reflecting on the brief speech he would make, if necessary, to whoever—reporters, officials or New Zealand travellers—awaited him on the docks. No one was waiting on the docks. By the time his story had been repeated in the family, and published in New Zealand newspapers sixty years later, many significant details had been added. It was said that, when he presented his credentials at the Colonial Office a clerk told him to 'put them there'. Then nothing happened until, several months later, he received the expected official envelope, which proved to be not an invitation to meet the Secretary of State, but a tax demand on income already taxed in New Zealand.[1] Though partially legend, the story at least accurately reflects the contempt with which (he often said) colonials were regarded among middle and upper-class Englishmen, in the great days of Victorian imperialism.

When he called at the Colonial Office, it is true, Chamberlain was out, but he was received (a London gossip columnist reported) with marked cordiality by the Under-Secretary of State, the Earl of Selborne, and the Permanent Under-Secretary, Sir Robert Meade. A few days later he had his first long interview with the great man himself.[2]

His situation was at first a little difficult because he was superseding Sir Westby Perceval, who did not want to leave, though he said he would sooner hand on to Reeves than anyone else. The 'Anglo-Colonial community' felt 'irritated amaze-

---

[1] Interviews with Mr. Eric T. Clarke, and Mrs. Beryl Clarke.
[2] *Auckland Star*, 25 April 1896.

ment' at the termination of Perceval's appointment, so (a reporter wrote) 'it was not to be expected' that Reeves 'would meet with a very cordial or enthusiastic welcome'.[1] However, Reeves showed more tact than they expected. When he moved into Westminster Chambers, 13 Victoria St., he wrote to Seddon that Perceval 'was quite civil to me when I came and expressed no resentment at not being reappointed'. Perceval was on the boards of three companies and had no intention of returning to New Zealand politics. Soon he was 'up to his neck in Gold Finance' and would not do 'a hand's turn of work' as the New Zealand representative at the Imperial Institute. Reeves reported that he was 'not hostile' but that his time was 'worth money' and he would 'give none without'.[2] So Perceval drifted quite out of his country's affairs and saw little of his old friend and colleague.

For a few years the New Zealand newspapers were full of news of Reeves. He became, almost at once, the most prominent agent-general the Colony had had, and put the suave Perceval, though not his other precursors (Featherston, Vogel and F. D. Bell), quite in the shade. He became the best known 'Anglo-Colonial' of the time. He became, moreover, one of the first New Zealanders to make a name for himself in London; the first notable example of the country's debilitating 'export of brains'.

To start with his deeds were trivial enough, though mostly dear to that large class of his countrymen that longed for a trip 'Home'. Within a few days of arriving he visited the House of Commons and dined with Sir John Gorst, the author of *The Maori King*, who had lived in New Zealand in the early sixties and was now a Member of Parliament. Reeves soon shared his enthusiasm for Toynbee Hall, the East End 'social settlement', and frequently talked to the working men there. He was dined, of course, by the Salters' Company and the Fishmongers' Company, finding these public dinners as tedious as he had at home—he was, it was observed, an abstemious eater, and confined himself to a single whisky and soda. He joined the M.C.C. and played occasionally for one of its teams. He was elected a Fellow of the Royal Colonial Institute, where he

[1] *Auckland Star*, 25 April 1896.
[2] Seddon MSS, 16 April 1896; 20 Feb. 1897.

lectured to the largest audience the Institute had attracted for years.[1] To the pleasure of the *Auckland Star* he forgot politics and delighted a large audience at the Hotel Metropole with a talk, illustrated by 'a lantern and some excellent limelight views', on New Zealand's scenic beauties. Surely, the *Star* thought, he could attract to New Zealand some of the host of Englishmen with spare capital.[2]

Reeves was an immediate success as a public speaker, equally effective and at ease at the London School of Economics, various Oxford clubs, or Toynbee Hall. In June 1896 he was the first 'colonial statesman' to address the Eighty Club (a Liberal discussion club founded largely by Haldane and named in celebration of Gladstone's victory in that year). Asquith presided; Sidney Webb sang Reeves's praises in moving a vote of thanks; and his lecture, 'Reform and Experiment in New Zealand', was published by the Club. Within a few days he also spoke at one of W. T. Stead's meetings for English-speaking union; dined with Chamberlain and then with Sir George Trevelyan, the historian and politician; was interviewed by *Commerce* and had an article in *National Review*. 'Altogether', a journalist wrote, 'it would hardly be possible for a colonial representative to be more *en évidence* . . . .'

The secretary of the Fabian Society, Edward Pease, said that one of Reeves's lectures on industrial arbitration was the most interesting yet delivered under Fabian auspices. Five hundred people, including George Bernard Shaw and Graham Wallas, the political scientist (or political psychologist) turned out to hear him.[3] He was inundated with invitations to give lectures, free or paid, to all sorts of organizations. There is no point in listing the large number of the talks which he gave in the next few years. Most of them, naturally enough, were about New Zealand and his own reforms. Altogether he contributed a great deal towards reducing the general ignorance about New Zealand. His lectures were not his only addresses. His wit, clarity, brevity and apparently inexhaustible fund of amusing stories, always appropriate (which he sometimes summarized in

---

[1] Seddon MSS, Reeves to Seddon, 16 May 1896. Most of the following details were reported in the *Auckland Star* 'Anglo-Colonial Notes'.

[2] 23 June 1896.

[3] *Auckland Star*, 23 Nov., 1 Dec. 1897; *Fabian News*, Nov. 1897.

PLATE 5

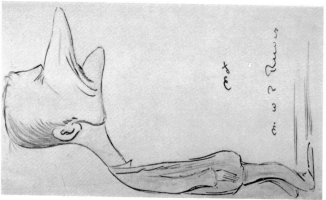

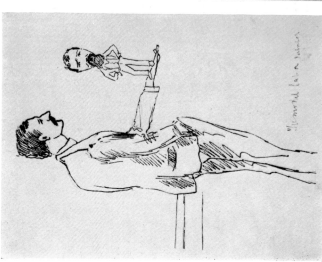

a. Cartoons by W. H. Montgomery (a and c) and Max Beerbohm

his journals for future use), made him an admirable after-dinner speaker. In 1898 an English periodical described him as one of the best in London.[1] At the same time Maud's services were in demand as a speaker on the women's franchise to ladies' organizations, such as a conference of the Women's National Liberal Association.

Reeves did not feel at home. He was shocked by the poverty and the snobbery. When his family arrived in London in May 1896 (after a bad trip in the *Rimutaka*, which broke down and was detained in Montevideo for seventeen days) the men who loaded their goods on a wagon at the docks ran several miles to their lodgings in order to get the job of unloading them. He was uncomfortable in another respect too. His appointment was for only three years, and his future thereafter was so uncertain that there was no point in buying a house. Consequently they 'made do' with rented furnished houses, first of all at 34 Brunswick Gardens, Kensington. The climate appalled him, and he suffered periodic attacks of neuralgia from the time he arrived. But in one respect he felt at ease for the first time in his life. He fell in with congenial groups of people who understood his political ideals and shared his intellectual interests. Their attention was both encouraging and flattering—though not as flattering as the unwary might suppose, for most of his new friends, though they were becoming important, were not yet famous. In particular, though he had long admired the Fabian leaders, he could not, as a successful politician, regard himself in 1896 as less than their equal.

The Fabians had known of Reeves before he left New Zealand. 'Pharos' had sent his pamphlet to Sidney Webb. Edward Pease had spoken of Reeves's legislation in 1895.[2] Reeves met them quite soon after reaching London. In December 1896 he wrote Fabian Tract No. 74, *The State and its Functions in New Zealand*, which eulogized state enterprise in the Fabian manner.[3] Writing it must have given him great pleasure. He thought it improper to belong to any political association while he was Agent-

---

[1] *Auckland Star*, 15 Feb. 1898, citing the *Echo*.

[2] *N.Z. Times*, 23 Feb. 1895.

[3] Reeves contributed to the discussions that lay behind other Fabian tracts such as No. 106, *The Education Muddle and the Way Out*. See E. Halévy, *A History of the English People*, Epilogue vol. 1, 1895–1905, Penguin Books, 1939, ii, p. 110.

General, but, like Haldane, the Reeveses became close friends of some of the Fabians without formally joining them. Some years later Maud did become a member.

In his *Memoirs*, Lord Samuel drew a quick portrait of the Webbs' house in those days:

When Sidney and Beatrice Webb were married in 1892 they took a house in Grosvenor Road in Westminster, overlooking the Thames. It was an ordinary London terrace house; but they made it something the reverse of ordinary. Mrs. Webb held there on a small scale the nearest approach to one of the intellectual salons of the eighteenth century that we have had in our day. Most of the leading spirits of what would now be called the Left, some also of the Right, would forgather there. She gave many dinner-parties, kept small by the size of the dining-room, and simple as a matter of principle. Sometimes a few others would be invited in afterwards for a talk on some special subject. Sometimes a throng of guests would make their way up the narrow staircase and strain the capacity of the drawing-room.

Haldane might be there, or H. G. Wells, or Creighton, the Bishop of London. At one of these parties I first met William Pember Reeves, soon after his arrival from New Zealand, where he had been a Cabinet Minister, to take up the post of Agent-General: he became one of my lifelong friends. The tall figures of Bernard Shaw and Graham Wallas would often be seen, overtopping the crowd—Shaw, bearded, amiable, emphatic, quizzical; Wallas, with his handsome, intellectual countenance, beaming benevolence through his spectacles; Sidney Webb, short, alert, unceasingly active, letting no opportunity pass to enlist interest in one or other of the schemes that he always had in hand.

But the centre of it all was Beatrice Webb herself. She combined a first-class mind with a striking and attractive appearance, and great charm of manner. Her musical voice had a welcoming, receptive tone; her smile was ready and sympathetic. All that she was and all she had she gave unstintingly to the service of humanity, with a devotion as complete as that of a medieval saint, and far more fruitful. The close partnership between her husband and herself, which developed in the course of years into a kind of dual personality, resulted in an output of literary work on their own special subjects, and of public activity, which has probably never been equalled.[1]

Shaw and Reeves enjoyed one another's company: they shared a physical fastidiousness, constant headaches, and a

---

[1] London, 1945, p. 29.

fondness for clever remarks. Later Reeves confessed that he had underestimated Shaw: 'before he became famous as a play-wright he gave me one or two of his plays to read in manuscript. I saw nothing much in them. One day, however, he read an unacted comedy to a small circle of friends of whom I was one; that opened my eyes. Shaw is the only literary man I have had the luck to meet who talked as brilliantly as he wrote and in exactly the same way.'[1]

Perhaps this was the same play-reading that Shaw described, in a letter to Ellen Terry, when he was staying at Sir George Trevelyan's house near Stratford-on-Avon in December 1897:

This is a gigantic house, with sixteen hall doors, rooms that no man has ever counted, a conservatory like the Crystal Palace, 76 bath rooms, and 1300 miles of corridor, with every door the exact counter-part of every other door, so that we have to crumble bread as we walk, like the child in the fairy story, to find our way back to the eating room. By a violent effort, a corner of the place has been made humanly habitable; and in this corner now dwell Trevelyan junior (our host) [Charles Trevelyan, the historian's son], the Webbs, the Reeveses... .

Reeves, he wrote, 'was a shining light of the Fabian Ministry which set our variety of Socialism on foot' in New Zealand: '(The Agent-General, snoring on the sofa, is going to wake—yes: there he goes.)' They went cycling and scattered sixpences on Shakespeare's tomb. One night, Shaw read them *The Devil's Disciple*.[2] If Reeves was backward, until then, in recognizing his genius, it is fair to add that Shaw was not yet well known: his only play produced in the West End, *Arms and the Man*, had been a financial failure.

The Webbs were known—and, in pursuance of tactics of Fabian opportunism, made themselves known—to the great, and especially to the rising. At their house, the Reeveses met Lloyd George, Balfour, Haldane, Winston Churchill, Ramsay MacDonald and many of the men who were to rule Britain in coming years. Reeves saw MacDonald often at the 'Rainbow Circle', a small discussion society of 'Liberals of the Left and Socialists of the Right', of which Herbert Samuel, J. A. Hobson,

---

[1] Reeves MSS, 'Memoirs'.

[2] C. St. John (ed.), *Ellen Terry and Bernard Shaw: A Correspondence*, 3rd ed. London, 1949, pp. 257–8.

the economist, and Charles Trevelyan were also members.[1]
When Reeves belonged, it met in a house in Bloomsbury Square.
At first he thought MacDonald merely 'able and industrious'.
But one day Reeves spoke to the group, at some length, on a
question of social reform. MacDonald explained why he thought
him wrong. Reeves 'went away and thought over his words and
came round to his point of view', he wrote in his 'Memoirs'.
(Lest it be thought that he habitually underestimated people, it
should be added that he confessed, in his 'Memoirs', to only four
such errors—Shaw, MacDonald, L. S. Amery and William
Massey.)

Herbert Samuel became a close friend. The Reeveses often
visited him at Porchester Terrace and at Cleveland, in Yorkshire,
where, in the evenings, they sometimes amused themselves by
writing parodies of well-known authors on set topics—one of
them was 'Coming Home at Sunset'—at which Reeves excelled.[2]
They were soon staying, too, at some of the great Liberal country
houses. No one could have been given a more heartening
welcome.

In their vacations the Webbs liked to work in the morning,
cycle in the afternoon, and read or talk at night. From them and
Samuel—and Shaw, with whom Reeves often went cycling—
the Reeveses caught this new enthusiasm. They joined the
Cyclists' Touring Club and spent many weeks, in the next few
years, cycling in Brittany, Portugal, Spain and elsewhere.
Reeves used to cycle to his office. He was said to be 'daring', but
the new 'safety bicycle' sometimes belied its name in his hands.
His understanding of anything mechanical was unusually dim;
things 'did things' to him; moreover, his habit of dreaming was
incompatible with riding with 'due care and attention'; so he
had a few spills.

Most of these new pleasures and activities, intellectual or
physical, were far removed from Reeves's duties; but not all of
them. His personal standing added something to the dignity of
his office which, though in Wellington it appeared almost
august, was in reality, and in London, a quite lowly one: at the
coronation of Edward VII the agents-general were seated near

---

[1] Lord Samuel, *Memoirs*, p. 24; J. Bowle, *Viscount Samuel*, London, 1957, p. 34.
[2] Interview with Lord Samuel.

the rear of the Abbey, behind the provincial mayors, from where Reeves could see nothing at all. In particular, his success as a lecturer made him the best public relations officer the Colony had had. In May 1896, after his successful address to the Royal Colonial Institute, he wrote to Seddon: 'I ... wish you would let me spend the part of the money hitherto chucked away on paying a financial adviser, on lecturing with limelights. I should not mind the trouble and I could get at a class of wealthy people which the ordinary lecturer cannot draw.'

The agent-generalship was essentially a commercial rather than a diplomatic post, which Reeves frankly recognized. When he said, in an interview in Australia, that his main business would be to help develop the New Zealand export trade, he was praised for renouncing the usual 'ambassadorial mimicry'. 'Canvassing, sample-rooms, tasteful displays in good shops, lectures, photographs, pamphlets, illustrated interviews are my notion', he wrote to Seddon in 1896 with regard to advertising New Zealand products: 'Give me the sinews of war and I will boom N. Zealand.'[1]

Much of Reeves's work, and much of his correspondence, were concerned with the export of butter, cheese, and frozen meat, the organization of which was still far from perfect. Both packing and handling required improvement. He found New Zealand butter stored alongside greasy wool at the docks. He was active in encouraging the building of further cool stores. Another constant worry was that butchers often sold New Zealand meat as Scotch, or River Plate meat as New Zealand. He sought to encourage shops to specialize in New Zealand meat. But this side of his job, though important to his country, is of little biographical interest other than showing, to the surprise of many people, that he had good business sense.

Even more surprisingly, Reeves became quite expert in the intricacies of London Finance. Here his connexion with the Pembers, two of whom were stock-brokers, and with his wife's relatives, the Carr-Saunders, who also were businessmen, may have assisted; but he carefully studied the money market himself. After a short time he was able to dispense with the services of a paid financial adviser—he was, he claimed, the only agent-general of the time to do so. He found it impossible to talk

[1] Seddon MSS, 28 Oct. 1896.

confidentially with the Bank of New Zealand people in London, and he had to 'scrutinise very closely, and suspiciously' any suggestions coming from the Bank of England. Consequently he was forced to rely increasingly on his own judgment and that of Walter Kennaway, one of his officers. His letters to Seddon were full of detailed information about raising loans, the sale of government stock, and sticky interviews with the Governor of the Bank of England.

Reeves was extremely thorough and saved his Government thousands of pounds through careful attention to details—and through constant pressure on brokers and bankers. For instance, he successfully urged the Bank of England to reduce its charges for inscribing New Zealand Government stock.[1] He was very skilful at raising loans. In 1899 he pushed through a £1,000,000 at 96 (which was much better than an Australian loan at the same time) and refused to pay the 1 per cent. demanded by the underwriters.[2] Seddon was most impressed[3] and relied more and more on him for advice on the best time and means of raising money. While Reeves's letters to the Premier discussed the tactics of borrowing, those to his friends as constantly denounced the policy.

Reeves's task was to assure British investors of the soundness, indeed conservatism, of New Zealand finances, so that the Government could borrow on the best terms. This involved him in endless manoeuvres to outwit, not only the 'Stock Exchange "bears"', who hoped to depress New Zealand Government stocks in order to profit from a new issue, but from the New Zealand Government's numerous enemies, who did all they could to depreciate the country's credit. Among them were many New Zealanders. Reeves told Seddon:

One of my greatest difficulties in trying to hold the fort here is the attacks made against us by New Zealanders. Every damaging article written against the Government and its finances in New Zealand is carefully marked and sent over here, and New Zealanders and ex-New Zealanders seem to take a sort of joy in running the Colony down. There is no Colony I know of, outside South Africa, which has

[1] Seddon MSS, Reeves to Seddon, 7 May 1898; PD, 1908, 145, p. 1112. J. G. Ward.

[2] *Auckland Star*, 16 March 1899.

[3] Reeves MSS, Seddon to Reeves, 20 March, 12 April 1899.

to meet nearly as much of this particular sort of enmity.... Added to that, nearly all the New Zealanders and members of firms doing business with New Zealand here are Conservatives.... Much the same may be said of nine-tenths of the New Zealanders who come over here on visits. Most of these people admit that the Colony is prospering, but they shake their heads over the finance and the labour legislation, and say we are borrowing too fast, and that the Trade Unions are becoming too powerful.[1]

But the Government's worst enemies were ghosts from Reeves's own past. The 'New Plymouth Harbour swindle' that he had helped so triumphantly to kill in 1888, and the unsuccessful Midland Railway Company that he had helped to launch, had left a large number of vituperative investors in England, who believed that they had been robbed by the New Zealand Government. In each case a misleading prospectus had been issued in England, but the Government had had nothing what-ever to do with the New Plymouth Harbour Board bond issue, and had not been responsible for the Midland Railway Company's statements. Reeves found 'the persistent libels of those papers which the Midland debenture-holders, New Plymouth Bondholders, anti-B.N.Z. [Bank of New Zealand] men, Tories and other enemies contrive to inspire' a continual trial. The disgruntled 'New Plymouth Bondholders' had appealed to the Council of Foreign Bondholders on the Stock Exchange to block Ward's loan in 1895, and when Reeves arrived were still actively denouncing the New Zealand Govern-ment in the 'financial rags'. Reeves helped to quieten them by interviewing the editor and financial editor of *The Times* and convincing them that his Government was involved only in the sense that it had refused to rescue the investors. But the Midland Railway investors plagued him for years. He urged upon Seddon that an amicable settlement might send New Zealand stocks 'up a point or so', but Seddon was not responsive. He was sorry himself 'at their losing their money, but as things stand, the capital value of the line is almost nil'. These two remarks were written in 1896 and in 1900 respectively. Between those years, Reeves was pestered by deputations from the investors, upon whom, while denouncing their 'preposterous claims', he used to

[1] Seddon MSS, Reeves to Seddon, 11 Dec. 1896, 29 Nov. 1901.

urge that 'it must be one thing or the other between us, either war or friendly negotiation.'[1]

When Reeves left New Zealand, Seddon asked him to answer any attacks on New Zealand. He found he had plenty to do. There was, he told Seddon, 'a strong tendency in this country to believe that Colonial politicians are as corrupt as Americans'. For years, almost single-handed, he waged war on New Zealand's enemies and traitors, in the correspondence columns of the Press. Within a few months of his arrival he was writing to the *Daily News*, the *Statist* and the *Economist*. He even replied to 'a most insolent and contemptible reference' to Seddon in the United States *Nation* because, he explained to Seddon, he fancied Chamberlain and his wife (an American) read it. On another occasion, when Seddon had been savaged, Reeves told him: 'If any paper of standing or importance attacks you ... I will not fail to defend you promptly and thoroughly. The credit of the Premier of the Colony is a matter of colonial concern and I do not think that any reasonable person would be able to suggest that it is outside my province to vindicate you.'

Reeves was no less touchy about his country's honour than his own, and he became a perennial correspondent of *The Times*, defending the New Zealand Government, its finances or his system of industrial conciliation and arbitration. In this rôle he was most effective; the great and the anonymous felt the whip of his prose,[2] though what effect his untiring apologetics had on public opinion is conjectural.

Reeves became Agent-General at the beginning of one of the most interesting periods of British imperial history, just after Joseph Chamberlain had launched his campaign to re-organize and reform the Empire. So great a man had never accepted the inconsiderable office of Secretary of State for the Colonies, but Chamberlain saw it as controlling the key to Britain's future. As Germany and the United States rose to industrial—and therefore military and naval—power, it seemed to him that 'splendid isolation' and 'little Englandism' had alike become anachronisms. The Conservatives had talked of strengthening imperial

---

[1] Seddon MSS, Reeves to Seddon, 10 July 1896, 31 May 1900.
[2] Some of his letters are in the Reeves MSS, small clipping book, pp. 168–171; see also *The Times*, 31 Dec. 1898; 6, 9, 19 Jan. 1899; 5 April 1900.

power since Disraeli's famous speech of 1872. Chamberlain meant to act. Business principles and capital investment would be applied to developing colonial resources; co-operation between the United Kingdom and the self-governing colonies would be extended, preferably by steps towards imperial federation; reforms of trade policy would make the empire an economic unit—he was talking in 1896, of forming an imperial *zollverein*, with internal free trade and tariffs against foreigners. As Britain declined, the Empire would expand to fill its rôle and, as a 'world-state', contest with Germany and the U.S.A. to control the future.

Chamberlain's campaign was to touch Reeves's life at many points. Within it he was to play a minor part, though mainly, as an agent-general and a Liberal, confined to the side-lines. It formed part of the context of many of his endeavours—even the most trivial, such as his negotiations with the Colonial Office over the award of honours to New Zealanders, a matter of great importance in a colony beginning to profess itself ultra-loyal, though Reeves must have regarded it with a quiet irony.

Before Reeves left New Zealand, Seddon had spoken to him about his personal feelings on receiving honours. In May, 1896, Reeves wrote to him:

I want to say a word or two in confidence to you about honours to yourself. I can get a K.C.M.G'ship for yourself but as regards the Privy Councillorship there seems a strong objection to breaking the precedent which reserves it for 'Imperial' services, and another objection to granting it without the K.C.M.G'ship. I enclose—in strict confidence—a note I have had from Onslow which sums up the position and tallies with what I had been told before. Now will you take a K.C.M.G'ship? or will you trust to my being able to persuade Chamberlain to make a new precedent and make you a Privy Councillor on the ground of your successful career as a N.Z. statesman, your influence with the Democracy and your loyalty to the Empire? You remember that in our private conversation before I left you told me that you would not have a K.C.M.G'ship. I thought you were right and I think so still. I would not take it myself. But if you have altered your mind please cable and I will set to work at once.

As to the P.C'ship I am by no means hopeless. Chamberlain wants to rally the Colonies to him. I go on the principle that he can't do that without making new departures. This unlucky African business [the

Jameson raid] is taking him up completely just now but that once out of the way he will push on with the Empire. If you could do anything to back him up in the Imperial Zollverein question that would establish a strong claim. As regards the Colonial Office that old request of yours to have all titles referred to NZ rankles a bit. I can see that from what Meade says.

Onslow, the ex-Governor of New Zealand, was now Under-Secretary of State for India. He had advised Reeves that he could not support an application for Seddon's appointment to the Privy Council, an honour rare and usually awarded only after the award of K.C.M.G. and for further imperial services.[1] On the other hand Seddon was not only unwilling to be knighted but, we may perhaps infer, shared Grey's view that the Order of St. Michael and St. George had been founded for the purpose of excluding colonials from the great traditional honours.

Reeves's attitude towards these matters was unusual. He was an ardent imperialist, in the sense of thinking the Empire was a force for good in the world, yet, at best, but a half-hearted monarchist. His attitude towards the court was ironically sceptical (even, in one letter to Waldegrave, 'atrabilious'). He loathed aristocratic formality and etiquette. The court dress which he inherited from Perceval was too large for him and he pretended not to be able to afford to buy his own. He declined to be presented or to attend any functions at court and similarly absented himself from Chamberlain's parties, which were very formal. He was, on democratic grounds, strongly opposed to accepting honours and declined a K.C.M.G. in 1897, 1899 and on other occasions.[2]

Late in 1896 the British Government offered to award further honours to the veteran New Zealand politician, Sir Francis Dillon Bell. Reeves had to see Chamberlain and indicate his Government's opposition. He reported to Seddon that Chamberlain 'seemed a little put out but spoke civilly enough

---

[1] Seddon MSS, Onslow to Reeves, 15 May 1896, enclos. Reeves to Seddon, 16 May 1896. The other letters referred to in this section are Reeves to Seddon, 11 Dec. 1896, 23 Jan., 20 Feb. 1897; and, Reeves MSS, Seddon to Reeves, 23 May 1901.

[2] Interview with Mrs. Amber Blanco White; *Auckland Star*, 15 July, 7 Aug. 1897; 17 July 1899, 3 July 1900; Reeves MSS, W. Kennaway to Reeves, 23 March 1901; *N.Z. Graphic*, 7 July 1900.

and intimated that they had no desire to press honours where honours were not wanted'.

Reeves took the opportunity of raising a delicate problem on which the New Zealand Liberals, after their unhappy experiences with governors, felt very strongly:

We then went on to discuss your request that the Government should be consulted prior to the appointment of the new Governor. I explained to him that there was no question of a desire on your part to interfere with Her Majesty's powers, or to exercise any kind of veto over them, but that my Government thought it reasonable that the names of any noblemen or gentlemen likely to be appointed should be submitted to them, in order that if any one appeared for a special reason unsuitable, the Government might courteously indicate this. He said that he quite understood that the Government did not wish to be unreasonable or dictatorial. After a long talk we came to this that while officially and publicly he could do nothing, still as Mr. Chamberlain he thought it quite possible that he could have a private talk with me, the result of which I could in strict confidence communicate to you. Then in due course any representation would pass through me to him. In this way you would practically get what you want. If you will permit me to offer advice, I do not think it would be wise to even suggest that he should publicly refer the possible names of appointees to you. I am positive that he would refuse to do anything of the kind, and the impression created in his mind would not be favorable to our Government. As you know, he is a very strong-minded man and by no means disinclined to fight. He intimated that the vacancy is not likely to be filled up until June, or at any rate, that the new man would not be likely to get his post until that month; this would give plenty of time. If I were you I should be satisfied to have a private and unofficial consultation, as it would be a great concession that hitherto I fancy has never been granted.

Chamberlain took the opportunity of pressing strongly upon Reeves the inadequacy of the New Zealand Governor's salary, which was only £5,000, whereas, Chamberlain said, a governor had to spend £8,000 a year.

After a further discussion with Reeves, Chamberlain agreed that the New Zealand Government should be consulted by the method suggested, but was 'evidently very anxious that no whisper of the matter should get abroad as in that case he would be angrily attacked by his Party here for surrendering a portion of the Queen's prerogative. I pledged your word of honour and my own that the matter should be an absolute secret.'

Lord Arthur Hill declined the appointment because of the expense. Reeves then discussed with Chamberlain the possible appointment of Lord Ranfurly: 'I particularly asked Mr Chamberlain whether Lord R was in any way personally obnoxious to the Irish Nationalists and both he and Lord Selborne said "certainly not!"—they had made special enquiry they added.'

Reeves then telegraphed to Seddon Ranfurly's name and details of his understanding with Chamberlain. Seddon had publicly announced that Reeves had been instructed to seek discussion between the Colonial Office and his Government before Glasgow's successor was appointed.[1] Now he was carefully silent. Thus, for the first time, the New Zealand Government had a say in the choice of a governor—a small addition to its powers of self-government.

Chamberlain also discussed with Reeves his plans for another Colonial Conference on the occasion of Queen Victoria's diamond jubilee. That for her golden jubilee in 1887, though significant in the growth of the Empire, had been a mere gathering of 'colonial notables'. Now something more impressive was intended. Reeves told Seddon:

nothing is to be spared to make it a very great ceremonial indeed. The Crowned Heads of Europe are expected. If the Colonial Premiers come Chamberlain hopes to hold an informal Conference of them and discuss with them a number of Imperial matters. This he told me in confidence at our last interview. I then took the opportunity of telling him that if he wanted to do honour to the Colonies in the Jubilee Year the best step would be to make the Premiers Privy-Councillors. I pointed out that nothing that he could give would please the Colonies half so much—it would be much better than making you Peers and fifty times better than making you K.C.M.G's. He seemed a good deal struck with the notion, and said that though as an ordinary matter they had to be very sparing of Privy Councillorships still in the Jubilee Year it *might* be different. He shook me cordially by the hand and said it should be considered at any rate.
Take my advice and come over if you can. Capt. Russell as a loyal

[1] *Auckland Star*, 26 Jan. 1897; Seddon MSS, Reeves to Seddon, 11 Dec. 1896, 23 Jan., 20 Feb. 1897.

Englishman can't refuse to facilitate parliamentary arrangements to let you away. Pleasant as it would be for me to represent New Zealand at the greatest Imperial Ceremony of our time I should like to see the Colony represented by its Premier.

Not knowing of this correspondence, Edward Tregear wrote to Reeves that he would have liked to see his face when he learned that he had to show the Premier round London—it was 'not so nominated in the bond' when Reeves left. And when the Seddons arrived, Reeves was, indeed, ill. But though Kennaway met them at Liverpool, Reeves—'looking very unwell'—turned up at Euston. He described the occasion in his 'Memoirs':

When Seddon first came to England as Premier, he was unused to official pomp. I met him, and we drove to the Hotel Cecil. There we were met by a tall, dignified official in black who informed us that he was charged with the duty of seeing to the comfort and convenience of the Premiers and their families. He showed us into Seddon's room, gave instructions about the luggage and so forth. Richard was obviously a little awed by him, as indeed was I, for I had been told that he had been sent across from Buckingham Palace. When his back happened to be turned, Seddon bent over to me and whispered, ' Shall I offer him a drink?' It was not yet quite noon, and I remembered a certain remark made by Mr. Winkle to Messrs Bob Sawyer and Ben Allen. So I whispered back; 'Not yet; it's rather early.'[1]

There immediately followed one of the most famous of New Zealand historical tableaux. Doddery old Sir George Grey called at the hotel and talked to Seddon for two hours. When he left, Seddon carried him downstairs in his arms.

Once again, Reeves was over-shadowed by his larger colleague. Seddon revelled in the celebrations; though he declined to be a knight, he loved to meet duchesses. Most of his countrymen probably enjoyed the spectacle of Seddon in the rôle of imperial statesman as much as he did acting it. Frank Waldegrave wrote to Reeves sardonically of the notion of the Premier 'in a royal carriage, wearing a court suit, and returning the cheers of the populace by raising his cocked hat' or being eulogized in Latin by a Public Orator. No doubt Reeves agreed, but the opinion was not general in New Zealand.

[1] On this and the following incidents, see also, *Auckland Star*, 10, 15 July, 7, 11 Aug. 1897.

At the Colonial Conference, while conceding that complete imperial federation could not be looked for in the near future, Chamberlain spoke for 'a great council of Empire to which the Colonies would send representative plenipotentiaries—not mere delegates'. Only Braddon of Tasmania and Seddon supported him. The Canadian, Laurier, and the other Australians blocked them, and the Conference resolved merely to hold 'periodical conferences'.[1]

On Seddon's birthday, 22 June, at a party in the Cecil, Reeves proposed the new Privy Councillor's health. Seddon replied that 'if he wasn't "Sir W.P." it was entirely his own fault, and because he preferred the principles of the party they both loved to a title.' And a few days later, at a luncheon given by the Fabian Society, still in an expansive mood, he suggested that Reeves should have a seat in the imperial Parliament, with power to speak on colonial questions.[2]

Defending, expounding, publicizing laws was a sad substitute for making them. Nevertheless, though writing books gave him less satisfaction than passing laws, his new job did allow him the leisure necessary to continue his writing and study. He collected most of his best verse in a volume, *New Zealand And other Poems*, which was published in January 1898 by Grant Richards, who published for the Fabians. It is not certain whether any of them were written in England, though several fragments from a long unfinished poem, 'Tasman', do not seem to have been previously published, and 'Rivers of Damascus' was possibly new.[3] Once again, his verse was favourably reviewed. The London *Echo* compared him with Gladstone, as a poet-politician, and thought it 'no exaggeration' to compare some of his verses with those of 'the great word-painters, Sophocles, Virgil and Tennyson'.[4] He was, indeed, a 'word-painter'. Though some of his verses like 'Nox Benigna' are successfully evocative of a mood, he generally describes nature rather than seeking to penetrate its meanings.

[1] K. Sinclair, *Imperial Federation*, London, 1955, pp. 27 ff.

[2] *Fabian News*, August 1897. The suggestion was not as absurd as it might now seem: at the 1902 Colonial Conference Laurier made the same proposal.

[3] Tregear had not seen the latter poem until late 1897 when Reeves sent him (it seems) the MSS or proofs of his book. Reeves may have written it in 1896. 'Letters from Men of Mark', Tregear to Reeves, 25 Nov. 1897. See above, p. 232, note 2.

[4] *Auckland Star*, 26 March 1898.

Late romanticism led him to strive for romantically-charged adjectives—'crystal radiance', 'limpid hyaline', 'stainless dome'—and to content himself, often, with 'clear seas', 'shadowy walls', 'phantom ranges', or 'shining abysses'. Sometimes he made greater efforts, as in 'An Old Ambassador's Pets', a monologue form derived from Browning, but he did not, in general, aim for more difficult things than would fit comfortably into the accepted poetics of his day. Though some of his poems deal directly with the life of the settlers he generally accepted without question the conception, common in New Zealand, of poetry as escape. Many years later he wrote to a Christchurch friend, 'As for the poetry you know what a solace and delight verse is, how it throws "the light that never was on sea or land" over the beaten and dusty thoroughfares of life.'[1] Though it may be unfair to quote here the words of a tired old man, there is no reason to suppose that he ever held a different opinion.

His best poems have charm; they are technically competent; a few are memorable; but they add nothing of note to English verse except their New Zealand subject. It is in terms of the beginning of writing in New Zealand, a new branch of English literature—not in comparisons with Tennyson—that the significance of his verse has to be discussed. The historian of New Zealand letters thinks the term 'occasional poetry' may justly be applied to Reeves's 'minor but historically interesting verses';[2] he was, in short, not a Poet, but (in the Canterbury tradition) a gentleman who occasionally wrote poems. He wrote them very well. As the first New Zealand-born poet of merit, he had an important place—an important rôle—in his own country.

Exile also gave him a motive and the time to reflect on the significance of his legislation in the light of the history of New Zealand; on the meaning of colonization, indeed of life, in those South Pacific islands, so far from the great powers, so far, many people would think, from history itself. Such questionings have since produced verse better than his, but they led him to write some of the greatest prose works yet to appear on New Zealand, including the most influential volume of history. From facts,

---

[1] Alpers MSS, Turnbull Library, Reeves to Miss G. Colborne-Veel, 25 April [probably 1925]. The complete letter is quoted below, p. 341.
[2] E. H. McCormick, *Letters and Art in New Zealand*, Wellington, 1940, p. 107.

18

imagination and feeling he created answers that moulded the New Zealanders' view of themselves.

A history of New Zealand had lain in his mind for many years. We may feel regretfully confident that he wrote the following paragraph in the *Canterbury Times* in 1889—for what other New Zealand state-lover could have envisaged a state-produced general history?

A readable, able, trustworthy history of New Zealand does not exist. The countenance of Government has not hitherto been of much service, while private enterprise, as represented by Mr Rusden, a prejudiced collector of unlimited dry-as-dust, has left a bad taste in the mouths of most people.... We have ... the material for history in the greatest abundance—official, newspaper and private. We have left the sifting of those materials to private enterprise, with the result that we have got no history, in the proper sense of the term. Were the matter put into the hands of a Royal Commission of the right men ... this reproach would be ended in a few years.[1]

He was commissioned to write a history of New Zealand by Horace Marshall and Son, a firm of newsagents, book-sellers and publishers, who were bringing out a 'Story of Empire' series, partly intended as board school text books.[2] *The Story of New Zealand* appeared in April, 1898, shortly after his poems. It was well received by reviewers. The *Daily News* said it was 'a brilliant little essay in the Macaulay style ... terse ... graphic'; the *Spectator*, while admiring its 'movement and lucidity', thought it too closely modelled on the Master. The *Sunday Sun* chose *The Story of New Zealand* for its book of the week, and published an interview in which the author appeared a different man from the one so often described by New Zealand journalists. He was now: 'A slight man, with a soft manner, a beautiful voice, and tones so rational, so conciliatory, so full of broadness and serenity of view, that you are inclined to think that this is an escaped scholar and not one of the leaders of a young and powerful democracy.'[3]

No sooner was his book out than he set to work to write for the same publisher a much fuller version, which he meant to call 'The Fortunate Isles' (a term which appeared in his poem

---

[1] 21 March 1889, editorial.

[2] Cecil Howard, *Mary Kingsley*, London, 1957, p. 241. Mary Kingsley was commissioned to write 'the story of West Africa'.

[3] *Auckland Star*, 2 Aug. 1898; reviews cited ibid., 24 May, 27 June 1898.

'At Vicar's Hill'), until he learned that it was already the title of a book on the Canary Islands. He then hit on 'The Long White Cloud', a translation of the Maori name for New Zealand, *Aotearoa*. In August he took his family across the Channel to Chinon, where he wrote in the mornings, cycled in the afternoons, and in the evenings read and thought about his next day's work.[1] His third book published in 1898 was out by November.

Once again, the reviewers were kind. 'C.T.'—probably Charles Trevelyan—wrote in the *Fabian News* that the chapter on Maori mythology would rank with anything in Grote's *History of Greece*. The *Spectator* congratulated New Zealand on having 'her home-bred historian': 'We measure our words when we say that the writer has produced a book which is remarkable for its freshness, force, and general accuracy.' But *The Times*, while acknowledging a 'tactful skill and an appreciative discernment', thought it 'a task almost impossible of achievement so to write the history of the rise and progress of a small community, removed by circumstances from intimate touch with the affairs of the great world, as to enlist the sympathies of those unconcerned'. In the case of a colony of which 'the influence on general movements is so indirect as to be scarcely recognised', the reviewer thought, 'the attitude of receptive egotism [a nice phrase] on the part of the public is of necessity lacking. The existence of New Zealand has not yet modified the affairs of the world in any very appreciable degree, and the world in general is proportionately indifferent to the history of New Zealand.'[2]

The occasional criticism and condescension did not much detract from the fact that Reeves had achieved a considerable success, which was not lost on his countrymen. Then, as now, a favourable London review, cabled out in full to the New Zealand daily newspapers, was worth any number of local notices, on the principle, generally if unconsciously accepted by a people few of whom understood the arts much beyond the level of painted, Christmas, biscuit-tin lids featuring 'The Blue Boy', that the value of criticism bore a direct relation to the distance of its origin from the reader.

---

1 'Letters from Men of Mark', E. Tregear to Reeves, 30 June 1898; *Auckland Star*, 2 Aug., 29 Aug. 1898.

2 *Fabian News*, Jan. 1899; *Spectator*, 15 April 1899; *The Times*, 3 Jan. 1899.

All of Reeves's experiences, growing up in New Zealand, his work and travel all over the country, had helped in the making of a book of great intellectual and imaginative sweep, in modern prose distinguished for its conciseness and clarity, a prose tempered over the years at his studies and at his editorial and ministerial desks.

Reeves gave to New Zealand development an intelligent and persuasive, a coherent interpretation which was almost universally accepted by his countrymen and scarcely questioned before the nineteen-fifties. Perhaps it would be more accurate to say that he discovered in its history a pattern, some parts of which were already accepted by New Zealanders, who were thus prepared to accept the rest. In terms of accuracy and balanced judgment it was immensely superior to anything that preceded it. Yet, when that has been said, it is possible to see most of it in terms of Reeves's own life—as a disguised autobiography.

The attitude towards the Maoris, whom he thinks to be dying out, is markedly sympathetic, as we should expect in the son of the proprietor of the *Lyttelton Times*, and in the man who made peace with Te Whiti. It was not the only possible attitude: the history of the Colony, up to that time, revealed widespread European hostility to the Maoris more frequently than friendliness, much more often than understanding. Great emphasis is given to the rôle of Edward Gibbon Wakefield and the colonizing companies in the annexation and settlement of the country—as we should expect from an author who grew up in Canterbury. Vogel's borrowing is defended, as it had been by the *Lyttelton Times* and his father. The 'continuous ministry' is seen as conservative; and the radical legislation of the Liberals is stressed. None of these attitudes is necessarily or completely unjustified; but none commands unquestioning assent.[1] It is not a prejudiced book in the obvious sense—he is charitable towards his opponents; surprisingly dispassionate, even, in discussing them. But it is a New Zealand Liberal view of New Zealand history. And a personal note is often unmistakable. The 'most marked failings' of the Colony's political life, he says, are 'the savagely

---

[1] Reeves's rôle in New Zealand historiography, and recent criticism of his views, are discussed in K. Sinclair, 'New Zealand Historiography', in a book on 'British Empire-Commonwealth Historiography' ed. Robin W. Winks, to be published by Duke University, 1965.

personal character of some of its conflicts ... lack of sense of proportion or humour'. He quotes Wakefield's 'terrible saying' that 'in Colonial politics "everyone strikes at his opponent's heart"'.

The opportunity and the time to write his histories were given by the fact that Reeves was in London; distance helped him to see in perspective the battles from which he had emerged. Yet, once again, it is clear that he had an important place in his own country; one left unfilled. For those few people in New Zealand who deeply cared about the growth of a native intellectual life, it was a tragedy that he was in exile. Guy Scholefield, William Downie Stewart, O. T. J. Alpers, the country's writers and scholars, corresponded with Reeves about their books, articles and reviews. He was not only the leader of Labour, but of the New Zealand intellectuals. That he lived in London was symbolic of the colonial status of the New Zealand arts: the relatively rich immigrant culture was withering, while what might replace it was with difficulty perceived. Frances Hodgkins, Katherine Mansfield and many lesser artists were to flee in their turn from philistinism and smug provincial conformity.

In 1896, with an instinctive defensive reaction which he soon shed, Reeves wrote to Seddon: 'If you hear of an article of mine appearing in the *National Review* here please don't think I am giving up my time to outside literary work. It happens to be an article I wrote in New Zealand.... Several people in N.Z.— including Tregear—read it before I sent it.'[1] A couple of years later, though he was a very active agent-general, he seemed to be living the life of a London literary man with strong political interests. The New Zealand newspapers reported that he was writing short biographies of Grey, Fox and Vogel for the *Dictionary of National Biography*, contracting to write a new book, refusing another offer. He was elected to the Savile Club, where he felt very much at home. He was a 'prominent member' of a Liberal club, the Articles Club.[2] His triumphant career as a public lecturer continued. His duties included the pleasant one of travel. He was reported in Budapest, in Berlin. In July 1899 he

---

[1] Seddon MSS, 16 May. See *National Review*, Aug. 1896, 'Five Years Reform in New Zealand'.

[2] On this club see R. B. Haldane, *An Autobiography*, London, 1929, pp. 104-5.

went to stay with the Shaws at Hindhead, where he caught diphtheria, and was dangerously ill. During his lengthy convalescence Shaw entertained him with amusing notes, and talked to him, from a safe distance, through the window.[1] Then he visited France with Maud and stayed with Uncle Pember in Hampshire. In September they sailed for the United States, with most of the other agents-general, to attend an International Commercial Conference in Philadelphia. To the Agent-General for Western Australia, who could not go, he sent a telegram: 'We float together. You float a loan.' The United States were endlessly stimulating. He attended a presidential reception. He saw Niagara Falls and wrote an article describing them. He visited many cities in the United States and Canada. He met Henry Demarest Lloyd, the American radical, who became one of his closest friends and one of the chief publicists of New Zealand's new legislation. Lloyd was, Reeves wrote on his death, one of those men who made him think more of mankind.[2] No one could doubt, reading the sometimes daily reports in the New Zealand papers, that Reeves was at the height of his powers and his power of living; that he was enjoying himself immensely.

[1] *Auckland Star*, August, September 1899.
[2] H. D. Lloyd MSS, document quoting Reeves.

17

BETWEEN TWO WORLDS
1897–1901

REEVES's main aim, when he landed in England, was to return to New Zealand politics at the earliest opportunity, a prospect which he discussed endlessly with friends at home. Reading the letters he received is like watching a merry-go-round with five horses of different colours. The first alone seems gay. The left wing Liberals (like Frederick Pirani, who had worked for the *Wanganui Herald* in Ballance's time) and the unionists, Reeves was told repeatedly, wanted him back. Tregear thought in 1897 that Reeves would inherit the leadership of the party.

The second circling topic is the advice, for example from one of his old friends, Mark Cohen, editor of the Dunedin *Evening Star*, not to return. Cohen would not ask him to return, he said, 'even if I believed the succession to the leadership of the Liberal party in this colony were within your grasp which, to be very candid, I do not'. Frank Waldegrave, his ex-secretary and now Under-Secretary for Justice, a refreshingly sardonic corres-pondent, agreed. Though the unions longed for Reeves's return, he advised, the time was not ripe. If he did come back, the only hope was to get a country constituency and 'talk freehold tenure, d——d loafing agitators, & the like'.

Waldegrave constantly observed (the third repetitive theme) that 'the whole tone of our public life' had sunk to 'a low level'. He was glad his friend was out of it, and did not have to defend the banks' and Ward's 'swindles'. He frankly did not think Reeves 'could ever come down to the pettiness of our politics. Fancy being Premier & having to decide whether you would give a billet as charwoman to Mrs Jones or Mrs Brown & what effect it would have from a party point of view.' The ministers went 'in fear and trembling lest some little trumpery departmental affair such as ordering a new coal scuttle or shifting a policeman' would be 'brought up against them in Cabinet' by King Dick.

On one occasion, when Seddon said he hoped other ministers would do more work in future, Waldegrave reported to Reeves that he 'felt inclined to reply "If you would give your team more of their head & less of the whip they'd be allright", but I refrained because that is the sort of jest Rich^d would repeat in cabinet.'[1]

Much the same testimony to the condition of New Zealand politics came from English friends who visited the Colony to see for themselves the results of his legislation. In 1897 Ben Tillett, the leader of the dockers in the 1889 strike, spent some time there. In 1898 the Webbs and Charles Trevelyan included New Zealand in a tour of the European New World. Samuel, who was to go too, married instead. Tillett thought the Colony as corrupt and 'low down' as the United States, but the Webbs, 'fresh from the Augean stables of America', were more discriminating. To them 'the customary Government favouritism and genial tolerance of fallen human nature' seemed 'peccadilloes'. They thought the wild accusations of corruption by T. E. Taylor and other left wing Liberals largely baseless, though it was true that Seddon had given himself a salaried position on the board selling off the Bank of New Zealand's properties.

When Seddon visited London in 1897, Sidney Webb had regarded him as 'a gross, illiterate but forceful man, more like a Trade Union official in such an industry as steelsmelting, than an M.P.'. But now the Webbs were as impressed by his courage (he was 'unabashed' by any attack or exposure) and skill as they were embarrassed by his vulgarity (he introduced his daughters as 'the Honourable Miss Seddons') and his roughness ('Take that bloody excrescence down!' he shouted to the Minister of Public Works in the presence of the Webbs and a gang of workmen). All these visitors thought Seddon's position as strong as a minister's could be.[2] Their only doubt—a fourth theme in

[1] The letters from Tregear, Waldegrave and Cohen are in 'Letters from Men of Mark in New Zealand', London School of Economics Library (microfilm copy in Alexander Turnbull Library, Wellington). Reeves's letters to them have not been traced.

[2] Ben Tillett's letter, 10 Aug. 1897, is in 'Letters from Men of Mark'. The opinions of the Webbs are cited from Webb to Reeves, 27 Aug. 1898 and Trevelyan to Reeves, 22 Aug. 1898 (both in Reeves MSS) and Beatrice Webb's journal, 1898, which includes an entry by Sidney Webb, 22 Aug. 1898 (Passfield MSS, London School of Economics).

Reeves's correspondence to which we shall return—was whether Seddon aimed at retiring to the agent-generalship. There was little comfort for Reeves in their letters.

The fifth theme in his correspondence was not much more cheering. Tillett thought the industrial arbitration system 'a monument' to his goodness, but its working involved endless difficulties which Reeves naturally wished he were there to solve, since Seddon could be expected to have little respect for its principles. Reeves anxiously read reports from Tregear (who called himself its 'step-father' or 'nurse') and from the Webbs and Trevelyan, who found the new arbitration court judge, W. B. Edwards, muddle-headed; and he anxiously wrote detailed suggestions to Tregear when amendments were in prospect. The main troubles lay in the working of the Conciliation Boards, which Reeves had thought would prove the most useful part of the system. Some union representatives kept up 'a continual scratching of labour sores', so that the Boards would go on sitting and they would get their thirty shillings fee each day —as well as expenses, which they 'shoved on', Tregear wrote, in 'shameless vouchers'. The employers thought there was 'too much conciliation and not enough arbitration', Seddon told Reeves. In 1901 Reeves's old enemy Willis 'log-rolled' among the more conservative Liberals and added to the amending bill a clause enabling disputes to be taken straight to the Arbitration Court. It was late at night; the House was tired; and despite the urging of Tregear and Cohen, Seddon did not fight. The result was a major alteration in the whole system; the Court (Tregear later wrote) became 'smothered with chaff the Board should have winnowed away'. It was very discouraging.[1]

Letters from New Zealand must have kept him emotionally slightly dizzy. The unions wanted him back; the country and his Act were going to the dogs; but the time was not ripe to return. He began to sound like a Bourbon in exile. He thought of coming back, he told Tregear in 1896, with the motto (which echoed the 'self-reliant' policy of the sixties as well as Ballance's) 'Alone but not a loan', and asked how it would be received. He was told that

[1] For the references in this paragraph, and for details on the development of the Act, see 'Letters from Men of Mark': Waldegrave, 9 March 1899; 16 Oct. 1901; Tregear, 3 April, 15 Sept. 1897, 11 Jan., 8 Aug., 31 Aug. 1900, 7 May 1901, 18 July 1906, 19 April 1907; Judge F. R. Chapman, 25 Nov. 1906, 23 Feb. 1907; Seddon MSS, Seddon, 15 Aug. 1901; *State Experiments*, ii, pp. 107 ff.

his countrymen now accepted loans as a matter of course; there had been a 'slackening' of Liberal principles—'you would indeed find yourself (as you say) a "political Ishmael".' But Tregear, who almost worshipped him, at other times assured him, 'we poor New Zealanders think of you with love and devotion.' He called him a Prince Rupert. He said that he was born of a virgin and had a halo: that he was a myth already, and everyone awaited his 'Second Advent'. But Tregear wondered whether he would think it worthwhile to give up London 'to come out to lead our ragged army', and exhorted him to remember that 'the post of danger is the post of honour'—'and better is one day among the clear light of swords than all the roses of Mayfair'.

There is no doubt that Reeves felt tired both at the recollection and prospect of battle. He had stood at that post too long. On the other hand, the enticement to stay in England for the time being was growing. In 1897 he wrote to Tregear that he had 'climbed to the summit of his life at forty'.[1] That was certainly his mood on reaching England, bitterly disappointed at being pushed out of New Zealand politics; and he was to sink into despondency often enough in years to come; but in 1897 it was a passing mood. His success in the society of the English left wing had opened up a new possibility, one perhaps dreamed of in 1874 when he was to go to Oxford, but long forgotten, of entering British politics. Many colonists and colonials—including Grey and Vogel—had tried and failed. But Robert Lowe, a lawyer-politician in New South Wales, had become a member of Gladstone's first cabinet. It would be guessing to attribute to Reeves an aim as high. On the other hand, he was far from agreeing with Charles Trevelyan, who wrote from Wellington in 1898: 'Supposing Seddon were to go, I cannot conceive what the result would be. There is no man fit for the position of Premier, except W.P.R.; but as said W.P.R. is wanted in a bigger sphere if he can stay there, and had better be a doorkeeper in the mother of Parliaments than dwell in the tents of antipodean authority, Seddon had better continue ... .'[2]

Reeves was sufficient of a realist not to delude himself that the shadow of London authority was superior to its substance in Wellington. We may suppose him to have had hopes of some-

---

[1] 'Letters from Men of Mark', Tregear to Reeves, 25 Nov. 1897.
[2] Reeves MSS, 22 Aug. 1898; copy in New Zealand National Archives.

thing better than a post as doorkeeper. British politics never gripped him entirely, as New Zealand's did, but in the late nineties to make a contribution to the causes of British reform seemed more immediately feasible.

A few years previously Reeves would have had little in common with either of the great political parties, though he would have found himself in agreement with individuals like Sir John Gorst (a Conservative) and Sir Charles Dilke, who combined a desire for social reform with a belief in the virtues of imperial expansion. But now many of the Liberals were moving away from Gladstonian liberalism towards some of the ideas and policies of the New Zealand Liberals. They were moved by the same causes that had influenced the New Zealand Liberals— especially mass demand for social reform—and were inspired by the same creeds.

In 1891 the Liberal 'Newcastle Programme' had included many policies of which Reeves could approve, including 'one man one vote', employers' liability for accidents, and the possible payment of members.[1] The 'idealist' philosophers, T. H. Green and Bernard Bosanquet, were inducing younger university men to modify individualism in the light of novel doctrines of state and social collectivism. Green had, for instance, plainly influenced Herbert Samuel, who was, when Reeves first knew him, writing a book to express the doctrines of the 'new liberalism'.[2] Green—and Samuel—and Reeves—thought that the state should 'hinder hindrances to the good life'; should give all citizens 'the fullest possible opportunity to lead the best life' (as Samuel wrote). Fundamental social reform was needed, Samuel thought, now that 'it was seen that Liberty was not a matter only of national independence, or of constitutional democracy, or of freedom of thought and religion and in the conduct of life; but that there could be no true liberty if a man was confined and oppressed by ignorance, by poverty, by excessive hours of labour... .'[3]

---

[1] R. C. K. Ensor, *England 1870–1914*, Oxford, 1936, p. 207.

[2] Viscount Samuel, *Memoirs*, London, 1945, pp. 24–26; John Bowle, *Viscount Samuel*, London, 1957, pp. 37–41. The interest of another Liberal Imperialist, Haldane, in German philosophy is well known. He was later a friend of Bernard Bosanquet. See Richard Burdon Haldane, *An Autobiography*, London, 1929.

[3] *Memoirs*, p. 25.

That was a path that New Zealand Liberals had taken ten years earlier.

Reeves's views were not identical with Samuel's, Trevelyan's, or those of more important Liberals such as Haldane and Asquith. He would, for instance, have stressed the state more than Samuel did and said less of liberty. Intellectually he was very much closer to the Fabians and the Independent Labour Party— ' " Out of Henry George by either Bellamy or Gronlund " was a true pedigree of the convictions held by nearly all the leading propagandists who set socialism on its feet in Great Britain between 1886 and 1900', R. C. K. Ensor wrote; and he noted, too, the influence of the *Fabian Essays*.[1] But, as we have seen, there were close connexions between Haldane, young Samuel and other Liberals with the Fabians. Reeves felt sufficiently near to the Liberals' views on social reform, to join them. And he was doubly attracted by the label 'Liberal Imperialist'. Rosebery, then Haldane and Asquith, and now younger men like Samuel had repudiated the 'Little Englandism' attributed to Gladstone. They saw (as Chamberlain did) social reform at home and imperial reorganization abroad as intimately linked in a progressive programme. Samuel wrote later: 'The same motives which led us to be social reformers at home made us favour, for the backward peoples, a stage of colonial administration, as the best means of helping them to reach a higher level of civilization. Besides, the existence of the British Empire assured, over nearly a fourth part of the globe, internal peace and tranquillity.'

Of the quality of this 'imperialism' there was (there will be) more to be said. For the moment it is sufficient to indicate that Reeves found that he had quite close intellectual ties with the 'Liberal Imps' (Beatrice called them the 'Limps') with whom he was friendly.

They were equally interested in him. For a few years New Zealand enjoyed a unique prominence in the thoughts of reformers. Not only Reeves's new friends, but many American and European scholars and radicals, like André Siegfried and Henry Demarest Lloyd, made the pilgrimage to the antipodean 'social laboratory' to watch the 'experimental' laws in action. In 1901 Seddon wrote to Reeves that applications for copies of

[1] Op. cit., p. 334.

their labour laws poured in from all over the world. By 1897 the *Auckland Star*, which had taken the lead in the process of expelling Reeves, was publishing smug assertions of New Zealand's pre-eminence in labour legislation.[1] New Zealand was 'out l.b.w.'—leading the bloody world! As a principal author of the new laws Reeves justly shared his country's brief glory. In 1897 Chamberlain himself sent to him for full details of the industrial arbitration Act and of every case in which it had been applied.[2] At every opportunity Reeves advocated its principles. At a trades union congress Ben Tillett moved in favour of compulsory arbitration, but was heavily defeated.[3] The British did not take up Reeves's measure; too many liberal feelings were offended by the loss of unionist liberties implicit in state arbitration; Churchill's Trade Boards Act of 1909 (earlier versions of which had been pushed by Dilke and Samuel) was based, instead, on the principle of a minimum wage that had been adopted in Victoria in 1896. But for some years, while many people were discussing means of preventing 'sweated' labour and improving working conditions, there was a keen interest in compulsory arbitration. Thus Reeves stood on a minor political prominence, from which there was some hope of advancing into parliamentary action.

From late 1898 until late in 1900 the New Zealand and English newspapers reported, from time to time, that Reeves was about to stand for Parliament.[4] He received many requests and suggestions that he contest various constituencies in what came to be called the 'khaki election' of 1900, and he gave much time to discussing the possibilities. In January 1899, for example, he was corresponding with Liberals in an electorate in Manchester. He was advised that it would need a great deal of 'working up', for though there was an Independent Labour Party candidate, there was no branch of the Liberal Party there.[5] The information was not encouraging. Imaginative journalists occasionally prophesied a brilliant future for him. The *Echo* thought he

---

[1] e.g. *Auckland Star*, 26 May 1897, editorial.

[2] Ibid., 8 Sept., 3 Nov. 1897.

[3] Reeves MSS, small clipping book, p. 154.

[4] Reeves MSS, small clipping book, pp. 12, 150, 152, 164, 165; *Auckland Star*, 21 Nov. 1898, 28 Feb. 1899 (quoting *Hull Daily News*), 8 Jan. 1900.

[5] Reeves MSS, W. Clarke to Reeves, 16 Jan. 1899; a 'Mr Scott' had also written on the subject.

'ranked with Sir Wilfred Laurier and Mr. Cecil Rhodes as a great Colonial statesman', and would 'soon find his way to the Treasury bench' if he entered Parliament. A writer in the *Chronicle*, drawing up a fanciful list of the next Liberal Government, suggested Reeves for President of the Board of Trade.[1] He had, in 1899, come so close to a decision that he wrote asking Seddon to reappoint him as Agent-General only for a year. But he had to decline this—and other—'offers' of constituencies,[2] despite the encouragement of his Liberal friends.

The immediate reason why Reeves decided not to stand for Parliament in 1899 was, quite simply, that he could not afford to. Herbert Samuel, who was elected by a Yorkshire constituency in 1902, wrote to his mother, 'you will not see very much returned out of £1,500.'[3] Members were not paid. Another factor was what Ensor called 'the stupid and grudging attitude of the local liberal associations': 'Each was run, as a rule, by a group of middle-class people, who had no use for a candidate without funds; and so, though organizations like those of the miners could buy their way into liberal seats, they were closed to individually gifted aspirants.'[4]

Reeves could not join the Labour Party, which was in process of formation—it was about to break away from the Liberals in New Zealand too. Some of his friends, like Charles Trevelyan, did so later, but he remained deeply committed to the idea of a Liberal party embracing all the progressive movements, and middle as well as working-class support and direction. Perhaps, in time, he would have felt at home in the British Labour Party (though scarcely in New Zealand, where there was greater suspicion in the Labour ranks of middle-class intellectuals). But in 1899, though he was friendly with the Labour leaders, he felt himself apart, and they agreed, if one may judge from a cordial letter which Ben Tillett wrote to him from New Zealand in 1897. Labour, in New Zealand, Tillett told him, 'is like Hamlet without the Prince with you absent. I am perfectly honest in this statement, although I do not relish the brutal fact, for I recognize the weakness of labour, when it is dependent upon *another* class

---

[1] Reeves MSS, small clipping book, pp. 152, 164; *Auckland Star*, 18 Dec. 1899.

[2] Reeves MSS, small clipping book, p. 165; Seddon MSS, Reeves to Seddon, 22 Sept. [1900].

[3] John Bowle, *Viscount Samuel*, p. 49.   [4] Op. cit., p. 222.

of man to represent it. It is good of you to bring your sterling powers, & your big humanity to help us, but while it reflects your goodness, it indicates our weakness.'[1]

There was speculation in New Zealand about whether he could be a Member of Parliament while retaining his appointment as Agent-General. It was argued that his duties in that capacity would be completed each day before the House sat, and even reported that the New Zealand Government was 'disposed to give the experiment a trial',[2] but it was certainly untrue. Farmers and businessmen would have protested about the country's main trade representative neglecting his task. There was some possibility of a paid position in the English Liberal Party, but no details can be learned of this.[3] In the end, he could find no acceptable way of earning a living while entering politics.

It does not seem that Reeves made serious efforts to stand for Parliament after 1899, but the idea continued to attract him for some years to come; remained, as it were, a door not quite closed, which formed an important element in his life. His English political aspirations were intimately linked with many of his activities in London, and must be kept in mind by whoever seeks to understand him.

How seriously did Englishmen regard Reeves's political prospects? The least kind view was put by a journal, *The Syren and Shipping*, in 1903: 'He was, and is, essentially a "*new* country man", which, being interpreted, means that whereas he was capable of distinction in a country whose men are mostly pioneers, he would have been easily overshadowed, and, perhaps, quite obliterated, by the sharper intellects of older countries.'[4]

He was, of course, eventually overshadowed by many of his new friends. But none of them thought that 'intellect' was a quality in which he was deficient. (Shaw wrote later that Reeves was 'quite as able as the Fabian founders'[5]—a view which perhaps may be taken as little seriously as that of a shipping

[1] 'Letters from Men of Mark', 10 Aug. 1897.
[2] *Auckland Star*, 27 March 1899.
[3] Both Reeves's daughters recall something of the sort, but are uncertain about the date and details.
[4] Reeves MSS, small clipping book, p. 188, 10 June 1903.
[5] Cit. *The Long White Cloud*, 4th ed., 1950, p. 13.

journal), though deficiencies they did naturally see. He was, Sir Charles Trevelyan thought, 'probably fairly tactless', while Viscount Samuel thought him rather 'hasty and hot—otherwise he'd have had a more successful career'.[1] But perhaps the fundamental circumstance was one which Reeves pointed out himself, in 1905, in an interview in which he first described how his childhood was spent reading about England:

Conversely, I have for the last ten years lived in London with my eyes turned half the time to the Antipodes. Thus all my life I have been, as it were, looking across the sea. Without ceasing to be a New Zealander I have also become an Englishman. Yet in talking over affairs with English friends our point of view seems almost always not quite the same. On the other hand I do not look at things quite as I should if I had never left New Zealand. It is a detached kind of position.[2]

Eleven years later he put it in another way when he wrote: 'I am neither a little Englander, nor a militant imperialist, and though some liberals have often urged me to get into the House of Commons, others, I imagine, think that my views might be troublesome.'[3] He was not, in short, quite an English Liberal. He was not quite an Englishman; was nearly a foreigner. As a politician he lacked deep roots in the society in which he lived. To begin again a political career with hope of success was, not impossible, but very difficult. Robert Lowe, who had become Lord Sherbrooke, had at least grown up in England.

Much of Reeves's life might be summed up in that one word: 'detached'. Or another image suggests itself. In June 1898, after Reeves had addressed the Labour Association, Herbert Samuel, who was honorary secretary of the Home Counties Liberal Association, moved the vote of thanks. He said that he hoped Reeves would go into English politics and help the progressive movement there. George Fowlds, an Auckland radical Liberal who was visiting England, in seconding the motion expressed his hope that Reeves would return and 'lead the labour party in the colony from which a conspiracy of conservative interests had spirited him away'.[4] Reeves hung, pulled in opposite

---

[1] Sir Charles Trevelyan to the author, 26 Oct. 1954; interview with Viscount Samuel.

[2] Reeves MSS, small clipping book, p. 110, *M.A.P.*, 19 July 1905.

[3] Reeves MSS, Reeves to Robert Donald, 17 Jan. 1916.

[4] *Auckland Star*, 27 June 1898.

directions, on a wire tautened between these two points, 13,000 miles apart, yet side by side in his mind.

For years Reeves and his family lived like temporary exiles. They had the air of campers, though campers with the servants and nannies to which their class was accustomed and which his £1,250 a year secured for them. When he was interviewed in 1900 for one of a long series of articles on 'Celebrities at Home' in *The World*, he still had not unpacked most of his library of two or three thousand books.[1] They had moved from Brunswick Gardens to another furnished house in Earls Crescent, near Holland Park, in April of that year, and again, in November, to 20 Cornwall Gardens, South Kensington. The journalist found there little that was 'characteristic' of him or his family, except 'a handsome Maori petticoat', though at his offices at 13 Victoria Street there were 'specimens of minerals and of Kauri gum' (in a large glass-fronted cabinet), a 'quaint egg-shaped lump' of gold-bearing blue clay, picked up by the Agent-General in Gabriel's Gully, a picture of the liner *Arawa*, a huge collection of photographs of New Zealand scenery and other antipodean bric-a-brac in abundance.

From the time of Reeves's departure, and especially after Seddon's return from the 1897 Colonial Conference, there were many rumours, reported in English and New Zealand newspapers, that the Premier was going to return to London as Agent-General. Continual uncertainty about his tenure added to Reeves's insecurity. He told a reporter that he had not heard of Seddon having such an intention and added 'that his own plans were not definitely settled'[2]—a statement that he might have made at almost any moment for years.

When his initial appointment ran out in 1899 he was re-appointed, at his own suggestion, for only a year. In 1900, despite the protest of William Russell, Leader of the Opposition, that the Agent-General's tenure should not so completely rest on the will of the Prime Minister, Seddon again gave him a one-year renewal, though he also raised his salary to £1,500 to cover the income tax that, to Reeves's resentment, he had to pay in two

---

[1] Reeves MSS, small clipping book, pp. 156-8, 7 Nov. 1900.

[2] *Auckland Star*, 7 Feb., 28 March 1898. On Reeves's appointment, see Seddon MSS, Reeves to Seddon, 22 Sept. [1900]; PD, 1898-1903, *passim*.

countries. Reeves wrote thanking him for his 'expression of confidence'—he would not, he said, forget it. With regard to Seddon's assurance to Russell that the Agent-General had not asked for a fixed term, however, Reeves admitted that he had not done so formally, but said he had told McKenzie and Ward, when they visited London, that now he had had to decline the 'offer' of a seat he did want a longer appointment. Seddon ignored his request and continued to renew his appointment annually. Eventually Russell, who had assumed the rôle of Reeves's chief protector, both from his sense of fairness and liking for him, said in 1903 that he knew Reeves to be dissatisfied: Seddon replied that Reeves had said nothing to him about wanting a longer appointment when he visited London in 1902. On this occasion several Members praised Reeves for his efficiency and his kindness to them when they were in London.

It was not easy to explain Seddon's behaviour. He was, to say the least, evasive, in his exchanges with Russell. Perhaps he liked having Reeves, among so many, under his thumb. But the most widely-accepted opinion was that Reeves was simply keeping a seat warm for him until he chose to go to London. Cohen, Waldegrave, the Webbs and Trevelyan all speculated, in letters from New Zealand, on whether Seddon intended to go. In 1900, when Reeves's appointment was discussed, Seddon flatly denied having any such intention; and it is, indeed, hard to believe that he seriously contemplated it; but his evasions encouraged uncertainty. Possibly it was a minor example of one of his favourite tactics: he was a despot whose joviality throve in an atmosphere slightly uneasy: his closest associates never quite knew what he would do next.

Reeves's life had lost its single-mindedness. Like Henry James, he realized that 'one must choose', and resented the 'terrible burden' of that choice between the Old World and the New. But, unlike James, he could not choose. So, physically, he inhabited England, but mentally much of the time he lived 'across the sea'. It might be possible to relate quite separately his experiences in England and his relations with New Zealand, but it would falsify the untidy story of his life at that time, for he led the two lives at once. They were constantly meeting and intertwining. Sometimes events in one place had immediate repercussions on his life in the other: imperialism, in particular, linked both.

Late in November 1899 Beatrice Webb noted in her journal that Reeves was 'out of spirits' over the Boer War.[1] His mood was shared by most of his political friends. All the larger liberal hopes (for which Gladstone, in particular, had stood) for a peaceful and more moral world, in which Britain would play a leading rôle, disseminating civilization and self-government, had been affronted by the spectacle of a British government bullying the small and apparently defenceless Boer republics. Though the extent of Chamberlain's complicity in Rhodes's plots was obscure, his aggressive intention was plain enough for collusion to be suspected. The radicals, Liberals like Morley and Harcourt or Lloyd George, and most of the socialists, like Ramsay Mac-Donald, denounced the Government and the war as inspired by chauvinism and the greed of the Rand mine owners. But to the 'Liberal Imperialists', though they were appalled by the origins of the war, the issues were more complicated, for they were faced with difficult questions: what did their new imperialism, proclaimed in years of opposition, really mean? How far could it be divorced from patriotism or from strategy? If imperialism was a beneficent process, ought not the empire be extended? In the end, while deploring (as silently as possible) the Jameson raid and Chamberlain's provocative policy, Rosebery, Asquith, Haldane and Grey supported the Government during the war. Campbell-Bannerman sat for a time uncomfortably between the so-called 'pro-Boers' and the 'Liberal Imperialists', before leaning decisively to the former with his famous speech labelling British tactics in South Africa 'methods of barbarism'.[2]

The Fabians were, if possible, even more disturbed, for they had thought very little at all about international or imperial affairs—indeed Reeves must have been almost the first person to talk seriously to them about imperial policy.[3] The left wing or radical Liberals and the left wing socialists among the Fabians

---

[1] Passfield MSS, 4 Dec. 1899.

[2] See, e.g., Samuel, loc. cit.; J. A. Spender and C. Asquith, *Life of Herbert Henry Asquith*, London, 1932, vol. 1; R. B. Haldane, *An Autobiography*, London, 1929; D. Sommer, *Haldane of Cloan*, London, 1960.

[3] See A. M. McBriar, *Fabian Socialism and English Politics 1884–1918*, Cambridge, 1962, pp. 119–20.

united against the moderates. After complicated struggle, Ramsay MacDonald and a few other 'pro-Boers' resigned from the Society; the majority, while not approving of the war, decided at least not to oppose winning it. The Society published a pamphlet, written by Shaw but endlessly revised by others, identifying itself with imperialism. Its leaders believed in the empire, in the sense of a community of self-governing nations, and of 'backward' peoples being helped towards self-government, though they hated 'jingoism', the crude bellicose chauvinism and xenophobia that filled the hearts of millions of British people, and some of their leaders, with elation and hatred. There was, however, among their unexamined assumptions (as in those of Samuel and other 'Liberal Imperialists') an acceptance of the superiority of British, or European, civilization, that could come close to brutal racialism. They rejected the internationalist attitude of most socialists and—as in the pamphlet, *Fabianism and the Empire*—effortlessly accepted the destiny of 'efficient' peoples to dominate the world.[1]

In the Fabian quest for 'social efficiency' Reeves was to be closely involved, though he was a good deal less interested in it than Shaw or the Webbs. Immediately he exactly shared their views. Though he was an 'imperialist', he was also a thoughtful colonial who could not ignore the bullying aspects of British policy in South Africa. He detested the hysterical enthusiasm of the public for the war. And this, his New Zealand friends advised, was the all but universal feeling in New Zealand. 'You can have no idea of the strength of the war spirit here', Waldegrave wrote—'So if you want to stand well with New Zealanders, or have any idea of trying your fortunes here, you must first of all be a Jingo & as we say now an Imperialist.'[2] And the others agreed. Reeves wrote to H. D. Lloyd, who was visiting England, that he did not believe there was an active 'pro-Boer' in New Zealand except a Wellington M.H.R., John Hutcheson, he had never met.[3] (T. E. Taylor, his old tormentor,

---

[1] Of the many discussions of the Fabian attitudes to imperialism the one I found most valuable was McBriar's book (see previous note), but perhaps he underestimates the element of racialism: cf B. Semmel, *Imperialism and Social Reform*, London, 1960. See also, M. Cole, *The Story of Fabian Socialism*, London, 1961 and E. R. Pease, *The History of the Fabian Society*, London, 1916.

[2] 'Letters from Men of Mark', 10 May 1900.

[3] H. D. Lloyd MSS, 12 April 1901.

was also denouncing the war: he was pursued and stoned by a mob which he bravely faced—and out-faced.)

Reeves was dispirited and divided. By an odd chance his countrymen sensed his mood at a time when they were completely unwilling to tolerate it. That they 'learned' of it by a quite inadmissable inference was almost beside the point.

McKenzie and Seddon detested the Press Association, which monopolized the sale of overseas news. When some small newspapers complained that they could not afford the Association's charges, the Ministers saw a chance of 'tilting' at the Association (Mark Cohen wrote).[1] They asked Reeves to telegraph the war news to the Government. Seddon released his cables to the Press —and the Agent-General suddenly found himself even more unpopular than the Minister of Labour had been. He did not present every defeat (and they were plentiful in 1899 and 1900) as a victory. Since his cables contrasted so markedly with the Press Association reports, which came from South Africa via London and Australia, sub-edited, embellished and amplified on route, he appeared to minimize the number of Boer soldiers and casualties and to ignore the ineffable heroism of 'our boys'. A telegram anticipating Cronje's surrender, 'as our men are five to one', was taken as an insult—the figures, presumably, should have been reversed. 'Warren abandoned Spion Kop during the night' was 'gloating' over British defeats. 'Buller making slow progress towards Ladysmith' was evidently wishful thinking—or else it implied cowardice. Reeves was denounced in the Press by editors and innumerable pseudonymous correspondents, and in the House, for 'lack of loyal accent', 'bias towards the enemy'. He was, it was reported, burned in effigy. The chairman of the Dunedin Stock Exchange denounced him for damaging the market. One of his ex-colleagues told Waldegrave that Reeves was 'funking it'. At home he was generally regarded as 'pro-Boer', while, at the same time, in London, the editors of the *Speaker*, a radical, 'pro-Boer' paper, were holding up an article he had written at their request 'on the ground of its ultra-Imperialist and warlike tone'.[2]

---

[1] 'Letters from Men of Mark', 6 May 1900.

[2] On this episode see AJHR, 1900, H-27, Reeves to Seddon, 20 April 1900; Seddon MSS, Reeves to Seddon, 7 May, 31 May 1900; Seddon to Reeves, 7 July 1900. The *Auckland Star*, 6 March, 8, 18 June, 1900 and the *N.Z. Herald*, 3, 5, 6 March 1900 provide specimens of attacks on Reeves.

Reeves's cables were simply cautious summaries of un-palatable news. Having no private sources of information, he had to be cautious—for instance he ignored Lord Rothschild's assurance, in conversation in May 1900, that the Boers would collapse in six weeks—and he had to be 'laconic and dry' to fit his messages into the government telegraphic code and save money. But the public thought him, at best, pessimistic, at worst 'pro-Boer'. When he cabled out evidence that his reports had been accurate, he was denounced for wasting public money 'for the purpose of proving his lugubrious vaticinations to be not absolutely contrary to fact'.

Seddon defended him. Privately he explained to Reeves that the 'press was at the bottom of the whole thing. The fact is we gave the news to some of the papers that were not on the list of the Press Association, and the morning papers had an advantage.' Eventually some newspapers did what they could to rescue his reputation. A letter he wrote to a friend was published:

I was an Imperialist before Imperialism was as fashionable as it is now, and have been for some years a member of the Executive Committee of the British Empire League, to which body most of the leading Imperialists in the Empire belong. I do not like wars of any kind, and believe that peace is, on the whole, the greatest of public blessings. When, however, my country is involved in a war, I sincerely hope and desire that she may triumph; and that is my heartfelt wish in the case of the South African war.

No doubt most New Zealanders soon forgot about it. In July Seddon assured him that 'you never hear a word about it now.' But those who disliked Reeves had one more reason for dislike. Massey and some other Opposition members never missed an opportunity of belittling him: one may wonder whether their malice was not, thereafter, partly inspired by memories of Reeves's cables. It is very noticeable that there was much less news about him in the New Zealand newspapers after 1900: one may also suspect that this was not only because, after his achieve-ments of the late nineties, he was becoming less newsworthy.

Reeves was, as usual, very hurt by the criticism. Once again he found himself out of touch with most of his countrymen whose warlike ardour made not merely doubt, but truth, a treason. Maud was one of a committee of New Zealand ladies who arranged for a stall at a bazaar to collect money for the Patriotic Fund and 'parcels of comforts for the contingents'. She, too, was 'rather worried by the silly and cowardly attacks', he wrote to Seddon, and 'very anxious to show that we have every sympathy with our troops'. It was, he thought, 'outrageous', 'shameful' that his 'honest effort' to keep Seddon 'posted up' should lead to such 'libelling and slandering' on a public servant who could not answer back.[1] Afterwards he made light of the incident. 'Isn't it comic?' he asked a journalist interviewing him in London. 'But it was an odd experience while it lasted, I can assure you!'[2]

It was, indeed, a depressing reminder of home. A New Zealand friend and admirer, Silas Spragg, wrote in reply to a letter that Reeves seemed to fear the militarism of his countrymen.[3] At about the same time there arrived another memento of antipodean pettiness. In 1897, after Alfred Saunders had published the first volume of his *History of New Zealand*, an unusual work in which phrenological insight reinforces prejudice, Reeves had written, 'I do sincerely trust that old Saunders will not live to continue his history down to the last decade.' The thought, he wrote, added 'a new terror to public life'. Two years later Volume II appeared. It recalled the 'luxurious indulgence' of Reeves's home; it complained of his 'unearned promotion' (over Samuel Saunders) to the editorship of the *Lyttelton Times* and to the Ballance cabinet. Saunders said that Reeves was 'neither physically, mentally, nor morally strong', and that 'no phrenologist would ever have chosen him for any post requiring the exercise of an honest and active sympathy in the welfare of the masses.'[4]

The thought of return had come to seem less attractive. When Henry Demarest Lloyd suggested, in about 1900, that he *should* go back, he wrote:

Sometimes I think I ought to go. Seddon is borrowing and spending a great deal too much money. I don't trust his finance and Ward

---

1 Seddon MSS, 7 May 1900.

2 Reeves MSS, medium clipping book, p. 55, *Admiralty and Horse Guards Gazette*, 13 Oct. [1900].

3 'Letters from Men of Mark', 12 Feb. 1903.

4 Hall MSS, Reeves to Hall, 1 Feb. 1897; A. Saunders, *History of New Zealand*, vol. ii, London, [1899], pp. 524-5.

seems worse than ever in the way of extravagance. But then in most other ways Seddon is doing very well and if I did go back I hardly see what I could do to put things right. I should have to work for my living and that would hamper me a great deal. I could not leave my old party (if I did reenter the House) and to support Seddon and at the same time restrain him would be the very deuce. It wrenches my conscience, though, to look on and see the fate of our policy and country in hands so ignorant and reckless.[1]

It was a letter at once realistic (for what *could* he do?) and yet weak (he did not mean to try).

By 1900, then, it seemed useless, for the time being, to go home. We know that he was right: New Zealand had six years of Seddonism ahead. As the 'khaki election' in England came nearer, he wrote to Seddon in July 1900, consoling himself for not standing for the House of Commons, that the Liberals, who could have carried the country in 1898, would be badly beaten (a vote for the Liberals was a vote for the Boers, government candidates proclaimed):

This is mainly the result of dissensions and the wretched jealousies of their Front Bench men. Ever since Gladstone left things have been getting worse and worse with them and there is now no leadership at all. This is not from want of ability—several of their men are able enough for anything—but from want of cooperation. Imagine things five times worse than they were with us in the days of Grey and poor old Montgomery and you can picture it. We are in for five years more of Toryism.[2]

Standing for the House of Commons and the House of Representatives were alike postponed. Once more, frustrated in politics, Reeves turned to his books. Throughout 1901, while he gave few public addresses and dropped out of the news as a potential Liberal candidate, he worked assiduously on *State Experiments in Australia and New Zealand*, a lengthy, two volume comparative account of the radical legislation of the nineties. It appeared in 1902. In Australia and New Zealand, he later wrote to Downie Stewart (the son of an old political rival), 'it was a complete failure—scarcely any copies were bought', but it was in demand among students of politics in the United

[1] H. D. Lloyd MSS, 7 Dec. [1900].
[2] Seddon MSS, 28 July [1900].

States and Europe, and the edition sold out within a few years.[1] Parts of it were translated into Russian and other languages. Less popular, less readable than his other books, it nevertheless contains some fine passages of prose description, as well as cogent and fair-minded analysis. It remains today an authoritative work which no one has sought to emulate, and seems likely to be his most lasting, as it is his most scholarly contribution to history and political studies.

[1] 30 June 1908. Letter kindly lent by Miss M. Downie Stewart. See also H. D. Lloyd MSS, 12 July 1901, 3 Jan. 1902.

18

IMPERIAL REFORM

1900-7

By going to London, it has become plain, Reeves had escaped from the irritating presence but not from the power of King Dick. He found his position tolerable, but still frustrating. He was simply employed as the Government's general agent. After Seddon visited London in 1897, and felt more confident in dealing with British officialdom, he only rarely gave Reeves the semi-diplomatic tasks that he enjoyed. Occasionally, however, it was necessary to call on him because a personal approach was necessary. In 1900, for instance, when the Colonial Office demurred at the award of a K.C.M.G. to John McKenzie and Ward (never having heard, it appeared, of the former, and having heard too much of the latter), Reeves's successful services in securing their titles were 'very much appreciated', Seddon wrote. The Government had made no recommendations for eight years, and Seddon did not propose, after this episode, to make any more.[1]

Reeves naturally felt that more use could be made of his services in political matters, and he wrote to him about this time:

By the bye I think you make a mistake in communicating so much with the Colonial Office through Lord Ranfurly [the Governor] instead of through me. For the last three years this practice has been growing ... and weakens my standing there very greatly as it will weaken that of my successors if it continues. The Colonial Office naturally like it well enough as if I am left in the dark I cannot ask questions or argue in such matters as Tonga and Samoa or the Trustees Investments Act or over Contingents or Defence proposals or half a dozen other things. It has always been the C.O's policy to give Agent Generals [sic] the go by. Some A.G's like this well enough as their only wish is for any [sic] easy life and no responsibility. My wish on the other hand is to do all I can for N.Z. and its govt. and I

---

[1] Reeves MSS, Seddon to Reeves, 23 May 1901.

think the matter worth your consideration. I have more than once meant to write to you and refrained, not wishing to bother you... .

Seddon promised to send him duplicate copies of his communications, through the Governor, with the Colonial Office, and Reeves replied: 'Something of that sort is just what I have always wanted, as the Colonial Office, though not discourteous, is wooden, and bound with red tape. A business matter might go on for 12 months between you and them and they would not tell me of it except by accident.' [1]

Seddon had a lower opinion than Reeves of the Colonial Office, and was frequently irritated by slighting treatment and dictatorial ways. (His feelings were more than fully reciprocated within the Colonial Office, where the notion that colonial premiers were of any importance was novel and faintly disturbing. 'Colonial statesmen', one official wrote of King Dick, who had written a 'pettish' memorandum in 1896, 'are very like children, and have to be treated accordingly.' When he came to the 1902 Conference, an official lamented that it seemed impossible to 'avoid giving him a *private* carriage & servants from the start': he seemed, as in 1897, 'determined to get a good start of all the others'.[2]) But Seddon had no intention of letting Reeves, or anyone else, share the honour or glory of the imperial campaign on which he embarked after 1897.

When Seddon became Premier, Grey had passed on to him his rich imperial mantle: 'Your position is a capital training for higher things—all the great questions between England and her colonies, and the United States are coming on the greatest the world has ever known—and men will be wanted fitted to arrange these—' [3]

Seddon needed little urging. As his ascendancy became assured, roads and bridges grew boring. He turned to 'humanism' and imperialism. 'Humanism' meant increasing attention to social legislation, especially old age pensions and, later, free secondary school places. It also involved him in revising Reeves's

---

[1] Seddon MSS, 28 July, 22 Dec. 1900.
[2] The first quotation, from a minute of 3 April 1896, is in the P.R.O., CO 209/256; reproduced in D. K. Fieldhouse (ed.) 'British Colonial Policy in relation to New Zealand', vol. i, p. 304 (mimeographed documents, University of Canterbury, 1956); the second is from a minute of 5 May 1902, in CO 209/264.
[3] Grey MSS, telegram 15 Sept. 1893.

labour bills, sometimes for the better, and in tempestuous struggles in committee and the House comparable with those of 1893–5: it was only after Reeves left that Seddon became the big-hearted, benevolent despot who is remembered. But even 'humanism' was not enough. He became one of the most loud-mouthed imperialists in the Empire. He won his own 'khaki election' and slaughtered the Conservatives. He took up Grey's—and Vogel's and Stout's—campaign to induce the British Government to annex most of the independent islands in the Pacific, and to hand as many as possible over to New Zealand.

In Seddon's attempt to build a New Zealand empire, Reeves was allowed only a minor rôle. He reported hints dropped in the Colonial Office: 'If the Fijian chiefs can be got to declare for some sort of union with New Zealand, I think that would go a long way to help. I have had a private & confidential talk about it with one of the permanent officials at the C.O., & that was the impression left on my mind.' Five years later, in 1905, he was able to send a letter from Alfred Lyttelton, the Secretary of State, indicating an intention of handing Tonga to New Zealand 'as some sort of compensation' for the loss of Samoa.[1] But the second trumpet in Seddon's imperial brass band was rarely audible above the first.

One of the few occasions when Reeves was allowed a larger rôle was when the Australian colonies federated in 1900, and then only because a conference was called by Chamberlain. The New Zealand Government wanted the Commonwealth Con-stitution Act, which was to be passed by the imperial Parliament, amended so as to give New Zealand the right, for say seven years, to join on the same terms as the original federal states. The Government was uncertain of the strength of public feeling in favour of joining—there was, for instance, an Australasian Federation League in Auckland—and wanted time to test opinion. Two other amendments to the constitution, with regard to defence and the right of appeal to the Privy Council, were also asked. Barton, the New South Wales delegate, and some other Australians, deeply resented New Zealand's attitude, perhaps because it partly supported the British Government's wish to amend the clause relating to courts of appeal and because the

---

[1] Seddon MSS, 20 Oct., 22 Dec. 1900; 29 July 1905.

protest had been made to the British, not to the Australians
themselves.

After the conference, where he spoke in favour of New
Zealand's suggestions, Reeves wrote to Seddon:

Neither Western Australia nor New Zealand has succeeded in
getting their amendments.... I am sorry that we have not got the
'open door' but in face of the opposition of the Australian Premiers
I did not expect to succeed. What people say here is 'We think
Australia might reasonably give this concession to New Zealand and
we are surprised she does not; but we cannot force the members of
a partnership against their will to accept a fresh partner'. That in
theory is an argument very difficult to meet, and though I have
honestly done my best to meet it, as you will see from the letters to
Chamberlain and the interview in the 'Daily News' and from the
article in the 'Morning Post' sent you by last mail and which I
inspired, I am not surprised it met with failure. The Australians, from
their own point of view, are very short-sighted not to grant the 'open
door' amendment because it would strengthen the hands of the
Federal Party in New Zealand immensely and at once, whereas their
rather overbearing and ungracious refusal should, I think, tend to get
up New Zealand's back.

I think your idea of Great Britain as an arbitrator between
Australia and New Zealand has sound sense in it and may be usefully
cultivated whether we try to enter the Federation or whether we
finally elect to stay out of it. Meantime the more I study the question
of appeals to the Privy Council the more certain I am that New
Zealand's interests demand that the right of appeal should be
preserved. That is equally the case whether we enter the Federation
or whether we stay out. The 74th clause of the Commonwealth Bill is
extremely badly drawn, and in the event of conflicts between New
Zealanders and Australians we may find ourselves deprived of our
right of appeal to England and remitted to an Australian Federal
Court whose prejudices would be all against us....

As regards the delegates and myself, Mr. Barton spoke to me the
other day and suggested that we should shake hands. As he made the
advance I did not like to decline it and I think the result will probably
be that the correspondence which has passed between us will be
withdrawn by mutual consent. Pending that I hope you will not make
it public in any way. With the other delegates I have been on excellent
terms throughout. Kingston has asked me more than once to send his
kindest regards and best wishes to you and he declares that New
Zealand would be welcome at any time into the Australian Federa-

tion. I am not so sure, however, that we should not meet with jealousy
and opposition from both Tasmania and Victoria. I do not say that
they would not let us in as an original State. But, as you know, that
would not be enough. We are certain to require special terms about
such matters as Maori representation and half-a-dozen others. It is
there that the opposition of Tasmania and Victoria would come in.
For my own part, as you well know, I do not think we ought to enter
the Federation though I do think we ought to make a working agreement with Australia on such matters as defence, customs tariff, etc.,
etc. However, whatever the Government's policy may be you may
depend upon my doing my best to carry out my instructions with
absolute loyalty.

Reeves continued to press for the amendment of Clause 74,
but eventually had to write: Chamberlain 'astonished every one
here by giving way to the delegates almost altogether'. Seddon
replied: 'In respect to Federation, Chamberlain has proved a
regular jelly fish and has fallen very much in my estimation, as I
thought he was a kindred spirit endowed with plenty of back
bone. The people in Australia did not care a dump about the
Federal High Court... .'[1]
Seddon not only sought popular 'mandates' for his actions,
but always professed to have them, claiming to know instinctively
what 'the people' wanted, in Fiji, Australia or elsewhere.
On most imperial questions Reeves substantially agreed with
his Government. For instance, when, a few years later, the
British Government agreed to the mine owners' request (already
approved by Milner, the Governor) to import Chinese
indentured labour into the Rand, Seddon and Reeves were
equally horrified. Seddon thought it 'a reflection on what our
sons have done during the war', and went on, writing to Reeves,
'To have as the first results hordes of Asiatics instead of Britishers
introduced into the new territories was almost heart-breaking.'
Reeves tipped him off when the best time occurred for an
official protest.[2] But this was an issue on which Reeves, the
English Liberal or Fabian, agreed with Reeves, the New Zealand
Agent-General. His friends in London felt as strongly as he.

[1] Seddon MSS, Reeves, 5 May, 31 May 1900; Seddon, 7 July 1900; AJHR, 1900,
A-5, Reeves to Under-Secretary for Colonies, 19 June 1900; J. Quick and R. R.
Garran, Annotated Constitution of the Australian Commonwealth, London, 1901, pp. 228 ff.;
R. M. Burdon, King Dick, Christchurch, 1955, pp. 220 ff.
[2] 'Letters from Men of Mark', Seddon to Reeves, 3 Feb. 1904.

Herbert Samuel, whose emotions were tinged with racialism as much as moral fervour against 'slave labour', helped to lead the Liberals in a crusade which took them into power at the next election.[1] And Shaw wrote in February 1904:

My dear Reeves

I hear, to my extreme disgust, that Chinese slavery has spread to the Passmore Edwards Settlement. Mrs. Humphry Ward, the patroness of the institution, has sent to say that if they dare to identify themselves with hostility to the Chinese, subscriptions will fall off. As far as I can make out, the mere whisper of your name has spread terror; and now, if you please, the meeting is to be kept as quiet as possible; Tozer (the usual resident chairman) is to take the chair; and a supporter of the Government is to be invited to flatten out Geary, who is not as yet a very glib speaker. Under these circumstances I should not dream of asking anybody to come to the debate; but if you feel that it would amuse you to protect Geary, you can go down and attend the debate with a sense of total relief from all consideration for the Settlement, and smash the emissary of the Rand into infinitesimal smithereens, drawing the obvious moral—support Shaw & Geary.

I feel furious for having lured you into such a business; but though the sons of Zeruiah have been too many for us as regards any sort of publicity, the satisfaction of annihilating them in camera may be better than nothing.

D——n their impudence!

P.S. They get rather a good working class audience—quite susceptible to insurgent oratory.[2]

But there was a major issue on which the English Liberals and Fabians disagreed with the New Zealand Liberals, and which made Reeves's position somewhat uncomfortable. In London, the ardent New Zealand protectionist soon came to accept the Liberal free trade dogma. The change was not intellectually inconsistent, for he had argued that tariff protection was needed by infant colonial industries; an industrial power was in a different situation. But it made difficulties for him, because the self-governing colonies wanted imperial preference, which would require Britain to introduce tariffs against foreign imports.

[1] John Bowle, *Viscount Samuel*, pp. 54–57.
[2] Reeves MSS, small clipping book, p. 187. Mrs. Ward, the Secretary of the Settlement, was, of course, the novelist; 'Tozer' was probably the Agent-General for Queensland, Sir Horace Tozer; 'Geary' was Sir William N. M. Geary, who stood with Shaw as a Progressive candidate for the London County Council in 1904.

Seddon was a vociferous advocate of imperial preference, and
not backward in suggesting that Britain should change her
policy—else the 'inevitable dismemberment' of the Empire
would follow. He denounced the freetraders as 'the sloths and
urchins of our public and political life'. At the Colonial Conference of 1902 he offered a tariff preference on British goods
imported into New Zealand, to encourage Britain to reciprocal
generosity. At a dinner given in his honour by New Zealanders
in London, at which Reeves presided, Seddon argued that
Britain had an unfavourable balance of foreign trade of
£161,000,000 (he had not heard of 'invisible exports') and 'had
to send out that many golden sovereigns to foreign countries to
meet the difference'.[1] Like many other New Zealanders, Reeves
found this sort of thing embarrassing and, as New Zealand's
representative, regarded with very mixed feelings the cartoons
and jokes about the Prime Minister which he placed in his
clipping books—in one satirical piece in *Punch* Seddon was
caricatured as saying that 'so long as there was mutton in New
Zealand he would never cease in his efforts on behalf of the
federation of the British Empire.' As a free trader, he found
Seddon's oratorical antics doubly distasteful.

When, in 1903, Chamberlain was converted to the colonial
programme of imperial preference, Reeves's position was even
more awkward. As Agent-General he might have been expected
discreetly to back Chamberlain, who resigned from the Government to press for 'tariff reform'. As a radical (and an erstwhile
follower of 'King Harry') he might have been moved by
Chamberlain's argument that tariffs would create employment
—though the English Liberals' defence of the 'free breakfast
table' equally had its precedent in the New Zealand Opposition
policy of 1888, had its potential appeal to his sentiment. But, in
the event, with most of the Fabians and the 'Liberal Imperialists',[2] he stuck to free trade. Since Seddon was now ardently
supporting Chamberlain, however, he had to do so quietly.

Distaste for Seddon's tactics, disagreement with some of his
views, but above all, frustration at his supine rôle as Agent-
General, encouraged Reeves to embark on an imperial pro-

---

[1] *The Times*, 18 June 1902.
[2] B. Semmel, *Imperialism and Social Reform*, London, 1960, p. 129.

gramme of his own. Years before, in 1889, he had been a member of the Canterbury branch of the Imperial Federation League which was started by G. R. Parkin, a visiting Canadian evangelist of the League. Parkin found the New Zealanders (Reeves conceded) 'torpid' about federation—so apathetic that his efforts fell flat everywhere but in Christchurch. Even there the committee met only two or three times.[1] The parent League itself collapsed in 1893, when it tried to draw up a programme satisfying at once its British free trade members and its colonial devotees of imperial preference. It left behind a few splinter groups and a series of incompatible programmes for imperial unity.

In 1897 and again in 1902, at the Colonial Conferences, Chamberlain advocated creating a 'Council of the Empire' to assist Britain, 'a weary titan', to bear 'the too heavy orb of its fate'. It would be a step towards federation. In 1897 Seddon supported him, but by 1902 even he was apathetic. No one thought federation practicable in the foreseeable future. Yet there were, as some men who believed in the Empire appreciated, a series of real problems which federation might solve. As the 'self-governing' colonies moved nearer to full autonomy, federation appeared the only alternative to dissolution, to which few Britons happily looked forward. The Boer War and the campaign for tariff reform added urgency to the problems which preoccupied 'imperialists'; and, as we have seen, challenged them to show that they were above mere 'jingoism'—which, L. T. Hobhouse said, was a kind of moral slang.[2]

Once again Reeves found himself playing an important rôle in what he felt to be important affairs, this time not of political deeds, but of thought and publicity, in one of the most pertinacious attempts ever made to reform the imperial constitution.[3] It was a position for which he was well qualified—none of his associates knew nearly as much as he did about the self-governing parts of the Empire.

At first his pronouncements differed little from those habitually issuing, at that time, from stuffed shirts after public

---

[1] *Canterbury Times*, 30 May, 29 Aug., 14 Nov. 1889; *Imperial Federation* (the journal of the League), June, July 1889. Reeves's rôle in the 'imperial council' movement is examined in detail in K. Sinclair, *Imperial Federation*, London, 1955.

[2] A. P. Thornton, *The Imperial Idea and its Enemies*, London, 1959, p. 72.

[3] See R. Jebb, *The Imperial Conference*, London, 1911, vol. ii and K. Sinclair, loc. cit.

dinners. At the inaugural dinner of the Liberal Colonial Club, a group of imperialist free traders, at the Trocadero Restaurant, he could be heard uttering patriotic platitudes, mere imperialistic noises; or at the Imperial Liberal Council (an anti-'Little England' group), in 1900: 'The British Empire was not a thing to be apologized for, but a thing to be proud of from their very hearts ... the British Empire [was] one of the most remorseless facts on the surface of the globe.'[1] At a discussion of imperial federation at a dinner of the London Chamber of Commerce late in 1900 he suggested that 'a small, well-informed Imperial Council, sitting, perhaps, in an advisory capacity, with the Colonial Secretary as President, would do much good, practical work', and that colonial peers should be created to 'assume the function and position of an Imperial Senate'.[2] Such suggestions for administrative reform begged all the questions. What, precisely, were to be the constitution, the purpose, the duties of these bodies? Federationists had talked vaguely on these lines for many years—but how were closer imperial ties to be reconciled with colonial self-government? In the next few years Reeves sought to find some answers.

Many of Reeves's friends shared his interest in thinking out an intelligent and non-jingoistic imperial policy. Sidney Webb hoped for the creation of a new party of 'national efficiency',[3] perhaps combining 'Liberal Imperialists' and progressive Unionists, in a programme of imperial development and social reform—which would create the conditions necessary for breeding 'an Imperial race'. 'But if some such combination was to come about, it must appeal to the country on a well thought out programme', L. S. Amery wrote:

That, in its turn, implied a body of men, a Brains Trust or General Staff, to evolve it.

---

[1] Reeves MSS, small clipping book, pp. 21, 159–63.

[2] Ibid., p. 162; *Daily News*, 22 Nov. 1900; *British Empire Review*, Dec. 1900.

[3] B. Semmel, *Imperialism and Social Reform*, pp. 72 ff. Webb possibly took the phrase from a speech by Rosebery in 1901 (E. Halévy, *A History of the English People, Epilogue* (1895–1905), Book 1, p. 163, Penguin Books, 1939. The 'co-efficients' are discussed by Semmel and in Bertrand Russell, *Portraits from Memory*, London, 1956, pp. 76–77; W. A. S. Hewins, *The Apologia of an Imperialist*, London, 1929, i, p. 65; L. S. Amery, *My Political Life*, London, 1953, i, pp. 223–5; H. G. Wells, *Experiment in Autobiography*, London, 1934, ii, pp. 760 ff. Wells uses the term 'social efficiency' in his novel, *The New Machiavelli*.

Such was the great thought with which the Webbs, one evening early in November 1902, plied a carefully selected company of friends at their house, 41 Grosvenor Road. The actual form the Brains Trust was to take was a small dining club, to meet at regular intervals for serious discussion and for the subsequent formation of policy. It was to be called the Coefficients, both to emphasize efficiency as the keynote of the new political grouping, and because policy was to emerge from the contributions of a body of whom each member was supposed to be an expert in his own domain. We were not to be more than a dozen to start with—all contributors, no passengers.

Their discussions made a tremendous impression on the 'Co-efficients'. Amery and W. A. S. Hewins both talked of the group in their memoirs. So did Wells in his *Experiment in Autobiography* and, in the guise of the 'Pentagram Circle', in his novel *The New Machiavelli*. The group appears, too, in Bertrand Russell's *Portraits from Memory*. Wells wrote that their discussions brought him closer than he had yet come 'to many processes in contemporary English politics' and gave him 'juster ideas of the mental atmosphere in which such affairs are managed': 'In certain respects our club represented something that seems now [in 1934], I think, to have faded out from contemporary English life. It had the gestures if not the spirit of free interrogation. It had an air of asking "What are we doing with the world? What are we going to do?"'

The Webbs asked Wells to join 'nominally for literature' but in reality, Amery guessed, 'for original thinking on all subjects'. Russell 'represented' science; Hewins, Director of the London School of Economics, the Webbs' pet project, was there as an economist; Reeves to present 'the colonial point of view'; Amery, the *Times* Boer War correspondent, was interested in army reform. Haldane and Sir Edward Grey represented law and foreign policy, while 'active Liberal Imperialism' was also represented by H. J. Mackinder, the geographer, who was then thought a coming man among the Liberals, but soon joined Chamberlain and 'tariff reform'. The dozen original 'Co-efficients' also included a naval officer, a journalist and a financier. They were later joined by Lord Milner, Henry Newbolt, the poet of 'Drake's Drum' and soon one of Reeves's friends, and others variously distinguished.

They made, Amery wrote, 'an excellent start, from the gastronomic point of view, by dining with Haldane' (later meetings were in the Ship Tavern in Whitehall and then in St. Ermin's Hotel), but the Webbs' hopes of the growth of a new party vanished after the brandy. They 'started straight away with the problem of closer political relations within the Empire' and found themselves sharply divided over 'tariff reform'—more markedly so when Chamberlain came out for preferences a few months later. Milner claimed to have converted Mackinder to tariffs, but most of the group had firm views. Wells found the younger imperialists unable 'to distinguish between national energy and patriotic narrowness'—and Russell left in disgust with the militaristic views of some of the club. Like Reeves, Wells thought the idea of tight economic imperial bonds was a chimera: the Empire had no natural economic unity. He said the Empire was not 'a clenched fist in the centre of Europe', like Germany, but 'an open hand all over the world'—an image unintentionally ambiguous.

I was still clinging to the dear belief that the English-speaking community might play the part of leader and mediator towards a world commonweal. It was to be a free-trading, free-speaking, liberating flux for mankind. Russell, Pember Reeves and Webb and possibly Haldane and Grey had, I think, a less clearly expressed disposition in the same direction. But the shadow of Joseph Chamberlain lay dark across our dinner-table.

'Anyhow the Coefficients, as a brains trust with a definite political object, petered out almost as soon as they began', Amery wrote, 'but as a dining club for the informal discussion of serious topics they flourished for five or six years.'

In 1903 Reeves and Haldane separately published schemes for imperial reform that clearly arose, at least in part, from these discussions, which encouraged the participants to clarify, if not modify, their individual views. In March Reeves wrote an anonymous article ('By a Colonial Ex-Cabinet Minister') on 'Federation—The Next Step', in the *British Empire Review*. His main point arose from his observation that little had been done, after the three Colonial Conferences, to follow up their recommendations, to investigate problems raised, or to prepare for the next conference. Double taxation, immigration laws, postal and shipping affairs, university education and many other subjects required co-operative discussion and action. He suggested the creation of an Advisory Council, to undertake such 'devilling' and act as a bridge between conferences. To allay colonial jealousy of anything which might encroach on self-government, the Council would be a mere secretariat, a subsidiary of the Colonial Conference, dealing only with matters referred to it by the Conference of premiers. The Under Secretary of State would act as chairman; a dozen or twenty members would be enough.[1]

This was a useful suggestion, which had the merit of arising from experience; a practical suggestion of one way in which imperial relations might be smoothed. Haldane had also been thinking as a working politician. In a talk to the Royal Colonial Institute in July he advised imperialists that they should drop all idea of a written constitution: what was needed was executive reform—'gradual and cautious changes in the modes in which the Sovereign takes advice'. He suggested the creation of a committee of the Privy Council, including members appointed at the request of the colonial Governments, as well as the Prime Minister and the Colonial and Foreign Secretaries, to advise the Crown on imperial affairs.

Later in the year both Reeves and Haldane became members of an esoteric committee of about fifty members, set up by a famous jurist, Sir Frederick Pollock. It arose among some imperialists who hoped to resume the work of the old Imperial Federation League. Many of the members of the committee were civil servants and the only names published were those of Pollock, Dr. G. R. Parkin, the Canadian federationist, Reeves and Haldane. They were mainly, it seems, free traders and Liberals. Their aim was to draw up a plan for an imperial council which might be a step towards federation. Here, as among the 'Co-efficients', Reeves continued to discuss imperial organization. About the end of the year, he wrote a signed article replying to Haldane,[2] whose 'Committee of Advice on Imperial

---

[1] *British Empire Review*, March 1903. The discovery of this article modifies my discussion of these suggestions in *Imperial Federation*, pp. 33 ff., and especially p. 35, n. 2. Haldane's article appeared in the *Review* in July 1903 as well as in the *Journal of the Society of Comparative Legislation*, 1903, v, part 1, pp. 66 ff.

[2] See K. Sinclair, *Imperial Federation*, pp. 34 ff., on these events.

Affairs' seemed to him too like the old idea of an imperial council —'a fussily meddlesome body composed of idle colonial absentees and distant Agents-General, leavened with an element of English bureaucracy'. It would be greatly distrusted in the colonies. Reeves now proposed that the Colonial Conference of the Secretary of State and the colonial Premiers should be turned into an Imperial Council, preferably as a committee of the Privy Council, but possibly quite independent. It would meet, perhaps, every two years. In addition a secretariat should be set up.

The report of the 'Pollock Committee', as presented by its chairman to the Royal Colonial Institute and reported to readers of *The Times*, substantially accepted Reeves's views, with the important addition that the Prime Minister should chair the proposed Imperial Committee of the Privy Council. But by now Reeves had been stimulated to further thought. Pollock reported that Reeves opposed the idea (which, immediately, came from Haldane) that the new imperial body should be a committee of the Privy Council, since such machinery was likely to be 'misunderstood and disliked': the colonists would allow no British constitutional paraphernalia to stand, or appear to stand, between themselves and autonomy.

There is no need to pursue the details of Reeves's scheme, as he finally elaborated it in articles and in a pamphlet. Essentially it involved turning the Colonial Conference into an Imperial Council, assisted by a secretariat. Together, these bodies would, he thought, give colonial governments a more direct method of expressing their views than in the existing 'irregular, unauthorised, and sometimes mis-informed way'. The Council would take 'the present loose, friendly Imperial union, and make the best of it in a practical and businesslike way'. He did not think these reforms would constitute an approach to federation. His detailed proposals arose from his (and his Government's) dissatisfaction with the existing administration of imperial relations and sought to provide immediate practical reforms, rather than from a preoccupation with the federal ideal. In particular, he hoped to take relations with the self-governing colonies away from the Colonial Office.

Because of his awareness of the colonists' attitudes—the growth of nationalism, jealousy of their rights of self-government

—he was moving from his youthful belief in federation towards a conception nearer to the modern Commonwealth, the British Commonwealth, as it became in his lifetime. He understood the significance of two of the elements that were to be important in the evolution of the Commonwealth: of co-operation over numerous legal, technical, educational and administrative problems; and of the system of Conferences, though he wished to introduce the term 'Council', with its federationist connotations. But he could not go all the way to join those Australian and Canadian and South African politicians who were already reaching towards the idea of 'dominion status' and separate foreign policies. He wanted the colonies to share in the discussion of British foreign policy before decisions were reached. In 1905 he argued that the colonial governments should not appoint Ministers of External Affairs—that the less they concerned themselves directly with foreign policy, the less they transacted business with foreign states, the better. The colonial premiers meeting in London at Conference or Council, were the best instruments for managing their countries' external affairs.[1] In this respect he spoke for his countrymen.

Reeves's scheme was, in 1905, adopted by the British Empire League, which urged it upon British and colonial governments and opposition parties. More important, after the resignation of Chamberlain, Reeves had the ear of the new Secretary of State, Alfred Lyttelton. In 1905 Lyttelton wrote to the self-governing colonies suggesting that the 'Colonial Conference' should be renamed the 'Imperial Council', and that it should have its own secretariat. The arguments he advanced, like his suggestions, closely followed Reeves's rather than those of the 'Pollock Committee', and at the annual New Zealand dinner in 1905, he freely confessed his indebtedness.[2]

Lyttelton's proposals were accepted by all the colonial governments except those of Canada and Newfoundland, but little came of them. When the 1907 Imperial Conference met the Conservative Government had lost office; Lyttelton had been replaced by Elgin, who was unsympathetic to the suggestions. Though the Australian premier, Alfred Deakin, and J. G. Ward, supported Lyttelton's suggestions, they were defeated. The

---

[1] British Empire Review, Feb. 1905, 'An Imperial Council'.
[2] British Australasian, 29 June 1905 (Reeves MSS, small clipping book, p. 108).

Canadians disliked the term 'Council', which sounded more formal than 'Conference', and feared that an imperial secretariat might become too powerful. The Colonial was renamed the Imperial Conference, over which the Prime Minister was to preside, and a sub-division of the Colonial Office was created to prepare for future Conferences—'an almost nominal change', Reeves wrote in *The Times*, 'redeemed from derision' by the attractive personality of Sir Charles Lucas, supervisor of the new Dominions Division.[1] Reeves had been fighting on the side of the losers, whom historians often ignore. In retrospect, it might seem that the reforms he wanted might have proved nominal themselves; but it would be a mistake to suppose that there was no chance that they would be adopted. In 1905 and 1906 he had some reason for optimism.

[1] 24 May 1909.

19

RESIGNATION
1906–8

In 1904, without consulting or informing Reeves, the Government passed legislation for the appointment of a High Commissioner to replace the Agent-General. The intention, Seddon explained to the House, was to follow the lead of Canada and Australia in raising the status of the country's London representative to a level appropriate to the new relations of the self-governing colonies with Britain. But there was a flood of speculation, for the position carried a salary of £2,000 and a £250 travel grant (when the Prime Minister received only £1,600) and was a three-year appointment (indeed, the bill at first provided for a five-year term). It was widely believed that Seddon had created the position for himself, particularly because he refused to tell the House whether he wanted it or not. Both Seddon and Reeves were severely criticized by Opposition members, notably Massey and Reeves's old enemy Duthie.

Reeves was mystified until letters from his allies in Wellington arrived. There had been a 'cabal' in the party, led by Ward and some aspirants to cabinet rank, to dispose of Seddon as he had of Reeves—a prospect which the latter must have regarded with mixed feelings. As his health deteriorated, many Liberals were tired of Seddon's growing indecision; of his continual search for a popular 'mandate' (the New Zealand talisman for political inaction). Ward told Mark Cohen's brother that Seddon would go 'in the fulness of time'; but, after a furious row, Seddon informed caucus that he refused to be 'shunted' off to London.

From these events, Reeves's correspondent, Atack, inferred that Seddon had encouraged his colleagues to hope, half believe, that he would go. Once they tried to make him do it, however, they learned that he had been bluffing.[1] The result was that, in

---

[1] 'Letters from Men of Mark', Atack to Reeves, 6 Dec. 1904, 17 June 1905. See also Cohen to Reeves, 16 July 1904, 16 June 1905; Tregear to Reeves, 23 Jan. 1905; Waldegrave to Reeves, 10 Aug., 31 Oct. 1904; PD, 1904, 131, pp. 825 ff.

1905, Reeves became New Zealand's first High Commissioner and received a three-year appointment—rewards deserved but not intended.

Reeves continued to treasure his hopes of a return to active politics in New Zealand. In 1905 he wrote to Cohen that if he came out he would stand as a 'temperance' candidate. Cohen assured him that he could have his old seat for the asking in the coming election, since T. E. Taylor meant to retire.[1] In the same year, at a meeting of the Political Labour League, an embryo Labour Party set up by the Trades and Labour Councils, the president, John Rigg, and other members had expressed their wish for his return, because it was under his leadership that Labour had made all its gains.[2]

In June 1906 Seddon died of heart failure. Now Reeves had to make a decision which might prove final. Ward was in Rome at a conference, and the political situation must have seemed as fluid as it was likely to be. All his old friends wrote offering their advice. But none of it was encouraging. Cohen and Waldegrave thought that only the Labour section of the Liberal Party would welcome him. The latter said there was much speculation about whether Reeves would return, but advised that 'the time for Labour to come out on top is not yet.' Tregear agreed. In a very long letter he at once claimed credit for influencing Seddon to introduce his 'humanist' legislation, and consoled Reeves for having to stay in exile. Ward, he said, was 'looked upon as the legitimate successor of Seddon' and people said, '"Let him have a fair show"—So, for three years he is probably safe.' But, Tregear said, if Ward failed to keep his Party united, 'then the eyes of all will turn (where many are looking already) to a man in London'.[3] Reeves's chances of beating Ward for the premiership were discussed in the Press too, but not highly regarded. The *Auckland Star* observed that a 'new generation', to whom he was little known, had grown up since his departure, and doubted whether he 'would care to leave a comfortable haven, in which he has rested so long, to try his fortune again on the troublous sea of politics.'[4]

[1] 'Letters from Men of Mark', Cohen to Reeves, n.d. [1905].
[2] Reeves MSS, small clipping book, p. 131, 15 June [1905].
[3] 'Letters from Men of Mark', Cohen, 16 June 1906; Waldegrave, 8 July 1906; Tregear, 18 July 1906.
[4] 14 June 1906.

Reeves apparently got as far as discussing arrangements for shipping his baggage;[1] but he did not go. By 13 June Ward was in London,[2] where he presumably met Reeves before sailing for home. In Wellington, Hall-Jones, who had joined the ministry when Reeves left, refused—as many Liberals urged—to form a new government and to oust Ward as Seddon had Stout.[3] By August Ward was Prime Minister and Reeves had gone to a quiet village in Norfolk for the summer.[4] Thus one of the crises of Reeves's life passed, leaving scarcely a trace for historians to find. To Atack, who met him at this time, he expressed some of his thoughts. Ward's succession to Seddon, Atack wrote, 'led to another outburst of pessimism. Almost the last words Reeves said to me when I took leave of him was [sic] a gloomy forecast of what was going to happen with Ward in full command.' In his 'Memoirs' Reeves wrote simply: 'I was almost heartbroken when I had finally to renounce all hope of re-entering political life.'

Ten years of exile, ill-health and disappointment had taken their toll. Atack found him, at the age of forty-nine, 'care-worn, and his appearance gave me rather a shock'. He was a sad-faced, sick-looking man. In 1904 Beatrice Webb, whom the Reeveses continued to visit frequently, noted in her journal that he was 'the same in opinion—but he has grown stale in English politics & is settling down to a certain plaintive dullness of spirit and aim.'[5] The self-pity that could be detected, at times, in his speeches in the nineties was sounding increasingly louder when he spoke of his political career. In 1902 he had written, while discussing his shop laws, 'The public loves to see social reformers laughed at, even when its conscience bids it support reform; it may obey conscience, but it owes a grudge to the men who have awakened it.'[6] In 1905, when chairing the annual New Zealand dinner in London, he referred back to the days when the Press likened him to Cassius, Robespierre, or Iago, and to the lack of encouragement from a democracy to its public servants, and

---

[1] Or so it seems from a letter from the firm of H. S. King & Co., 31 July 1906, in the Reeves MSS.

[2] *Auckland Star*, 13 June.

[3] 'Letters from Men of Mark', Waldegrave to Reeves, 8 July 1906.

[4] *Auckland Star*, 10 Sept. 1906 (report dated 3 Aug.).

[5] 2 May 1904 or shortly afterwards. The exact day is not clear.

[6] *State Experiments*, ii, p. 187.

remarked 'how gratifying and delightful to its servants are a few kind words frankly expressed ... .'[1]

But was he altogether 'the same in opinion'? During his years as 'a socialist on a shelf' (as he put it in 1903),[2] had he not become perceptibly less socialist? The quality, the tone of his opinions, had changed. In New Zealand, in the vanguard of the proletariat, he had seemed and sounded more radical than he did now, among the Fabians. Perhaps it is difficult to take seriously the socialism of an agent-general who talked with Rothschild and appeared on platforms with the arch-imperialist, Lord Brassey. The same doubt legitimately touches the Fabian leaders at that time. Reeves had become a public figure, but of a very different kind from the one New Zealanders had known. In 1905 he estimated that he had spoken at 267 dinners and nearly as many luncheons in nine years. Those four or five hundred speeches served a useful purpose for the Agent-General, but otherwise they involved much waste of his time and effort, and were an ephemeral and trivial achievement. He had not, like many colonials visiting London, been seduced by royalty or aristocracy from his democratic ideals, but one might think that he had been beguiled by another kind of glamour. He had become a 'safe' man, if not 'sound' in his opinions, in the eyes of the City. Even the name by which he had come to be known, W. Pember Reeves, hinted at the metamorphosis.

There is clear evidence of changing attitudes in his endless correspondence with Tregear and others about industrial arbitration. He was becoming more hostile to strikes, at least in the New Zealand context of his Arbitration Act, and more concerned with the rights of employers. As early as 1901 he wrote asking Tregear whether a union could cancel its registration under the Act at will, and thus enjoy an unrestricted right to strike. He did not like the idea that any union could be strong outside the arbitration system; if necessary, he thought unions should be 'coaxed or "commandeered" inside'. And he thought it unfair that a union should be allowed to get outside an Act to which employers were subject. In 1906 he was still writing on the same theme. In his reply to Reeves in 1901 Tregear had already foreseen (with approval) how an Act, originally intended to

---

[1] *British Australasian*, 29 June 1905, Reeves MSS, small clipping book, p. 109.
[2] 'Letters from Men of Mark', Silas Spragg to Reeves, 12 Feb. 1903.

encourage unions, could be used to dragoon them—was, indeed, to be so used by Massey's Reform Government in 1912 and thereafter. If no registered union existed—if a union had cancelled its registration and gone on strike—a small number of persons could form one, register, and secure an award applying to all the workers in the industry. It could be argued that, in his concern to see that strikes were prevented, Reeves was merely trying to defend his system, which might collapse if they occurred. Nevertheless the emphases of his thinking were moving to the right. There is no doubt that he approved of a 1905 amendment which made strikes illegal while an industrial award was in force, of which Tregear wrote with enthusiasm and for which he claimed the credit. John Rigg, the unionist leader, had opposed it. When, in 1906, the first strike for a decade occurred in New Zealand, Reeves was sad.[1]

That Reeves was diminished is also plain from his writing. In 1908 he produced another book, published by A. and C. Black. *New Zealand*, which was illustrated by two Auckland painters, Frank and Walter Wright, was a kind of travelogue, or survey of New Zealand scenery and social life. It was chatty, interesting, but naturally lacked the bite or depth of his earlier books.

He rarely wrote verse now. In 1902 an English newspaper had suggested that the London atmosphere had killed his 'gift of versifying'.[2] Two years later he gave it the lie by publishing in the *Monthly Review*, which was edited by his friend, Henry Newbolt, what is often regarded as his finest poem.[3] 'A Colonist in his Garden' explored, as fully as he could, a theme he had touched on before, and in a dramatic form which suited his rhetorical talent.[4] The Englishman writes to the Colonist:

> Write not that you content can be,
> Pent by that drear and shipless sea
>   Round lonely islands rolled,
> Isles nigh as empty as their deep,
> Where men but talk of gold and sheep
>   And think of sheep and gold.

---

[1] See 'Letters from Men of Mark', Tregear's letters, 7 May 1901, 18 July 1906, 19 April 1907; *The Long White Cloud*, 3rd ed., London, 1924, pp. 318–19.

[2] *Echo*, 10 Feb. 1902, Reeves MSS, small clipping book, p. 166.

[3] May 1904.

[4] Cf. Verse 11 of 'A Ball in the Old Provincial Council Chamber' in *Colonial Couplets*.

A land without a past; a race
Set in the rut of commonplace;
    Where Demos overfed
Allows no gulf, respects no height;
And grace and colour, music, light,
    From sturdy scorn are fled.

And, in his mind, the Colonist replies:

Here am I rooted. Firm and fast
We men take root who face the blast,
    When to the desert come,
We stand where none before have stood
And braving tempest, drought and flood,
    Fight Nature for a home....

'No Art?' Who serve an art more great
Than we, rough architects of State
    With the old Earth at strife?
'No colour?' On the silent waste
In pigments not to be effaced,
    We paint the hues of life.

It expressed the wish to return of a man who had worn himself
nearly out in the strife, and lost the courage to face the blast
again. Its biographical poignancy arises from that—that it was
an affirmation of faith by one who, somehow, could not bring
himself to live by it. Thereafter his poetic impulse wavered.

In ten years Reeves had written, in no negligible series of
books, almost all he knew of New Zealand. His passion grew
feebler, though there remained an abiding warmth that is a kind
of love. The politician had found no roots in English politics;
now the writer was becoming rootless too. Meanwhile his hopes
of going home had virtually vanished; his belief in his country
was shaken by Ward's ascension; his work for imperial reform
had come to nothing. It was time to change his life.

In January 1909, 'after eighteen years of public work in or for
my Country', Reeves wrote in his 'Memoirs', 'I quitted her
service, taking with me two old Despatch Boxes, a well-worn
Portfolio and a prefix of Honourable.' His other relics were
'memories of men and movements, laws and books, political

battles, political dreams, all of which had made life worth living
and had been the main things that interested me'. With these his
unfinished autobiography was, he wrote, to be 'chiefly concerned'; as is this biography.

The New Zealand circumstances that immediately led to his
resignation are obscure. When G. H. Scholefield asked him about
the 'final severance', Reeves wrote: 'it would scarcely do for me
to begin talking about my official experiences or views. That
could only be done if (1) The ending had been serene and
pleasant or (2) If I wished to plunge into controversy. As neither
is the case I say nothing.'[1]

In 1907 and 1908 there had been growing criticism in New
Zealand of Reeves's re-appointment, mainly on the grounds that
he had been absent so long that he had lost touch with the
country. But he was re-appointed in 1908, only to resign
shortly afterwards, in July, while offering to continue to act as
High Commissioner until November. Ward praised him for the
money he had saved the country. The *Auckland Star* made some
amends for its past assaults on Reeves, by praising his versatility
and accomplishments. It said that it was absurd to speak of
Reeves as though he were an alien. Nevertheless, the suggestion
that he was 'out of touch' was probably not unfounded, for the
New Zealand Reeves remembered was still depressed. Now the
average standard of living was one of the highest in the world.
In December 1909 the Conservatives fired another shot at
Reeves by defeating the Government on a vote of £400 to pay
him for his services as financial adviser to the Government,
which continued for some fifteen months after he left the agent-
generalship. The money was eventually approved, but it was an
unexpected reverse which the Government had not experienced
for years.[2]

The background to Reeves's resignation is clearer in England,
where he had accepted appointment as Director of the London
School of Economics and Political Science and also as a director
of the National Bank of New Zealand. Nothing much need be
said of the latter appointment, though it astonished some of his
school friends, who fancied that a banker (like a teller) should be

---

[1] G. H, Scholefield MSS, 3 July [1908].

[2] NZPD, 1907, 142, p. 892, 953 ff.; 1908, 143, p. 779, 145, 1112; *Auckland Star*,
11 June, 25 July, 1908; *N.Z. Herald*, 4, 6, 7, 30 Dec. 1909.

'good at figures'. An agent-general's extensive knowledge of the economic life of his colony, and his experience of London trade and finance, made him an obvious choice for the board of a bank. When F. D. Bell was New Zealand Agent-General he was several times pressed to accept directorships of banks;[1] and Perceval moved into the world of finance. Nevertheless, that Reeves was acceptable to a bank shows how far his reputation had moved towards respectability. His parsimony, and his careful attention to detail in raising loans, were traits that had led him in that direction, from labour bills to banking.

His appointment to the London School of Economics arose from his interest in education and Fabianism. It was a position holding out great promise to a man of Reeves's views. The L.S.E. was the Webbs' favourite child, an institution unique in Great Britain. It had been established, mainly by Webb, in 1895, to advance the impartial study of economics, politics and what would now be called 'social studies'. Haldane, who worked with Webb in remodelling the University of London in the late nineties, also lent a hand, because of his desire to increase the number of universities in the country. The foundation was made possible when a Fabian left some £10,000 in trust for the purposes of the Society. Webb, one of the trustees, managed to interpret the will so as to spend about half the money on the School. At the same time (he was an incomparable committee man and wire-puller), as a member of the London County Council, he managed to have the Technical Education Board set up and to induce it to make annual grants to the L.S.E. from funds derived from a licence fee imposed by temperance reformers on sellers of liquor. Thus, Janet Beveridge wrote, 'the impartial School of Economics was floated, by a combination of whisky money and money for the Fabian Society'.[2]

The School was opened with great enthusiasm but, despite the aid of other benefactors, little money. Its first three directors were all 'Co-efficients': the aim, Beatrice Webb wrote in 1902, was to 'increase national efficiency'. The first, an Oxford don,

---

[1] W. D. Stewart, *Sir Francis H. D. Bell*, Wellington, 1937, p. 15.

[2] *An Epic of Clare Market*, London, 1960, p. 28 and *passim*. See also, Beatrice Webb, *Our Partnership*, ed. B. Drake and M. I. Cole, London, 1948, pp. 84 ff. and S. Caine, *The History of the Foundation of the London School of Economics and Political Science*, London, 1963.

W. A. S. Hewins, left in 1903 to join Joseph Chamberlain's Tariff Reform Committee. The second, H. J. Mackinder, the geographer, was also converted to tariff reform and resigned in 1908 to stand for the House of Commons as a Liberal Unionist. Sidney Webb decided that the next director must be a free trader, lest people think the Fabians and the L.S.E. were 'Fair-traders in disguise'.[1] The Webbs tried to induce Herbert Fisher to take the post and then G. M. Trevelyan, who, Beatrice wrote in her diary, was 'a Fabian ... young and enthusiastic, and ... would put life and magnetism into the work'. Both refused. Then they considered several other academics and 'our old friend W. P. Reeves, who *might* be induced to accept the position, who is a good administrator, with experience, with colonial connexions, the right opinions. Mackinder prefers Reeves to Trevelyan—he fears so young and inexperienced a man.' Reeves accepted, with a salary of £700, in addition to '£200 or so' as director of the bank and £400 as financial adviser to his Government. It was a big drop in salary, for he continued as financial adviser for only fifteen months. But, Beatrice wrote, 'We are quite content and he begins with enthusiasm.'

[1] Janet Beveridge, p. 64. See also, Beatrice Webb's diary, May 1908, and entries for 15 June, 8 July 1903, Passfield MSS.

20

IN THE DAYS OF THE COMET
1906–9

FROM about 1904 to 1918 the family lived in a large house at 43 Cornwall Gardens. The children were brought up by 'nannies'. The two generations did not share each other's lives. When Reeves was out to one of his innumerable dinners, the children were sometimes permitted, as a great treat, to take high tea with their mother. Otherwise, while they were small, they were cleaned up and taken to see her before bed-time. But though, like other men of his class and place, Reeves saw little of his children, and though his nerves could not stand their racket, he was a fond parent. In his diary he noted stories about Fabian: 'Fay, gazing thoughtfully at the water in which he has just washed a pair of dirty hands. "It is curious what a colour the London soap turns water to".' Fay was a clever boy, 'musical' like Beryl, and sturdy. One of Reeves's greatest joys was coaching him at cricket, as he had once coached his younger brothers. Fay went to St Paul's 'Prep' School.[1] Lord Samuel recalled how nervous Fay had been of the other boys, at breakfast before his first day at the school. By the end of the day he was full of the school slang, and reported that 'Those Bewsher's chaps aren't half bad.'

Soon after 1900 Maud's sister, 'Effie' Lascelles, came with her two girls to live with the Reeveses, when her husband was accidentally killed in Christchurch. One friend, who often stayed with them, thought Reeves was always 'rather out of it', in a house full of women.

By the early nineteen-hundreds Maud was leading a busy public life of her own, giving lectures and reading papers on such subjects as the economic position of women, or 'the Disabilities of Mothers as Workers'.[2] She was a member of the

---

[1] The headmaster of the school, Colet Court, was James Bewsher.

[2] e.g., *The Needs of Little Children*, Papers by Mrs. M. McMillan, Mrs. Pember Reeves, etc., Women's Labour League, London, 1912; *A Summary of Eight Papers and discussions upon the Disabilities of Mothers as Workers*, Mrs. Pember Reeves etc., Fabian Women's Group. London, 1910 (private circulation).

National Anti-Sweating League and, as a member of the executive of the Central Society for Women's Suffrage, an active 'suffragist'. In April 1906 she spoke, without notes, to a crowded meeting in Clifford's Inn Hall, on the women's franchise in New Zealand. In December 1907 she was a speaker at a meeting in Paddington which was packed by hostile medical students. After several speakers, including G. P. Gooch, failed to make themselves heard, Maud spoke to them. Her first words—'You wanted to hear a suffragette; I am the nearest approach to one on the platform' (*The Times* reported), 'delighted them amazingly, and they cheered her enthusiastically for several seconds.' But they soon 'wearied of their better behaviour' and began smashing the furniture, until driven off by police.[1]

Maud joined the Fabian Society in 1904. In 1906-8 she was a central figure in the most famous drama in its history when H. G. Wells, who had joined in 1903, tried to take over the leadership. He hoped to turn it from a 'drawingroom society' to a mass movement. At that time, he wrote, the Fabians 'permeate English society with their reputed Socialism about as much as a mouse may be said to permeate a cat'.[2] The executive committee empowered him to set up a special committee to consider his proposals of expansion. One of those he nominated was Mrs. Reeves. They brought out their report, but in the subsequent debates, Wells, a mumbling speaker, was massacred by G. B. Shaw. While the discussion of the special committee's report was in progress, Maud led a further attack on the executive. As leader of many women members, she demanded that the Basis of the Society should be revised to include votes for women, a proposal with which not all the men agreed. Some argued that the franchise was a question of democracy, not of socialism. Shaw was appointed to negotiate with her, and he came off 'distinctly the worse'. He reported that the women would vote in a body for the special committee's report unless their demand was granted. The executive gave in.[3]

In the elections for the executive in 1907 Wells came fourth, following Sidney Webb, E. R. Pease and Shaw. Maud was sixth.

---

[1] *The Times*, 6 Dec. 1907; *Fabian News*, April 1906, April 1907.
[2] M. Cole, *The Story of Fabian Socialism*, London, 1961, p. 120; cf. E. R. Pease, *The History of the Fabian Society*, London, 1916, ch. ix.
[3] M. Cole, pp. 127-8; Pease, pp. 175-7.

But Wells lacked the skill of Shaw and Webb in committee and soon tired of such work. In 1908 he resigned from the Society. Maud was a very active member, from 1907 to 1909, and remained on the executive until 1919.

At this time Wells was intellectually one of the most exciting men in England, bubbling with energy and ideas about the reconstruction of society. Following his stories of 'science fiction', he was producing a series of original works on sociology or politics and beginning on his novels of social life, which were to include some of his finest work. The Reeveses had become very friendly with him and saw him frequently. When Wells sent him his *Food of the Gods* in 1904, Reeves thanked him with a post-card:

> 'The Food of the Gods'
> From Heaven's Grub St! Cry through London Town,
> Good Critics, cry this fare that genius sells,
> The Gods' Ambrosia, washed divinely down
> With nectar from their Wells.[1]

Whereas the Webbs and most of their friends, like the Reeveses, lived very conventional lives and held conventional views on most questions other than political, Wells's radicalism extended from politics to the basic institutions and customs of social life. Nor were his revolutionary theories merely academic. In 1906, in an address to the Fabians, he denounced 'the family'. He held that the state must go further in protecting children from their parents, and wished to substitute 'public for private morality in the education and support of the young'.[2] *In The Days of the Comet*, published in 1906 (like *A Modern Utopia* the year before) was a fictional representation of some of his views on the subject of sexual freedom. His hero, Willie, marries Anna Reeves but continues to love Nettie. After the passing of a comet, humanity rises to a utopia of free love, in which Anna, Nettie and their husbands all live together. By 'free love', he later explained,[3] he meant, not sexual promiscuity, but, indeed, a more moral relationship than could be formed by men and women in the chains of archaic and often repressive law and custom. By this time Beatrice Webb was becoming hostile to Wells, because of

---

[1] Reeves MSS, MSS diary and note-book.

[2] Pease, pp. 175-6; Passfield MSS, Beatrice Webb's journal, 18 Oct. 1906.

[3] *An Experiment in Autobiography*, London, 1934, vol. ii, pp. 467 ff.

his 'underhand manoeuvres and violent bluster' and his 'naïve little lies' during the Fabian row. Now, when he observed to her that it was only possible truly to know another person sexually, she wondered (in the privacy of her journal) 'whether with all the perturbation caused by such intimacies you would have any brain left to think with'. Maud Reeves, however, 'claiming to be "advanced" in her opinions ... did not object' to the novel.[1]

Amber Reeves was drawn into the Fabian circle through her parents. In 1906 she joined the Society. She was at Newnham College, Cambridge, where she had gone somewhat against her father's wishes, and only after Edward Pember offered to pay her fees if Will withdrew his objection. The offer was declined, and Amber went on from her prizes at Kensington High School to higher honours. In 1907 she gained a first in the first part of the Moral Sciences Tripos. Gilbert Murray and other professors wrote congratulating Reeves on his daughter's brilliant success. In 1908 she was top again, and graduated a Bachelor of Arts with first class honours.[2]

It is not difficult to imagine her excitement at knowing so many famous and clever people. Once, at a Fabian gathering, she was dancing with a member of the executive, Dr. Stanton Coit, the leader of the Ethical Movement (to which Ramsay MacDonald and J. A. Hobson were at one time attracted), which sought to find sanctions other than supernatural for leading a moral life. G. B. Shaw, who was watching, said to her afterwards, 'That's not dancing, it's the ethical movement.' She was, one may guess, stimulated and flattered by their attention and conversation, and they by hers.

Their ideas she would not have found wider, or bolder in their questioning of the bases of society, than those of her Cambridge friends, as Edwardian youth, seeking to shrug off Victorian prohibitions and destroy Victorian shibboleths, endlessly discussed new causes, Fabianism, Votes for Women, or Free Love. Some of their feelings were being expressed in the new plays and novels, for instance, in Shaw's *Mésalliance*, by Hypatia, whom Beatrice Webb thought a portrait of Amber.[3] Shaw

---

[1] Passfield MSS, B. Webb journals, entries, 1 March 1906, 18 Oct. 1906, 5 Dec. 1906, 23 July 1909. A distinguished English academic described Mrs. Reeves to the writer as 'would -be advanced', one who would 'take up the latest advanced thing'.

[2] *The Times*, 16 June 1908; letters in Reeves MSS.

[3] Journal, 27 Dec. 1909.

described her thus: 'an opaque white skin, black hair, large dark eyes with dark brows and lashes, curved lips, swift glances and movements that flash out of a waiting stillness, boundless energy and audacity held in leash'. Hypatia says, 'I'm fed up with nice things: with respectability, with propriety!... I dont want to be good; and I dont want to be bad ... I want to be an active verb.' And: 'Men like conventions because men made them.' Or, in *Fanny's First Play*, in 1911, another of Shaw's 'new women', Fanny O'Dowda (a member of the Cambridge Fabian Society), says, 'That's all our respectability is, pretending, pretending, pretending!' On the first night of this play two of the 'respectable' characters, Mr. and Mrs. Knox, were made up to look like the Reeveses.[1]

In September 1908, at a Fabian Summer School on the mountainous coast of North Wales, when hundreds of Fabians, their friends and a dozen students were meeting to discuss, listen and laze, Beatrice Webb noted in her Journal:

The young folk live the most unconventional life.... Stealing out on moor or sand, in stable or under hayricks, without always the requisite chaperonne to make it look as wholly innocent as it really is. Then the 'gym' costume which they all affect, is startling the Methodist Wales, and conversation is most surprisingly open. 'Is dancing sexual' I found 3 pretty Cambridge girl graduates discussing with ½ dozen men. But mostly they talk economics and political science.... There is some really useful intellectual intercourse going on between the elders, and between them & the younger ones.

Among Beatrice Webb's visitors were Rupert Brooke and

the brilliant Amber Reeves, the double first Moral Science Tripos, an amazingly vital person & I suppose very clever, but a terrible little pagan—vain, egotistical, & careless of other people's happiness. This may be a phase, for she is a mere precocious child, but the phase is unpleasant and not promising for really sound work. However, the little person can work & work easily & play at the same time. A somewhat dangerous friendship is springing up between her & H. G. Wells. I think they are both too soundly self-interested to do more than cause poor Jane Wells some fearful feelings—but if Amber were my child I should be anxious.

[1] Interview with Mrs. A. Blanco White.

In mid 1909 the inner circle of Fabians were shocked to learn that H. G. Wells and Amber had gone off to France. In an 'impudent letter' to Reeves, Wells suggested that 'Mrs. Reeves by her admiration of *In The Days of the Comet*' had condoned their conduct in advance. The Reeveses, Beatrice wrote, were 'shrivelled up with the pain' of it all: 'the poor conventional father ... now takes up an almost melodramatic attitude of furious indignation against the "Blackguard Wells and his paramour"' (not that her own comments were less angry or conventional). Reeves denounced Wells, with little discretion, as a 'vile impudent blackguard', 'a dirty little beast'.[1] Wells added insult to injury by immediately publishing a novel, *Ann Veronica*, of which even the title plainly referred to his new love. Reeves was not merely described but caricatured in the opening pages: 'a lean, trustworthy, worried-looking, neuralgic, clean-shaven man ... with a hard mouth, a sharp nose' who rode a bicycle and wrote nonsense to his daughter: '*You have no grasp upon the essential facts of life (I pray God you never may)*.' Today, *Ann Veronica* seems tepid and clumsy, but at the time very many people were deeply shocked by a novel in which a young woman acknowledges her desires—and makes the advances. By early 1910 Beatrice Webb found Amber very changed, 'shy and subdued', 'sweet and frank'. She married happily and wrote a distinguished series of novels and books on social, political and psychological subjects. Wells went on to greater achievements and further experiments.

The effect of these events on Reeves was immense, though incalculable. His views on sexual morality were rigidly conventional and almost morbidly puritanical: he did indeed act like a stereotype of the outraged father. He could not console himself with such thoughts as Beatrice Webb's: 'all of this arises because none of us know what exactly is the sexual code we believe in—approving of many things on paper which we violently object to when they are practised by those we care about.' Unlike Maud, he had not pretended to approve of the new morality. To someone so proud and thin-skinned, the wide notoriety of the affair, which he helped to spread, was a calamity. When Sidney Webb was 'helping him into the saddle' at the

---

[1] Interview with Dr. G. H. Scholefield; B. Webb Journals, 1909–10, Passfield MSS. See also, Lance Sieveking, *The Eye of the Beholder*, London, 1957, pp. 223-4.

L.S.E. the students were talking of nothing else but the current literary gossip. As he took his seat at lunch in the Refectory, one student thought, he looked like 'a condemned man'.[1] There can be no doubt that his domestic tragedy made it much more difficult for him to change his occupation than might otherwise have been the case. Another result was that he fell out with most of his Fabian friends. Shaw's attempts to smooth things out in 1909 made him furious. And though, after a period of strain, Beatrice noted in her Journal in August, 'All is right between us and Reeves', he was never again as close to the Webbs as he had been. This, too, made his path at the L.S.E. much more difficult than it might have been.

[1] A number of students of the time have testified, in interviews, on this point.

21

SCHOLARS AND GREEKS
1909–19

WHEN Reeves went to the London School of Economics he had a general knowledge of its management, for he had been a member of its Court of Governors since its foundation.[1] He knew something of one of its problems, relations with the University of London, because he had been one of the four members appointed by the Crown to the University Senate since 1902. He had also delivered courses of lectures at the School on public administration. But he had no university training or experience of daily academic life, which was a considerable handicap. In choosing Reeves, however, Webb had considered this and decided that the task was essentially one involving negotiations with the business and professional world.[2] Probably he, too, underestimated the peculiar problems of academic administration. It is likely that the feeling that Reeves was an outsider accounted for some hostility he encountered among the teachers.[3]

Among the staff were some outstanding and eventually famous scholars. It would not have been easy to find men more likely to advance towards the objective of the school, the discovery of a science of society. Their quality testifies to the Webbs' reputation and influence. They included L. T. Hobhouse, the philosopher, Lilian Knowles, the historian, G. Lowes Dickinson, another historian, who helped to found the League of Nations, Edwin Cannan, the economist, Mackinder, Graham Wallas and Sidney Webb himself.

The students were, for those days, an unusual group. Some had already graduated and were working for higher degrees. Already the School had begun what has been perhaps its greatest achievement, to attract students from all over the

---

[1] LSE Archives, S. Webb to Vice Chancellor, 9 June 1908, (Finance and General Purposes Committee).
[2] Ibid.   [3] Interview Mrs. Beryl Clarke.

Empire. Many were Indians and Chinese. Some daytime lectures were repeated after five o'clock, because the majority were 'evening students', who had worked in offices or class-rooms all day. Most of the students were twenty-three to twenty-eight, while some were even older. One student said, 'We were an odd job lot at those evening classes! Clerks and students and teachers, young and old, men and women of all sorts and conditions.'[1] The L.S.E. was then quite small. In 1910 there were 614 students, with another 1,000 coming for 'special classes'. By 1914, enrolments on the general register had reached 1,231, while 900 came for 'special classes'.[2]

Reeves found the finances of the School in a mess. Its income was only about £7,000 a year from 1908 to 1913.[3] Although Webb had been pressing on Mackinder that 'everything must be subordinated ... in his mind' to raising more money, they had decided that the 'best course' was to continue the expansion of courses offered, although this involved extra expense, hoping that a new public appeal, or the London County Council, would provide funds. Sidney Webb wrote to Beatrice, 'It is a hazardous game; and I am alive to the risks. But the commitment will not be great or irrevocable; and we shall not move without help.'[4]

Reeves learned in 1909 that there was a large deficit in the building and equipment account and that the general account was heavily over-drawn. It made him feel at home: plainly a new Ballance policy was called for. 'The administration', he wrote, 'had to be marked by intense caution, if not by down-right parsimony.' He was forced to wipe out the depreciation reserve, and use working receipts for capital expenditure.

The result was gratifying. By the end of the year the loss of the Refectory had been reduced from £200 to £6. By mid 1910 the School had £1,500 on deposit after (he reported) 'a thrifty use of the year's current receipts', and finances were better than they had yet been, though part of the administrative fund was still

---

[1] E. M. Forster, *Goldsworthy Lowes Dickinson*, New York, [*c*. 1934], p. 98; Janet Beveridge, *An Epic of Clare Market*, London, 1960, pp. 75–76; Passfield MSS, x, 2(i), 104, 'Brief Report on the Work of the School since 1895', 1899.

[2] LSE Archives, Minutes of Court of Governors, 14 July, 16 Dec. 1910; 2 July 1914.

[3] Janet Beveridge, p. 67; LSE Archives, Minutes of Council of Management, 1913.

[4] Passfield MSS, ii, 3 (i) 61, 22 Feb. 1908.

being spent on equipment and building.[1] At the end of 1911 Reeves was able to recommend a substantial expansion of all the activities of the School. Most of the teachers were paid very inadequately; several thousand pounds were needed for the library and scholarships; the London County Council was providing a site for a further building, for which £20,000 was needed. He hoped to double the size of the accommodation. A public appeal was launched for £25,000, but initially it fell flat. By mid 1912 not much more than £1,000 had been donated or promised. A mere £2,200 was spent on additions to the existing building in Clare Market, the Strand.[2]

Reeves continued, though not energetically, with his writing. In 1911 a new poem, 'Greek Fire. A Byzantine Ballad', appeared in the *Spectator*. It's metre owed too much to Scott's 'Young Lochinvar'; the rhetoric was too full blown in its pursuit of the exotic.[3] He also wrote various articles and chapters of books, such as one on New Zealand in *British Dominions*, edited by W. J. Ashley, in which he sincerely regretted that his country was borrowing so fast.[4]

Maud wrote something much more important. As one of a Fabian Women's Group, she spent four years investigating the effects of a good diet on pregnant women. They selected a large group of wives of men in the Lambeth district who earned 18s. to 26s. a week. The women were taught to keep careful accounts of their weekly expenditure. In 1912 she wrote a Fabian tract, expanded next year into a book, *Round About a Pound a Week*, describing some of their findings. She showed how far these poor people were from the middle-class stereotype of them as feckless loafers: how much thrift, wisdom and regularity were needed to exist on so little. She showed how the poor lived, and called on the state, as a national responsibility, to care for the health of children as well as their education, by introducing school clinics and midday meals. Her book, summarizing a pioneering piece of sociological research, was a best-seller.[5]

---

[1] LSE Archives, Minutes of Court of Governors, 1908–10.
[2] LSE Archives, Minutes of Council of Management, 1911–12.
[3] 16 Sept.
[4] London, 1911; also W. P. Reeves (ed.), *Studies in Economics and Political Science*, LSE, 1909, 1910, 1913.
[5] *Family Life on a Pound a Week*, Fabian Society, 1912; *Round About a Pound a Week*, G. Bell, 1913.

Each year Reeves gave a course of lectures on such subjects as old-age pensions, electoral systems, land taxation or colonial history. He was at ease with the students and saw a good deal of them on informal occasions. Many of them retained pleasant memories of his 'charm of manner and wealth of wit'.[1] His repartee was as quick as ever.

Sir Alexander Carr-Saunders, a relative of Maud (and later a Director of the L.S.E.), thought Reeves's verbal wit quite remarkable. On one occasion, he recalls, Reeves was sitting listlessly scanning a newspaper when someone, reading a letter, announced, 'Oh, Ella Fortune has had twin girls.' Instantly Reeves looked up and said, 'Well, little misfortunes never come singly.' A typical pun was his remark that an army class, attending lectures in economics, was 'seeking the bubble reputation, even in the Cannan's mouth'.

One secretary of the Students' Union later said that, in his relations with staff and students, Reeves was 'thoroughly democratic but he always maintained his dignity and expected to be obeyed'.[2] Mr. and Mrs. Reeves began the practice of inviting students to tea in the board room. He ate his lunch each day at the head of the centre table in the Refectory, with Miss C. S. Mactaggart, the Secretary of the School, at his right hand.

The 'voluptuous Miss Christian', as Shaw called her, was an Australian who joined the Fabian Society in 1897 and stood unsuccessfully for the executive a year later.[3] When Reeves arrived at the School she virtually ran the day-to-day administration. She had had a rival for some of her duties, her cousin, John McKillop, but he had retired defeated to the Library. In 1909 he resigned. Miss Mactaggart was, in effect, the registrar, as well as hostess, accountant and deputy director.[4] None of the first three directors was full-time, though what Lady Beveridge wrote, that Reeves was 'less of a full-timer' than Hewins or Mackinder,[5] was almost certainly untrue. His only other occupation during his first years at the School, the directorship

---

[1] *Clare Market Review*, June 1919.

[2] LSE Archives, 'History of the School', G. V. Ormsby, 'The L.S.E., 1911-14' (essay).

[3] *Fabian News*, April 1897, May 1898.

[4] LSE Archives, A. L. Bowley address, 18 April 1945, 'History of the School'; S. Caine, pp. 54, 69.

[5] *An Epic of Clare Market*, p. 67.

of the National Bank, was scarcely arduous. Until 1913 or 1914 he seems to have given almost all his time to the L.S.E.

According to Miss Mactaggart, Reeves resented the influence of Webb, the other power at the School, and tried to keep him in the background. In any case Webb had to resign his position of Chairman of the Governors in 1910, on the insistence of the railway companies that subsidized the Railway Department at the School, after he supported a claim by the railwaymen for higher wages.[1] He continued to exert what influence he could. There remained, however, Miss Mactaggart.

Reeves seems, at least during his first years at the School, to have confined her to the day-to-day details of administration, while keeping important decisions in his own hands. She greatly resented what she regarded as his inefficient despotism. Jealousy eventually became hatred. Years later she was to recall that he was 'jealous almost to madness, and vain almost to madness'.[2]

She sorely tried his limited patience. For instance, during World War I, when Amber was working at the Ministry of Munitions for a tiny salary, Reeves decided that she was underfed and suggested that she might lunch with him at the School. Miss Mactaggart, instead of telling him or Amber that she objected, wrote to Maud saying that if Amber came again she would protest, on moral grounds, to the Governors.

On one curious matter, which much impressed the students, it is difficult to distinguish the Director's from the Secretary's hand. One secretary of the Students' Union recalled that, in about 1912, they had 'a hard tussle' to persuade Reeves 'to relax his regulation against women smoking in public and it was indeed only after his wife had convinced him that smoking by women was not necessarily associated with moral degradation that he modified his opposition.' Reeves, this student thought, was 'peculiarly Victorian in his views on women's behaviour'. A woman student of the same generation, however, attributed this rule to Miss Mactaggart, who always said that it was a 'convention' that women did not smoke in the Refectory. It seems improbable that Maud persuaded Reeves to relent. She disliked smoking and discouraged him from smoking at

---

[1] *An Epic of Clare Market*, pp. 65–66; LSE Archives, C. S. Mactaggart interview, 11 Feb. 1933.

[2] LSE Archives, 'History of the School', interview, 11 Feb. 1933, letter to Director, 30 Nov. 1935, and 'Recollections', Feb. 1942.

home, so he generally had his after-dinner cigarette while walking
to the corner for a newspaper.[1] But probably both stories were
substantially true; it may be that Reeves warmly supported
Miss Mactaggart's 'convention', or that she had invented it to
justify his prejudice.

Reeves's main enterprise at the School during the years 1913
to 1915, which may briefly serve as an example of his work, and
one which affected his reputation, was an unsuccessful attempt
to purchase the building of the Smith Memorial Institute. This
was a hall adjoining the School which was used for meetings of
local clubs, a factory girls' dining club and other charitable
purposes. In 1913, when the School desperately needed enlarged
premises, the trustees of the Institute were in difficulties and
approached Reeves to see whether the School could, in some
acceptable way, take over or lease their property. At this time
some £5,000 was available, from gifts and a benefaction, but
Reeves had allocated it to extending the existing building.
Reeves and the Chairman of Governors, Russell Rea, were
negotiating with a friend of Haldane's for a large gift. When this
came to nothing, in December Reeves suggested to the trustees
that their trust should be transferred to the L.S.E., which would
use the building, create a chair or scholarships to perpetuate
W. H. Smith's name and devote an annual income to continue
the charitable work of the trust. Reeves then left Webb to
continue the negotiations while he visited Greece during the
Christmas vacations.

In Reeves's absence, Webb drew up a detailed draft of an
agreement to transfer the trust. 'I have made much of what we
would do', he wrote to Miss Mactaggart, 'but it does not really
amount to very much. It is desirable to mention recreation as
well as instruction'. The trustees, however, wanted more than
Webb had suggested. They wished to spend the income allocated
to continuing the trust and wanted the hall to continue to be
available for local clubs. On his return Reeves wrote to Webb,
in March 1914, that his life would not be worth living if the
trustees gained the powers they wanted. Webb wrote to Miss
Mactaggart that, though some of the proposals would not do,
'they are clearly willing to deal, & to transfer as we wish; and

[1] LSE Archives, G. V. Ormsby, 'The L.S.E., 1911-14'; Janet Beveridge, p. 81;
interview with Mr. Eric T. Clarke, Reeves's son-in-law.

they are only putting the terms in the way most favourable to them, as a try on.' He was confident that a further meeting with the trustees would be successful, and added in a patronizing if not openly contemptuous postscript: 'I don't particularly want to come. I think the Director had better land the fish.' Years later, Webb recalled, in an interview with Sir William Beveridge, that in Reeves's absence he 'had practically arranged for the purchase of the Smith Memorial. It was a matter of getting some of the Trustees replaced by others; but when Mr. Reeves came back to the School: "he lost us the Smith Memorial".' Reeves was not in Webb's class at that sort of manoeuvre.

At this time Reeves was negotiating for a very large donation of perhaps £30,000 from a financier who had gone as far as to instruct his architects to draw up plans for a new building. When this fell through, and a fresh offer could not be made to the trustees of the Institute, Reeves turned down their terms. In October, however, the Carnegie trust offered £6,000 for the purchase of the Smith Memorial hall, but in 1915 the Smith trustees declined Reeves's new offer. It was for mishandling this phase of the negotiations that Webb's ally, Miss Mactaggart, later blamed Reeves. The Smith trustees valued their property at £10,000, and wanted £8,000. Years later she claimed that Reeves had told the Carnegie trustees that he could purchase the Institute 'at a perfectly ridiculous figure'. It is not, however, certain that she was right. The original Carnegie offer had come when Reeves was approaching that trust for help in expanding the library. In mid 1915 Reeves asked for £10,000. Only when this request was declined did he, at least formally, offer the Smith trustees £6,000.[1]

This episode had a decisive influence on Reeves's administration of the L.S.E. It coincided with the beginning of the 'Great' War. Now the expansion of the school was impossible. Enrolments fell; new building was postponed. 'Rigid economies' in staff salaries and even book purchasing were essential. The Council was very pleased that Reeves had had the foresight to establish a reserve fund for times of emergency.[2] The episode

---

[1] This episode is copiously documented. See LSE Archives, Minutes of Court of Governors; Minutes of Council of Management; File 206/3 (re the Smith Memorial Institute); 'History of the School', Webb and Mactaggart interviews and letters; Passfield Trust MSS, xi, folios 11–17.

[2] LSE Archives, Minutes of Court of Governors, 10 Dec. 1914.

marked virtually the end of any energetic attempt by Reeves to master his new task. But, though the war certainly enforced idleness upon him, it was not solely responsible for his failure to make a notable success of academic administration. It is evident that by 1915 little could be expected of him.

Nothing shows more clearly how badly things were going than the attitudes of those who cared most deeply about the school, Webb, Miss Mactaggart and Graham Wallas, Webb's confidant on the staff for many years. In March 1915 Reeves told Webb that he regretted that Wallas so rarely confided in him and that he would welcome Wallas's advice. Webb, who had asked Wallas in 1908 to do what he could to help Reeves, now suggested a fixed weekly hour of consultation, such as Webb had had with Hewins and which he thought 'of the greatest value as an administrative service': 'I hope you won't mind my suggesting it; & that you will go in next Monday & see him.' But Wallas thought the request quite unreasonable, and criticized Reeves, evidently with some heat. Webb then wrote to him:

Reeves has done very well as Director in many respects, greatly to the advantage of the School. We could not have done without the special services he has rendered—notably all the salaries might have had to be scaled down, as has happened elsewhere. (Put out of your mind any apprehensions as to speculative finance. The School has no mortgages. Its funds are on deposit at the banks, or in the war loan. My criticism on our finances is that the management has been *too* cautious. I like a debt and a deficit—in all but my own personal affairs. Reeves apparently is exactly the converse!)

It is a blunt comment on Reeves's remoteness from the teaching staff that one of the leading scholars thought his finances speculative.

Webb went on: 'Ill-temper is a terrible handicap and personal defect, all the more so because other people find it very hard to treat as they treat blindness or deafness in those with whom they have to deal. We all have to put up with it with such patience & sympathy as we can develop.'[1]

At the New Zealand offices in London, Reeves's impatience and irritability had become well known, but the senior staff had

[1] Passfield MSS, ii, 4, g. 1 and g. 2, Webb to Wallas, 12, 15 March 1915; also ii, 4, d. 24, 7 July 1908.

felt great affection for him. At the L.S.E. no one seems to have been able to 'develop' any sympathy. His bad temper was becoming notorious and was to grow worse with the years—a product of constant ill-health, strained nerves and the disappointments he had suffered before joining its staff.

By 1915 Reeves's health had begun to deteriorate. In that year he resigned from the M.C.C., where he had spent many happy hours, and from the Political Science and Philosophy Club. His health, he wrote to the latter (as he had to Ballance twenty-three years before) was not of the strongest: 'The result is that I have got into the habit perforce of doing nothing that I am not obliged to.'[1] At sixty he did not, however, seem to everyone a spent force. In 1910 Reeves had become friendly with Herbert Hoover, who, in 1915 or 1916, tried to induce him to come to Stanford University as a professor.[2]

He still had plenty of energy for travel, which had constantly delighted him since he came to England. In September 1914 Maud and he went over to France—'odd as it may seem, for the sake of peace and quietness. The atmosphere of London is naturally warlike and anxious to a degree and I thought that in north-east France, so long as one kept well out of reach of the Germans, a wandering Englishman, armed with proper passports, would probably be left very much to himself.' To go to Arras, which had just been recaptured from the Germans, certainly was an odd place to expect to find peace. His visit there, near the front, coincided with troop movements. He was immediately thought a spy, and was taken to the police station for lengthy questioning. He wrote an amused account of this 'comical little episode', though conceding that suspected spies were being shot daily.[3] While he was sitting in the Boulogne railway station a German plane tried to bomb it, but missed. Reeves promptly went to inspect the damage. He thought, 'To drop such things may be called war: to me it seemed a clumsy attempt at murder.' His disregard for his physical safety

[1] Reeves MSS, 23 Sept. 1915.

[2] D. S. Jordan, *The Days of a Man*, Yonkers-on-Hudson, 1922, ii, p. 333. According to the family, he was asked to be president of Stanford (and Hoover was, indeed, looking for a president at that time); according to Hoover (letter to the writer, 1957), he asked Reeves to give a course of lectures. Jordan was probably right.

[3] 'A Corner of France in War Time', MSS in the possession of Mr. Tristram Reeves, Christchurch.

22

continued to be noteworthy. In 1917, when he was in the Refectory at the L.S.E., bombs began to fall near by. Everyone but Reeves took shelter in the basement. A professor related that Reeves refused to move, and said, 'You young people certainly go, but I am too old to bother about my safety.' And there he stayed 'in solitary equanimity'.[1]

It was no accident that led Reeves to leave the L.S.E. and travel to Greece during the important negotiations with the Smith Memorial trustees. He had found his last great love, which took up all that remained of the ardent temper of his youth.

Since his boyhood in a 'new country' he had been fascinated by the ancient civilization of the Greeks. His studies of classical literature and history had not seemed a dull imposition, but, like reading Byron, were imaginative fuel. For most of his life he had been a devoted phil-Hellene. He visited both Greece and Crete some time before 1905, and thought both the people and their country very like his own.[2]

At the L.S.E. his favourite talk was of the Greeks. 'He never tired', one student recalled, 'of ... drawing parallels between ancient Greece and modern New Zealand.'[3] Now, during the Balkan wars, as the Greeks (and their allies) confronted the Turks, he took up their causes as his own. Disappointed in New Zealand and in England, he adopted a country—a country of the mind, where the romantic could walk at ease; but also one which called on its citizens for action in causes that touched his deepest self in a way that his work had not done for years. The Greek peninsula and islands became his new New Zealand, his new Empire. Greek nationalist ambitions provided his last crusade. Though he was not built for the nervous wear and tear of continuous action, always he had felt drawn (as in Paris in 1875) to heroic enterprises: it was, indeed, a need so strong that, as a young man, he could not resist viewing his own in that light. The contest in which he now joined, with the feeble means at his command, was not as far in spirit as it was in distance and time

---

[1] LSE Archives, 'History of the School', E. J. Urwick to Director, 30 Nov. 1943.
[2] See *The Long White Cloud*, 4th ed., pp. 9-10.
[3] LSE Archives, 'History of the School', G. V. Ormsby, loc. cit. Reeves's longest surviving letter, to O. T. J. Alpers, 11 Jan. 1903 (Turnbull Library), is about a comparison, suggested by Alpers, between the Liberals' legislation and those of the Roman reformers, Tiberius and Gaius Gracchus.

from his first fight for Canterbury's provincialist ambitions: 'if I could not sympathize with a brave community fighting fiercely against great odds for much less than bare justice', he had written to William Montgomery in 1887, 'I should not be proud—still less if they were my own people.'[1]

In December 1913 with Alexander Ionides, a member of a Greek family long settled in England, who had retired from the Stock Exchange to devote himself to 'literary and scientific studies', Professor R. M. Burrows, of King's College London, and D. J. Cassavetti, a lawyer who had been a correspondent in Greece for *The Times*, Reeves took the lead in founding the Anglo-Hellenic League. Reeves became the chairman and Cassavetti the secretary. Immediately, their aim was to counter the active pro-Bulgarian propaganda campaign in England, which followed Bulgaria's attack on Serbia and Greece, after they had jointly defeated the Turks. The League aimed 'to defend the just claims and honour of Greece'; to remove prejudices, spread information, promote travel and economic and cultural relations with Greece.[2]

In the same year Reeves wrote two pamphlets, *Albania and Epirus*, published by the League, and *A Plea for a Civilised Epirus*, published by the Aegean Islands Committee, in which he argued that Greece, not the newly-formed Albania (which he feared would be a hot-bed of feuds and foreign intrigues) should take over Epirus. At the end of the year Ionides and he set off for Athens to form a branch of the League there. His travels he described in his 'Memoirs':

We landed at Patras in the darkness of a winter morning. Our steamer lay at some distance from the pier and we fell into the hands of the only surviving band of brigands in Greece, the Patras boatmen. A Sirocco was blowing and the foam of the waves blew over the boat. I sat on the leeward side and let Ionides take the seat to windward where he got the seas on his back. After disembarking, we plodded through the mud to the railway station, to be informed that the train would be two hours late because a flood had carried away a bridge. However, a kind-hearted Greek friend on the steamer had sent a

---

[1] See above, p. 64.

[2] Information about the Anglo-Hellenic League has been derived from its correspondence and the minutes of the Annual General Meetings and of its Executive Committee; from its numerous pamphlets; from letters in the Reeves MSS; and from an interview with Mr. D. J. Cassavetti.

message to the Customs Department explaining that a distinguished English gentleman who wrote much in London newspapers in the cause of Hellas was to be treated as well as possible, so our luggage was passed through. His kindly credentials however, involved me in some trouble. At that time, much the best English writer on Near Eastern matters was Mr. [J. D.] Bourchier, the very able correspondent of *The Times*. Mr. Bourchier had lived in Greece and became of good repute there as a Phil-Hellene and a friend of Venizelos. After going over to Sofia he espoused the Bulgarian cause and some letters of his to *The Times* had greatly wounded Greek feeling. He was very unpopular at that moment. For some reason or other the people who received the message about me from the steamer got it into their heads that I was Kurios Bourchier. All along the railroad we were treated to dark looks from guards and porters. Towards evening we reached K—— where there was a restaurant. Cold, damp and half-starved, we were received with sullen ill-will. When we asked for milk, it appeared that there were no cows in the district. How then could we expect cheese or butter? Meat?—surely we knew that a number of Orthodox Greek fast-days came together at that precise time. Cakes? Figs? Oranges? They were to have come from Athens that afternoon but had not arrived. Bread? Yes! Black Coffee? Yes! Sugar? No! However, the exasperated Ionides found some sugar in a corner, the coffee was hot, we did what we could. On our way to Athens, Ionides announced that he meant 'to make those fellows sit up'. On reaching Athens, however, we learnt that the Bourchier legend was circulating amongst our friends—everything circulates in Athens—and causing much laughter....

The upshot of it all was, that a party was arranged. Ionides and I were taken back to K—— as honoured guests. Waggonettes were provided; we were driven about the country and showed ruins and selected scenery. We were given a dejeuner, a well-cooked dejeuner, worthy of a City company. I was privileged to occupy the same waggonette with a very attractive young lady who, when we parted, swore to remember eternally that I was not Kurios Bourchier.

In Athens, dressed in clothes borrowed from Ionides, a professor and other friends, he had a half-hour's audience with King Constantine. A branch of the League was set up, with Princess Alice as patroness. His work was not unappreciated. The University of Athens awarded him a doctorate of philosophy —his first and last degree. And he accepted his first honours (other than his title, 'the Honourable'); he became a High Commander of the Order of the Saviour. He travelled, rapidly, to Korfu and Crete, where he wrote a new poem, 'The Sphakiot's Return'.

On his return he became one of the Greeks' chief, honorary, publicity agents. Because of his political and journalistic experience and of his many contacts with politicians (including Liberal cabinet ministers), businessmen, academics and editors, he was skilful at the task. He wrote letters to the *Daily Chronicle*, the *Morning Post*, the *Westminster Gazette* and (from time to time) articles, signed 'Plinthos', in the *New Statesman*, defending the Greeks against criticism or advancing their claims.[1]

He and his friends in the League soon had plenty to do. The League was formed at the height of modern Greek power and (in England) prestige. At the Treaty of Bucharest her territory was nearly doubled. The Prime Minister, Venizelos, enjoyed a considerable reputation far beyond his country. Reeves became his friend and unqualified admirer. Though he was not, he said, given to hero-worship, he did 'most utterly and completely trust Eleutherios Venizelos'.[2] This devotion was to involve him, and the League, in the desperate faction of Greek politics, which made those in Wellington seem a parlour game.

Venizelos wanted Greece to join the war on the side of Britain, France and their allies; the King leant towards neutrality, and, indeed, sympathized with the 'Central Powers'. In 1914 the King forced Venizelos to resign. Reeves wrote an article comparing the incident with the overthrow of Chatham by George III (who was 'animated by teutonic ideas quite unsuited to the English race').[3] The League sent Venizelos a telegram expressing 'grief for his resignation', and made representations to the Foreign Office. But the cause of a neutral Greece was hard to defend: Reeves wrote to Samuel, who was now in the Government, that the Foreign Office regarded outsiders who meddled in Balkan affairs as cranks or scoundrels.[4] He was, he wrote to Ionides in 1915, 'a very sad-hearted Phil-Hellene'.[5] Neverthe-

---

[1] Anglo-Hellenic Leaflet No. 3, Reeves and Burrows, (letter in *Morning Post*, 25 Nov. [1913/14?]); *Daily Chronicle*, 11 April 1914; *Westminster Gazette*, 27 June 1914; 'Plinthos', *New Statesman*, 13 March 1915, 5 Feb. 1916. Reeves possibly also wrote the *New Statesman* articles on Greece of 11 Oct. 1913 ('Machiavelli in the Aegean'), 25 Oct. 1915 and 23 May 1914.

[2] Anglo-Hellenic League, minutes of General Meeting, 5 July 1917.

[3] *New Statesman*, 13 March 1915.

[4] Reeves MSS, 27 Nov. 1915.   [5] Ibid., 13 Nov. 1915.

less, his enthusiasm persisted. In January 1916 he wrote to another
friend that he was devoting all his spare time to learning modern
Greek, of which he was 'now acquiring a pretty fair knowledge':
'I find it a much better language than I had supposed, with much
of the flexibility and trickiness of the old classic tongue. ... I have
interested myself very much in Balkan politics, and tried to do
for the Greeks some of the services which Sir Charles Dilke so
generously rendered them.' [1]

In the mid year he suffered a serious break-down of health.
At first he caught a cold, then had 'neuralgia in the eyes'. In July
the doctor told him to rest for a month. Then, in August, his son
Fabian, who had left King's College, Cambridge, to enlist in
the Royal Naval Air Service, had a bad flying accident. Reeves
now collapsed altogether and the doctor sent him out of town.
In November Webb saw him, recovering from a 'fever': 'He was
very friendly & professed to be quite well. But he was terribly
pulled down & shaken. He was very cheerful about the School,
& full of praise of Steel Maitland [Sir Arthur Steel-Maitland,
the Chairman of the Governors].... His son has just taken a
seaplane in loops round the South East Coast, & is doing well.' [2]

He now had to take another, this time a terrible, blow. On
6 June he was informed that his son, a Lieutenant, was missing.
He was flying a Nieuport in a fight over Griencourt, involving
twenty or thirty planes, and was shot down. For the next two
months the family was tortured with uncertainty and grief.
It was reported that he had died a prisoner, but no one knew.
Not until September was he reported killed in action. In
November they learned, from the International Red Cross, that
he had died in his plane. One of his masters at St. Paul's School
wrote that Fabian was 'one of the very few original thinkers I
have had under me'. Reeves wrote simply to a friend, 'I will
only say ... that a better son no man ever had and that until his
death I never knew what it was to feel anything but pride and
pleasure in him.' [3]

The effect on Maud was tragic. She was now at the height of

[1] Reeves MSS, Reeves to Tuckwell, 19 Jan. 1916.

[2] There are a large number of references to Reeves's health in letters in the Reeves
MSS and in the correspondence etc. of the League. See also, Passfield MSS, Sidney
to Beatrice Webb, 9 Nov. 1916.

[3] *The Times*, 17 Sept. 1918; Reeves to R. H. Hooper, 27 Feb. 1918, and many
letters in the Reeves MSS.

her powers: in *The Times* there were more references to her than
to her husband. In 1916, because of her 'expert knowledge of
domestic economics', she had served on a Board of Trade
Committee to investigate the causes of the current rise in prices
and to suggest possible remedies. In March 1917 she, and another
woman, were appointed the Directors of Women's Service in
the Ministry of Food. Their duties were to direct propaganda in
connexion with the Government's appeal for voluntary rationing
—urging, for instance, the consumption of mangel-wurzels as
a substitute for potatoes.[1] After Fabian's death she continued this
work, but at the end of the war, like many thousands of people
in Great Britain who had lost their children, she was caught up
in a wave of 'spiritualism'. Mrs. Leonard, the spiritualist, and
others of her kind, at endless séances, sought to put her in touch
with Fabian. She accumulated many volumes of closely-covered
pages of 'spirit-writing' which cruelly purported to include
obscure messages from the dead. Fay seemed, Maud told Lord
Samuel, 'absent-minded like Will'.

Reeves was never quite to recover from Fabian's death. Sick
and dispirited, he felt savaged by life. Of his work at the L.S.E.
not much remains to be said. In 1917 and 1918, several days a
week, always ill, he was to be found wrapped in rugs in his room
there. But he did very little. Professor A. L. Bowley's (much-
repeated) quip, that 'Pember Reeves reigned, while Miss
Mactaggart ruled', was certainly true now, though it could not
have been said before 1914. Now she began to sign most of the
correspondence. He spent much time helping to plan and
organize a degree in commerce, a subject on which he wrote,
in June 1917, and again in 1918, long reports, but it seems that,
even here, Webb, who induced Sir Ernest Cassel to give the
necessary money, was the main force.[2]

Reeves was not merely ill. He had largely lost interest in his
work at the School. Since 1909 he had sat on the Board of the
National Bank. In October 1917 he was elected Chairman of
Directors. Webb later said that, by this time, things were 'not
going too well' at the School and he 'asked a person he trusted
[probably Graham Wallas] to let him know when the School was

[1] *The Times*, 17 June 1916, 3 March 1917.
[2] LSE Archives, S. Webb interview, 24 Nov. 1932; M. Cole (ed.), *The Webbs and
Their Work*, London, 1949, p. 51.

really suffering as a result ... .' In April 1919 Beatrice related in her Journal the circumstances of Reeves's resignation:

In the intervals of other business Sidney has been busy with his old love—the School of Economics. His position as a Cassel Trustee, dispensing the £150,000 [*sic*] a year to be devoted to a faculty of Commerce, has given him a position of vantage for the reorganisation of the work of the school.... This unfortunately required him to undertake the unpleasant task of telling an old friend—W. P. Reeves —that the time had come for him to resign from the Directorship. Sidney felt that some one had to break the news and though there was very great discontent with Reeves's Directorship on the part of staff & the Governors & an open breach between him and Miss Mactaggart—the real administrator of the School—no one volunteered to say the decisive word. Sidney felt that he was responsible for Reeves [appointment] to the School there to be Director more than ten years ago on the express understanding that he should retire in seven years. But he failed to do so & had even altered the superannuation age of 60 as laid down by the University. He clung desperately to the Directorship but gave practically no thought to the work of the School & has by his [illegible] egotism alienated most of his colleagues. As he is very well off there seemed no reason to keep him on out of pity. It was a painful interview—but Reeves took it well, merely remarking that Sidney was ruthless in the pursuit of his causes & allowed no personal considerations either on his own behalf or on other peoples, to stand in the way of the success of an Institution or movement which he believed in. Which of course is true.

Nothing in earlier records supports this suggestion of a seven-year appointment.

Everything was done with due decency. Reeves was praised for his achievement in stabilizing and expanding the School's finances. He wrote the usual letters explaining that, in future, the Director would have to be full-time; that he was resigning because of his health. To an old friend, the New Zealand parliamentary librarian, he wrote that the strain of running the School and the Bank was too much: 'but I shall hope to go on with the Bank for a year or two longer. After that there will remain nothing to be done unless I have strength enough to write one more book, as I am anxious to do.'

He would not, he said, write any more verse: hard work and sorrow had taken too large a toll.[1]

[1] Reeves MSS, to Charles Wilson, 9 April 1919.

PONDOLAND

1919–32

REEVES was now sixty-two. Of the next four or five years of his life there is little to be said. He was frequently ill and always in bad health, plagued by headaches and sleeplessness, which often kept Maud up with him half the night. The life of the family now—as for some years—was largely organized round his health.

He went in several days a week in the mornings to the bank, but there is no evidence to suggest that his duties there were demanding. His experience of New Zealand life and his financial caution must have weighed in the formulation of the policy of a bank traditionally cautious and 'safe'. With help from senior officers of the bank he wrote the annual reports, which annually complained of the high level of New Zealand taxation and the level of government borrowing. In 1922, noting the absence of labour conflicts in New Zealand, he expressed his great faith in the commonsense of the Dominion's workers: 'I refuse to believe that they will let their country down by holding up industry in a year of trial like this.'[1]

He saw almost nothing, now, of his friends of 1900. In 1923 he heard that Webb had 'broken down' and sent him a generous gift. Webb told him he was merely ill, and though his resources were strained, he returned the money.[2] He had lunch and played billiards in either the Reform or Savile Club each day, where his sense of humour and constant joking were long remembered. One old friend at the former, A. G. McArthur, once said that he was surprised, with all Reeves's public service, that he had no honours. Reeves replied that the only honour he had coveted was to be a J.P. McArthur arranged for him to be appointed a J.P. in Kensington.[3] Although he was presumably unaware of it,

[1] 50th Annual Report, National Bank of New Zealand Ltd.
[2] Reeves MSS, Webb to Reeves, 14 Nov. 1923.
[3] Interview with Mr. A. G. McArthur.

Reeves had once come close to much higher honours. In 1911, when the Liberal Government was fighting the House of Lords, he had been on Asquith's list of proposed peers.[1]

A group of old friends formed 'Ye Sette of Odd Volumes'. Reeves was called 'Maori'. They published small books in small editions numbered in odd numbers. For instance, 'Hydrographer', Lt. Commander R. T. Gould, R.N. (Retd.), their president, wrote *The Sea-serpent*, of which 167 copies, numbered 1–333, were issued in 1926.[2]

As his mind dwelt increasingly in the past, during the twenties he began to write, or more usually to dictate, his autobiography, some of which has been quoted in these pages. It never, however, advanced beyond the stage of discontinuous sections of chapters, sometimes inaccurate (because uncorrected) or inconsistent, relating isolated episodes, anecdotes or impressions. Most of it was about New Zealand, but a lengthy section was a whimsical account of his relations with royalty, which he scorned but not to write of. The first 'royal personage' he heard of as a boy, Prince Albert, he recalled, had just died. He had been presented to many rulers since then, and so many of them had shortly afterwards been assassinated, that an Italian once (with 'a disgusting gesture') accused him of having 'the Evil Eye', and denounced him for having declined to meet the Kaiser shortly before the war. He pretended to feel uncomfortable about the risks he represented for royalty, and while disbelieving, felt there was 'something in it', as his mother used to say of the Tichborne claimant.

Many of his best stories against himself, generally about some defect of dress, related to these encounters. As Agent-General he had been unable to avoid being presented to Edward VII, shortly before his coronation. Consequently he was, at last, obliged to acquire court dress. On this occasion he arrived at the palace with the tissue paper still on his buttons. The attendants quietly removed it. Maud, however, surpassed him. Instead of the expected satin train, she wore yards of chiffon with 'gum dew drops', which she thought would make a party dress for Amber. Edward VII immediately became ill, so that the coronation had

---

[1] J. A. Spender and Cyril Asquith, *Life of Henry Herbert Asquith*, London, 1932, i, pp. 329–31.
[2] Information from Mr. Thomas Blanco White, who has this volume.

to be postponed. Reeves wrote an irreverent but kindly coronation ode:

> And every 'growler' yelled to every cad
> 'It ihn't no go! Ole Teddy's regler bad'.[1]

The next time Reeves spoke to the King was shortly before his death. He declined to be presented to George V.

From 1918 to 1925 his main interest in life continued to be the Greeks. He went on interviewing cabinet ministers and other authorities, and writing numerous letters, on their behalf. When he left the L.S.E. he donated three hundred books on economics, social reform and history to the University of Athens. King Constantine had fallen; Venizelos was back in power and had brought Greece into the war on the side of Britain, to the delight of the Anglo-Hellenic League and Reeves. Even when the war progressed badly, he could write, 'The sky is dark in the Near East but I have faith in Providence and Venizelos.'[2]

In 1917 and again in 1918–19 Venizelos was in London and Paris, trying to create a 'Great Greece'. In 1918 Reeves wrote another pamphlet, *An Appeal for the Liberation and Union of the Hellenic Race*. Only about half the Greeks, he argued, had yet been 'enfranchised' from foreign bondage—especially to the Turks, who were 'quite unfitted to govern'. (The Bulgarians he thought as bad. In a letter in 1918 he wrote, 'For twelve hundred years those cruel savages have been the curse of the Balkans.')[3] He pleaded for the creation of a very large Greece, including all Greeks, even the hundreds of thousands who were in a minority in their districts, as in Thrace—for the Greeks were more progressive, humane and civilized than their neighbours, Turk or Bulgar. Cyprus and Rhodes, Thrace and Macedonia, the ancient districts of Lydia, Ionia, Caria, most of Lycia ... all should be Greek. Greek nationalism could go further only by going to Constantinople. The London Committee of the Un-redeemed Greeks distributed 20,000 free copies.

For a time it seemed Greek wishes would come true. At the Treaty of Sèvres (which was not to be ratified), Greece gained very large areas of Turkey. In 1919 Venizelos was defeated in the

---

[1] Reeves MSS, small clipping book, pp. 112–13.
[2] Ibid., Reeves to R. M. Burrows, 1 Feb. 1918.
[3] Ibid., Reeves to A. Andreades, 9 Oct. 1918.

elections (in his pamphlet Reeves had granted him the integrity
of Aristides, the resourcefulness and vision of Themistocles, the
courage of Leonidas); in 1920, against the wishes of the Allies,
King Constantine came back with popular support. Now Reeves
thought the position 'dark and doubtful'. With some of his
fellow enthusiasts, he published in the *Westminster Gazette* a
manifesto of the League, regretting the election results and
denouncing the Turkish nationalist leaders as 'a blood-stained
and merciless gang'.[1] When the allies abandoned the Greeks,
after encouraging them to land at Smyrna, and left them to fight
the Turks, the League was powerless, while some local Greeks
were becoming impatient of its 'Venisdist' tendencies. Reeves
wrote one more pamphlet, denouncing Turkish atrocities,
The Great Powers and the Eastern Christians. Christiani ad Leones!, in
1922. But the League seems to have been weakening, becoming
divided in opinion and losing its enthusiasm. It had achieved
very little, except to keep pro-Greek sentiment alive in Britain
during the war, at times when the reputation of Greece was low,
and to encourage social contacts between people of the two
countries.

After the fall of Smyrna in 1922, and in 1924 when he spoke in
Greek at the University of Athens on the occasion of the Byron
centenary, he visited Greece again. But there seemed little he
could do now to further the Greek cause. In 1925, after serving
for twelve years, he resigned his position as Chairman.

Nothing in Reeves's public life, after he left New Zealand's
service, gave him as much satisfaction as his work of love for
Greece. And he knew it was appreciated. In 1920 he was made a
Grand Commander of the Order of George I. Many Greeks,
including the Archbishop of Cyprus and the committee of the
Cypriot 'Enosis' Club wrote thanking him for his help. At some
time, late in life, he wrote his own epitaph:

> Were a New Zealander this stone to pass,
> 'Tenákoe!'[2] I should mutter 'neath the grass,
> Or if a Briton deigned to glance and stay,
> 'Goodmorrow Sir!' I might presume to say,
> But when a Greek his way doth hither wend,
> Then '$Καλῶς ἦλθες$!',[3] for 'twill be a friend.

[1] Anglo-Hellenic League, minutes of general meeting, 6 Dec. 1920.
[2] 'Pleased to see you.'   [3] 'Welcome.'

But in the mid twenties, though his Mediterranean affections may not have diminished, his thoughts were turning more and more from the isles of Greece to Pacific islands. One of his old obsessions was refreshed by a request to write a preface to a book on Chinese coolie emigration. Even now, he confessed, he could not speak of the Chinese—and their 'loathesome' vices—without emotion.[1]

At about the same time, George Allen and Unwin began to take an interest in his historical writings. They bought from the Receiver the rights to *State Experiments* when Alexander Moring Ltd. went into liquidation. It is typical of Reeves's financial scrupulosity that, when he learned that they were under no legal obligation to pay royalties, he informed them that he 'saw no reason why in that case' they should. Sir Stanley Unwin later recalled: 'We equally firmly insisted that there was a moral obligation, to which he responded that in that event the amount we had paid the Receiver ... must be a first charge on the royalties, and thus it was finally arranged.'[2] (In the same spirit, when he was High Commissioner, though he occasionally bought shares through the firm of Pember and Boyle, he would not purchase New Zealand shares, because he might be profiting from inside information). *State Experiments* was reissued, un-revised, printed by a photographic process, in 1923.

Allen and Unwin had also, in 1914, acquired the rights to *The Long White Cloud*, and now, in 1923, proposed a third edition. After a good deal of urging, Reeves agreed to help. In the end he made very extensive revisions, including the addition of three new chapters on the Liberal Government up to the death of Seddon. Cecil J. Wray, an Englishman whose work kept him 'in close touch with the New Zealand statute-book',[3] added three chapters bringing the story up to the end of World War I.

The new chapters, especially 'King Dick', which includes material he had been drafting for his 'Memoirs', are as fresh and vigorous as anything Reeves ever wrote. He is generous to Ward, who was still alive—and was to become Prime Minister again in 1928. He writes of Seddon, despite some typical barbed jokes,

[1] P. C. Campbell, *Chinese Coolie Emigration to Countries within the British Empire*, London, 1923.
[2] Letter to the writer, 7 Aug. 1953.
[3] *The Long White Cloud*, 3rd ed., preface, p. 9.

with warmth, even affection: 'His head made one think of iron wedges, stone axes and things meant to split and fracture. And the pallor of his face was lit up by two alert blue eyes and by a peculiarly pleasant—nay, sweet—smile... .'

He was, Reeves reflected, 'almost the converse of the merry, witty king who never said a foolish thing and never did a wise one'. He 'went on, year after year, making laws that were sound for the most part and speeches that were, for the most part, sound'. Yet Reeves also recalled that Seddon's great popularity began only after he had been Premier for five years—by which time most premiers had no popularity left. Reeves remarked that Seddon 'was not over-fond of intellectuals and had a propensity for breaking with the clever young men of his party'. But, though Seddon had not been 'encumbered with either theories or ideals', Reeves naïvely consoled himself with the thought that the 'popular leaders of New Zealand in the future seem likely to be men with definite theories of Government and Society up to which they mean to work'.

It was hard to think of Seddon as dead—to imagine him 'asleep, inert, or passive in any world, however vast and remote', when one thought of his 'extraordinary power of defying fatigue', of 'his general air of hopeful good-humour'. Did he, Reeves wondered, when he met Charon, 'take the helm when crossing the river'? And he thought of his old 'chief' 'smilingly haranguing Elysian mass meetings in fields of amaranth and asphodel, where there is no time-limit for speeches'.

Occasionally Reeves glanced wryly over his shoulder, as when he recalled that not once, while he was minister, was he asked to devote a public speech to his labour legislation: 'Only after the laws were fully at work and social students came from other countries to study them did New Zealanders begin to think that they might be something better than a pile of raw rubbish palmed off on the public by an ignorant demagogue.' But he was no longer as sorry for himself as he had been; rather, he basked in a quiet satisfaction at the continuing success of compulsory arbitration and other reforms.

In 1925 rumour reached New Zealand, and was reported in the Press, that he was renewing his youth, regaining interest in the things that had concerned him at the height of his powers.[1]

[1] *Evening Post*, 17 May 1932, (citing 1925 report).

He spent much time, now, revising his verses, which he had printed on loose leaves—as he had in about 1912—for distribution among his friends. He also, in old age, often copied out verses by others that appealed to him. It was apparently in 1925 that he wrote to Miss G. Colborne Veel, sister of a Christchurch poetess whose verses he had sometimes admired, a letter which speaks more strongly than anything else of his mood:

You cannot think how grateful I am for your more than kind letter. In public life such things do not often come to a man. Now and then, only, some friend writes one a letter of real sympathy and honest approval. A few such I have, but none that have pleased and touched me so much as yours of yesterday. Perhaps it is a confession of weakness for a politician to admit that the ceaseless course of fault-finding, abuse and more or less spiteful and unjust accusation affects him in any way. But I will admit that sometimes in moments of weariness and depression one is tempted to wonder whether there are such things as friendship and just appreciation left—whether there are people who can understand that a man can have ideals and battle for them. Of course fits of depression pass away: but letters like the two you have written me help them to pass away. I shall keep your letters and value them I assure you. As for the poetry you know what a solace and delight verse is, how it throws 'the light that never was on sea or land' over the beaten and dusty thoroughfares of life. Perhaps a public man is rash to let his name be linked with verse in a country where provincial taste and middle-class feeling are as strong as they are here. Perhaps he ought to treat it as

'A thing to retain and say nothing about
Lest if used it should draw degradation through doubt'.

However I have run the risk. On the whole I have nothing to complain of though an M.H.R. did tell me in debate that I was 'worse than Nero' for writing the 'Toi-Toi In Church' whilst there were Unemployed in the country. Even if I had done anything but laugh, as I did, at his tirade your letter would outweigh a hundred such insults many times over. Believe me when I say that it came like manna in a wilderness of barren correspondence.

Yours gratefully

W. P. Reeves.[1]

---

[1] Dated 'The Bank 25th April'. Turnbull Library. His other surviving letter to her is dated 22 Sept. 1924.

What he thought his best verse he collected in a new volume, *The Passing of the Forest*, privately published for him by Allen and Unwin in mid 1924. It included poems from each of his previous volumes, some sentimental and second-hand wartime verses and some, previously unpublished, of greater biographical, if not literary, interest. There is one curious poem, 'The Gate of Fame', which was written before 1912, and probably after 1900.[1] It recounts an allegorical sea voyage of an anonymous hero, who is reborn from a long, dreamless sleep— 'A youth again, and on a morning sea!'—and 'running with the wind' in 'blithe, expectant confidence', towards the gate of a dream-city. After many dangers and trials he reaches the out-works:

> God! 'Tis the goal. But from those silent walls
> No warder challenges, no welcome calls.
> I stagger onward: lo! Ambition's fate—
> —A pit before the gate!

In his preface to the new edition of *The Long White Cloud*, C. J. Wray wrote of Reeves, 'Ill health has kept him off the stage for so many years that not very many remember the work he did or the manner in which it was done.' That was not true in New Zealand. In November 1925, the same year when he laid down his hand in Anglo-Hellenic affairs, the Bank sent him on a tour of New Zealand, in order, it is believed, that the office could be reorganized in his absence.[2] His tour, all over the country from North Auckland to Invercargill, was a triumph. He felt warmed and happy at the welcome he received, everywhere, from old friend and foe alike. When he addressed a hundred Wellington businessmen, the president of the Chamber of Commerce introduced him with the recommendation that he 'was not influenced by any party bias'.[3]

He wrote a good deal about his trip in a confidential report to the Bank, in his next annual report, and in the preface to a new

---

[1] It did not appear in *New Zealand* (1898)—from which, however, he omitted 'By the Solent', so the omission may not help to date it. It appears, however, among some printed poems, dated 2 Dec. 1912, in the possession of Mr. Thomas Blanco White, London.

[2] This is the recollection of his son-in-law, Mr. Eric Thatcher Clarke. I am much indebted to the London Office of the National Bank of New Zealand for permitting me to read his confidential report and other documents.

[3] *Dominion*, 16 March 1926.

edition of his travelogue, *New Zealand*, in 1927. Every day he was astonished and fascinated by the changes he saw: a New Zealander, Gordon Coates, Prime Minister; the people twice as numerous, taller, healthier and more sober. Though he could not refrain from comment on the high proportion of farmers working for their post-war mortgages, and on the government debt, such unwelcome details seemed small shadows in a sunny land. Arbitration was working. The employers had a better attitude towards the unionists—none of whose grievances were not 'susceptible to civilised and peaceful arbitration'. Fertilizers had brought great areas of land into production. Secondary industry was developing rapidly.

The bush was still being cut, but extensive tree planting was helping to make the country the most beautiful, he thought, of the eighteen he had visited. He smiled his way through the land. In Wellington he was thought a delightful conversationalist. At the Hermitage, in January 1926, he was invited by his friend, Sir John Findlay, to write some verse about Mount Cook. He wrote his last poem, 'Aorangi'.[1] Frank Wilding took him see to 'Risingholme', but he was too upset to go inside. Only his family seem to have noticed the sour old man whom many people in England knew. When he met his sisters and brothers in Canterbury, all old too but none distinguished, Crosbie fell asleep while he was talking. 'Wake him up!' he snapped.

He described New Zealand as 'a children's Paradise'—but that thought scarcely tempted him to stay. And Maud said, 'Thank God we left!' 'Cheered and full of confidence in the future of such a country and such a people', he wrote, they sailed off to visit Beryl and her family in the United States, as they had on their way from England.

He was fortunate to revisit his country before it was hit by another depression, not as long, but psychologically more devastating than that of the eighties. He surveyed its effects from afar, noting the Government's 'curiously close reversion' to the 'retrenchment' policies of fifty years ago—cuts in civil service salaries and unionists' wages, and the like. He congratulated the Government on its determination to balance the budget 'at

[1] *New Zealand Alpine Journal*, iii, no. 14, p. 259.

whatever sacrifice'.[1] When the Bank of England sent to the
Dominion a financial emissary whose name still sounds chilly,
almost sinister, to many New Zealanders, Reeves wrote to
G. H. Scholefield, in 1930, 'I am glad to see that Sir Otto
Niemeyer thinks that our New Zealand finances are sound. He
has a good head where money matters are concerned and his
verdict will undoubtedly carry weight in London.'[2]

A greater New Zealand poet than Reeves was then writing:

> The heart is gold, the name is Otto,
> 'Women and children first' the motto.[3]

Reeves's warm sympathies for the employee had not altogether
congealed, however, into cold metal. In 1930 and 1931 he fought
a successful battle against some of the shareholders who were
dissatisfied that the National Bank had reduced dividends
without cutting staff salaries or reducing the Board's contribution to the Pension Fund. At the 1931 annual meeting he
determinedly resisted the onslaught of the malcontents:
'... no, we are certainly not going to meddle with the Pension
Fund. (Hear, Hear.) The Pension Fund is an independent thing,
not under the control of the Directors at all. It is a large and, I am
happy to say, thoroughly solvent fund, and it makes all the
difference to the life and hope of our staff, and the idea of our
cutting down and meddling with the pensions is repulsive to me
personally.'[4]

He also flatly refused to agree to salary reductions. At a time
when other banks were cutting salaries, many poor employees
of the National Bank were grateful for his leadership, and
remember his generous instinct still.

In 1930, Scholefield asked why he didn't bring *The Long White
Cloud* up to date, and Reeves wrote:

There is no doubt that I ought to tackle a concluding part between
the death of Seddon and the present time. I should have done so
already but for a sort of moral cowardice. The truth is much has
happened during the last twenty years with which I cannot agree—

1 National Bank of New Zealand archives, article for *Financial Times*, 17 Feb. 1931;
59th Annual Report, 1931.
2 G. H. Scholefield MSS, 20 Oct. 1930.
3 A. R. D. Fairburn.
4 Report of proceedings of annual meeting, 1931, National Bank of New Zealand
archives.

PLATE 6

W. P. Reeves, 1930–32

reckless finance, public and private; a selfish and short-sighted land policy with its concomitant crazy speculation; the antics of the Federation of Labour in 1912–13; and other things. I am so proud of New Zealand and so wrapped up in her future that I have not the heart to sit down and write chapters, parts of which might seem like the pessimistic complainings of a disappointed old man. However, if I can live a while yet I shall take up the job and try to look as much on the bright side of things as honesty will permit.[1]

At about the time he left the L.S.E., Reeves bought a house at 31 Pembroke Square. In 1929 he bought, as well, a property called 'Badlands' near Wisborough, in Sussex. It consisted of a 'bungalow', really an old Tudor farmhouse, and several acres of land. There he spent much of his time, near the end of his life, cutting weeds endlessly with one of his collection of fancy swords. The company of his grand-children, Anna Jane, Margaret Justin and Thomas, and of his nephews and nieces, gave him great joy. For them he wrote, in about 1929, some doggerel, 'Poems of Pondoland', recounting, for instance, 'The Buying of the Bungalow':

> It was Aunt Maud who fixed it. She stood pen in hand
> And settled the Uncle with one brief command.
> 'Sign this cheque!' she said firmly, 'And bother the cost'.
> And he signed and was done for like poor Dr. Faust.

—or describing his wielding of the sword against the weeds.

Much of his time he spent reading in his library, a converted barn. He grew ever more absent-minded. Once he put his pen in a bottle of quick-drying rubber solution and called to Maud that he couldn't get it out of the ink. The arm-chair caught fire from a cigarette and he left the room without noticing.

In December 1931 he resigned his chairmanship of the bank, but continued a member of the board until his death. In 1931 he read his name in the Press among a list of distinguished representatives of the University of London who were dead. 'Proud as I should be to be ranked with the illustrious dead,' he said, 'I suffer from a vital disqualification.' About that time he learned that he had cancer of the prostate, which he kept a close secret. He died on 15 May 1932, at the age of seventy-five, leaving £12,547, and was cremated at Golders Green cemetery.

[1] 11 April 1930.

INDEX

Peacock, John Thomas, 63, 68
Pease, Edward, 248–9, 313
Pember and Boyle, 339
Pember, Edward Henry, 6, 9, 38–39, 243–5, 268
Pember family, the 8–10, 253
Pember, Francis, 30
Pensions, 92, 217, 231
People's Political Associations (1890), 114, 117, 120, 121
Perceval, Sir Westby Brook, education, 65; during 1887 election, 65, 67, 77; in Parliament, 81, 110, 113, 124, 146; during 1890 election, 115, 116, 122; Agent-General, 133, 203, 234, 246–7, 258
'Pharos', 99–104, 196, 249
'Phiz', see Evison, Joseph S.
Pike, Vincent, 94
Pinkerton, David, 179
Pirani, Frederick, 269
Plimmer, John, 142–3
'Plinthos', 331
Political Labour League, 304
Political parties (absence of, before 1887), 66–67; origins of, 65–73. See also, Labour Party, Liberal Party, Reform Party, Conservatives
Political Reform Associations (1887), 65–69, 71–73, 74, 76–77, 79, 118
Political Reformer (1887), 76
Political Science and Philosophy Club, 327
Pollock, Sir Frederick, 299–301
'Pre-Adamites', the, 11
Press, The, (Christchurch), 25, 30, 51–52, 59, 65, 66, 67–68, 75, 78, 84, 95, 128, 159, 227
Privy Council, 290–1, 299–300. See also, Honours, royal
Progressive Liberal Association (Christchurch), 190, 217
Prohibition, 177–9, 188–92
Prohibitionists (in Parliament), 178–9, 193, 194–5, 216. See also, Prohibition; Stout, Sir Robert
Protection League, 71, 118. See also, Tariff protection
'Provincialism', 33–34, 61–62, 65, 69, 70, 77, 78, 82. See also, 'Development'
Public Tenders, Contracts and Works Bill, 228–9
Public Works, see 'Development'
Punch, 294

Queensland Worker, 110, 237

Rae, C. J., 120–1
Railway Commissioners, 106, 112
Railway League, 53. See also, Midland Railway Co.
Rainbow Circle, the, 251–2
Ranfurly, Uchter John Mark, Earl of, 260, 288
Rangiora, 5, 15, 17, 77, 114, 120
Rangitikei Political Asssociation, 142
Rea, Russell, 324
Rees, William Lee, 134
Reeves, Amber (Mrs. Blanco White), 58, 88, 243, 312–18, 323, 336
Reeves, Beryl (Mrs. Clarke), 58, 243, 312
Reeves, Ellen, 6, 8–11, 17–19, 24–25, 30, 36, 57–58, 129
Reeves, Fabian, 243, 312, 332–3
Reeves, Herbert, 128
Reeves, Hugh, 128–9
Reeves, Magdalene Stuart, 214, 219, 243, 279, 322–4, 327, 335–6, 343, 345–6; marriage, 57–58; character, 58, 160; becomes editor, 96; feminist views, 58, 180; organizes women voters, 189; lectures in England, 249, 313; and Boer war, 284–5; and Fabians, 312–18; writes book, 321; and Fabian's death, 332–3; Director of Women's Service, 333
Reeves, William, 22–24, 41, 50, 61–62, 70, 136–7, 154; arrives in New Zealand, 5–6, 10–11; family of, 8; marries 8–10; early career in New Zealand, 5–6, 16–20; and Lyttelton Times, 20–21, 30, 51–56, 95–96, 105, 128–30; and W. P. Reeves, 22–24, 29; builds 'Risingholme', 31–32; character, 29, 33–34; elected to Parliament, 32; joins cabinet, 32–34; financial difficulties and death, 128–30
REEVES, WILLIAM PEMBER: WRITINGS AND POLITICAL VIEWS Verse, 39, 47, 49, 55–56, 58, 77, 96, 97–99, 108, 127, 153, 224–5, 232–3, 243–5, 262–3, 307–8, 314, 321, 331, 334, 341–2, 343; Short stories, 97; Historical writing, 99–104, 183, 248–9, 263–7, 286–7, 339–40; Articles on Imperial Council, 298–301; Pamphlets etc. on Greece, 329, 337–8; Travelogue, New Zealand, 307, 342–3;